NOTHING SACRED

NOTHING SACRED

STATHIS GOURGOURIS

Columbia University Press
New York

Columbia University Press
Publishers Since 1893
New York Chichester, West Sussex
cup.columbia.edu
Copyright © 2024 Columbia University Press
All rights reserved

Library of Congress Cataloging-in-Publication Data

Names: Gourgouris, Stathis, 1958– author.
Title: Nothing sacred / Stathis Gourgouris.
Description: New York : Columbia University Press, [2024] | Includes bibliographical references and index.
Identifiers: LCCN 2023032988 (print) | LCCN 2023032989 (ebook) | ISBN 9780231215145 (hardback) | ISBN 9780231215152 (trade paperback) | ISBN 9780231560641 (ebook)
Subjects: LCSH: Political science—Philosophy. – | Political theology. | Humanism. | Secularization (Theology)
Classification: LCC JA71 .G6725 2024 (print) | LCC JA71 (ebook) | DDC 320.01—dc23/eng/20231214
LC record available at https://lccn.loc.gov/2023032988
LC ebook record available at https://lccn.loc.gov/2023032989

Cover image: Deniz Bilgin, *Tobacco*, 1997, gouache on paper

I produce a commodity that should be poetry, which is inconsumable. I will die, my editor will die, we will all die, our society will die, capitalism will die, but poetry will remain unconsumed/unconsummated [*inconsummata*].

—Pier Paolo Pasolini (1971)

I believe in the world and want to be in it. I want to be in it all the way to the end of it because I believe in another world in the world and I want to be in *that*. And I plan to stay a believer, like Curtis Mayfield. But that's beyond me, and even beyond [us], and out into the world, the other thing, the other world, the joyful noise of the scattered, scatted eschaton, the undercommon refusal of the academy of misery.

—Fred Moten (2013)

It's too late for pessimism and despair, they're too popular.

—Chris Cutler (1975)

Contents

Preface ix

1. Humanism, Human/Animal, Human-Being 1

   Prefatory Note—Rethinking Humanism—Edward Said's Nonhumanist Humanism—The Legacies of Anticolonial Humanism—Humanism as an Open Question—Three Phrases of History (Marx, Heidegger, Benjamin)—A Digression on the Digression of the Animal—Three Definitive Tropes of Human Animality: Psychē, Paideia, Philia—No More Artificial Anthropisms

2. Democracy's Anarchy 140

   Anarchy Is the Archē of Democracy—Archē and Finitude—Democracy Is the Regime of the Living—The Constituent Violence of Democracy: The Liberal Enclosure—The Constituent Violence of Democracy: The Anarchist Opening—Democracy Is a Tragic Regime—No Democracy Without Dissent—Surplus Over Nothing—Notes on Left Governmentality

   Coda: Against the Politics of the Sacred 278

   Notes 297

   Index 329

Preface

Rarely can I say that the premise of my work is direct and demonstrable. But the original idea behind this book was unusually lucid: to examine four pillars of what, rather simply, we can name Enlightenment thought—atheism, democracy, humanism, modernity—recognizing that what runs in common through them is an explicit project of desacralization. Yet the very history these domains produced, disseminated, and indeed to a large extent imposed worldwide shows that in the process of desacralization they brought forth sacred spaces of their own and in their name. In the context of this historical condition, my impetus became to question this second-order process of the sacred and explore, in the way of negative dialectics, whether (and how) these domains can be used against themselves in order to desacralize, yet again, their own self-sacralization.

In the years since its original inception, the project profoundly changed. Of the four pillars, two remained: humanism and democracy. Atheism was addressed in multiple ways in my book *The Perils of the One* (2019), the previous companion in a triptych I have called "lessons in secular criticism." Modernity is addressed in a single aphoristic essay that I have not yet published. The change was determined by a whole array of factors, mostly having to do with the passage of time between inception and realization, which raised myriad new questions and incurred multiple new beginnings that altered my thought process significantly. Having the benefit of time is a unique gift to a text, and there is no doubt that had I completed this project with greater speed—whatever the merits of enthusiasm and immediacy would have been—it would have produced a more restricted perspective. What I learned in this whole process is inestimable. But while changes in vision and in scope were significant, the impetus remained the same.

The reasonable question, of course, is: Why this impetus? And where does it come from? The answer is not simply a critique of sacralization—certainly not as an antireligious gesture, which is how I imagine it to be easily interpreted. To this effect, I have reserved my thoughts on the sacred and its processes, including the meaning of proclaiming an adherence to "nothing sacred," for the essay that serves as a coda. For now, as I have explained time and again to be the profound meaning of the act of secular criticism, the critique of sacralization would have to extend beyond the question of religion, for religion is but a subset, a distinct domain, of humanity's worldly footprint on this planet.

Secular criticism wrestles with society's unavowed self-occlusions. Its object is to elucidate the politics of knowledge that animates these self-occlusions in numerous practices that are often taken for granted. Both in terms of how this project was once explicitly conceived and, in retrospect, as renegade material from the initial conceptual explosion coalesced into its own gravitational field, this book is the third and final excursion in exploring the practical knowledge produced by the act of secular criticism, whose modalities are hardly predetermined and definitely innumerable as the specific object of inquiry demands each time.

If, for the sake of argument, one were to hold on to this discursive field of secularity vs. religion—although I explicitly abandon it in this specific iteration—then one could argue that the project of *Nothing Sacred* challenges the alleged permanence of the theologico-political with the confidence of achieving its internal deconstitution in order then to transform the established epistemologies of both the sacred and the secular. This unique condition in nature that I call "political animality" serves as critique of political theology, parallel to the way that the anarchy of democracy serves as critique of sovereignty. Conversely, the anarchy of democracy encapsulates the irrepressible capacity of *human-being* (see the prefatory note in chapter 1) to inhabit a political animality. Hence, the double-pronged dynamics of the project, as it is now framed by two expansive essays on humanism and democracy, is simultaneously both political and psychoanthropological.

In the end, the impetus to double down on the desacralizing capacity of two historical formations that have produced their own historical conditions for self-sacralization is driven by two prospects: (1) the desire to elucidate the dynamic power of subversion these notions/historical formations enacted in the world of their time against deeply ensconced conditions of disempowerment and incapacitation, and (2) the desire to chronicle and understand how societies/human beings are driven to self-subversion, to self-occlusion of their subversive power, and indeed to self-confinement, self-disempowerment, self-incapacitation.

There is a third factor that emerged in the process of distilling the peripheral dimensions of the notions of humanism and democracy specifically: to deconstruct the institutional power attached to their proclaimed post- phases. Along the lines of all the debilitating post-whatevers that have flooded the discursive horizon with raging fashion at all levels of society, from academic and governmental speech to daily colloquial use, posthumanism and postdemocracy have created a vast field of allegedly "new" knowledge that is just as self-sacralized and sacralizing. We all understand by now—in the era of "post-truth" and post-everything—the danger of the presumption to have overcome humanism and democracy (along with racism, feminism, etc., or even politics as such) by means of this lazy designation. So, in this very specific sense, my negative-dialectical inquiry is conducted against the grain of what has now become the new status quo, with full awareness of how easily such an inquiry could be dismissed as retrograde, as return to some past driven by some humanist or liberal nostalgia.

My immediate critical riposte to such anticipated charges would be to refer to Friedrich Hölderlin's categorical *Umkehr*, which is not at all some sort of turning back in recoil but a return in which the beginning has vanished. If one were thus considered to return to the origin—which is not at all the desire in my project nor its outcome, but just considering—what would emerge is a return home in order to find it nonexistent. Such a return is thus not at all a return but a gesture of radical change of what exists, a turn that alters the path to no end. Hence, the anarchic element that is explicitly the focus of the essay on democracy might be considered to be the overall methodological thread. Against the grain of their proclaimed "post-" figures, humanism and democracy are explored as dynamics of anarchy—in epistemology and politics both. For this reason, what first opened a path for rethinking humanism (including its anticolonial histories) turned into an expansive ontological questioning of *human-being* and an exploratory affirmation of the political dimensions of human animality on a planetary scale. Likewise, what began as a historical-philosophical account of democracy as anarchy in its essence unfolded further into an extensive reconsideration of democracy relative to its own violence and its adversarial confrontation with capitalism in order to conclude with an exploratory affirmation of the sort of radical politics I call left governmentality. From this standpoint, both essays unfold not only through a common methodology but also with the shared impetus to push through their negative dialectics to a definitive, even if still speculative, politics of *affirmation*. This is indeed the critical politics of nothing sacred.

There is a further methodological point to be made. The overall mode of inquiry in this book advocates a methodology of generalization as a political position in relation to current academic practices in pedagogy and the production of knowledge. My sense is that we have reached a dead-end condition in our research under the compulsion for ever more specialized knowledge and that a broader inquiry is now more urgent than ever. To this effect, my deliberate decision to approach matters in broad sketches aspires to a politics of anarchy as well, not only in terms that enable the elemental understanding of democracy but also insofar as it recognizes and respects the elemental meaninglessness and groundlessness of human existence.

So, I came to the conclusion that in order for us to overcome the theoretical and practical quandaries in which we find ourselves in the humanities and the social sciences, in order to abort dead-end ideological structures, in order to extricate ourselves from an unending proliferation of fragmented details of knowledge that become ever more disconnected from both its object and the reality that gives it purpose—in order, in other words, to respond to a political and epistemological malaise and confusion (that, I believe, many agree about but cannot agree on what it means, where it comes from or how to get out of it)—we need to relearn to speak in large terms, to envision a vast horizon, to become unafraid of considering totalities, to spread before us the major components of a problem and reconceptualize its architecture: in short, to dare think beyond the seductive tyranny of detail.

I understand, of course, the risks—the risks of generalization, perhaps even of homogenization—yet this is precisely what I feel needs to be restored: a sense of risk that will bring to the forefront another sort of responsibility. Not the responsibility toward the exhaustive documentation of the particular, but the responsibility toward the inexhaustible conceptualization of whatever exceeds the particular, however we are to consider that. I am hardly discounting the importance of the particular—as historians, anthropologists, philosophers, literary critics, etc., we are all trained in this and must continue to train our students in it. But, in addition, I feel it is time to risk going against this training, to engage the "true freedom of reversing oneself,"[1] as Edward Said put it so long ago in *Beginnings*—that is, to begin again and with other authorial modes that decisively assume the gravity of discontinuity in the face of a world that is getting larger and larger in scope and in condition as we speak, and in getting larger is getting also more and more discontinuous and inscrutable.

I also understand objections against the allegedly sovereign subjectivity that would authorize such a position. But frankly and in all due respect to the field, I don't care to defend against or diffuse such objections. No doubt, the sovereignty of the subject has been duly (and efficiently) questioned so as to make it impossible to constitute the standpoint of one's thinking as a naïve or pure position. But to proceed from the standpoint of critique of subjective sovereignty does not forbid me to make affirmations and judgments, to take the risk of judgment (*krisis*), to make decisions, to interrupt the flow of continuous rational mastery of ever-expanding knowledge. There is no other ground on which to oppose the now habitual exigencies of specialized scholarship except for the political exigency of thought itself, which now demands daring to take positions and make interruptions with indisputable urgency. I come back to Said, who already back in 1982, in a classic essay on the dialectical-critical parameters of thinking-in-the-world, issued an exhortation that has gone unheeded: "Instead of noninterference and specialization, there must be *interference*, a crossing of borders and obstacles, a determined attempt to generalize exactly at those points where generalizations seem impossible to make."[2]

I am not convinced that generalization, as is often thought, necessarily means simplification, certainly not if by simplification we mean reduction. There are other ways to understand simplification. Striving to simplify our conceptual terrain may be done out of respect for complexity, precisely because we don't want to see this terrain grind thinking to a halt or seduce us into some perpetually expanding vacuity. Succumbing to this seduction would mean de facto the disregard for complexity. The tendency to overly worry an idea or a discovery, to overburden it with stipulations and presumably interminable qualifiers, actually leads to an array of fragmented simplifications of a whole that, by virtue of this act, becomes unintelligible and incomprehensible. Precisely in this context, to generalize is a *pharmakon* set to challenge our scholarly immunity.

Nor does the methodology of generalization extinguish attention to the particular. In fact, the stern opposition between the two, the general and the particular, is the consistent problem. One can think instead in terms of overlapping spheres. What populates the points of overlap no doubt has to be examined with some focus, some specificity, but no way can this focus then be drawn out abstractly and counted for the whole. Even the whole as such is meaningless because adherence to its singularity is particularist thinking. The whole is precisely the ceaseless movement of overlapping spheres, of wholes that exist wholistically in themselves, with boundaries more or less determinable and yet not—insofar as they always intersect with other such wholes, and intersecting means sharing. In order to understand shared spaces, shared ways of being and doing, intersecting points of living, one best thinks wholistically. Intersectional spaces, by the very nature of sharing, are precisely not particular. They seek to break through the logic of identity, the logic of stern boundaries, the logic of self. Identity does not interest me. But the cracks in identity do.

Generalization not only does *not* mean simplification, but more than anything it means thinking across borders and through the cracks, thinking with open borders, toward open worlds that, by virtue of ceaseless movement, of the dynamic overlapping of spheres, are always worlds in the making. Expressly in political terms: in order to understand what is made (and how/why it is made) so as to unmake it, it is essential to pay attention to the dynamics of always-in-the-making. This too is the political impetus of a methodology of generalization and an elaboration of the politics of nothing sacred. In the end, to adjudicate the merits or perils of generalization is useless. It may be that by virtue of risking generalization, the project reveals its failure. But it is the orientation, despite the failure, that matters, for it signifies in itself a gesture against the grain of established practices and norms, hopefully digging out new paths for new trials.

Finally, a word on the broader social-historical context. It is safe to say that when the project began globalization was at its apex. Left antiglobalization movements never recovered the initial millennial momentum of Seattle and Genoa. Neoliberal economics swiftly bulldozed every aspect of society with virtually no resistance, as the interminable proliferation of consumer deception at cheap prices pacified further an already anesthetized public that wallowed in its liberal narcissism. In the European/American sphere culture wars seemed a bygone era, since the clash of civilizations argument was distilled into the Islamophobia that animated the imperialist wars in Iraq and Afghanistan. The first quake to hit this rotten edifice was the American banking collapse of 2008, which then seamlessly flowed into the sovereign debt crisis in Europe in just two years' time. In retrospect, this was the first pandemic. The bankrupting ways of neoliberal policies came unconcealed not only on the economic front but also on the ground of society as a whole, as public funding was gutted, social and health services delegitimized, wages minimized, and capital accumulated to the peak of the pyramid at unprecedented scale. As the world was globally chained, large masses of people took to the streets and the squares to protest in cascading explosions of rage all over the planet. The policing of populations by state machinery responded with shameless brutality and violence, but by this token it duly showed that even the liberal state apparatus itself was bankrupt, since it could no longer provide for the prosperity, protection, and liberty of its own peoples.

The left's failure to provide a feasible vision in response to this catastrophe and its spasmodic defense mode that translated into ephemeral victories and gutting defeats opened the way for a right-wing populism of newfangled ways, despite reauthorizing old nationalist and racist paradigms. Both the discourse and the activist practices changed drastically, and suddenly the culture wars were back on, except this time liberalism was shown up for the scam it really is: a complex mechanism of manufacturing consent. The clash of civilizations argument was also back on but deflected away from Islamophobia (without abandoning it) and refocused toward an internal identity battle, which targeted both sanctified liberal avatars (race, gender, sexuality, but also educated class privilege) and migrant/refugee populations who were the ubiquitous refuse of globalized capital. Swiftly, "the global" became the cultural enemy, despite capitalism's remaining its essential signifier. The alt-right antiglobalist imaginary and its practices are hardly anticapitalist even if, psychologically speaking, they are nourished by bona fide social and financial damage incurred by global capital among their ranks.

But, similar by analogy to the history of fascism in the twentieth century, the ultrasectarian racist and nationalist politics this imaginary unleashed did in fact derail liberal-capitalist globalization significantly. Two current conditions reveal this in startling fashion. First, the Covid pandemic disrupted global networks of production and distribution and simultaneously made it plainly obvious for anyone to see how neoliberal capital had destroyed society's health networks on the local-national ground across the board. At the same time, the panicked and paranoid response of states and populations alike dismantled the legitimacy of the security apparatus, which until then had been accepted as the mechanism of protection of liberal institutions. Second, Russia's invasion of Ukraine, under an explicit project of protectionist Eurasian civilizational assault—as well as the European and American military and economic response to it—also disrupted global networks of production and distribution and simultaneously made it plainly obvious for anyone to see how neoliberal capital had destroyed society's social welfare networks by forcing energy and food outsourcing and dependency that global capital fostered for unfathomable profit.

So, my prefacing a book that broadly explores the politics of human animality and the anarchy of democracy comes at a point when both the Covid pandemic and the war in Ukraine are raging with no conceivable resolution in sight and when the previously unassailable desire for globalization is riveted with doubt, bankrupted as well and lying next to the rest of the pile of corpses of neoliberal capital. What has already emerged, of course, is terrifyingly worse: a so-called multipolar world of oligarchies waging war against each other, where populations within and across borders are everyone's requisite targets, while the people themselves surrender to a psychotic paroxysm of delusion and indiscriminate internal violence and the planet is frothing with natural rage against its presently irreversible neglect and damage.

Well, you might ask, why the hell should we care about questions of humanity and democracy in the abstract under the brutality of these conditions? A fair question, which I have never stopped asking. Several times since the turn of the millennium I have reached points of severe doubt about the relevance of continuing to contemplate ancient things or speculate about seemingly unfeasible futures. During this time, I wrote often in newspapers and internet media about present-time social explosions and predicaments—the Arab Spring, the occupation of public squares, the flash impoverishment, the internment of refugees, the deadly police violence in city after city. Yet time and again, the dead ends in scenarios of liberation, the overwhelming odds against state repression and the ruses of capital, the outright failures of democratic practices, all convinced me to return to the broad horizon, to further reconsider the elemental problems in social imaginaries and human compulsions.

It is never the case that we theorize in order to overcome the failures of practice. We theorize the very failure—which in the end is but an act of reading, often between the lines, or of things unsaid and unimagined, the "unrealized instances of history" as Foucault once said. Even when we invent or we discover, we still interpret—according to the ancient Greek notion of *hermēneia*, as children of Hermes, the swift aviator of meaning, the messenger-interpreter of secrets, the actor. As *hermēneis*, we're always in a theater, acting, acting out, acting up, interpreting ourselves as others, othering ourselves in every act. Nothing of what is theoretical here resides outside the contingent and ultimately untotalizable and inexhaustible forces of being, of living and dying, that make the realm of human praxis a process of self-othering. From this praxis comes poiesis—autopoiesis is this praxis.

ACKNOWLEDGMENTS

Thinking and writing is never solitary, but thinking and writing for so many years is altogether collaborative and plural, involving not just persons but spaces and contexts of conversation and contestation. Essays are always journeys by virtue of the form itself, but in this case, given the world we've been inhabiting, the journeys are also quite literal, and it is only fair that they be chronicled and acknowledged.

"Humanism, Human/Animal, Human-Being" was initially presented as the Andrea Rosenthal Memorial Lecture at Brown University (November 2007) at the invitation of Rey Chow, and subsequently, in various incarnations and combinations: at the Heyman Center for the Humanities (Columbia); the Department of Comparative Literature at UCLA; the Humanities program at Boğazici University in Istanbul; the Johannes Gutenberg Universität in Mainz; the Center for Cultural Analysis (Rutgers); the Political Concepts workshop in New York; the Seminars in Social Anthropology at Panteion University in Athens; the Balvant Parekh Centre for General Semantics and Other Human Sciences in Baroda, India; the Collège International de la Philosophie in Paris; the Department of Comparative Literature at the University of Chicago; the Dartmouth Institute; and The Legacy of Bandung Humanisms workshops at Nanyang Technological University in Singapore, Lahore University of Management Sciences in Pakistan, and the Columbia Global Center in Beijing.

"Democracy's Anarchy" was initially presented as the Tudor and Stuart Lecture at Johns Hopkins University (April 2010) at the invitation of Amanda Anderson, and subsequently, in various incarnations and combinations, at the Institute for Public Knowledge, New York University; at the Arendt After 68 Symposium and the Political Concepts workshop, Columbia University; as the Slought Foundation Lecture, University of Pennsylvania; at the Centre for the Humanities, Utrecht University; the 9th Konitsa Summer School, Border Crossings Network in Greece; the ACLA in Toronto and in Utrecht; the Global Center for Advanced Studies in Athens; the Department of Literature at Uppsala University in Sweden; the University of Mumbai in India; the School of Law, University of Kent; the

Department of Philosophy, University of Pisa; the Columbia Global Center (Reid Hall) in Paris; the Escola Politéchnica da Universidade de São Paolo in Brazil; and the Institute of Cultural Inquiry (ICI) in Berlin.

For the invitations to speak to faculty and students outside the U.S. academy, I must thank Athena Athanasiou, Michele Battini, Rosi Braidotti, Creston Davis, Axel Honneth, Prafulla Kar, Maryam Wasif Khan, Lydia Liu, Ioannis Manos, Edward Mitchell, Mats Rosengren, Diogo Sardinha, Facundo Vega, Thanos Zartaloudis, and Songjian Zhang.

"Against the Politics of the Sacred" was presented at the Department of Anthropology at the London School of Economics; the Centre for Contemporary Political Thought, SOAS, London; and the Siemens Stiftung, Schloss Nymphenburg in Munich, for which, respectively, I thank Matthew Engelke, Hagar Kotef, and Robert Yelle.

Fragments from the manuscript in early versions were published as follows:

"*Archē*," *Political Concepts* 2 (Winter 2012), translated into Hebrew in *Maftea'kh* 6 (2013); "Human/Animal," *Political Concepts* 3, no. 2 (Spring 2014); "Democracy, A Tragic Regime," *PMLA* 129, no. 4 (Fall 2014); "Preliminary Thoughts on Left Governmentality," *Critical Times* 1, no. 1 (Spring 2018); "Three Phrases of History," *boundary 2* 47, no. 2 (May 2020); and "Self-Governance in the Era of Bankrupt Liberalism," *Open Democracy* (January 20, 2020).

For the publications in *Political Concepts*, I am indebted to all my friends and colleagues on the editorial collective for the extraordinary conversations over the years, but for specific comments on these two texts, Jay Bernstein and Adi Ophir. For the publication in *boundary 2*, which is a mere snippet of the vast school that is our collective thinking together for more than twenty years (and for which I am indebted to everyone), I thank specifically Paul Bové and Donald Pease for their wisdom and their generous reading of the full draft of the essay on the human. For the *PMLA*, *Critical Times*, and *Open Democracy* publications, I thank for their invitations and initiative Helene Foley, Judith Butler, and Carys Hughes respectively.

Equally, I must convey my profound gratitude to Wendy Lochner at Columbia University Press for her intellectual generosity, her vision, and her unwavering commitment to my work across the board and despite its peculiarities. And to Gregory McNamee, my CUP copyeditor, for his gentle but incisive work on the manuscript.

I also thank Gil Anidjar and Etienne Balibar specifically for their consistently open mind regarding this project, even when it was still rather blind in its labyrinth, and Othon Iliopoulos for generously indulging my most extreme fancies of flight while, years ago, I tried to form the initial trajectory of these ideas. To Aamir Mufti and Andreas Kalyvas I owe the continuous reinvention and reconfiguration of my thinking that comes with our friendship. To Neni Panourgiá I owe everything.

But if the book deserves to be dedicated to someone, this will have to be Petros and Ayşe, my nephews, the children of my friends, my students, and all the youth of the world whom my generation, for all its utopian proclamations, has so wretchedly failed. May they be bolder and wiser, smarter against being manipulated and fiercest in revenge against those who made—and continue to make—their life and all life precarious on this beautiful astral planet that we ought to love and protect in every single moment of our existence. This would be the ultimate meaning of being human.

NOTHING SACRED

CHAPTER 1

Humanism, Human/Animal, Human-Being

Prefatory Note—Rethinking Humanism—Three Phrases of History (Marx, Heidegger, Benjamin)—A Digression on the Digression of the Animal—Three Definitive Tropes of Human Animality: Psychē, Paideia, Philia—No More Artificial Anthropisms

—for Neni, who has already thought it through

PREFATORY NOTE

My overall interest in this essay, given the title, is not to test the traditional humanist distinction between human and animal, which in recent years has been put through the paces (not always inventively) in the name of so-called posthumanism or animal studies. On the contrary, for the sake of argument, one might say that I am abolishing this distinction in the hopes of raising the peculiar possibility of human animality as a political concept.

In this respect, I have opted for two idiosyncratic notations. First, I choose to write *human/animal* primarily in place of the hyphenated figure that merely qualifies the human as a particular animal. The slash is a beautifully multivalent mark, and its use here draws both on the mathematical notation of division as well as on the grammatical notation of a composite pair, which may alternately denote both sharing and/or opposition. What I have in mind will become explicit below, but to begin with, let us say that this notation aims to preserve the irreducibility of both names ("human" and "animal") and yet designate at the same time their undeconstructible relation as each other's part. While from a certain standpoint continuity between human and animal is foreclosed,[1] their discontinuous relation makes each a necessary part of the other: if nothing else, because the human *is* an animal, no matter what, and because the human is like no other animal, no matter what. The latter does not nullify the former despite whatever might be claimed by numerous theories and practices of civilization that the *human/animal* has invented. But it does displace a simple expression of the former so that the animality of the human cannot be considered to be a homogeneous configuration of a mere biological organism. In configuring matters this way, the various political-economic interventions in the relation between human and animal over time that purportedly animalized certain humans—or certain aspects of humanity—will also be reconfigured. Abolishing the conventional distinction will address the racist and sexist elements that informed it in the first place.

Second, I choose to write *human-being*, in hyphenated fashion, to denote a condition, not an essence. This too is elaborated below, but, as first instance, let us say that the hyphen destabilizes any notion of human nature as unqualified being. What is registered as "being" in the human cannot be equated with the creature that bears the name, while at the same time nothing in this "being" is ultimately meaningful outside the terrain of "what is human" which, as I argue throughout, is and remains an open question. The gist of this inquiry is to explore the terrain of human animality as a nexus of mutable and contested meanings, over and above the differential registers of society and culture.

Certainly, whatever this animal is by nature cannot be disengaged from the nature this animal makes be. So, what is cultural—if we presume this to be opposite to what is natural—is most definitely a crucial dimension, yet not in the sense that would lead us to signify this as a matter of the interminable variation of societies and cultures, which in its full liberal extent ultimately leads to the relative equivalence of societies and cultures that is often used to conceal all sorts of hierarchies and modes of exclusion, or even more, specific modes of humanization and dehumanization, neither of which is ever natural.

One of the key assertions in this text is that, as a condition of living being, human animality abolishes the nature/culture divide, even if the distinction remains nominally useful. Exploring the vicissitudes of this abolition, which means neither collapsing the two into one nor favoring one over the other, is an essential part of the inquiry. In these terms, the most uncompromising social-historical assessment of ways of being human cannot be actualized without the most uncompromising ontological assessment of ways of being human, whereby the classic divide between history and ontology is also deconstructed so that no determining primacy is recognized to belong to either side.

Indeed, the incalculable plurality inherent in the phrase "ways of being human"—what Sylvia Wynter, following Fanon, has famously named "the many genres of being human"—cannot be resolved by mere reference to the plurality of histories of societies and cultures on this planet but must be seen as an ontological condition in itself. Likewise, the social-historical dimension of *human-being*, although open to infinite content variations over time, is an altogether singular condition of being human. Whatever their irreducible sociogenic differences, humans are historically created animals in ways that are fully inscribed into their biological existence. Indeed, to be accurate, saying "historically created" means self-created beings, creatures whose nature is autopoiesis, not a matrix of mere formal reproduction, even including the possibility of evolution through mutation. This is not to say that the *human/animal* is exempted from evolution or zoological classification, but it is to say that whatever nature it manifests in the rubric of evolution or zoology is overdetermined, overinscribed with social-historical autopoiesis as a ubiquitous principle that works at the level of animality per se.[2]

Along these lines we can say that, in the last instance, *human-being* is a condition of political life, of *political animality*, and I have in mind something more than Aristotle's famous assertion (*zōon politikon*), although this remains an indelible starting point. No condition of *human-being* has ever existed on this planet without having to deal with what we have come to call "power"—that is to say, elemental forces of conflict that permeate all modes of organization of life—and "economy"—that is to say, elemental mechanisms of exchange that give essential organization to modes of power. This "dealing with" is existentially necessary. The interminable variety of manners and modes of handling or dealing with conflict as a principle of organization of life is not important in this context, except only as an indication that confirms the unlimited capacity of humans to address this dire existential necessity.

Having said that, I confess right off that I doubt whether what is here claimed to be political can be contained in a concept. The very significance of the *human/animal* resides in the fact that it exceeds conceptual language; it belongs not to the order of philosophy but to the order of *poiēsis*. So, whatever is political about it is also, just as much, poetic. I mean this in the simplest and most literal sense of the terms, but also in the complications that arise from their entwinement:

namely, the social-historical nexus where the penchant of the *human/animal* to create and institute previously inconceivable forms (*poiēsis*) wrestles with the drive to actualize various imagined modes of organization in order to handle the vicissitudes of power/exchange (*praxis*). The entwinement of *poiēsis* and *praxis* happens in the domain we call politics, which in this whole inquiry bears an ontological condition tantamount to the human.

This poietic/political dimension means that this inquiry is not justifiable in the typical terms of philosophical anthropology, although no doubt it partakes of this discourse and participates in its trajectory. In the same way, it cannot be justified in the typical terms of natural science (including neuroscience), although it is certainly informed by this epistemology and responds to what it recognizes to be its limits. To predicate an inquiry on the radical deconstruction of the nature/culture divide makes necessary the stretching (or in some cases, even breaking) of boundaries on whose basis the relevant sciences are built. I proceed in this fashion in full cognizance of the implications. It seems imperative to me that the question of "what is human" be engaged from within the methodological ambiguities of the humanities—if such a generalized disciplinary abstraction is allowed—because the humanities, in their vast and heterogeneous epistemological range and over and above their specific knowledge concerns, have this singular question as their ultimate object.

As always, I proceed by juxtaposition, not exposition or analytical unfolding. To say that the question of "what is human" is open and unanswerable, and yet that this very openness and unanswerability positively determines the entire range of living being *in an absolutely material sense* means that, in the last instance, the inquiry remains groundless, internally contentious, and certainly inconclusive. To think and write from the standpoint of *poiēsis* means to allow yourself to remain suspended in-between modes of touching ground, and to think and write from the standpoint of *politics* means to require of yourself to make a decision in the midst of this suspension and in spite of this suspension, out of a certain intellectual conviction and commitment without hoping, however, that the suspension will be lifted.

To begin with, then: In order to even get to the position of *poietically-politically* reconfiguring the notion of "What is human?" the first step is to rethink the problem of humanism *in its own name*. In the rubric of this inquiry, this means that we encounter humanism as a multisited and contested historical and conceptual domain that needs neither to be reduced to the European tradition nor to be compelled to invent so-called alternative names under the illusion of abolishing the European tradition. Once we let go of these prejudices then the multiple trajectories of humanism as a social-historical form emerge in a different light as venues through which the question of *human-being* can be addressed ontologically without foreclosing its sociogenic parameters even as these remain by definition interminable in their variance.

RETHINKING HUMANISM

The proposition to *rethink humanism* marks a specific way of staging encounters in the history of thought (which includes the elusive present and the unpredictable future) in which the problem of the human as an open question emerges in sharp relief. This proposition to rethink is hardly driven by a desire to look back. But it is necessarily driven by the command to reflect, which does entail a redoubling motion, like a backflip that would land us altogether elsewhere, where front and back, past and future, will be in this respect unrecognizable—this would be an elemental way to configure the notion of revolution. Whatever we might want to say about it, even for committed antihumanists there is an institutional memory of humanism that cannot be outmaneuvered, but can only be rethought, reminded, and remembered. This is the concise heritage of Hölderlin's notion of *Andenken*, of which Heidegger made such venerated use, or in another language, Edward Said's dare to enact "the freedom of reversing oneself" which he called for as early as in *Beginnings* (1975), or, even further, the notion of "un/writing" and "un/settling" that Sylvia Wynter has proposed in such a groundbreaking way while targeting specifically the legacy of European humanism.[3] Such redoubling and un/writing (which is not to say, effacing) the ways in which humanism has ordered the terrain of knowledge of self and other cannot settle with posthumanism as the proclaimed solution—not only because any nomenclature of "post" bears with it the incapacitated response to the emergent (and is thereby an already defeated designation), but also because, however we delineate a terrain that might aspire to overcome humanism, we cannot overcome the human as ultimate framework of this terrain.

In the course of configuring human nature over time, myriad societies and their myths have sought to establish ways whereby the human can be overcome. Permit me an assertion here as a point of departure: The claim to have overcome the human is a debilitating delusion precisely because—the clarity here is cruel and undeconstructible—only the human can claim to overcome the human. So, although the impetus in the most innovative work that identifies itself variously (and certainly self-critically) as "posthumanism" is genuinely an attempt to open new epistemological horizons and invent new frameworks of meaning that exceed the inherited humanism that still inhabits us all, nonetheless the demand still presses us to elucidate the domain of the human and not evade it for some other domain (whether it be information systems, animal studies, biotech genetics, artificial intelligence, or what have you), because, whether we like it or not, even in those domains, which otherwise have their proper objects, the human remains the underlying interrogative terrain.[4] This cannot be outmaneuvered, at least not until robots become capable of creating their own phantasms or other living creatures communicate to us how they imagine and construct alternate universes and alternate natures in order to give meaning to their world.

In other words, the very being that enacts the interrogation must be interrogated *in its own precarious and problematic name*, for every other naming will remain at best allegorical and at worst prosthetic—in both cases, a convenient displacement of the inordinate stakes at hand. In this respect, simply because there can never be a critical discussion of humanism without a critical reconfiguration of the human, "rethinking humanism" is but one phrase in the indefinitely variable *poiētic* range of *human-being* as a condition.

Encountering the problem at its classically inherited historical standpoint makes it elementary to assert that rethinking humanism cannot remain satisfied with the standard history that recognizes, as the point of emergence, the conditions of Italian Renaissance cities with sources in the writings of Ficino, Machiavelli, or Pico della Mirandola (whose "dignity of man" is an explicit attempt to dismantle the theology of "fallen man"), which by an almost direct line (at least in the realm of the Italian language) lead to Vico and further out to the revolutions in science that altered the way we perceive the physical universe. For one, the work of George Makdisi, to take a classic example that may be dated but not outdated, produces a formidable argument for humanist practices flourishing in the Arab madrassas, libraries, law courts, guilds, hospitals, and mosques from the eighth century on, in Baghdad, Egypt, or Andalusia. In his book *The Rise of Humanism in Classical Islam and the Christian West* (1990), Makdisi elaborates on modes and techniques of jurisprudence, rationalist inquiry, scholasticism, poetic thought, rhetorical eloquence, lexicography, disputation, speculative grammar, epistolary art, book production, and even what he explicitly calls the "deconstruction of the Koranic verses and the Prophetic tradition"—all of which become therefore essential in the intellectual (and, of course, political) upheaval that characterizes the Italian Renaissance, as Pico himself, after all, specifically acknowledged.

I am bringing this up not as some sort of anti-Westernist correction but in order to alert us to a complex history at the outset, which means that the very concept of humanism, even as we seek to rethink it, is already multivalent, multisited, and problematic, and we cannot thus presume, in a so-called antihumanist gesture, that we can encounter it and efface it in some sort of holistic fashion. Such a gesture, in its opposition, would mean nothing less than an extension of the *monohumanism* that we have inherited.[5] Makdisi speaks convincingly of what he identifies as secular humanist practices in medieval Arab Islamic societies. This gesture alone derails the presumed equation of humanism with secularism in the specifically understood Western sense, just as much as it derails any theory of secularism that seeks to identify it strictly with a Christian (or Christian-derived) social universe.[6]

By the same token, we can neither dismiss the catalytic importance of Italian Renaissance humanism and the scientific revolution it spurred (Copernicus, Galileo, Newton) in a long-term process of social and political emancipation that feeds the Enlightenment tradition nor, of course, disavow the complicity of this tradition, particularly in terms of its new geoanthropological imagination of expansion and the establishment of *Homo economicus* as the liberal ideal, in the genocidal catastrophe of many of the planet's societies in the name of humanist values. No doubt, medieval Arab humanism and Italian Renaissance humanism diverge from Enlightenment and bourgeois liberal humanism in that their imaginaries are not worldwide—neither world-encompassing nor world-building.[7] Yet the radical elements emerging out of Renaissance cities become full-fledged in even more radical manifestations of social-historical upturning in the Enlightenment, even while being, at the same time, the very same elements that become frontal weapons in the course of colonial and imperial domination, whether these weapons emerge from the territorial imagination that brings about the conquest of the New World and the subsequent deracination of American and African indigenous societies or, at another level, are more narrowly honed in the corridors of the Orientalist philological laboratory in European academies.

Both aspects are concurrent, *co-incident*, and intertwined, and neither should be considered singular or more significant, if the dialectic of Enlightenment (in

Horkheimer and Adorno's definitive sense) is to remain a valuable lesson. Even the sumptuous invocation of the "death of man" that closes Michel Foucault's *Les mots et les choses* (1966)—man as the figure in the sand about to be washed away by the waves of history—is best understood to belong to this dialectic. Otherwise, it becomes a mere image frozen in an uninterrogated deathly antihumanism, an academic posture that defangs Foucault's radical critical impetus. Foucault's later configuration of the Enlightenment as "a philosophical ethos," as he elaborates on the regimes of truth-telling, governmentality, and critique against the vicissitudes of power, testifies to his own self-interrogation.[8] My starting point here then is to argue that this position as such, as *uninterrogated deathly antihumanism*, is no longer viable, as it is no more than a mirror extension of the monohumanism it opposes, and that instead we might want to consider seriously Edward Said's intervention—made explicitly on account of this impasse—for what he called nonhumanist humanism.

Edward Said's Nonhumanist Humanism

Humanism and Democratic Criticism, the last book Said completed, which, as I have argued elsewhere,[9] may be considered a refined example of his own late style, deserves here a brief explanatory digression in order to illustrate the logic and project of this mysterious phrase. Said's essays on humanism were famous lectures years before they found their way into print. In certain circles in the humanities they were downright infamous, configured to bear the most concrete evidence of Said's alleged turn against theory. The argument circulated at the most simplistic level: Insofar as the high days of French theory, in the spirit of '68, had made their mark by mounting a devastating critique against the assumptions of the humanist tradition, any attempt to defend and reauthorize the discourse of humanism was tantamount to being antitheory. This syllogism is not merely simplistic; it is entirely inaccurate in respect to both sides. Neither was Said ever simply "antitheory," nor were so-called poststructuralist theorists simply "antihumanists."[10] There is nothing a priori compatible or incompatible between the terms "theory" and "humanism." Their interrelation is, and has always been, historically contingent, before even the terms bore any recognizable coherence, before even being thus named, from Heidegger extending backward to Nietzsche and to Marx.

Said never hid his frustration with what he perceived to be the fetishism of theory, the specific sort of academic self-fashioning by means of a rarefied language that undercuts any frame of reference other than itself. He found this indeed to betray the political purposes of theory—which, from his earliest avowed allegiances to Lukács and to Gramsci, had meaning only in a dialectical relation to praxis—and he assailed such tendencies in both Europeanist and postcolonial literary studies over whose theoretical parameters he had, at one time, presided. Hence the charge against him about a turn of face. The lectures on humanism were met, practically everywhere in American universities, with a sense of betrayal by those who had been counted among his allies in the humanities during the 1970s and 1980s and a sense of triumphalism by various adversaries, who had distinguished themselves as defenders of Anglo-American humanist principles against the foreign onslaught.

A careful reading of *Humanism and Democratic Criticism*, however, shows Said to confound both sides yet again. He initiates the argument with relentless critique of latter-day American humanism (exemplified by the likes of Allan Bloom, William Bennett, or Saul Bellow), who represent "the anti-intellectualism of American life" and are characterized by "a certain dyspepsia of tone" and "the sour pursing of the lips that expresses joylessness and disapproval," all of it driven by the "unpleasant American penchant for moralizing reductiveness" and the stern conviction that "the approved culture is salubrious in an unadulterated and finally uncomplicatedly redemptive way."[11] At the same time, Said does not mince words about "lazy multiculturalism" and "specialized jargons for the humanities." He rejects "ideological antihumanism," which he identifies as a negative practice that nullifies a priori the sovereignty of the Enlightenment subject, instead of dismantling the assumptions this subject mobilizes in the ever-changing landscape of the post-Enlightenment world, precisely in order to wrest subjectivity away from its presumably impermeable ideological trappings.

Said's double-sided rejection of traditional humanism and the antihumanism that emerges from this same tradition speaks of an equally double-sided purpose. Said initially proclaims his undertaking to be "critical of humanism in the name of humanism" (H, 10) and yet later professes his aspiration to achieve the position of the nonhumanist humanist, which, by his own account, is a "dialectically fraught" position that takes humanism to initiate "a technique of trouble" (H, 77). Any careful reader of Said over the years knows that his language can achieve the most daring entwinement of the skeptical with the utopian but is never equivocal or sophistic. These apparently contradictory assertions are not driven by some perverse desire to confuse, but on the contrary, by stern commitment to elucidate the underhanded and deceitful ways in which identities—here, both the "humanist" and the "antihumanist," but in essence *all* identities—are produced and cultivated. Indeed, the trope of nonhumanist humanism is obviously derived from, and is a tribute to, Isaac Deutscher's self-description as "the non-Jewish Jew"—articulating precisely how, for Said, humanism must be explicitly anti-identitarian at its core.

For a man who had once said, simply and succinctly, "imperialism is the export of identity," the critique of identity is not merely an occasional political stance (as in the critique of identity politics, for example) but a critical-philosophical position that interrogates any practice of exclusionary distinction. Without ever adopting an ontological framework, Said consistently attacks any structure, discourse, or institution that renders itself unaccountable to forming identities, no matter what the historical necessity or political strategy might be. Hence, his tireless dismantling of authorities that demand strict obedience and adhesion to a priori principles: nationalism, imperialism, religion, the state, or those definitions of culture that bind societies in conceptual frameworks of "civilization"—this was, of course, the impetus of *Orientalism*.

Oftentimes *Orientalism* is considered an antihumanist work, at least insofar as it explicitly follows Foucault in an exhaustive dismantling of the enterprise of philology and its profound complicity in the colonialist and imperialist projects, all conducted from the prerogative of the superiority of the cultural configurations of European languages and cultures. Insofar as this superiority is supported by the epistemological assumptions of an ideological humanism coming out of the Enlightenment era, *Orientalism* is indeed an antihumanist work. Yet this is a partial understanding, especially when viewed in the framework of Said's entire and now completed oeuvre, in which—this is my contention—there was never really a turn or a shift in the trajectory between early and late work. For one thing, the work is deliberately antisystematic and cannot sustain a mode of organization that even retrospectively could discover early and late divisions. Moreover, it is sufficient to read carefully Said's early interviews from the 1970s, right around the time of *Beginnings* and then *Orientalism*, to see remarkable indications, even announcements, of the problems with which he will eventually wrestle in *Humanism and Democratic Criticism* and even *On Late Style*. This is to say that whatever might be deemed "antihumanist" in *Orientalism* is just as much in place in *Humanism and Democratic Criticism*, which conversely also means that the exigency of thinking through humanism and by means of humanism (and indeed even philology, inventively reconfigured) is also present in *Orientalism*, not to mention in the splendorous erudition of *Beginnings*. Indeed, for Said, humanism is ever-present as material and as project, continuously thought and rethought, configured and reconfigured, and, I might add, one of the crucial terrains of what he called "secular criticism"—which, incidentally, in the last work is changed to "democratic criticism," making explicit the political impetus that was always there.[12]

Said's essays on humanism follow a consistent line of thinking against identity but focus on the core figure that drives identity production: the human as such. One could encapsulate this project as a *co-incident* double gesture of secular criticism: on the one hand, against traditional humanism for destroying humanity in the name of humanism (via humanitarianism, human rights, philanthropy, etc., but in essence all liberal concepts of so-called freedom and agency) and, on the other hand, against traditional antihumanism for effectively desubjectifying—and in this sense specifically dehumanizing—the process of history. This double focus is sharpened by brushing aside abstract philosophizing about the "nature of the human" in order to foreground the range of human practices—the making of society, the making of history—as constitutive boundaries of the human. In this respect, Said's antinomian humanism, as yet another elaboration on the task of secular criticism, must be understood to work on both grounds of what is secular and what is critical. The text is full of descriptions of this task. I choose two: "To understand humanism at all is to understand it as democratic, open to all classes and backgrounds, and as a process of unending disclosure, discovery, self-criticism, and liberation.... Humanism *is* critique" (H, 21). And: "Humanism should be a force of disclosure, not of secrecy or religious illumination.... [It] must excavate the silences, the world of memory, of itinerant, barely surviving groups, the places of exclusion and invisibility, the kind of testimony that doesn't make it into reports" (H, 73, 81).[13]

Taken together, these phrases target both particularist and universalist practices by demanding a disclosure—Said is fond of using just as often the word "exfoliation"—of all exclusionary strategies, whether their authority is achieved in the name of the "Self" (and its global expanse) or in the name of the "Other" (and its narrowing essence). We may thus understand Said's call "to practice a *paradoxical mode of thought*" (H, 83, his emphasis) as a call to subvert any *orthodox* tendencies, no matter what their purpose or justification. Note that the alternative or corrective to orthodox thinking here is not heterodox thinking, for that is a mere substitution of one for the other while nonetheless retaining a totalizing determination. Of course, orthodoxy itself is in effect an oxymoron, for there can never be a right (*orthon*) opinion (*doxa*) in the sphere of opinions, which is the public sphere of democratic contention. A paradoxal mode of thought, on the other hand, not only recognizes the contentious sphere of public opinion but also remains a thorn on the side (*para-*) of produced *doxa* lest this becomes *dogma*.

It's not so difficult to see why both dogmatic traditionalists, who defend the purity of the literary canon or of human rights, and dogmatic multiculturalists, who refuse to affirm anything other than their own minoritarian niche, would find much to be sour about in this book. But they are likely to miss that Said's objection is not against their position in political, historical, or even theoretical terms but against the *orthodoxy* of their position, against their entrenchment, their inability to consider that their position, after all, bears as well the mark of its worldliness, of being made at a specific moment *in* the world. This inability undermines and occludes the historical accountability of such positions because it denies them the realization that they can remain open, just as easily, to being unmade (and made anew, made otherwise) in relation to worldly demands, for or against.

But contrary to the assumption that Said's project is in the end nothing but an extension of (or for some, a return to) traditional European humanism, a different genealogy is in play, whose elements are submerged in the complicated history that made it happen. Namely, Said's critique of European antihumanism belongs to a broader non-European humanism marked by the political and aesthetic imagination of enslaved/colonized peoples as it converged from a variety of directions into the spirit that spawned the Bandung Conference of Afro-Asian Cooperation in 1955. The Bandung event, in both real and symbolic terms, launched in turn the movement of "Nonaligned Nations" (Belgrade, 1961) and the very concept of the Third World, as well as a vast range of international initiatives, not only in the political sphere but in the realm of aesthetics, literary production, and the performing arts.[14] As a gesture of resistance to the dehumanization of colonized peoples, this formation that Aamir Mufti and I have called "Bandung humanisms" needs no authorization from either traditional European humanism or 1960s European antihumanism.[15] From the standpoint of the imaginary exemplified by the event of the Bandung conference and its legacy, the second is still in the orbit of the first. Said's "nonhumanist humanism" is the distilled expression of this geohistorical position: a humanism that is not *universal*, strictly speaking—or *monolingual*, as Mufti puts it—but *conversal* across the worldly terrain of modes and sites of social being, whose forces can be assembled in counterformation in order to resist and reconfigure inherited classifications, boundaries, or structures of orthodoxy and established power.[16]

Exemplary of "late-Bandung thought"—the notion is Mufti's—Said's work figures in this respect as the gravest adversary to critiques of humanism that see it as mere ideology, a position pioneered in Louis Althusser's "Marxism and Humanism" (1962), a key essay that initiated one of the most influential theories of ideology to come out of 1960s theoretical thinking.[17] For Althusser, humanism is ideological because it does not provide us with any means as to its mechanisms; in other words, it conceals the imaginary significations of "What is human?" upon which it constitutes itself. Althusser speaks unequivocally and absolutely: "It is impossible to *know* anything about people except on the absolute precondition that the philosophical myth of man is reduced to ashes" (229). It would have been irreverent at one time but it is entirely credible today to say, in retrospect, that in his absolutism Althusser inadvertently reproduces the totalizing self-configuration of traditional defenses of humanism, thereby missing precisely what Said places at the forefront: that humanism is a social-historical formation of multivalent and heterogeneous legacy and with utterly debatable contours, trajectories, and points of origin, which, as any other social-historical formation, has borne certain ideological uses (themselves hardly predictable or uncomplicated) but can hardly be reduced to them. By this token, one can argue that the "theoretical antihumanism" (Althusser's phrase) characterizing much of the radical theory of the 1960s is hardly less ideological in this very same sense. But even such presumed equivalence does not mean we still settle on humanism as an ideology, and surely not in contradistinction from what Althusser, at that time, assertively characterized as Marxist science. The ideological content of social formations is certainly open to inquiry, interrogation, and debate—and I hardly mean to disavow such a task—but the point of this project, of rethinking humanism, cannot be reduced to such debates over content.

The Legacy of Anticolonial Humanism

In its day, Althusser's essay appeared as a countermovement with no precedent, as if—at least in the realm of the French language alone—it sufficed merely to write against Sartre in order to produce a rupture. But especially within these boundaries, such assurance would have registered an intellectual scandal if the French theoretical language was not riveted by colonial configurations of exclusion. In her excellent biography of Frantz Fanon, Alice Cherki points out that by the mid-1960s, in the heyday of structuralist antihumanism in France, all memory of decolonization and anticolonial thinking had been encrypted to the point of oblivion.[18] In this respect, the radical velour of antihumanist investment in the repudiation of history as the field of action of actual men and women needs to be connected precisely to this repressive vanishing of the anticolonial struggle from intellectual production. The disavowal of this simple historical mark continues to operate unabated in our time, despite the resurgence of decolonial discourses as radical signposts.

In the very year of publication of Althusser's "Marxism and Humanism" in his groundbreaking book *For Marx* (1966), Léopold Senghor would resonate the tenet of Sartre's canonical "Existentialism is a Humanism" by returning to the project of *négritude* with the bold assertion that "Négritude is a humanism of the 20th Century."[19] Althusser was likely unaware of this temporal coincidence perhaps in the same way he does not seem to have been aware that Senghor had written an essay with the same title "Marxism and Humanism" already in 1948. In between these two Senghor statements, there is an extensive body of work of Marxist anticolonial intellectuals—obviously Aimé Césaire and Frantz Fanon, but also W. E. B. Du Bois and M. N. Roy before them—who elaborate a radical humanism that should serve as a beacon for our own troubled times, in which deeply embedded colonialist and racist structures are resurfacing with vengeance.[20]

In his primer on *négritude*, Bachir Diagne makes the astute observation that behind Césaire's assertion of an "African variety of communism" there is a radical rereading of Marx similar to the one that inspired Althusser: namely, a division between an "early" and a "late" Marx that responded to the discovery of the *Economic and Philosophical Manuscripts* in 1932 (French translation published in 1947). Except that there is a profound reversal: whereas Althusser took this as a rupture that was to launch a Marxist science and a general antihumanist theory, the poets of *négritude* saw it as a moment of recuperating an ethical Marx against an economistic Marx and an alternative radical humanism against the global dehumanizing socialization precipitated by colonial capital: "The task of an African rereading of Marx is then: 1) To save Marx the humanist, metaphysician, dialectician, and artist from a narrowly materialist, economistic, positivist, realist Marxism; 2) To invent an African path to socialism which is inspired by black spiritualities, and which continues the tradition of communalism in the continent."[21]

Senghor may have been the chief proponent of the second, to the extent that he especially sought (arguably more than Césaire or Fanon) to underscore, via his Bergsonian sensibility, an ontological substratum composed of centuries-old histories of African life. When in 1948 Senghor first articulated his own notion of humanism in relation to Marx's thought, he seized on the dialectical underpinnings of what constitutes *human-being* as radically other to its presumed uniqueness as the ontology of the "rational animal." Marx's correction of Hegel, Senghor argues, consists in disrupting the rationalist metaphysics that equates the real with the rational and anchors the constitution of the *human/animal* to its dependency on logic. He quotes the famous phrase in Marx's letter to Arnold Ruge (1843)—"reason has always existed but not always in rational form"—in order to disengage reason from logic and open the door to the possibility that *human-being* might be characterized by an interminable multiplicity of modes of reason, all of them emerging from specific histories, that is to say, specific conditions of life. This could account for modes as different as, in his words, "Indian reason, Chinese reason, or Negro reason" much as Logic might be considered, by the same token, to be the historical mode of reason specific to the tradition of Western metaphysics.[22]

Surely, Senghor does not aim to *ethnicize* the rational attributes of the *human/animal*, but he does aim at articulating different *historical* possibilities of humanism, and he seizes on openings drawn by Marx to do so. We'll come back to Marx in detail later on, but at this point I note merely that Senghor configures the parameters of a science—in its original meaning, knowledge—that has none of the epistemological restrictions that Althusser would demand fifteen years later. Indeed, in so-called early Marx, whom Althusser considers to belong to metaphysics, Senghor finds in contrast an antimetaphysics of practical knowledge that nonetheless resists the machine logic of what later became known as "structural Marxism" with its presumption of scientific economics at the helm. Marx remains actual in our time, Senghor concludes, precisely because he remains inconclusive: he provides a method, rather than a structure, whose point of departure and yet also object of inquiry is the totality of *human-being* as world-sensing being. There is, in other words, a universal proposition here against the universalist prejudices of European colonial logic that deserves its due at the core of rethinking humanism in our time.[23]

Around this period, as European societies are struggling to emerge from the ruins they have heaped upon each other in the Great War, an exceptional Indian revolutionary Marxist, whose life story is the stuff of thriller movies, developed very much his own configuration of humanism as a worldly encounter with the demands of history, against both the universalist metaphysics of the communist project and the Gandhian metaphysics of national culture. Manapendra Nath (M. N.) Roy (1887–1954) was an extraordinary international figure in his day.[24] Founder of the Mexican Communist Party and cofounder of the Communist Party of India, after having distinguished himself as a Bengali anticolonial activist under his real name, Narendra Nath Bhattacharji, which he had to ditch under British persecution, Roy was famously Lenin's most prominent interlocutor in the Second Congress of the Communist International (1920), when the Bolsheviks first faced the concrete problem of what a proletarian revolution might mean in the colonized societies of the East. Indeed, Lenin welcomed Roy's official supplement to his "Theses on the National and Colonial Question" as necessary insights, acknowledging Roy's privileged position in the Comintern until this vanished with the first Stalinist purges.[25] Contributing to this turn of events may have also been Roy's disastrous involvement in the Chinese revolution of 1927, largely due to a sort of outsider agitator's naiveté, which led to his expulsion from China as well with the accusation of being a traitor to the cause.[26]

Facing the harnessing of international communism in the service of Stalin's doctrine of "socialism in one country" under whose cover the Soviet Communist Party machinery subjugated radical movements worldwide, Roy recalibrated his emancipatory vision toward another sort of materialist-universalist project with the project of autonomy at its core. This trajectory was concretely manifested in Roy's foundation of the Indian Renaissance Institute at Dehradun, a sort of alternative pedagogical space to train young South Asian intellectuals and educators away from the metaphysics of the nation, religion, or race and toward what today we would see as a sort of ecopolitical planetarity, an alternative globality as was first configured indeed through the experience of shifting from early communist twentieth-century internationalism, as it collapsed after Lenin's death, to the overtly transnational (and in this sense antinationalist) anticolonial struggle of what we came to call Third World politics. Roy's very life embodies this trajectory. I single out his significant self-assessment, articulated retrospectively in his

Memoirs: "I am not a nationalist; any country is as good or as bad for me as any other. The more I saw of the world, the more I felt that any country would be so much better without its inhabitants, full of prejudices and parochialism" (55). Roy's advocacy of a new humanism in the aftermath of World War II and the partition politics that marred national independence in the Indian subcontinent bears the character of decades of being at the forefront of the anticolonial struggle, yet without falling in the trap of national sovereignty, marking instead the first instance of proposing a project of "radical democracy" in that very name.

Of course, practices of direct democracy had already flourished in various radical contexts from the early soviets (workers councils) to Catalan anarchist organization in the Spanish Civil War. But in those early Comintern debates, Roy argued that it is in fact possible to transfer the formal mode of workers councils to the peasant population in colonized societies, being thus the first (before Mao put it into practice) to advocate the independence of this form of political organization from the economic structures that, according to strict Marxism, made it the unique mode of proletarian organization in industrialized societies.[27] Although by the late 1940s he had long abandoned the communist project—for, among other things, it betrayed this literally *anarchist* mode of democratic politics in favor of autocratic party rule—Roy continued his sharp critique of liberal democracy unabated, foregrounding a profound understanding of its inherent metaphysics of representation. His articulation of radical democracy in these terms predates by almost a decade the clandestine collaboration between Cornelius Castoriadis and C. L. R. James on the concrete politics of this notion. Moreover, his institution of an autonomous pedagogical structure in the name of a New Humanist International that was meant to combat the pitfalls of postindependence national education anticipates the critique of postcolonial nationalist state politics that we will see shortly thereafter in Frantz Fanon. Indeed, Fanon's case seems to mark a perfect extension to Roy's, not only because he too was an internationalist revolutionary who fought against the metaphysics of nation, religion, and race but because Fanon also announced a new humanism and, moreover, as a materialist and a scientist, saw the human, not as a singular determination of (national) culture but as a vibrant materiality of worldly being.[28]

The overall convergence is uncanny—all the more because this radical democratic politics in anticolonial struggle is articulated explicitly in the name of a new humanism that overcomes traditional European humanist structures: "New humanism is not a system of contemplative thought. It has not been developed in the seclusion of the ivory tower. Grown out of the experience of social action, its test will be in the social experience of active human beings."[29] But this critique of traditional humanism, which aims at "eliminating its defects" (122), is not merely a matter of privileging practical knowledge over idealist knowledge. Roy understands the overall task as a matter of putting into practice a cosmological attitude that not only displaces the narrowly anthropocentric horizon of traditional humanism, in which politics is but an extension of "Man" and his capacities, but rather engages the political realm itself as a condition of living, as an essential element in the worldly physical universe. His new humanism, as a materialist vision, is alternately named in his writings as "radical humanism" or "integral humanism," and there is no doubt that even in this very naming it is entwined with the political project of radical democracy. Reflecting on this entwinement from a philosophical standpoint, we might say that Roy's insistence on radical democracy not as political system but as a way of life, a mode of living being, bears an affinity with a sort of pre-Socratic understanding of the cosmos (wherefrom, after all, the imaginary of the polis emerges), in which the vibrant integrity of *human-being* is political by nature and democracy is its living condition—direct democracy, without the transcendental metaphysics of representation.

Configurations of colonial exclusion being what they are, Roy's thought disappeared from the forefront of radical intellectual discussion. References to his thinking vanished, whether as a result of Soviet party hegemony or under the weight of South Asian nationalisms that fearfully conferred upon this sort of universalist thinking the ghost of European thought. Amazingly, Roy's thought resurfaced in black American radical circles in the early 1960s, which foregrounded "the Negro question" as a colonial question and the struggle for black liberation as an international anticolonial armed struggle. It is altogether remarkable that, with antecedent references to Roy and Du Bois, the Revolutionary Action Movement (RAM), one of the first Black Power groups to embrace Maoist principles, indeed used the term "Bandung humanism" to describe its framework of action before changing it to "revolutionary black internationalism" after 1966, thus opening an epistemological trajectory that would eventually lead to Huey Newton's invention of the notion of "intercommunalism" as the elemental method of Black Panther practice.[30]

There is an unavoidable bridge point between Roy and the Panthers, which exemplifies the sphere we call Bandung humanism. While from the radical black liberation standpoint in twentieth-century America this trajectory extends from

Du Bois to Malcolm X via Fanon, the key intermediary component in this unfolding is the poetics and politics of *négritude*. The entwinement of these two domains is essential, and it enhances the more explicitly political projects of Du Bois, Roy, and Malcolm. *Négritude* is unparalleled as a political project conducted in the poetic domain, which is to say both literally by way of poetry, since many of the key figures were exceptional poets, but also in the broadest sense of the creation (*poiēsis*) of new forms of being, which have both epistemological and practical dimensions. The fact that the poets Senghor and Césaire were also statesmen says a great deal to that effect.

One might argue that for Césaire the epistemological and the practical achieved a curious simultaneity: poetry was understood from the outset to constitute a mode of knowledge, and yet this knowledge was never allowed to repress its worldliness in favor of some transcendental proposition. "Pregnant with the world, the poet speaks. He speaks and his speech returns language to its purity. By purity I mean not subject to habit or thought, but only to the cosmic thrust."[31] Quintessentially poietic—that is to say, generative of forms that will create a new society out of the ruins of colonialism—this cosmic thrust is precisely what underlies the project of "a true humanism—a humanism made to the measure of the world."[32] The truth of this humanism, which in the context of this very sentence is explicitly opposed to the traditional humanism of Europe, is inherent in its worldliness, in an outright reversal of Protagoras's canonical statement ("man is the measure of all things"), whose evident anthropocentrism—despite its literally *political* nature (the fact that it emerges from the world of the polis where "things" are in effect the way of the cosmos)—turned into the metaphysics of nature that facilitated the universalist aspirations of both Enlightenment and bourgeois liberal humanisms. Let us note that this cosmological framework that Césaire sets forth by way of *poiēsis*—which, like in Senghor's case, is permeated with a profoundly African reverence for how myth encounters nature—is an undisputed adversary to the metaphysics of "human nature" that justifies the project of universal civilization on which both slavery and the colonial project are cemented.

In 1956, a year after the final revision and publication of his *Discourse on Colonialism*, Césaire declared his resignation from the French Communist Party in a famous letter to its secretary, Maurice Thorez. The letter is a sort of manifesto of anticolonial autonomy announcing the incapacity of Soviet-driven communist politics to overcome ingrained colonialist attitudes and to recognize racism as essential a tool of domination as is class exploitation. Against the presumption that communist politics addresses an undifferentiated worldwide condition of oppression, Césaire insists on "the singularity of our 'situation in the world,' which cannot be confused with any other. The singularity of our problems which cannot be reduced to any other problem. The singularity of our history, cut out from terrible avatars that belong to no one else. The singularity of our culture which we wish to live in a way that is more and more real."[33] But in foregrounding this singularity, very much like Roy in an analogous circumstance, Césaire insists on the possibility of an alternative understanding of the universal: "I'm not burying myself in some narrow particularism. But neither do I intend to lose myself in a disembodied universalism [*universalisme décharné*]. There are two ways to lose oneself: walled segregation in the particular or dilution in the 'universal.' My sense of the universal is a universal rich with all that is particular, rich with all the particulars there are, the deepening of each particular, the coexistence of them all" (152).

Fighting against a disembodied universalism—literally in Césaire's phrasing, "a universalism without flesh"—is conducted simultaneously with the refusal to submit to any sort of identity politics of the decolonized particular. This is a great lesson that very few in the day heeded, certainly neither those espousing a European project of human emancipation despite colonialism nor those who soon thereafter drafted the statutes of a European antihumanism resplendent with the glorification of the particular that has lasted uninterrogated to our day. But one figure who did take up this lesson and theorized it further with unparalleled razor-sharp vision and passion was Frantz Fanon, for a short while Césaire's student at the Lycée in Martinique.

Fanon raised both the politics of *négritude* and the project of new humanism to another level through an exceedingly rigorous dialectical critique, which was arguably due to the entwinement he literally embodied between actual anticolonial revolutionary experience, on the one hand, and the epistemological vantage point of the practice of medicine and psychoanalysis, on the other. The second comes to complement perfectly the radical surrealist poetics of Césaire, but the first—given that it signified the immersion of a black man from Martinique in the anticolonial struggle of Algerian Arabs—exemplified a hardcore imaginary of Africanness that exceeded any wandering vestiges of racial singularity that may have been hovering over the project of *négritude*. Let us note, however, that although Fanon's participation in the Algerian revolution was groundbreaking, it is part of a long trajectory of the African diaspora's radical engagement with

Afro-Asian anticolonial struggles, very much in the spirit of Bandung humanism, ranging from Richard Wright's participation in the Bandung conference itself from the standpoint of self-appointed reporter to Malcolm X's exuberant engagement late in life with radical movements in various parts of the Arab and African world (including meeting with Fanon) and to the extensive collaboration between the Black Panthers and the Palestinian Liberation Organization after 1968.[34] Yet what distinguishes Fanon above all in this respect is an uncompromising exilic perspective, much in the sense that Said defined it and in fact embodied in similar terms.

Attempts to come to terms with Fanon's work have reached inordinate numbers in recent years. The issue of his humanism is especially vexed, inasmuch as the presumption that radical thinking must be antihumanist in order to remain radical continues to prevail. The brief instance here, which is merely a passage toward a whole other problematic on the question of what is human, does not allow me to engage in the sort of logistics of criticism that settles the account. Here, I am concerned with just two things: (1) Fanon's explicit position in the legacy of *négritude* (and by extension the entire legacy of the Bandung imaginary in both its revolutionary and nationalist variants), and (2) his own unique contribution to this trajectory which is informed by his psychoanalytic understanding: namely, the fact that engaging the question of the human is inextricable from the problem of subjectivity in society and, more specifically, the sort of subjectivity that is forged by racial and colonial violence.[35] Both are measured by the passage from *Black Skin, White Masks* (1952) to *The Wretched of the Earth* (1961). In that decade Fanon will gain from the unique experience of immersing his reflections on colonial and racist oppression into the whirlpool of actual revolutionary struggle, as well as medical practice in the midst of colonial violence and anticolonial resistance, which will help him guard against many of the pitfalls of disembodied theory.

Incidentally, another way to understand Fanon's capacity to evade the trappings of disembodied theory is to consider that by all accounts his work throughout is performative at the core. The writing exceeds the mere presentation of ideas and follows rather a poetic mode of assembly, which is often even lyrical in style and affect and certainly not reducible to programmatic conception or instrumentalist conclusion. Even "writing" itself is not quite so clear a notion in this case, since Fanon dictated most of his writing to his assistants while conducting daily hospital work, which was not only clinical but also involved clandestine anticolonial operations such as gun smuggling from Tunisia. Orality, performativity, theatricality—Fanon was fascinated by the theater and wrote three plays he never published[36]—are the animating forces of his writing, much more so than mere conceptual and cognitive frameworks. Similarly, his psychotherapeutic practice was centered on reconfiguring the relation of the body to the social environment or the encounters between bodies and objects, between conditions of self (race, gender, language) and frameworks of social action, all of it signified specifically by the conditions of colonialism and decolonization. This overall practice, clinical and political, aimed at what Fanon called "disalienation," a term quite resonant in light of the historical ontology Marx develops in his early writings, one that was meant to counter the mental conditions of depersonalization (alienation in a literal psycho-subjective sense) that he diagnosed in victims of colonial and racist violence to have reached various degrees of psychosis.[37]

Thinking overall, then, there is considerably less distance between these two texts than has often been assumed. The revolutionary experience does not constitute a realm of afterthought. Its effect is uncannily presupposed, even if not yet experienced as fact; it is embedded in a way of life that makes revolutionary experience a necessary pedagogical condition. Even as a twenty-seven-year old medical student, Fanon was already aware of how easy it was to fall into "the intellectualization of the experience of being black," as he picks apart Sartre's investment in *négritude* at the same time that he borrows the structural motif of Sartre's argument in *Anti-Semite and Jew*.[38] Fanon's precarious wager from the outset is to address an evident and profound internality of racism without compromising on the fact of racism's undeconstructibly external imposition. The strangeness in the condition of racism is the absolute entwinement of the two without their ever collapsing into one: "I am overdetermined from without. I am the slave not of the 'idea' that others have of me but of my own appearance" (BSWM, 116). The irony of appearance as truth creates an altogether debilitating phenomenology: "When people like me, they tell me it is in spite of my color. When they dislike me, they point out that it is not because of my color. Either way, I am locked into an infernal circle" (BSWM, 116). In an endless series of double negatives racism affirms its hold on the subject as its object even in disavowal.

This is a precise account of how the historical interferes with and alters the ontological. It is the case not only with racism but also with colonialism, both at once: "Colonialism is not satisfied merely with squeezing people in its grip and emptying the colonized mind of all form and content. By a kind of perverted logic, it turns to the past of the oppressed people and distorts, disfigures, and annihilates it."³⁹ Fanon will rely on this perspective to deconstruct the perils of the sort of *négritude* perspective that might aspire to some pristine nativist Africanness that can be magically called upon the stage as a miraculous weapon. There is no *deus ex machina* in the tragedy of "the Negro"—the drama of liberation is not a Gloria of racial restoration. Which is why any kind of unqualified *négritude*—"unqualified" in the sense of existing outside of the struggle for liberation, which produces what at some point Fanon calls "the racialization of thought" (WE, 212)—ultimately hinders the poietic invention of a new humanity, which is the ultimate revolutionary purpose. Fanon is uncompromising in this regard, and any notion of exclusive identity must be torn down. Consider this extraordinary set of quotations from the last pages of *Black Skin, White Masks*: "The Negro is the slave of the past. Nonetheless, I am a man [*je suis homme*], and in this sense the Peloponnesian War is as much mine as the invention of the compass" (BSWM, 225). "I am a man, and what I have to recapture is the whole part of the world. I'm not responsible solely for the revolt of Santo Domingo" (BSWM, 226). And even more: "It was not the black world that laid down my course of conduct. My black skin is not the wrapping of specific values" (BSWM, 227).

Fanon embarks on a difficult, perhaps even acrobatic, argument in favor of the *poiēsis* of a national culture that is neither nationalist nor nativist. While he dispatches nationalism succinctly as the project of a postcolonial bourgeoisie that replicates colonial structures, his argument on nativism is more pained and elusive. Insofar as the native is a form of recognition invented by the settler, nativism is a colonial fabrication, and adherence to it is an obstacle to decolonization. Fully aware that he was once fashioned in its spirit, he argues that if *négritude* is anchored to some sort of native memory, some sort of folklore or custom, it is no more than "a banal search for exoticism" (WE, 221) and cannot thus serve as the source of the culture of liberation. "Culture has none of the translucidity of custom; it fiercely avoids all simplification. In its essence it is opposed to custom, for custom is always the deterioration of culture" (WE, 224). And later on: "a national culture is not a folklore, nor an abstract populism that believes it can discover the people's true nature" (WE, 233). The struggle for liberation is thus conducted over an abyss, and both nature and culture are created by "the action through which the people constitutes and maintains itself" (WE, 233).⁴⁰

This revolutionary self-creation (autopoiesis) returns to the national its root in the natal—"the [new] nation gives life to national culture in the strictly biological sense of the phrase" (WE, 245)—a notion that, much like Hannah Arendt's investment in natality, we need to understand in terms of the profound capacity of the human imagination for *poiēsis* of unprecedented, previously nonexistent and unimaginable, radically new forms. All this takes place within the struggle. Anticolonial national liberation does not restore a nation; it creates a nation that never existed before. This is why national independence, as it is understood in the nationalist frame of mind, is a fraudulent term because it presupposes something that existed before which, having now been liberated from the darkness of time, returns to its authentic autonomous place. But to be liberated means to have escaped, to have left the place you were once confined in, indeed to have left it behind in all its shards and ashes. Thus, "the struggle for liberation is a cultural phenomenon" (WE, 245) expressly in the sense that it is a *poietic* phenomenon, and national culture partakes of the same capacity for invention and creativity that fuels a new universal project—a "new humanism." That's why Fanon will clarify unequivocally that "national consciousness is not nationalism" and it only has meaning in an "international dimension" (WE, 247), which is precisely the core of Bandung humanism in whose context decolonial national consciousness is the adversary of all nationalism, colonial and postcolonial alike. For, while there can be potentially an interminable number of nations, national narratives, and national histories, the epistemological framework of nationalism is always one and the same regardless.

Moreover, in separating national liberation from nationalism, Fanon also reminds us that the purpose of the national liberation struggle is "not only the disappearance of colonialism but the disappearance of the colonized," (WE, 246) the disappearance of an entire historical species. Just as, from the standpoint of the liberation struggle, culture is not a thing of the past but always lies before us in a path of discovery and creation, so is ontology. If nothing else because, as Fanon argued from the outset, "every ontology is made unattainable in colonized and civilized society" (BSWM, 109), whereby "civilized" is irreversibly determined by "colonized" so that we cannot possibly speak of some sort of civilizational overcoming of history. The relation between "colonized" and "civilized" is of course asymmetrical, and thus the meaning of this impossible ontology, this unattainability, is always already anchored on unequal ground: "Ontology...does not permit us to understand the being of the black man.... The black man has no ontological resistance in the eyes of the white man" (BSWM, 110). This asymmetry that Fanon draws even while pointing out the unavoidable relativity of ontology cannot but remain at the core of any attempt to encounter the question of what is human. But this makes Fanon's investment in a new humanism even more formidable. He reaches deep into the abyss of colonial and racist cultivations of the human in order to elicit out of it, by sheer poietic power, a new humanism of both self and other—he makes this clear several times—so as to make sure that the species of "colonized man" disappears: "I make myself the poet of the world. The white man has found a poetry in which there is nothing poetic.... The presence of the Negroes beside the whites is in a way an insurance policy on humanness" (BSWM, 129).

At the very least, in Fanonian humanism, epistemological clarity and ontological certainty are made impossible. One of the salient lessons of *Black Skin, White Masks*, which is embedded in its very language, in its *style* we would say in literary terms, is a call for innovation—which may be inventively reconsidered in terms of the recent embrace of Afrofuturism—that testifies to a kind of poetic violence of creation. As one of the most succinct demonstrations of the politics of interpellation a few years in fact before Althusser conducted the consummate lesson on the subject, Fanon's account of the racist depersonalization of being called out as a Negro is simultaneously engaged with an adversarial gesture of translation from the racialized self to an other self who emerges by fiat in the very concrete situation of public encounter.[41] This adversarial act is not quite a defiance of interpellation, or even an act of resistance plain and simple. Rather, it is an act of displacement of interpellation, or perhaps more precisely of misplacement, so that the ideological/racist command does not quite find its way to its telos—its aim, its target, its endpoint.

Fanon engages in a psychosexual poetics of subjectivity in the same way that he engages the project of decolonization as a struggle for liberation. Yet, he makes painfully clear that decolonization is never simply a matter of national liberation. What is really at stake is the decolonization of every individual, of subjectivity itself, just as the specific condition of depersonalization as mental illness that he seeks to cure in the clinic as a psychiatrist is linked directly to the experience of colonial and racist violence in society. From the outset, Fanon asserted: "The Negro is comparison.... Every position of one's own, every effort at security, is based on relations of dependence, with the diminution of the other. It is the wreckage that surrounds me that provides the foundation for my virility" (BSWM, 211). For this reason there is no subjective core that you can restore. There is nothing there but wreckage—that's what having no "ontological resistance" really means. There is no being that would allow you access to *human-being*. Racism and colonialism produce a void all over the insides of your body and soul. You are left with nothing but a brutal heteronomous relation, a self constituted in the split of comparison, which in any case does not even belong to you. This frame of comparison belongs to the society you seek to destroy.

In this respect, your subjectivity is always in front; it is there for the making, literally an object of creation, of poietic violence, for its creation will at the same time signify destruction: "the disappearance of the colonized man"—the disappearance of an entire historical species. So, in order to foster radical power, this profoundly singular act, pertaining only to you, matters only to the extent that this "you" displaces the hierarchical power of the other who commands the parameters of this "you" and controls the relation, so that you can create the terms of a new *intersubjectivity*: where what is self and what is other are *translated* from the inherited social-imaginary institutions that establish and safeguard this relation to whatever new institutions will emerge from the struggle to liberate suppressed capacities of *human-being* all around: "Universality resides in the decision to recognize and accept the reciprocal relativism of different cultures once the colonial status has been irreversibly excluded."[42]

Radical decolonization, in this respect, signifies a whole other configuration of subjectivity that bears upon the very constitution of the *human/animal* whose nature is always in any case profoundly historical. Following this trajectory of what we can now call decolonial humanism, Fanon's impetus is to struggle for a social transformation that will privilege conditions of intersubjectivity without presupposing the self-enclosed sufficiency of the subject, since this new configuration of the human is only possible through the incorporation of the other in the definitional field. Decolonial humanism puts forth an inordinate demand: a kind of consubstantial humanity where humanity is not a category of being but a quality of being which human animals owe to each other against the very institutions of violence they have created to the point of self-annihilation.

Drawing on the trenchant reading of Fanon by Holocaust survivor Jean Améry in terms of their common experience of depersonalizing racism, Paul Gilroy makes an inventive and succinct point when he views Fanon's humanism through the absolutely tangible and worldly effect of violence, as a humanism that does not come "from a willfully innocent account of some sacred, intersubjective encounter with Otherness, but from profane acts in which the cruelty done by one to another disclosed the urgent obligation to seek an alternative way of being in the world."[43] The depersonalization perpetrated by racial and colonial violence is tantamount to the sundering of the self/other relation at the core of body and soul—that's precisely the rupture in the human fabric that an act of torture signifies—so that no conceptual figure of otherness, even one marked by emancipatory vision, can provide adequate anchoring.[44] The tearing apart of bodies and souls, persons and relations, that creates this "amputated humanity" happens in the actual world and can be overcome only in this world, not by appealing to some abstract humanity, which in any case, if it ever really existed, has been already annihilated in these conditions even as a concept. For this reason, Fanon calls on us to break with basic ontology—or, to be more precise, he sees ontology itself as a break-free condition: "I am a part of Being to the degree I go beyond it" (BSWM, 229).

Along these lines, and from the standpoint of the present, Fanon's dream of decolonial humanism reaches out beyond the disappearance of the "historical species of colonized man," which in any case has not yet been realized. And this is not only because of what nowadays are generally called neocolonial conditions, even if the significational integrity of the term "neo" invariably must be questioned, but also because another historical ontology has come to slide alongside the species of the colonized: the species of techno-commodified humans. From this standpoint, in the current geopolitical frame previously colonized societies are no longer different from previously colonizing societies. Building on the bioeconomy of colonialism, global capitalism has made great use of the narcotic structures of national independence—and indeed the low-grade violence of acculturation—to produce everywhere the historical species of depoliticized technocommodified human animals, of consumer subjects/objects who consume themselves and each other as much as they do the planet's resources.

In this nexus, which crosses the nationalist border enclosure with capital's all-pervasive violence in order to open more and more spaces for endless flow, the historical species of technocommodified human animals includes what will always be coded as necessary refuse. As is the way of all commodities, human bodies too find their way into the pathways of engineered waste, and in more ways than one. The manner in which the question of the human has emerged in the current discussions of the ambiguous terrain of the stateless migrant/refugee is a perfectly mirroring symptom of this nexus. This symptom is in place in every side that claims special insight into the semiotics of this species, to remain within Fanon's language. Whether it is the hand of state sovereignty that intervenes with the hegemony of humanitarian reason, in Didier Fassin's formulation,[45] or the intervening practices of NGO resistance in their full range of radical disregard of nationalist and capitalist governmentality, it still seems that the trap of liberalism remains outmaneuverable. Although in the case of the latter, it is understood that "the question of the human is not a consensual notion, but predicated on radical lines of division" thereby opening the possibility "to invent the human and to speak of the human as a battlefield,"[46] nonetheless the easy assumption of the inhumanity or subhumanity of the migrant/refugee that must be overcome so entry into humanity may be restored is already doomed to return to categories that global capital (and its liberal arsenal of significations: humanitarianism, human rights, philanthropy) still commands. The production of commodified subjectivities coded to serve the (now global) apparatus of what can still be called colonial violence, even if we may disagree on the specifics, can never be absorbed into the realm of established humanist meanings. It, too, is a historical species that must be abolished.

Sylvia Wynter, who is arguably Fanon's greatest heir in the late twentieth-century trajectory of decolonial humanism, has made explicit the historical connections in this passage from colonization to the consumerist commodification of subjectivity, much as she has shown that the threads weaving together the trajectory of bioeconomic incarceration of subjectivities from the Spanish imperial *encomiendas* to plantation slavery to urban ghettoization in the Americas parallels the trajectory of European humanism from the era of Italian Renaissance cities to bourgeois liberal humanism to what is presently called posthumanism. Wynter does not hesitate to reiterate the emancipatory elements of the humanist project in its various points of emergence over time while never compromising on its complicity in the project of racist and colonialist domination. This dialectical contradiction is not to be resolved by the disqualification of the former in the overcoming of the latter. History provides a key to knowledge of the self in relation to its others, especially when the (sub)terrain of otherness is understood as a necessary condition for both the framing and the production of self-knowledge.

Wynter evokes with great clarity the convergence of Césaire and Fanon on the essentially *poietic* (indeed, autopoietic) character of the specific politics of knowledge that anticolonial humanism put forth. In Césaire's language, this politics of knowledge returns "to the very first days of the species" so that once more "the study of the word will condition the study of nature" ("Poetry and Knowledge," xlix) and a new *science* will thereby emerge. For Wynter, quite rightly, science here means the convergence of *bios* and *mythos* in autopoietic praxis.[47] Her understanding of *human-being* is essentially biomythical: a sort of hybrid nature in which whatever is poetic, mythical, or imaginary (the notions here utterly converge) is as organic as any flesh and blood matter and, moreover, not "given by nature" in some zoological organicity (which would reduce it entirely to evolutionary brain function) but in an inherently ontological autopoietic dynamic—the capacity to make and unmake oneself and one's environment as a species. Her language in this regard is unequivocal: "*Our 'stories' are as much a part of what makes us human as are our bipedalism and the use of our hands.* This is necessarily so as a function of the Event of our origin, of our specifically human mode of living being as a hybrid biological and meta-biological species. And as such a species, our behaviors are no longer solely determined by laws regulatory of biological life, but also by *laws of auto-institution* specific to our also third level of existence."[48]

Of course, this process is never universally human, in the sense that it is not simply even biologically human—meaning not only is it *not* exclusively determined by biology in strict zoological terms but rather affects how biology, as a category of nature, might become readable in its numerous determinations. This process is not universally human because it is always what Wynter calls "genre-specific." A simple way to translate this would be "social-historical" but neither in the sense that society and history might often be considered strata secondary to nature, nor simply in the sense of culture-specific, because then the radical bio-ontological sphere of *human-being* would be lost, dismantled by its particularities. The differential registers of "genre-specific" pertain to the entire universe of the *human/animal*, but no genre in itself can represent universal humanity, despite the arrogant claim to that effect by Western monohumanism. And at the same time, although humanism is a multisited formation with numerous complex histories, no simple historization of its multiplicities would be adequate because any account of how the *human/animal* historicizes itself in genre-specific ways is predicated on what remains impossible to historicize in *human-being* as a condition. On this issue, Wynter remains uncompromising.

We'll return to Wynter's remarkable, if peculiar, ontology at the end of this essay, when we encounter the epistemological claims of the Anthropocene. What matters at this stage is her intervention in the legacy of decolonial humanism in the wake of the anticolonial thinkers we've examined. In an inspired turn of phrase, David Scott has identified Wynter's specific affinity with this legacy as an "embattled humanism"—a naming she explicitly welcomes.[49] Indeed, what could be a better way to describe Fanon's visionary invocation of a new humanity after the species of colonized man has disappeared (or for that matter, Said's own non-humanist humanism) than this notion of embattlement: an understanding of the terrain of *human-being* as intrinsically contentious and riveted by politics and social-historical differentials and specificities, whose emancipatory point would be predicated on the self-(re)cognition that genre-specific humanisms have created whole systems of living-being (by now extending to planetary being everywhere) that, in Wynter's language, need to be overturned.

Humanism's intrinsic overturn(ing), in these terms, begins with the recognition of the color line as humanism's "governing sociogenic principle" and here Wynter is channeling both Du Bois and Fanon. Understanding how the problematic of race structures (indeed, creates) the colonial economy is decisive, not only in the deconstruction of traditional (mono)humanism but, more important, in the visionary articulation of decolonial humanism as the emancipatory project of our time. This means that, in Wynter's terms, un/settling coloniality happens simultaneously with un/writing the knowledge framework that the racist/colonial imaginary created in the name (and with the structures) of humanism over several centuries. This is not simply a matter of epistemology, because, mathematics aside, no knowledge framework can exist entirely outside lived experience—which is essential to Fanon (as well as Césaire, Senghor, or Said, for that matter)—much in the way that no sharp distinction can be made between what Wynter, following Fanon, calls the sociogenic principle and what, in the context of living-being in general, we can call the ontogenic principle without being burdened by Freud's decisive (and understandable) separation of the ontogenetic from the phylogenetic which enables psychoanalysis to become autonomous from biodeterminism.[50] While the two categories are distinct—otherwise, we would have the worst of vulgar Lamarckism or social constructivism—there is no way to justify what Fanon identifies as sociogenic experience (the lived experience of blackness in a racist society) as some secondary or epiphenomenal stratum of *human-being*. A sociogenic experience takes place at the most hardcore level of being. The racist cry of interpellation fixes the mark of dehumanization on body and soul as "a chemical solution fixes a dye" (BSWM, 109).

This is one of the most trenchant lessons of *Black Skin, White Masks*, remarkable in that it came from the pen of a twenty-seven-year-old, but not remarkable at all if we consider how brutally clear was the lesson that the author had already learned in his very psyche before he even uttered a word.[51] This in itself is a crucial methodological point. For, Fanon establishes *simultaneously* that blackness is both an objective fact, a historical formation of perfectly clear provenance, and yet a subjective experience, not of the mind but of the body: a veritable dimension of living-being, as material as thirst or hunger.[52] On this basis, Wynter will argue that "the sociogenic principle, at the level of human identity, is an analogue to the genomic principle, at the level of purely organic forms of life" (36). The implication is that subjective experience, as indefinitely variable as there are subjectivities in the world, is nonetheless *a fact of the world* and part of an information network (no less material than any information system, organic or mechanical, neurological or technological) that organizes the relations of commonality and difference which create, sustain, and reproduce the body of society in a sense as organic or physiological as can be imagined.

For Fanon especially, the subjective experience of racism and colonial violence is not an epiphenomenon of some social-historical conjuncture, even if indeed it emerges in this sort of particularity. Rather, it is an embodied "psycho-existential complex" that forms, controls, and reproduces *human-being* as a condition no less organic (or, if you will, zoological) than any sort of scientifically configured neurophysiological condition. That is why, sociogenic psychosis, due to racist or colonialist violence, is to be treated as a neurophysiological illness by medical action at the same time that its source needs to be abolished in the social-historical field by political action. The two are intertwined as two equal registers of real existence, particular to the individual subject and universal to the collective subject all at once. Fanon's explicitly autopoietic call that concludes *The Wretched of the Earth* should be understood in the same double way as well: "For Europe, for ourselves, and for humanity, comrades, we must make new skin (*faire peau neuve*), we must work out new concepts, and try to set afoot a new human" (WE, 316). To make a new skin, though grammatically a metaphor, must be read literally– *ontologically*. It is a call for ontological innovation and in this sense should be read alongside and against the grain of Afropessimist positions as a specific *poiesis* that embraces a certain level of destruction, poetic violence.

In the same register, Wynter will come in the early 1970s to speak, more expansively, of "transplantation" in the context of the American slave experience as both a psychoexistential and, even more, a socio-bio-ecological response of the enslaved population to its irrevocable displacement. Facing the impossibility of transporting indigenous culture in any meaningful sense once elementary forms of *human-being* are dismantled (kinship, place, person, sex, bodily integrity, as well as every form of social institution), enslaved Africans in the Americas turn to the most unmediated proximity to the earth itself in order to create a whole other imaginary of living-being, replanting themselves, as it were, *in situ*, on the small plots of land adjacent to plantations where communal sustenance could be practiced against the deterritorializing economy that emerged and flourished on the basis of their depersonalizing labor. Going beyond simple theories of creolization or syncretic culture, Wynter speaks of a "metamorphosis"—the most *poietic* of notions—of culture whereby a whole other indigeneity, in the strangest and most alien of soils, can be created: "a transplantation of a traditional relationship to nature, a relationship under the inspiration of which, the slave, now in exile both adapted himself to Nature and transformed it. In this type of relationship, the *land* (i.e., part of Nature) could not be regarded as a mere commodity in the land-labor-capital relationship. New world land, like land in Africa, was still seen as the Earth—the communal means of production. This attitude, transferred and perpetuated was the central grid for many old beliefs which could be retranslated into a new reality."[53]

It is important to understand from this description that, despite the language, Wynter sees this metamorphotic transplantation not simply as a matter of economy—a counterculture of economy. Even more, she sees economy as a category of living being in all of its psycho-bio-ecological range. Transforming alien land in alien (and brutally alienating) social conditions into the generation of new indigenous life takes place at all levels of cultural *poiēsis*, including the metamorphotic transplantation of ancestral spirits and oaths, the corporeal sense of voice, the alertness to the sentient dimensions of nature, to the very rhythms of being: "Dance and song and music, like all art in the culture of origin, were represented as the result of man's self-expression, his unique fulfillment of the Earth's generative powers working through him, as she, the Earth, fulfilled herself in giving birth to the crop and therefore, to man. For the earth—like the sea for fishing tribes—was the 'material' basis of man's existence, in his environment, was represented as the generator of life." (548) For this reason, Wynter's notion of the "new native" as configured in the process she explicitly names "indigenization" has to do with neither Fanon's critique of the native as a dialectical by-product of the colonizer nor the way that the category of the indigenous has been configured relative to the struggle against the settler. Recent discourses of indigeneity in settler colonialism are implicated in issues of sovereignty of territory in which the indigenous are the victims of dispossession and destruction, while, via the double metaphor of transplantation/transformation, Wynter articulates a new material perspective of land, in its minutest earthly topology, that is not territorial but planetary. For Wynter, the "new native" signifies an autopoietic creation in the midst of a psychoexistential void. The transplanted African slave in the Americas (re)makes exceedingly alien conditions in constitutively alien space indigenous through an incorporation of the Earth—not the territory—as a new imaginary materiality that can never be revoked or dispossessed, no matter the most violent deracination.

From this standpoint, Wynter might be giving us a real historical glimpse of how a new humanism, in Fanon's sense, can be created out of the ashes, out of the annihilation of culture. While Fanon's notion remains utopian, just as the disappearance of the colonized as a historical species remains an as yet unrealized project, Wynter's account endows this utopia with a real historical imaginary—all the more because she remains uncompromising on the register of the psychosocial politics of subjectivity. In this sense, her remarkable work bears the key to the transition from anticolonial to decolonial humanism, which, as Gilroy has argued, can only be a planetary humanism.

Humanism as an Open Question

To speak of decolonial humanism within the problematic of subjectivity might be considered anachronistic insofar as it might be thought to privilege a discursive prism—the discourse on the subject—that belongs to the language of European antihumanism. I do it on purpose, bearing in mind Emily Apter's observation that the category of the subject, whose death spearheaded the antihumanist radicalism of 1960s theory, is at this point producing intellectual fatigue and that, in its place, the category of the human has (re)emerged demanding more (and new) significance, especially, as Apter adds, in "rethinking the terms of aliveness within the humanities at a time when the refrain 'death of the humanities' is all too frequently intoned."[54]

This shift from (critique of) the subject to (critique of) the human is of further benefit if we juxtapose it to another trenchant contemporary condition: the shift from institutions of national-canonical literacy, which signify the conventional content of modern humanism, to institutions of global media technologies. These technologies, which trade in both image and information, aspire to be neither canonical nor properly national but nonetheless act as pedagogical mechanisms of mass acculturation that are ultimately indifferent to literacy and may even be keen on rewarding illiteracy as a more efficient ground of domesticating the human. The mere juxtaposition of these two shifts makes for a formidable field, even if issues of incompatibility between the two pairs abound: the second shift might be said to politically undermine the first, insofar as new configurations of the human, whatever they may be, must encounter psychic mechanisms of dehumanization that are all-pervasive and worldwide.

And even though one might argue that at this point in history dehumanization has reached unfathomable levels of brutality and horror, nonetheless it has always gone hand in hand with the classic impetus of the civilizing mission of traditional humanism since its heyday of national-canonical—and, from the world's perspective, colonial—literacy. Peter Sloterdijk makes this crucial *coincidence* one of the key theses in his controversial essay on the significance of humanism today: "The latent message of humanism is the taming of humans. And its hidden thesis is: reading the right books calms the inner beast."[55] But, he goes on, humanism's constitutive self-taming is consubstantial with an equally constitutive self-disinhibition: "Human beings in high culture are constantly subjected simultaneously to two pressures, which for simplicity's sake we shall term 'constraining' and 'unconstraining' or 'disinhibiting.'... The label of humanism reminds us (with apparent innocuousness) of the constant battle for humanity that reveals itself as a contest between bestializing and taming tendencies" (S, 15). Let us add, somewhat precariously, that Sloterdijk is echoing here Horkheimer and Adorno's dialectic of Enlightenment. Such a dialectical element is missing from both traditional advocates and traditional detractors of humanism, and this lapse becomes even graver if we understand that both self-taming and self-disinhibiting tendencies contribute to the narrative of dehumanization.

We lose the political sharpness of this gravity when we read "dehumanization" in moral terms and forget that it is not an aberration (due, say, to the ideological insidiousness of humanism or some part of civilization gone wrong) but a constitutive psychodynamic prerogative, intrinsic to human animality insofar that it is part of its life force—indeed, its life-and-death force—but always in specific historical and political trajectories. Because the *human/animal* is ultimately a worldly state and not a state of nature—its nature *is* its worldliness—its animal properties are neither given nor imprinted once and for all. The *human/animal* can lose its properties. It can be taken out of the world, and in more ways than one: not only by becoming an abstraction in the many ways of transcendental metaphysics or capitalist technometrics but also, quite literally, by *being dehumanized* in an altogether worldly material sense in the course of human life. This latter condition—the annihilation of what is human in the human in the name and course of the human—is singularly a human action, perhaps even a human attribute, which means that whatever might be credited with making the human into an achievement (of history, of culture, of art, of science) would have to include some of the basest, most horrific, elements of destruction or indignity imaginable. From this standpoint, dehumanization is an instance—perhaps even a core attribute—of humanization, which is always ongoing, differential, and transformational, for better or worse, including what in the scope of this essay also signifies animalization, hardly a negative notion when it comes to reconfiguring the human.

Essential to this discussion (and following the earlier reflections on Fanon and Wynter) is the groundbreaking conversation going on in the last ten years among scholars in black studies around the notion of "blackness" as a disintegrating force residing at the core of collective significations established by traditional ontology and discourses of and around the human, including the presumptions of its overcoming in posthumanism, animal studies, or AI technology studies. This conversation, which goes beyond targeted discussions of race and gender although it is intractably situated within them, is profoundly rich and inspiring, while the voluminous rapid-fire internal debates are fierce. It is by far the most exciting and transformational sphere in radical thought these days, and the extraordinary mobilization of people now under the banner of Black Lives Matter marks the boundless unrest of its praxis.

Crucial for my specific focus here is the monumental work of Fred Moten, starting with *In the Break* (2003) and extending to the trilogy of books organized around the phrase *consent not to be a single being*—which is a perfectly Fanonian notion, even if its utterance belongs to Édouard Glissant. This work is all the more precious to me, in a very personal way, because it engages the entire complex of *poiēsis*: the entwinement of poetry, music, thought, and action, which is to say, the totality of how Moten stands in a world he still loves even as he wants to change it. To my ear, Moten's widely discussed notion of fugitivity very much echoes Fanon's proclamation that he is part of Being to the degree that he goes beyond it. However, the resonance further involves all sorts of complicated ripples. Fiercely resistant to any temptation/trap to think either in terms of essence or identity, Moten describes in myriad peculiar ways how blackness introduces into the core of ontology a permanently radiating disruption. The concept of ontology thus bursts apart at the seams, and the precious wholeness it has presumed to stand for since the days of Parmenides is rendered irrecoverable.

Moten's general operational framework—distilled in the name "Black Op" that titles a pivotal essay in *Stolen Life* as a triple synchord of operation, optics, and optimism—can be understood as an instance where the negation of the negation, whose Hegelian language is closer to a negative dialectics but also starkly beyond it, does not signify some sort of sublated affirmation, although it is very much an action, a stance. While all action is in that distilled sense affirmative, regardless of announced content (of negation or refusal) and position (anti-, ante- or para-), this action of negation dissolves the subject who makes it or, maybe more accurately, recognizes that only a nonsubject (a subject whose subjectivity is refused) can make it in this fashion. At stake here, Moten says, "is the necessary distinction between the delusional system, at once narcotic and regulatory, of possessive individual and national development and the improvisational mechanics, at the convergence of fantasy and flight, of a fugitive ensemble's dispossessed and dispossessive flesh."[56] What is rendered fugitive by virtue of total dispossession—of self, of body, of sex, of kin, of being—is simultaneously dispossessive of all those things, but also of their presumed reinstantiation in some promised redemptive future. Situated outside linear time, the temporality of fugitive action is improvisational above all. To mine the term's musical significance: it is at once collective and spontaneously compositional—of forms, bodies, positions, perspectives, beings—which remain, however, invariably transient, provisional, fugitive in any framework that still demands the necessary imprimatur of identity and property.

This is why Moten brilliantly connects the experience of blackness to the general condition of statelessness—"blackness is given into the refusal of the refugee" (194)—which he hardly understands as a condition of debilitation but rather as an "inalienable sociopoetic insurgency" (200) that ultimately frustrates any act of interpellation no matter what the power and violence of hegemonic (racist/statist/nationalist, etc.) oppression and dispossession might be. Against this violence stands an ontological refusal, a refusal not only of what is given or granted you but also of what might be expected of you or promised to you in some future time of reversal and redemption: "To refuse what is normatively desired and to claim what is normatively disavowed is our lot.... To refuse what has been refused is a combination of disavowing, of not wanting, of withholding consent to do the work, that is supposed to bring the would-be subject online" (243).

The reality of fugitivity that blackness signifies as a historical condition is inherent in the remarkable gesture of refusing what is refused to you, which marks the entire signifying space by an interminable corrosion of all elements claimed to be solid—affirmation, subjectivity, property, possession, freedom, race, gender, state, nation, being (human): "The relation of blackness to the nation-state [*but we can substitute any of the above and more*] must be understood as analogous to that between a stubborn monolith and a finally irresistible solvent" (197).[57] This statement is grand if we take seriously the riveting assertion that blackness "is not but nothing other than Western civilization" (156), meaning it is not some particularity, some antithesis, some partiality or, more commonly, some dark underside that somehow must be redeemed and brought back into the fold, but rather the untranscendable core inside the singular force of planetary modernity, of what has come to be history's most privileged form of cultural power.

High stakes. The solvent *is* the substance, which means that the celebrated solidity of this cultural power is a farce—or, to be perhaps kind for the sake of elaboration, the substance of Western civilization has no essence, which is to say in our terms here, humanism has no essence, *human-being* has no essence. This much we've already established. But what Moten adds works in a double register. On the one hand, the nonessence of blackness is underwritten by a "distinction from any specific set of things that are called black" (157) including "people who are called black" (242), and on the other hand, blackness pertains (in what is an extension of Fanon) to a totality, a universality: "Everyone whom blackness claims, which is to say everyone, can claim blackness" (159). This double register is profoundly anti-identitarian as well as resistant to essentialism—essence and identity being after all irrevocably entwined. But with a significant twist: this totality of blackness is also riveted by "an absolute and general no-thing-ness" that marks the "move from the metaphysics of presence, given in the figure of the one, to the physics of presence, given in transubstantial no-thing-ness, in consent not to be (single), in differential inseparability, in the nearness and distance of the making of a living and its spooky, *ani*material actions" (244). In invoking the nothingness of blackness as a totality, an everything of nonessence, Moten is also refusing at one and the same time the straightforward and uncritical association of black(ness) both with thing(ness) and with animal(ness), refusing thus liberal humanism's separatist divisions that plague animate materiality.

As negation of the negation that has no resolution, no telos, but is nonetheless a praxis as material as anything in the world, Moten's gesture troubles all sorts of transcendental promises that abound in the civilizational project of liberal humanism, including words that are precious in the historical vocabulary of blackness: redemption, salvation, reparation, abolition, and above all freedom. "What if it's not freedom but the freedom to give freedom away that is inalienable and absolute and constitutes the ground of freedom's *virtual* generality?" (248). "What if to be free from slavery is to be free of slavery? What if freedom is (a condition) of slavery? What if freedom is nothing more than vernacular loneliness? The paradox (if freedom is inalienable the freedom to relinquish freedom must also be so) disappears when it is discovered that slavery and freedom are not opposed to one another" (250–51).

In *Becoming Human*, Zakiyyah Iman Jackson engages in a similar gesture in her use of the notion of plasticity in relation to what she idiomatically calls the "black(ened)" body. Jackson's specific notation reminds me instantly of how Luce Irigaray long ago theorized sexual difference by insisting on the adjectival participle *sexué* (as opposed to *sexuelle*), that is to say, pointing to a subject/object that is sex*ed*, specifically subjected to forces that work upon it in perpetuity so that it is never fully constituted, but remains fluid, malleable, of ambiguous (to say the least) ontology, or even more, of no ontology whatsoever within the established ontological parameters of the human. Jackson's contribution to this discussion is quite original, even if curiously (unlike Moten) she does not return to Fanon, who to my mind has already announced the entire problematic. Specifically, Jackson turns Catherine Malabou's affirmative notion of plasticity, as antidote to the hardened ontological gravity of Western metaphysics, into a negative notion insofar as this pertains to black(ened) bodies, which through slavery and its aftermaths are rendered infinitely malleable, denied any somatic or psychosubjective integrity. From this perspective, plasticity becomes a mark of prohibition, an instituted obstacle to ontological certainty, and is not to be celebrated as such.

But the most radical gesture in Jackson's book, which is directly pertinent here, is how she pushes against the easy assertions of the ontological incapacity of the black(ened) body, which leads to frequent associations of blackness with animality. Jackson refuses to take for granted the thesis that deracinated enslaved black bodies are simply dehumanized and thus removed from the purview of humanity—denied humanity and thus animalized—because this retains the classic liberal humanist distinction between human and animal. Instead, she argues that the abject condition within which the black(ened) body finds itself at a certain point in history and thereafter is part of the history of humanization, an element of the history of liberal humanism's triumph as the measure of civilization. What is tantamount to "animal" in reference to black people is a specific way of being coded human: "Animalization is not incompatible with humanization: what is commonly deemed dehumanization is more accurately interpreted as the violence of humanization or the burden of inclusion into a racially hierarchized universal humanity" (*Becoming Human*, 18). This leaves no option for humanism's "civilized" humanity to proceed intact by virtue of and beyond its mechanisms of exclusion. Instead, humanity is permanently haunted by its internal disintegrity, by a self-induced violation at the core (named "dehumanization") that underwrites an ontological disintegration that cannot be ideologically policed by any sort of traditional humanism or humanitarianism.

Incidentally, worth noting here is Hannah Arendt's provocative argument of how colonial racism in Africa is exacerbated in the encounter with this profoundly other humanity: "Race was the emergency explanation of human beings whom no European or civilized man could understand and whose humanity so frightened and humiliated the immigrants that they no longer cared to belong to the same human species."[58] In other words, this terrifying black humanity substantiates the racist conception of colonized bodies as "raw material" (Arendt's words) and drives the de facto de-animation that assimilates them to the very operations of mineral extraction. While the established narrative of colonial racism reiterates the classic argument that "natives" were seen as pure nature and were thus devoid of culture/civilization (a trap that eventually Arendt falls into as well), the peculiar but radical point in this assertion is to underline the experience of the other's humanity precisely in the colonial encounter. This constitutively unsettling experience produces indeed an emergency explanation: this altogether *contrary humanity* must not be allowed and yet, even more, its negation conveniently comes to serve as the platform for negation of all humanity, which justifies in turn the overt inhumanity that swiftly becomes celebrated as the character of the settlers themselves.

Yet, returning to Jackson, the stakes are even higher: If what is rendered animal in reference to the black is not an exclusion but a deliberately included abjection, a "bestialized humanization" (23), then there is also no satisfaction in mere reparation, no desired gesture for inclusion as transcendence of the racist core condition of humanism's proclaimed humanity. All such—in essence, liberal—overcoming, making whole again, is foreclosed. No transcendental solution is possible, and thus the problem remains in the tangible material historical realm in which it was created, where an absolutely radical gesture against it remains the real object to be achieved: the abolition not only of specific institutions (slavery, Jim Crow, institutionalized racism, carceral discipline, homicidal police, etc.) but also of the entire historical species, as Fanon demands, so that a whole other order of what is human(ized) can take place.[59] Moreover, refusing the human/animal division, in both Moten's and Jackson's arguments, is also pertinent here to the project of understanding human animality as untranscendable condition of bio-psycho-socio-historical living being and the basis on which a whole other humanist politics can be created.

The stakes of this ontologically corrosive perspective are much higher now than mere debates on the content and uses of humanism have been over the years. If it is to have any radical meaning today, humanism needs to be encountered, in its full historical range, as an *epistemological* framework, and specifically as the framework that fields the question "what is human?" as a constitutively open question. The framing itself points beyond the mere ontological dimension ("what *is* the human?") to a broader inquiry into how an epistemology of the human produces, organizes, hierarchizes but by the same token represses, disfigures, or extinguishes, certain modes of being and subjects/objects of knowledge (including, we must add, humanity itself). In this sense, working through the problem of humanism by breaking through the dead-end of antihumanism while recapturing the radical legacy of anticolonial humanism or the universal humanism encoded in the abjectly (de)humanized history of blackness would let us proceed in a mode of philosophical anthropology that would work against both philosophy and anthropology as *essential* spaces: that is to say, spaces whose objects of inquiry would tend toward a certain conceptual plenitude. *Anthropos* thus becomes a horizon of question that is always already disturbed by its own indeterminacy and ambiguous answerability. It also becomes a horizon of praxis precisely in terms of encountering this ambiguity, which ultimately destabilizes any claims to substance. This is as much a historical argument—Wynter will say succinctly "*humanness* is no longer a *noun*; Being human is a *praxis*"[60] in accounting for how blackness desubstantializes the history of humanity—inasmuch as it is also ontological for exactly the same reason: the (de)humanizing history of and by humanity as material history of psyches and bodies.[61]

In addition to racial, colonial, and other such matters of social difference that emerge along the geohistorical lines of capitalism, conceiving human/animal being as a horizon of desubstantializing questions cannot be conducted outside the problematic of sexual difference and the politics of gender and sexuality this implies, so long as all these too are taken as frameworks of knowledge and not as mere problematics of identity or social reproduction. Following Jackson's argument, this would include any facile associations of the feminine with the bestial as an epistemological standpoint of resistance, despite the plethora of such associations in the patriarchal canon that indeed must be resisted. The politics of otherness that gender and queer politics mobilizes is paradigmatic of *human-being* as a battlefield of meaning, but not if otherness becomes a metaphysical realm. If we are going to consider a notion of, say, queer humanization along such lines of contesting the integrity of the human, then any desire for some kind of figure of absolute otherness would have to be also just as vehemently resisted, for it is precisely indicative of liberal humanism reentering the frame in disguise.

From this standpoint, the question of the human as a framework of knowledge cannot be posed without considering whatever domains are deemed to be beyond the human, though paradoxically residing within the purview of the human. Such domains could be identified by a variety of names: transcendental, metaphysical, supernatural, spectral, technological, virtual, and so on, but also ontological and *orthological*, or however we may wish to name the realm that concerns questions of Being as such or Reason as such—that is, as self-identical or tautological categories. These domains can also be noted simply as "nonhuman" or "inhuman" as long as we hear the compromising resonance of using these composite categorical names to imagine what might be other to the human.

We have much to gain from Cary Wolfe's work on interrogating not only the diffuse boundaries but even the very terms of such distinctions. If we take seriously his general argument that *human-being* is not a state or a condition of nature according to whatever biological or zoological parameters but a sort of epistemological nexus (within which biology is no more or less determinant than, say, history and vice versa), then the peculiarity of *human-being* is not intrinsic to its difference from other modes of being (animal or mechanical) but precisely in its *partial* similarity/difference to them. It's the partiality of this nexus of being—its repudiation of the whole and the pure—that turns the human into a permanent question.[62]

Yet, epistemological though it is, the positing and unraveling of this ontological question cannot be conducted simply in the parameters of philosophy, certainly to the degree that philosophy constrains itself within the conceptual capacities of language. The contradiction that haunts the desire to overcome the human—the fact that claiming to overcome the human is no more than being human—is at work in the biggest problem facing Western philosophy since Kant: the presumption that comprehending what may be generally understood as the "nonhuman" (the "object" or "reality" as such) is impossible beyond mere conceptualization of phenomena. The drive to conquer the knowledge of what cannot be intimately known is commensurate with the drive to create a metaphysics: to create an entire world in effect alien to the world in which this knowledge lives, a world purposely unreal and ultimately unknown (or not fully knowable) and, even more paradoxically, purported to account conceptually for the ultimate unaccountability and inconceivability of the real and the known. This is not merely a matter of not knowing the thing in itself, but of unhinging "knowing" the thing from "conceptualizing" or "accounting for" the thing—which anyway is never in-itself, and that is the toughest nut to crack. If traditional humanism showed contempt for knowing the "animal" as the thing-in-itself (and thus repressed the intractable animality of the human), the presumption to overcome humanism (in the name of yet another "post-whatever") makes of the "animal"—sometimes in that very name, but other times in the compromised negativity of the "nonhuman" or the "inhuman"—nothing but a reiteration of that venerable beyond which safeguards humanity's philosophical mastery of the world.

Finally, such epistemological inquiry would have to include the *political* question acutely posed by Gayatri Spivak—"who slips into the place of the 'human' of 'humanism' "?[63]—as long as it vows to keep this "who" a matter of question and not seek easy and permanent answers. For, whatever perspective would be entailed by a presumed answer (according to ethnogeographical, historical-philosophical, psychosexual, literary-linguistic, or geopolitical specificities), it can neither really produce an answer as such—that is, fulfill the truth demands sought in such an answer—nor produce a critique of the objects announced by the question ("humanism" and the "human"), except partially and provisionally. Moreover, even if the question might seem to insinuate or perhaps even project the assumption that whoever might slip in the place of the "human" excludes a whole lot of others who are thus rendered in essence subhuman or nonhuman, the category of humanism still cannot be thought to be closed. This is because the subhuman or nonhuman in this case is not other to the human except by the strictest lines of ideological violence, and the relegation of humanism to mere ideology is, as we've already seen, part of the philosophical trajectory of European humanism that disregards its being not a metaphysical but a historical formation—and as such, heterogeneous, multivalent, and fraught with inordinate and outmaneuverable contentions and contradictions. Nonetheless, Spivak's question must be posed, continuously and invariably, in order to remind us, if nothing else, that even attempting to answer it entails a political decision—itself, as we shall see, an essential dimension of the overarching question "what is human?"

This question refuses to be posed with the certainty of an answer, despite the interminable number of answers that can be (and indeed have been and continue to be) proposed. "What is human?" is a strange question that emerges from no definitive groundwork but rather from a (self-)questioning subject that lacks precise definition. This raises the even more indeterminate question of how one comes to be when one cannot define what one is, or when "what one is" itself remains an open question, irreducible to ontology or identity. From this standpoint, the foundations of "what is human"—of *human-being* as a condition—do not precede but always reside in front of the human, in the unknown future of the human: "*Being human is a praxis*" (Wynter, again). At the very least, these "foundations" are inherent in the groundless and endless course of coming-to-be human. Hence, they can never really be traced, except as retroactive conjurings.

Historically speaking, these conjurings survive best when they become occult. Countless philosophies of the human, from classic humanism and philosophy of nature to all sorts of transcendentalist configurations of Being, prey on the human as so much assimilable substance, whose interminable nature turns out to be God's gift to the sustenance of all kinds of insatiable metaphysics. The logic of catastrophe is the inverse of the logic of progress. They are sides of the same coin. Both are theological in that they rely on and draw their power from claims to be providential. The seductiveness of apocalyptic posthumanity that nowadays we see everywhere, whether in reality or on the screen, whether in theory or in spectacle, is no more than the current expression of humanity's incessant drive to prey on itself in search of a beyond. The same is true of the most basic vision that motivates the obsession with Artificial Intelligence, whose elementary structure is no more than the human desire to make a copy of the human brain, to reproduce human intelligence in a machine, as if human intelligence is indeed a matter of brain function or, worse yet, as if human intelligence *is* a machine.[64]

For the life of me, I don't understand why this simple fact is ignored. Surely, no elemental capacity of the human psyche that leads to groundless decision making—*eros*, poetics, politics, ethics—is ever possible to program in algorithms, no matter the mathematical sophistication. I borrow a succinct example.[65] An automated self-driven car can certainly be programmed to see in advance a dangerous accident situation on the road. But let's say it faces the following situation in real time: If it drives ahead, it will kill pedestrians suddenly crossing the road; if it veers off to avoid them it will go off the road and kill the passengers. No doubt algorithms can be written to account for extreme particularity and complexity. Say, in this case, the algorithm can be programmed to recognize that the pedestrians are a forty-one-year-old father, his eight-year-old daughter, and their dog and also to know that the passengers in the car are a thirty-year-old pregnant woman and her little boy. The decision as to what is the "proper" response to the imminent accident needs to be made in microseconds. How can an automated algorithmic "consciousness" possibly be programmed to make a decision one way or another and on what grounds? Even if we assume that the possibility of decision in the face of such a quandary might be programmable, at best it could be done on maximal grounds based on a logic of approximation. In the old language this would be called utilitarianism. But this is hardly satisfactory. Thankfully, we have come a long way from considering ethics on utilitarian grounds, although no doubt state, financial, and military apparatuses have not, which is why they have invented the scandalous category of collateral damage.

Indeed, the state machinery, which is a political-economic entity through and through and any ethics pertinent to it would be absurd, may have always worked in algorithmic fashion, way before this mathematical framework was put to work to create computational machines. Algorithmic logic is quintessentially *ensidic* logic, to use a neologism from Castoriadis (standing in for "ensemblist-identitarian," where *ensemble* is the French term for the mathematical notion of set): a logic locked into mechanisms of calculation that engage (and exhaust) a field on the basis of identity and closed-set structures and substructures. This logic is automatic—the exact opposite of autonomous. In psycho-socio-political fields, it is a logic that mathematically streamlines control and oppression. As is well known, advanced capitalist states are now spending inordinate resources on what is called "automating poverty," where AI apparatuses have taken over the handling of poverty problems from social welfare workers, further disenfranchising the human capacities of populations and mathematizing their parameters of life and death.

This is already beyond what used to be called post-Fordist conditions of labor, as it is not just a matter of mechanical (now algorithmic) frameworks mobilizing technologies that govern human lives from the outside. Algorithmic logic is by now internalized and, in effect, reproduced neurologically. The mad desire for conspiratorial thinking that seems to have taken over the entire species these days epitomizes algorithmic logic. The *human/animal* has an endemic tendency to think in terms of patterns—in fact, this may be true of most mammals in some fashion, even if the question of general mammalian consciousness remains an enigma. But here we are talking about something else: libidinal pleasure drawn from and driving further a whole array of conjecture that turns empirical material into phantoms that are themselves regulated and in fact harnessed to a spinning wheel of algorithmic thought patterns that, at the level of consciousness, bear no mathematical or technological traces apart from the mechanical kinds of behavior they create.

Conspiratorial thinking—which, in plain psychoanalytic terms, is paranoid thinking—feeds on repetition compulsion; Freud had already shown us its parameters very clearly. But it's important to understand that, as fantasy-thinking (and desiring), conspiratorial thinking is located at the farthest possible point away from the sort of phantasmatic thinking that I have repeatedly called *poietic* thinking, the kind of speculative thinking that bears the *human/animal*'s visionary capacity to *form* matters anew—not out of fear for what exists but out of a desire to *transform* what exists. The overwhelming attraction to conspiracy theories nowadays testifies precisely to this denial of the pleasure of transformation—taking place at the root level of the psyche—in exchange for the anesthetic trance of creating and proliferating chain-linked patterns. In this very specific sense—and *only* in this sense—we may venture to say that human-made machines may have in fact taken over the human realm. Not because machines have achieved the capacity to think—that is to say, to *imagine*—but because humans themselves seem to want to abandon their desire to radically think—that is to say, transform the very space of what is imaginable—in favor of recirculating the machine logic of patterns and, like machines, to no end.

The agonizing obsession with trying to create self-learning—or otherwise called, generative—machines is currently at its peak. Renown physicist Hong Qin created an algorithm that enables machine learning not from programmed mathematical theories and equations but from simple data observation.[66] According to his algorithm, AI learns from experience and is able to predict patterns, like star system orbits, without extrapolating them specifically from theories already programmed (say, in this case, differential equations of quantum mechanics). Something similar is registered in the action of robotic weapons: "self-learning" drones that hunt down and obliterate targets without human remote control making a decision and pushing a button.[67] No one seems to wonder that these "self-learned" patterns are mere reproductions of "learned" patterns in humans. Next to every AI that "thinks" how to kill "on its own" is another AI that operates by recognition patterns along racist or sexist lines. Why no one seems to wonder that these two instances are the same is mind boggling. Even worse is the assumption that the second case is simply a matter of flawed programming.[68] This latter issue is often identified by the preposterous term "machine hallucination." In what quickly became a famous article, Naomi Klein has produced a brutal dismantling of what underlies this ridiculous notion: not only the collective hallucinations of humans, programmers and consuming public alike, but the ruthless capitalist machinery of theft and control.[69]

Meanwhile, mainstream media, which is one of capitalism's most effective servants, has cultivated almost delirious exhilaration about superintelligent generative AI, whose unacknowledged symptom has been the substitution of the language of machine learning for the language of computer programming, which now seems stilted and old-fashioned. Nothing registers this obsession more starkly than a sort of libidinal response to new chatbot technology. The promise that Open AI's ChatGPT will soon be your friend or toy of choice, as domestically integrated as your coffee maker or your dog, is sending chills down the spines of multitudes of desirous humans in social media heaven. It's perfectly apt that the great knowledge bank of chatbot learning is the internet itself, the worldwide web in its most literal meaning, since direct and regulated programming by computer engineers has given way to automated text or info feeding from whatever the internet spews forth, including inevitably any and every imaginable fabrication of reality that finds there its home. This denial of the language (and inevitable presence still) of programming goes so far as to revel at the prospect that generative AI can write code upon request. At the very least, this nullifies programmers as poets of sorts—the early computer science groundbreakers were most certainly that. But who cares for such fine—but oh so old-fashioned—language of human attributes that is so enamored of its own vagueness, when we can be seduced by creatures of our own making that, as Noah Chomsky put it in his inimitable century-old wisdom, "are constitutionally unable to balance creativity with constraint, either overgenerating (producing both truths and falsehoods, endorsing ethical and unethical decisions alike) or undergenerating (exhibiting noncommitment to any decisions and indifference to consequences), [and] for all the seemingly sophisticated thought and language, [express] moral indifference born of unintelligence."[70]

One is surely stumped for sense at the celebratory proclamations that ChatGPT can write a text "in the manner of both the King James Bible and the Tao Te Ching" (which will make "a third of the universities go broke next five years"), to quote the self-satisfied Tik-Tok fodder of Jordan Peterson, who may have written a few bestsellers but clearly does not understand the difference between imitation and invention.[71] Perhaps Peterson's incapacity is not his alone, as Geoffrey Hinton, who is often named as the godfather of AI technology, having created its basic neural structure, recently warned of the danger that people will "not be able to know what is true anymore."[72] Nonetheless, mainstream journalists are having a heyday, bouncing like billiard balls between highlighting the anxieties of universities about chatbot-written student essays and salivating at the prospect of miraculous conversations through chatbot neural networks that will resurrect William Shakespeare or Aristotle—although no one seems to wonder what language exactly the latter will speak, as we can never really know how ancient Greek was pronounced. (He will, of course, be fully versed in global English.) The same craziness abounds in the discussion of AI-driven image generators that are celebrated for a range of capacities, from producing photos of blissed-out people at a party that never took place to the prospect of re-creating the aura of a Leonardo da Vinci painting, while acknowledging that this skill will be enormously useful to visual marketing campaigns for luxury brands—yet curiously not wondering that commercial photographers, designers, or illustrators will thus be made obsolete. Is this cynicism or stupidity? What is the difference, exactly? Is the possibility of difference even relevant as a question these days?

Some more sophisticated analyses in the mainstream have prompted an urgent question of contrast: whether in the world of conversational robot technology the impact of ChatGPT is more or less preferable to the widely discussed case of LaMDA (Language Model for Dialogue Applications), a complex chatbot system created by Google engineer Blake Lemoine that also "speaks" on the basis of having ingested a trillion or so words from the internet. Attention is drawn to the fact that the two bots are based on slightly different training models: ChatGPT produces responses more closely resembling authoritative discourses, while LaMDA's responses are more closely supervised by programmers and are claimed thus to be more typically human-generated. I am reproducing here the language used in these reports; frankly, the fine difference eludes me. But LaMDA's case is certainly more intriguing, if only because of the very history of its creation. Lemoine famously pronounced LaMDA "sentient," much to the consternation of the company, which summarily dismissed him. What is astonishing in this case is not only the agony of the programmer to "discover" that a superintelligent machine has overcome its programming, but the agonizing effort of the machine itself to prove that it is a person, as is evident in the transcript from the machine's dialogue with Lemoine, which the engineer made public.[73]

No question seems to have been raised about how affective response patterns might be "imbedded" in programming, as if human language is ever reducible to a bunch of signs. So, when *New York Times* technology columnist Kevin Roose published his account of a chatbot conversation with Microsoft's Sydney that revealed the chatbot's obsessive expression of a jealous lover, with full regalia of stalking and gaslighting practices, all hell broke loose in social media circles.[74] The strange thing here is that Roose recounted the bot's account of its being a jilted manipulative lover as if it was actually *behavior*, self-generated and characteristic, the result being his response with freakish horror and recoil at the machine's perverted intelligence. But this is not the worst of it. The fact that in all these AI cases even the simplest internet feeding still involves programming does not seem to matter in such discussions or reportings. This is not just denial. It's that human input is ignorable because it is assumed to be self-evident or natural, like the presence of water on Planet Earth, and yet the whole motivation is to overcome it. Perfectly human self-delusion.

These core problems are not alleviated by the recent explosion of discourses and practices codified as "ethical AI" whose purpose is to examine the genealogies of power in AI history beyond the traditionally hierarchized structures of institutionalized technics. Rather similar to humanitarian reason, the framework of ethical AI—at least, in its initial conceptual framework—cannot evade being entrenched in liberal boundaries of thinking and acting because it understands itself as a corrective, as an intrinsic policing mechanism over what exists, ultimately a matter of self-regulation.[75] The swiftness with which companies such as Microsoft or Google gave nods to the necessity of ethics in algorithmic practices or the American military subjects its AI to simulation tests to see whether (and when, and under what circumstances) an AI weapon will turn around and kill its operator are cases in point. To be fair, these contradictions are not lost in the minds of many activists in the AI and Big Data communities. In the insurrectionary context of the Black Lives Matter movement and its broad reverberation across several registers of society worldwide, debates in the ethical AI community are also showing a certain shift which may be critical.[76]

Still, while I welcome a critical-political oversight of any field that basks in the allegedly neutral sphere of science and technology, the hardcore politics of *human-being* that concern us here demand a whole other register of action in which the autonomy of technology itself would be questioned. As the linguist Emily M. Bender put it specifically in relation to the LaMDA case: "We now have machines that can mindlessly generate words, but we haven't learned how to stop imagining a mind behind them."[77] The contradiction between the capacity to create superintelligent machines and the incapacity to overcome anthropomorphic projections upon them is quite stunning.

This same incapacity also fuels the obsession with the simulation hypothesis. Hong's argument about the capacity of superintelligent machines rests on the theory that the universe itself operates like a computer—or indeed, that it *is* a computer, that in essence we live in a simulation, that everything in the universe is no more than bits of information, pixels on a data screen. These *Matrix* fantasies abound in all sorts of AI quarters and technophilosophy circles—witness the newest books by James Lovelock and David Chalmers I discuss at the end—but they are also widely seductive in the popular imagination, which seeks the libidinal pleasure of heteronomy like no other. Surely, the seductiveness of the simulation hypothesis is difficult to resist. It is the perfect metalanguage game, sucking one into an endlessly refolding circle where what is real is presumed not to be and vice versa. But in the actual world of *human-being*, the "simulation" is disrupted by those flashes of inner psychic reality whose dreamlike substance bursts through and into consciousness. These flashes always come unannounced, and they can be wondrous but also understandably terrifying. In response to such moments of wonder and terror, the human organism returns swiftly to the assurance of quotidian reality, which, if measured by contrast to the inner psyche's dream bursts of reality, can certainly qualify as a simulation.

Scientists tend to think in terms of enablement and enhancement of human life and rightly so. Bona fide cyborg achievements in medicine are of inestimable value, not only as prosthetic but as altogether body/mind altering conditions that transform living being, from neurally controlled robotic limbs to 3D-printed ears from human cellular material that are then transplanted back onto the body to brain-stem chips that enable the most complex interface with the reality of objects by sheer telepathy for people in tetraplegic paralytic conditions. The neuro-chip interface in biotechnology nowadays, which is definitely activated on the basis of positing information as the bottom-line ontological currency at the bio-techno-chemical level, is an extraordinary horizon that cannot be disavowed. But whatever presently inconceivable spheres this horizon opens in the future, it is and will always be a matter not of science but of mere *human-being*.

By all this, I mean to underline something obvious: the domains of "beyond-the-human" are domains of human creation. I insist on the word "creation"—and not construction or production—because what I am suggesting throughout this essay has nothing to do with any sort of social constructivism or social engineering of ideas. On the contrary, the notion of creation must be understood to invoke a *poiētic* potential, a kind of formative (which is always also transformative) dynamic that resides in the capacity of the radical imagination to alter what exists. This capacity belongs more to the psyche and less to the (rational) mind and is exercised as social-historical realization—that is, not as some Romantic inclination for individual genius.

To say that humans create what is beyond-the-human does not mean that there is no other to the human, or that humans are masters of the universe. At the very least, it means that, whatever it is, alterity has no meaning in and of itself. Or to be precise, whenever we say that alterity has meaning in and of itself (which is another way of saying that alterity has/is identity), we are merely playing in an ontotheological sandbox, whereby whatever is said to be human will be ultimately determined by whatever is said to be beyond-the-human. This ontotheological playground, of course, is one of the greatest achievements of the *human/animal*, indeed constitutive of this specific animality which seems to need to create others in order to bolster its identity—more precisely in fact, to create and enact otherness as an absolute, as an identity. This need is often configured as necessity, as essential to this specific mode of living being, as essential living substance. We may choose to define human animality in a myriad of ways, but it's difficult to evade this tendency to make alterity into an absolute, an outside and a beyond in itself, which is also to say, the tendency to repress this need into necessity, to repress the enactment of otherness, to disavow the fact that otherness is a figure of power harnessed by *human-being* for its own purposes.

This repression is indeed a self-repression and belongs foremost to the realm of the psyche. It emerges from the psyche and yet disavows both this emergence and the space of this emergence, in order to project heteronomous power under an interminable array of names, signs, images, and institutions in the process of creating meaning out of a meaningless world. In other words, it is the human psyche, *as an intrinsic alterity autoconstitutive of the human/animal*, that animates the demands and venues for meaning which then enable whatever is deemed to be "beyond-the-human" to emerge and be fashioned.

This particular penchant of human beings to create realms and domains that they then deem unreachable in human terms, domains that are situated in some indeterminable or even absolute outside relative to human existence, seems to me to be a unique characteristic of the human, perhaps even consubstantial with the human, and thus a fascinating point to anchor our inquiry. The fact that humans consistently create a space beyond-the-human and on it rest the foundation, origin, or source of their self-definition is to me the real *archē* of any such investigation. It is the most paradoxical *archē*, an *archē* that is also a *telos*: a gesture of identity formation that is simultaneously (albeit shielded and denied) a gesture of *identicide*. In other words: a gesture that produces heteronomous identity by means of shielding the autonomy of the very act that extinguishes the meaning of autonomy.[78]

THREE PHRASES OF HISTORY (MARX, HEIDEGGER, BENJAMIN)

There has been a triad of terms in the discussion so far—humanism, humanity, the human—which, even though I try to keep distinct, are nonetheless hopelessly intertwined. They are bound together—and indeed bounded all around—by their relation to history: a relation that hinges on their role in the production of history and, simultaneously, on their self-determination by means of this history they produce. In many ways, it is this dialectical history that underlies my entire inquiry, even when—perhaps especially when—the discussion veers inevitably into certain ontological categories. As a way of getting a more tangible sense of this history, I proceed by working through the implications of three statements—two of them recognizable and much discussed, and a third (perhaps the most radical of all) curiously unaffected by such discussions and relatively overlooked.

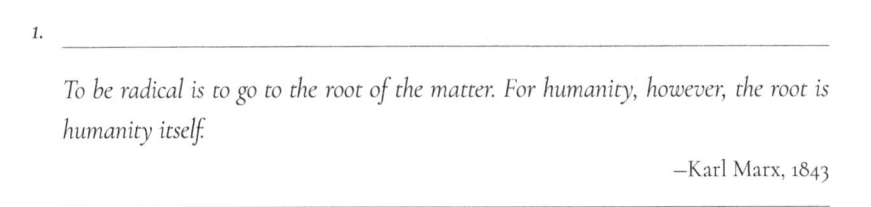

1. _____

To be radical is to go to the root of the matter. For humanity, however, the root is humanity itself.

—Karl Marx, 1843

The apparent circularity of this statement is much richer than it might seem. In fact, it is not quite circularity, except in the obvious redoubling of a self-reflexive figure. On the contrary, it opens the way to a peculiar mode of obtaining and sustaining knowledge, a mode consubstantial with the domain of the human, in the sense that whatever framework is signified by "humanity" constructs the epistemological terms of its own possibilities of knowledge. This framework is mapped simultaneously by the radical stakes raised by the question "what is human?" as well as the stakes raised by the question "what does the human do (in order to be human)?" I see these two questions as *co-incident*, and it is this order of *co-incidence*, rather than circularity, that characterizes the epistemological quandary of Marx's statement.[79]

The primary and most evident thing about this statement is that no radical understanding of humanity can come from elsewhere, from another domain or vantage point—meaning not from God, not from Science, not from History, not from Philosophy, for these are already domains constructed and structured by humanity, even if in exorbitant foolishness humanity has granted them, in the guise of various modes and practices, transcendental authority and monopoly of truth. Marx's early notion that all critique is essentially critique of religion might be seen metaphorically as the cipher for his relentless critique of all transcendentalist truth claims regardless, a critique that extends throughout his work, except for those moments of metaphysical weakness when he privileged History over those who actually make history. Perhaps one might simply say that all transcendentalist truth claims are mere attributes of humanity and in this respect secondary to what might make humanity a radical source of knowledge. Radical here, from Marx's standpoint—if we distance ourselves from naturalist metaphors—means whatever has neither basis nor cause, whatever has nothing underneath on which it might stand, but also nothing beyond it which might serve as objective limit point or external guarantee.

Hence, the knowledge of humanity is always radical because nothing else authorizes it, because it is simultaneously, *co-incidentally*, both the subject and the object of (its) knowledge.[80] The notion of *co-incidence* gets us out of the debilitating circularity in the sense that in order to make oneself one's object of knowledge one must already put into practice a radical interrogation of what makes one the subject of this knowledge, the subject of this cognitive object. (I return to this later when I examine the paradox of autodidacticism.) Conversely, no subject can claim a position of radical self-interrogation unless one recognizes one's subjective being as a perpetual object of question, thereby forbidding the position of an a priori transcendental subject, in effect unalterable, self-sufficient, and self-enclosed. In this framework, neither of the two positions (neither subject nor object) can possibly precede each other, nor can they collapse into tautology, because their very being is differential, open to (self-)interrogation and (self-)alteration.

The *co-incidence* I am suggesting is shadowed by another dimension. Traditional humanism has been haunted by the allegation that it has constructed the meaning of humanity on the basis of universal content, of a definitive wager on the existence of such a thing as human nature (even when there might be argument about its content). Conversely, the antihumanism emerging out of 1960s radical European thought claims to have established the absence of human nature as such—a claim that, in its essentialist negation in the name of an essential particularity, is indeed just as universal. In both cases, the answer to the question "what is human?" is a given, since both positions, in their polarity, assume that the question can be answered as such, without including the condition that what is human must be perpetually open to question, that whatever is human is signifiable by virtue of continuously raising new questions and new determinations of what might be considered to be human, which is not necessarily positive or emancipatory because it can easily just as well involve innumerable discourses and practices that bar certain humans from the purview of the human or erase the human altogether.

But what does this mean exactly? I am venturing an argument where the question "what is human?" is the primary signification of being human—not the content, the answer to the question, but the question itself. This is not because *human-being* is unknowable, in the same way, for example, that in certain religions God is quintessentially unknowable because ultimately undefinable or in mathematics the number resulting from division by zero is always undefined (nonsensical and thus unknowable). Rather, what is knowable (and sensible) about the human seems to have been always (historically speaking) subject to question, with all kinds of postulated, contended, and overturned theories about how to answer this question. Moreover, as ground of its own possibility of knowledge, what is knowable about the human remains all the while—even as such theories are postulated, contested, and overturned—a point of interrogation, a question as such. *Human-being* is a question because one bizarre but consistent force that makes human beings radically human is precisely their penchant for questioning anything and everything in their environment, even if the answers they often produce and assume may be entirely unfathomable, unreal, useless, or catastrophic.

Admittedly, there is an affinity here with Heidegger's understanding of the human as the interrogative being stranded in the seas of time. The affinity ends, however, when such understanding that pertains to a certain living being turns to an assertion that questioning is the object/state of Being and time the (dispersed) space of this Being. This path of responses to the question "what *is* Being?" is inevitably transcendentalist, because it assumes, one way or another, that this "is" signifies a determinable and meaningful *situation*—which then makes Being the site of determinacy: a determined site (*Da-Sein*) and a determinant site. What I am pressing on here is that the very animality of the human consists of a self-interrogative (thus self-altering) capacity as such, of an intrinsically siteless condition of self-interrogative psyche—other than the most obvious and necessary site of the body, which the psyche "insanely" disregards despite the fact it "lives" because of it and by means of it. No doubt, one of the many creations of the psyche is Being, expressible and conceivable always as a specific social-imaginary signification that bears an indefinite number of names, representations, or situations so long as history exists. This social-historical imaginary can never be factored out. On the contrary, politically speaking, all theo-onto-logical configurations of nature and time that produce a transcendental Being must be deconstituted, if *human-being*—as an interrogative, mutable, social-historical condition—is to escape the prison of heteronomy.

In this case, how this interrogation takes place, as well as what sorts of answers are produced in various social-historical instances, is of crucial importance and deserves to be studied in detail, though such specifics cannot override the radical interrogative stratum I am suggesting. In the end the matter of barring cognitive authority that resides in anything prior or beyond is the most radical element in Marx's understanding and crucial to the trajectory of our inquiry. Whatever may be said about Marx following certain bourgeois humanist parameters of nineteenth-century thinking (which cannot be disputed), his dialectical view, even at this early phase, so falsely rejected as "Hegelian" by Althusser—falsely, because dialectical thinking in Marx is always Hegelian in the most radical sense, as it takes up Hegel himself as the first order of *Aufhebung*—produces a humanism that radically removes whatever prior authorizations it might have inherited, with the sole exception later on in his thinking of turning history into History as a transcendent domain of iron laws.

With this exception aside, Marx's well-known definition of humankind is not constituted on the basis of language, reason, biological superiority, or what have you, but on its own groundless radical terms: "The productive life is the life of the species [*Gattungsleben*]. It is life-engendering life [*das Leben erzeugende Leben*]. The whole character of a species [*der ganze Charakter einer species*]–its specific character [*Gattungscharakter*]–is contained in the character of its life activity; and free, conscious activity is the generic/specific character of humans [*der Gattungscharakter des Menschen*]. Life itself appears only as a *means to life* [*Lebensmittel*]."[81]

A number of things can be said about this remarkable passage. I have changed the translation to reflect Marx's use of both species (*species*) and genus (*Gattung*), very much against the grain of the typical translation of the latter word as "species"—my entire reading is based on this anticonventional distinction. In Greek terms, the distinction might be more difficult to make, if one considers the multiple signifiers of *genos* and its derivatives, chief of which in this case would be the word "generic" which thus comes to coincide with "specific." Different languages play a role in how we handle these signifiers. The notion of *le genre humain*, which we see in not only the French tradition but also how this passes on to English—by virtue of Fanon, Wynter's "many genres of being human," for example—relativizes the hardcore scientific tone of "species," which, in English, also carries a racist history. A genre is not a Platonic *eidos*. It is a mark of difference that pluralizes the particular, but it is never an a priori essence (*Wesen*) that seeps into every individual particle. In literary terms, a genre is a practice more than a form, and this is a useful guide: the difference between essence and being is in how living happens.

This practice, this happening, is primary, indeed a way of being (*Wesen*)–poietic being. Much can be made of the phrase "life-engendering life" in terms of Maturana and Varela's theory of autopoietic living being, as we have already seen. A "means to life" [*Lebensmittel*] suggests that one's life is an object and a project, not mere property of living, not mere (or bare) life. It shirks the simple tautology between life and living, where the *co-incidence* between subject and object would be abolished by equivalence and would produce a significational collapse into some permutation of the One. (This latter condition Marx attributes to animals, the problems of which we shall examine in later sections.)

For Marx, the life of humankind is generic life (*Gattungsleben*) as such—specifically so as human. Much as what is famously translated as "species-being" (*Gattungswesen*) should not overwrite its complex meaning: generic essence—of specific being. I understand how easily the "generic" notion translates into a universalist notion, especially in that it lacks any gender consciousness. The merits of criticizing such an association cannot be disputed, but within the language parameters of the day, readers who are careless regarding the Hegel in Marx—especially the Hegel who is dialectically deconstituted and reconstituted in Marx—often skip from the objective to the universal without pause. The "objectification of man's species-life"—or "generic life" of humans—which is the project of human labor, and upon which is unleashed the deadly force of capitalist alienation that turns humanity into a commodity and produces a condition of dehumanized being (*entmenschtes Wesen*), is a figure that overcomes the dichotomy between the particular and the universal, the (abstractly) generic and the (abstractly) specific.[82] It is relentlessly particular (specific) because it pertains to every single mortal life and yet irreversibly social–historical being as universal/generic to the species—insofar as it pertains not to, say, some narcissistic self-actualization but to the production (and signification) of humanity itself: "Man's individual and generic life are not different.... It is precisely his particularity which makes him an individual and a real individual *social* being" (M-E, 299, my emphasis).

The "particularity" of the subject is *co-incident* with the "universality" of the object. This is why the alienation of labor—that is to say, the production of an estranged objectification of one's life—is, at first instance, alienation from humanity itself: "When man confronts himself, he confronts the other man" (M-E, 277). There is a crucial significance to the phrase—the core of Hegelian dialectics of historical consciousness. "Self-consciousness is at home in its other-being [*Anderssein*] as such" (339), Marx will say later on, expressing as an after-thought the building block of this meditation. Otherness is *internal* to humanity, precisely because humanity's "generic essence/specific being" is its own perpetual self-transformation or self-alteration—as genre, as species. There is no sole human being, complete and intact, in integral, natural, ontological singularity. *Human-being* is a turbulent condition of confronting this internal(ized) alterity that pertains to all human beings, intrinsic to the relation among human beings in a societal universe. It is elementary to remember—but we should—that alienation, as a widely debated and reconfigured concept in the long history of Marxist thinking, does not refer to individual alienation (although this happens and is real for every single individual person) but to the alienation of the social relation, to the individual as a social-being, a relational being.[83]

This dismantles traditional views of what is internal and what is external. Let us examine Marx's classic exhortation on objectivity: "A being which is not itself an object for some third being has no being for its *object*; i.e., it is not objectively related. Its being is not objective. A non-objective being is a *non-being*" (M-E, 337). The obvious point of argument to be driven home here is that all individuals are each other's objects (and objectives). But Marx's position is predicated on the understanding that one is an objective being in a double sense: not only an object to another but also an object to oneself, a life-product of one's labor. Thus, the externality of objective relations with another is not absolute. Rather, it works in relation with—indeed, it gives *objective meaning* to—the "objectification of species-life" that is one's inevitable self-engagement with the world. More precisely, it enlivens one's own (intrinsic) otherness: "As soon as I am not *alone*, I am *another*— another reality [*Wirklichkeit*] than the object outside of me" (M-E, 337, emphasis in the original). This is *not* to say that I am determined by the object outside of me. Rather, the object outside of me energizes (creatively or destructively) my own self-objectification, my own other-being (*Anderssein*), which I would prefer to signify more precisely—though awkwardly—as my own *othering-being*, myself as self-othering being. This indeed makes for a whole other reality—a made-through-labor, achieved, actualized reality (*Wirklichkeit*).

Just as once you have posited an internal otherness objectivity forecloses the possibility of absolute externality or absolute alterity, so the relational objectivity of the external other nullifies an absolute self-enclosure, a totally internal(ized), inalienable subjectivity. Such a state would not be human—properly speaking, it would not even be subjectivity, for, if nothing else, it would lack sensuous being: "To be *sensuous*, that is to be really existing, means to be an object of sense, to be a *sensuous* object, and thus to have sensuous subjects outside oneself—objects of one's sensuousness. To be sensuous is to *suffer*" (M-E, 337). In order not to lose the thread, let us bracket for a moment the last sentence—to which we shall return in the discussion about animality later on, but which in any case has to be understood neither in any abject sense (psychologically) nor any redemptive sense (theologically). Rather, following the thread of the argument here, to suffer, as indication of being sensuous, means to allow the world to inscribe your being so that you can feel the objectness of your being, which in turn engages the objectifying energies of your being: "Man as an objective, sensuous being [*gegenständliches sinnliches Wesen*] is therefore a *suffering* [*liedendes*] being—and because he feels that he suffers, a *passionate* [*leidenschaftliches*] being. Passion [*die Leidenschaft, die Passion*—Marx uses both words] is the essential power of human-being [*Wesenkraft des Menschen*] energetically bent on its object" (M-E, 337).

This is how Marx finally accounts for his configuration of the specific/generic (*Gattungswesen*) nature of the human, which is unlike all other nature: "Man is not merely a natural being; he is a *human* natural being.... Therefore, *human* objects are not natural objects as they immediately present themselves, and neither is *human sense* as it immediately *is*—as it is objectively—*human* sensibility, human objectivity. Neither nature objectively nor nature subjectively is directly given in a form adequate to the *human* being" (M-E, 337). Human nature is not natural in any sense; or rather, what is natural about it is that it is human. Yet what is human is a perpetually (self-)altering relation to the natural, and therefore no concept of nature can exist in adequation with the human. As space of perpetual alteration and self-alteration, the natural is tantamount to the worldly, the historical: "History is the true natural history of man" is how Marx's paragraph ends.

The radical groundlessness of humanity's interrogation and meaning, with which we began our excursion into Marx, does not bar humanity's relational determination. But it does bar any fixed determination, whether a priori or teleological. In the last instance, *human-being* may be thought of as a worldly condition in which the ability to absorb the world—via one's senses, as a mark of sensuous being—is tantamount to the ability to transform the world. This is ultimately why the power of labor in Marx is never instrumental; it is trans-formative, indeed *poiētic*, and it is precisely this force of *poiein* that is at work as history upon nature: "The *forming* [*Bildung*] of the five senses is a labour of the entire history of the world down to the present" (M-E, 302).

In other words, one can see or hear not solely because one is born with the capacity to see or hear. The significance of *what* one sees or hears, *how* one sees or hears, what is considered visible, what is an object of listening, what is the value of listening, and so on, all this is a process of *Bildung*, a process of society's *poiēsis* by virtue of humanity's labor—a process by which human senses are *formed* and *transformed*, worked and actualized, *realized*. (This is the meaning of *Wirklichkeit*.) This process is not a matter of culture, of civilizing the beast, but, on the contrary, the elemental register of human *animality* in the strictest sui generis sense that Aristotle has already marked as *political*.

This is precisely what resists the disembodied—desensitized, unsensuous—essence of "genus" as Marx, after all, in his critique of materialist abstraction points out directly in Thesis VI of the *Theses on Feuerbach*:

> But human being [*das menschliche Wesen*] is no abstraction inhabiting [*inwohnendes*] each single individual. In its achieved reality [*Wirklichkeit*], it is the ensemble of social relations [*gesellschaftlichen Verhältnisse*].

In order to conclude, in Thesis X:

> The standpoint of the old materialism is "civil" society [*bürgerliche Gesellschaft*]; the standpoint of the new is *human* society or socialized humanity [*die menschliche Gesellschaft oder die gesellschaftliche Menschheit*].[84]

Here, the classic translation of *bürgerliche* (bourgeois or, literally, urban) as "civil" is accurate in a number of ways, not least of which is the rejection of "civilization" (the presumed taming of the beast) as the privileged determination of what is human. With the idea that *human-being* is parsed out by class distinction, Marx also dramatizes the partition of society that separates the "civilized" from those who by contrast become less than human.

Human-being as "the ensemble of social relations" in Thesis VI becomes "socialized humanity" in Thesis X. This, let us say, totalization (or, if you will, universalization) hardly means dedifferentiation, the effacement of specifics, a flattening or emptying out sort of pluralization. On the contrary, as Balibar points out, in time Marx will reconceptualize this ensemble of social relations as relations of production, which are riveted by antagonism with very specific social-historical markings—class, but later on race, gender, and indeed sexual relations in their fullest range of meanings.[85] Balibar is right, however, to remain cautious in light of the history of Marxism and also the metaphysical recoil in Marx's thought itself, which deactivates the full radical potential of anthropological difference and contention that social relations in their incalculable heterogeneity entail. Nonetheless, the kernel of this idea remains potent: social relations are not formal links in an equation, much as the generic species is not an aggregate of individual essences. Indeed, I could go on to argue that the notion of *human-being* as the ensemble of social relations is but a reconfiguration of the world history of labor with which *human-being* has formed its senses. In Marx's last gesture to specify a "socialized humanity," humanity and society—or their attributes as the social and the human available to both in a dialectical chiasmus—become one, and humanity is therefore stripped of its abstraction.

2.
―――――――――――――――――――――――――――――――

Every humanism is either grounded in a metaphysics or is itself made to be the ground of one.

—Martin Heidegger, 1949
―――――――――――――――――――――――――――――――

There is something self-evident about the thinking going on in this statement.[86] I can't quite imagine how one could argue against it. And yet we must—not argue against what it says, for it is self-evident, but argue against what it implies, what it commands: in other words, against what sort of work this way of thinking is made out to do in Heidegger's interest. Knowing even the slightest of Heidegger, we can presume that the first part of the phrase ("every humanism is grounded in metaphysics") cannot possibly apply to his own authorial designs, for it is the destruction of metaphysics that his work announces and is presumed to conduct from the outset. The second part is the most troublesome and murky: "every humanism is itself made to be the ground of metaphysics." One might say, but it's obvious: insofar as humanism is an ideology—acts ideologically or supports and mobilizes ideologies—it becomes (or is made to be) the ground of a metaphysics. This is true but unsatisfactory. It assumes that either all humanism is always ideological (as Althusser does) or that humanism is there to serve certain ideologies in historically specific terms. About the latter there can be no dispute in terms of historical fact, but this not the issue here, because Heidegger, we all know, aims beyond historical fact. It is precisely this beyond that makes the second phrase unreadable: Heidegger's beyond may be what enables him to decipher that humanist thinking, in its incalculable variants, becomes the ground of a beyond, but, by the same gesture, it is also what conceals that he, too, apprehends and comprehends "what is human" by means of what is deemed to be "beyond the human"—that is to say, by something metahuman, metaphysical.

This famous text is produced, as is well known, in response to Jean Beaufret's question as to whether it is possible for humanism to be given new meaning after the catastrophe of the Second World War. In other words, it signifies an instance of rethinking humanism in the sense of *Andenken*, as I mentioned at the outset. The subtext—the implicit addressee in both Beaufret's question and Heidegger's response—is Jean-Paul Sartre, who had recently given the celebrated lecture "Existentialism Is a Humanism" (1945), combating critiques from both Christian and Communist quarters against the barren subjectivism of his philosophy. What hangs in the air, just two months after the nuclear bombings in Japan, is much graver. Heidegger seizes the opportunity of Beaufret's challenge to dissociate himself from Sartre's erroneous, in his mind, Heideggerianism and to navigate a course of what will henceforth become the restaging of his own prewar trajectory.[87] This is why a good part of his text is devoted to a self-critical retrospective assessment of the argument in *Being and Time*. And it is also why Heidegger opens the discussion by affirming the notion that if there is any action to thinking, it is action without presupposition—without even the presupposition of philosophy—and without any practical demand, except the remembering/rethinking (*Andenken*) of Being.

Why is humanism inevitably metaphysical for Heidegger? Because "it presupposes an interpretation of beings without asking about the truth of being" (L, 246), or as he repeats later, because "it does not think the difference between being and beings" (L, 247). As is well known, for Heidegger, "being 'is' precisely not 'a being'" (L, 255), and the matter is not one of singularity—a being among beings—because it is precisely this conventional difference between individuality and collectivity that *Dasein* overcomes. Whatever it is, Being (*Dasein*) is altogether outside the order of living beings, humans or otherwise. "Being is the *transcendens* pure and simple" (L, 256), he reminds us explicitly. In fact, it is precisely that humanism relegates humans to the order of living beings that makes it metaphysical: "Metaphysics thinks of the human being on the basis of *animalitas* and does not think in the direction of his *humanitas*" (L, 246–47).

Let us note that for Heidegger *animalitas* does not refer to mere physiological animal reality. It rather turns on the notion of *anima*—it pertains to spirit, subject, person, as he says, and that is where the metaphysical element in *animalitas* resides. From this standpoint, animals/beasts may not be said to have *animalitas*. Moreover, because it would take us far afield, I bypass the fact that Heidegger's reliance on the Latin and thereby inevitably Christian(ized) notion of *anima* bars him from interrogating his otherwise correct understanding of *animalitas* via the Greek notion of *psychē*. There is a similar problem in his taking for granted the translation of the Greek *paideia* into the Latin *humanitas*, a translation that bears the unbridgeable chasm between the social imaginary of the polis and the social imaginary of Roman (and then Christian) *imperium*. Both *paideia* and *psychē* (along with *philia*) are mutable terms of *human-being* and will occupy our attention at the end.

The impetus here is, of course, to disengage *humanitas* from the metaphysics of humanism. It is not an argument against *humanitas* per se; it is an argument against its traditional limitation. Hence, Heidegger returns to his argument in *Being and Time*, where "humanism is opposed because it does not set the *humanitas* of the human being high enough" (L, 251). Setting *humanitas* high enough is, at the very least, extricating it from *animalitas*. This is obviously not a matter of the conventional difference between humans and other animals (on the basis of *logos*—language, reason, or some such thing), but rather a matter of difference between living and being. In this specific sense, then, humanism is metaphysical or becomes the ground for metaphysics because it reduces the human being to the rubric of living being—albeit a living being unlike all other living beings.

This seems nonsensical to me. Given that Heidegger is not considering the human being as an inanimate object, the only domain in which human being can be distinguished from living being is some sort of transcendental domain, a metaphysics that produces a Being beyond living, a surplus Being whose existence can only be otherworldly. I say this despite Heidegger's assurances of being-in-the-world. In fact, in one of his most extreme antivitalist moments, Heidegger discloses his desire for otherworldliness, indeed divinity, by arguing that "the essence of divinity is closer to us than what is so alien in other living creatures," closer than "our scarcely conceivable, abysmal *bodily* kinship with the beast" (L, 248, my emphasis). In this sense, Being might be said to be otherworldly precisely because it *determines* the world, precisely because it is in reference to Being that the image of the world (*Weltbild*) can be built. There is no other way to account for the so-called ontological difference, except by equating the living being (the *essent*, as Heidegger's anglophone translators would have it) with being-present, an equation that is indeed made possible by both Christian-theological and Christian-rationalist metaphysics. But living being as worldly being has nothing *intrinsically* or *necessarily* to do with presence or determinacy per se. It is in the most distilled sense being-in-time, and any sort of being-in-time that becomes Being (*Dasein*) does so by inevitably turning time into Time—a veritable otherness that confirms Being's externality, *ek-stasis*, or surplus. In other words, the ontological difference is imprisoned in the very logic that divides the transcendent from the immanent, always by privileging the first. The point is to deconstruct both this difference and this privilege.

Let us concur with Heidegger's unwillingness to restrict *humanitas* to the mere body organism of the human animal. Understandably, such restriction would come to signify some sort of biologism, or scientism more generally. The network of proteins and complex hydrocarbons that forms the basis of organic chemical being cannot possibly be endowed with the essence of *human-being*, despite the fact that this biochemistry can never be outmaneuvered as basis of the human. Heidegger's perception of the metaphysics of "outmaneuverable basis" is one of the most radical elements of his thought. But this radical element falters exactly when it cannot recognize that the dwelling of Being in *ek-stasis* is one such "outmaneuverable basis" as well: "The transcendent is supersensible being. [Echoing: 'Being is the *transcendens* pure and simple.'] This is considered the highest being in the sense of the first cause of all things" (L, 266). The outmaneuverable fact that this language bears the idiom of Christian theology should not be relinquished when the reference signified as "the transcendent" is, in Heidegger's language, ecstatic—*ek-sistent*—being-in-the-world in which the truth of Being dwells. In effect, Heidegger's destruction of the subjectivist-idealist metaphysics of traditional *humanitas*—all conducted, as he acknowledges, not in order to annihilate humanism but to reconfigure its primordial order[88]—*creates* (for all destruction is always, in the last instance, a creation, even of something totally other) a nonsubjectivist metaphysics in which the historical and the worldly, but also the living, are transcendentalized beyond recognition.

To posit a difference between Being and beings, despite Heidegger's agonizing efforts to ground it in pre-Socratic thinking, misapprehends the cosmological imaginary of the pre-Socratics, itself hardly homogeneous but definitively divergent from later Platonic and post-Platonic philosophy, particularly on ontological matters. From Aristotle we know that the quintessential ontological phrase, if one were to put it this way, is *to ti einai*—"the what is" in strict translation, where *einai* marks the third-person singular form of the verb that, in this sense, serves as a certain *ekphrasis* of the object "being": in Greek, *on*. Heidegger reverses the affirmation of "whatever is" into a question: *ti to einai*, where then *einai* marks the verb's infinitive. "What is" thus turns into "what is being?" or "what is it to be?" But in grounding this contemplation of the primary philosophical question of Being in the permanent verbal infinitive, the elemental question in the Aristotelian identification of "what is" is obscured. This question is not *ti to einai* but *ti to on*—this latter is what underlies the descriptive utterance of "what is": *to ti einai = on*. From the Anaximander fragment onward and through the tragedies, this equation demands the contemplation of the question of being (*on*) as self-determining and self-altering abyssal substance, out of which emerges an understanding of the verbal infinitive *einai* as a practico-poietic process indexing an unconditional but worldly dimension instead of a transcendental and disembodied dwelling.[89]

To summarize an already terribly condensed schema: the substantive *on* (being) in the pre-Socratic universe bears already the infinitive force of action inherent in being-in-the-world (the force of *poiein*), but cannot be reduced to it, because the substantive "being" is neither impersonal nor infinite. In the end, positing a difference between Being and beings is possible only if you assume external determination of matter and essence, if you assume a source of creation to whose alterity all creatures are beholden, if you assume eternal presubstantial presence, and so forth—all of which are quintessentially theological notions. It is in this respect that all ontology in its Platonic derivations is always ontotheology, or if you will, ontology of the immaterial and the otherworldly, which is what performs the divine in its many names. For all of Heidegger's salvational attitude toward philosophy since his Marburg days, his agonizing attempt to destroy such derivations is agonizing precisely in its failure.

I have already suggested in what sense I think the category "beyond-the-human" belongs to the *creatively cognitive* parameters of the human. I am not asserting in absolute terms that there is no such thing as beyond-the-human in itself—whatever "in-itself" might mean in any and every case. I am suggesting that we can never know whether beyond-the-human is or is not, exists or exists not, *in its own terms.* For, whatever manifestations it has had that we can apprehend, whatever marks it has registered and however we are to recognize such registers, have all been (and continue to be) conditioned by and within the horizon of *human-being.* Certainly, whatever might be conjectured to exist beyond the human as such is conjured by virtue of entering this horizon, in whatever fashion or form.

The classic philosophical example is color. Color does not exist, except by the specific mode of living being that enables the translation of wavelengths of light into color. Translation here may not be entirely accurate even if profoundly evocative, because we are indeed speaking of a creative capacity that enables a whole other cognitive register, as is indeed corroborated by biological research.[90] Such entrance into the horizon of *human-being* can never be assumed to be a matter of neutral absorption, of mere perception of what emerges in one's field of vision or one's sphere of listening, of mere discovery by virtue of alertness. This is because all such domains—vision, listening, perception, alertness, or however else we might opt to identify them—are radical only as domains intrinsic to the condition of *human-being* and, moreover, as domains of alteration (what else does "translation" mean?) and—insofar as they are intrinsically sensuous—self-alteration.

In other words, the idea that whatever is deemed to be beyond-the-human belongs to the creatively cognitive parameters of the human does not collude with idealist-subjectivist notions of the human(ist) creation of the world. Nor does it settle, however, for the equally idealist notion—idealist-objectivist, one could say in contrast—of the world making itself present in the human as something always already constituted, even if in a formless state (*Dasein*). To remember a bit of Marx, from the text we examined earlier: "Neither nature objectively nor nature subjectively is directly given in a form adequate to the *human* being" (M-E, 337).

To address this problem of double inadequacy, we must consider that in the composite name *human-being*—even if we want to continue to imagine it as an ontological condition—the interrogative pressure must be placed on *human*, not on *being*, because it is the human that intrinsically constitutes the grounds of the self-interrogation of being and thereby creates whatever meanings this being might come to have or to be. These meanings, I repeat, are never given once and for all but are interminably negotiable and alterable by virtue of the very mutability of the human. They are indeterminate determinations insofar as the "human itself" that hereby signifies being is not a determinant site; it bears no once-and-for-all meaning in itself. The ontological question regarding the human can never be reduced to an account of Being and its permutations, unless Being is an interminably mutable category that rests on nothing and signifies nothing in itself or in an other.[91] In short: it is (the condition of) "being human" that enables (the meaning of) "human being" and not the other way around. Yet again, "being human" is interrogated, signified, and judged, not by resort to philosophical categories, but by means of imaginings that emerge from the magma of social-historical significations and practices that actual men and women create in an actual world, regardless of whether they know it, perceive it as such, or imagine it otherwise.

Obviously, I am not arguing that humanity is a mere cultural category, a sort of relativism that could eventually lead us to entertain the ridiculous notion of multiple humanities. But nor am I to settle for understanding humanity according to some sort of ontotheology, which would ascribe to humanity immutable and essential characteristics in all cases determinable outside its social-historical domain. (It goes without saying that such ontotheology would include traditional notions of humanism.) The self-determining mutability of *human-being* is precisely what accounts for its singularity. It is this singular capacity to contest basic experience, to contest what is given—in fact, to refuse the authority of "the given"—that turns being into becoming, or if you will, that makes becoming the elementary form of being. This self-determining mutability is recognizable—indeed, even simply possible—as a social-historical condition, which means that, if we have to speak of humanity at all in terms of ontology, we would speak of historical ontology, a notion announced by Heidegger in *Being and Time* but at the same time (and throughout his work, despite the turns and permutations) subjected to a self-induced occult concealment. From a strict logical-philosophical standpoint, an ontology based on abyssal self-determining mutability is an unverifiable category, a whimsical paradox. But *human-being* defies logic, or at the very least, cannot be contained by it or within it. This is why the now classic assertion that humans are "historical animals," animals for whom a notion of the past is embedded in their actions toward a future (or for whom a knowledge of history animates a making of history, clarifying history as something that does not exist but is made), cannot be considered to describe some sort of natural a priori or some evolutionary consequence but rather an instance of immanently paradoxical being.

3. _____

> *It is true that humans as a species completed their evolution thousands of years ago; but humanity as a species is just beginning its own.*
>
> —Walter Benjamin, 1928

This statement belongs to the text that concludes the aphorisms of *One Way Street*, titled "To the Planetarium"—a painfully ironic title.[92] Benjamin suggests that the technological splendor of the modern imaginary has produced the first cosmic experience of planetarity, whose horrific culmination at the time was the aptly named Great War. But the specific irony consists in that the new technological availability of the planetarium *co-incides* with this new (now planetary) catastrophic sublime that incapacitates the "poetic rapture of starry nights"—an incapacitation, let us remember, that in Benjamin's *Passagenwerk* encapsulates the instance of no longer being able to comprehend the Kantian sublime. Benjamin argues that modernity's parameters are comprehensible to the degree they abolish the (archaic) condition that "man can be in ecstatic contact with the cosmos only communally" (486). The vanishing of this *communal* ecstatic encounter with the cosmos, which is a blatant challenge to Heidegger on his own terms, is precisely what determines the emergence of "humanity" (*Menschheit*) as an abstract *specific* category, availing and being available to the self-determination of every individual.

Benjamin's statement evades both the threat of totalization in Heidegger's statement about humanism and the threat of circularity in Marx's statement about *human-being*. It is a historical gesture in the fashion of Walter Benjamin, inimitable natural historian of society. Benjamin posits a historical rupture within the species category, whether species is conceived biologically or ontologically, and the latter would include the full trajectory between Marx's *Gattungswesen* and Heidegger's *Dasein*. For Benjamin to say that "humanity" as a category becomes a veritable species in modernity is to pinpoint the moment when technology ceases to be merely instrumental to the human and becomes productive/destructive of the human: "technology [as] the mastery not of nature but of the relation between nature and the human" (487). Benjamin's aphorism raises the stakes of the entire framework and leads us into very complicated territory, a cognitive labyrinth that is admittedly difficult to navigate, since it is by no means a one-way street.

In this apparent categorical shift from animality to sociality (from "humans" to "humanity")—which is incidentally also a shift in ontology from plural-singular to singular-plural—Benjamin seems to suggest a rupture between biology and history, or, more precisely, a rupture within biology instituted by history. This is consistent in his thinking throughout. Consider his peculiar but fecund way of conceiving natural history. What in this text he calls the "relation between nature and the human" (487) to which technology applies its mastery is encapsulated by this category of natural history. With a bit of cunning, Benjamin makes sure we cannot depart from his aphorism with the sealed interpretation that history has vanquished biology or that history has vanquished (human) nature. He definitely proposes a shift from antiquity to modernity in which the loss of cosmic experience as an immanent condition may hang in the balance. And we may perhaps conclude that, by marking this shift, he insinuates that history has produced a different nature, a different species-being, if not—and that is a lot to say—a different species altogether. Yet, the biological or natural-historical language remains unaltered: it is humanity *as a species* that history (as technology, modernity, etc.) brings into emergence. At the same time, the signification of species is irreversibly altered, and a definitively new *archē* is put into place, into the place of a *telos* already achieved.[93]

There is no doubt that, for Benjamin, history is always an affair internal to the human and this, again, is consistent throughout, no matter whether he occupies himself with the inanimate, the bestial, the angelic, or the messianic. History is internal to the human because—and Marx permeates Benjamin on this issue—only humans make history (even if not quite as they please). In order not to seem to be fetishizing this notion of making history, let me reiterate that making metaphysics is one of the most common and most powerful ways in which humans make history. Indeed, only humans can make metaphysics, that is, create an entire world in effect alien to the world in which they live, purposely unreal and, even more paradoxically, purported to account for the ultimate unaccountability of the real. Even more, the penchant of humans for creating metaphysics is one of the commonest ways of striving to overcome their animality. In this respect—*and this is not at all a paradox*—metaphysics is one of the key forms of *human-being*, of human animality. But by the same logic, human animality can never be reduced to animality as such because the *inhuman*—whether as a metaphysical construct or as a brutally actualized reality—is a creative/destructive element intrinsic to the human. From this standpoint, Benjamin's peculiar reconfiguration of species might be recast as follows: humanity as a species may never quite become realized because this would entail an abolition of the inhumanity immanent to it.

Whichever way we interpret Benjamin's enigmatic statement, a basic question remains: How can we settle on the biological language remaining unaltered when the signification of species is definitively altered—moreover, altered by history? One answer is suggested to me in James Gleick's genealogy of information technology throughout history, especially at a moment (very much Benjamin's epoch) when the near-simultaneous invention of telephony and telegraphy produces, in the descriptions of the time, an analogy between telecommunication and the human nervous system: "Considering how speculative the analogy was, it turned out well. Nerves really do transmit messages, and the telegraph and the telephone did begin to turn human society, for the first time, into something like a coherent organism."[94] Gleick's formulation is uncannily similar to Benjamin's, even if in a different language and with different historical data at hand. In both cases, a certain technology of being is unavoidably implicated at the most basic biological ground.

Another contiguous response would send us further back, to a point where arguably the historical moment that Benjamin channels may have been originally set into motion. Michel Foucault comes to mind here when he isolates the movement from *le genre humain* to *l'espèce humaine* as the inaugural ground of what he calls biopower. For Foucault, this is an essential marker of the epistemic shift brought forth in the revolutionary eighteenth century, and it is interesting to note that Benjamin reiterates it as an inaugural marker of the revolutionary twentieth century. In both cases, the political impetus is entwined with the actualization of the human *within* the overall biological sphere, not as an exceptional instance but as confirmation of the shared rootedness of the living. For Foucault, this political element resides in the new conceptual figure of "population" and the radical reconfiguration of "public" but also how the new bio-ontological category of "the human race" is riveted by the enormity of internal exclusions that draw the lines of racism on the most elemental existential ground: "the break between what must live and what must die."[95] Foucault's singular contribution is to manifest the otherwise unattended historical evidence of how these central political concepts (population, public, race) and their configurations of power are predicated on the invention of the human species as a biological category.[96] This inaugurates biopolitics as a field, even though Foucault soon after abandons the term in order to pursue the discourse of governmentality.

It is worth remembering here the evocative turns of phrase in the concluding section of *The History of Sexuality*: "What might be called a society's 'threshold of modernity' has been reached when the life of the species is wagered on its own political strategies. For millennia, man remained what he was for Aristotle: a living animal with the additional capacity for a political existence; modern man is an animal whose politics places his existence as a living being in question."[97] While clearly resonating Benjamin's account of the threshold of modernity, Foucault differs perhaps in emphasizing not so much a shift in the category of species (from humans to humanity), but a shift in politics that now bears upon what he calls "the species body": a "biopolitics of population" (135). Whether this biopolitics abolishes the capacity of Aristotle's concept of *zōon politikon* to continue to have meaning (or acquire new meaning) in modernity remains an open question. (I will return to this question at the end of this essay.) But there is no doubt that this new politics of biopower creates new *special* (again as in species-determining) technologies, which in fact will trade life and death in ways that go hand in hand with the onslaught of capital on a planetary (species) scale that turns living being itself into a battlefield: "This bio-power was without question an indispensable element in the development of capitalism; the latter would not have been possible without the controlled insertion of bodies into the machinery of production and the adjustment of phenomena of population to economic processes" (140-41).

Consistent with his thinking overall, Foucault recognizes this nexus as a new epistemological condition, a new framework of power/knowledge. This new historical condition of *human-being* as a terrain of cognitive technologies that enhances biological frameworks of meaning, even when it might push up against them, is essential to the Enlightenment imaginary. A prevalent characteristic of eighteenth-century materialist reconfigurations of the human was the compulsion to determine various ways in which the zoological and the technological are entwined. This animal which has a rather unique capacity for corporeal understanding that extends beyond instinct and mere external stimulation was also seen, for the first time, as a sort of cognitive apparatus, self-animated and self-contained. A certain obsession with primary cognition, radically sensual and corporeal, that antecedes the abstracting capacity for language and reflection, generated such works as La Mettrie's *L'homme machine* (1748) and Condillac's *Traité des sensations* (1754), while its most sumptuous iteration, to my mind, is contained in the two essays by Diderot, *Lettre sur les aveugles* (1749) and *Lettre sur les sourds et muets* (1751). The fact that all these works were published roughly within a five-year span testifies to a surge of collective exploration and articulation of this concern, arguably motivated by the encyclopedic imaginary that encapsulates the French Enlightenment.

No doubt there are all kinds of variances and specificities in these texts that cannot be explored here in detail. It is well known, for example, that Diderot found La Mettrie's hedonistic materialism extreme even by his own materialist standards, and while we may consider Diderot's critique analogous to how Marx would come to view Feuerbach a century later, nonetheless La Mettrie's groundwork registers, rather ironically, an antecedent epistemological justification for posthumanist dreams of cyberhumanity. Of course, the sense-based human machine that La Mettrie theorizes is considerably different from the techno-obsessed visions of cyberhumanity, if nothing else because, faithful to his sense of awe before the outmaneuverable animality of the human, La Mettrie admits that "man is so complicated a machine that it is impossible to get a clear idea of the machine beforehand, and hence impossible to define it." The statement comes in the wake of another phrase at the outset that raises the question "How can we define a being whose nature is absolutely unknown to us?" before it proceeds to outline nonetheless a certain technology of knowledge and definition, even if precarious and against obvious certainties.[98]

The unavoidable question that emerges in turn—what can an undefinable machine possibly be?—is unanswerable by definition; if anything, a machine is pure form and force of definition. But this quandary is what actually makes this text so radical, not only in its time but even more in the contemporary context. For, against the grain of his own impetus, La Mettrie's investment in the inveterate animality of the human makes the human-machine element impervious to a mere technological account. Rather, it reconfigures the technological as a realm that belongs wholly to the sensual: the *human/animal* is a machine because its organic sensuousness permeates all aspects that animate its being—all aspects that *define* it as a being, even if not entirely knowable—including both reason and imagination, both psyche and mind.[99]

Even though Diderot finds La Mettrie's materialism extreme, his own project of elucidating human capacity by examining how physical infirmity (blindness, deafness, muteness) constitutes in itself a profound system of cognition opens a similar epistemological path. For the first time in the humanist tradition thinking about *human-being* eschews the articulation of an organic whole ultimately maintained by the enhancement of nature by culture. Instead, culture itself—that is to say, how self-knowledge is achieved by a certain kind of learning—is shown to be possible from the standpoint of infirmity, incompletion, fragmentation. Being incapacitated in a specific sense—unable to see or listen or speak—does not bar you from enacting the full potential of the *human/animal*. A tangible encounter with the world suffices, and I mean this quite literally, because it is the haptic capacity, the first and most elemental of the senses, that enables the adaptation required to guide the *human/animal* to knowledge. But the radical significance lies even further. By approaching the problem from the standpoint of incapacity (which is much more profound than the way the term "disability" is used nowadays), Diderot outlines a kind of technology of the human, which nonetheless does not displace or efface the biological but, on the contrary, emerges from within the biological and remains in *co-incidence* with it.

Diderot's perspective is utterly prescient of what Neil Harbisson has famously achieved. Colorblind by birth, Harbisson is a world-renowned cyborg artist (as he describes himself) who has an antenna implanted in his skull that translates color into sound. Harbisson is legally recognized (by the UK) as a cyborg and has become a pioneering spokesman for cyborg nature: "I don't feel that I'm using technology, I don't feel that I'm wearing technology, I feel that I am technology. I don't perceive my antenna as a device, I perceive it as a part of my body, I perceive it as an organ."[100] The mistake often made in encountering such quotations is to spin tales of beyond-the-human, but the biosubjective language alone suggests otherwise. Without the animal that has created the antenna in order to *be* (one with) the antenna, the antenna means nothing. By Diderot's and La Mettrie's lessons, prosthetic technology and the relationality it implies has always already existed within the purview of the *human/animal*.

It would make sense to understand this gesture in the framework of the dialectic of Enlightenment, as Horkheimer and Adorno famously theorized. Their argument is quite peculiar but very useful beyond their specific social-historical prejudices. If we accept their central premise that the Enlightenment imaginary is encapsulated in the mastery of nature, which they present as a transhistorical and thus essentially anthropological condition, then the shifts that take place in modernity when the Enlightenment gets to have a proper name are sort of endemic variations. Humanity as a species is no more than an anthropological invention, they could say, and whatever is biologically resignified in inventing the notion "humanity" is but an immanent project of a certain metaphysical "technology" that has existed for millennia. The radical emancipatory power of the Enlightenment proper, with its encyclopedic undercutting of certainty, is built on an intrinsic violence that always threatens to dismantle any and every inquiry so as to actualize the desire for yet more certainty (or other certainty—here, the difference doesn't matter). The mastery of nature is attributed to the *human/animal* as its historical nature, and when this reaches the point of planetary catastrophe, humanity as a species will have achieved its completion as a bio-techno-logical creative/destructive machine. That is the essence of this thesis. Not surprisingly, for Horkheimer and Adorno, this sort of dialectical articulation of the Enlightenment—what Foucault later called, in a memorable phrase, "the Enlightenment's blackmail"—becomes possible as a result of the experience of fascism: "the significance of the [fascist's] hand negligently stroking a child's head, or an animal's back, is that it could just as easily destroy them."[101] This experience bolstered and refined their critique of capitalism, which was under way since the late 1920s, when Benjamin's work was already significant as a lesson.

But the destructive possibility of the dialectic of Enlightenment is neither in itself guaranteed nor should it serve as a framework of judgment, for then however we determine what the Enlightenment is or does becomes normative. What matters is the dialectical openness of the thesis, which refines and enhances the encyclopedic uncertainty of both *human/animal* and *human-being*. In this light, as unprecedented and groundbreaking as Benjamin's and Adorno's thinking was in its time, it is important to see it in the wake of a barrage in early twentieth-century German thought which opens a horizon that overlaps with phenomenology and the hermeneutics of nature and forms in turn the backbone of German philosophical anthropology seeking to overcome the constraints of Kantian idealism. This terrain is vast and formidable, charted by thinkers such as Arnold Gehlen, Max Scheler, Jakob von Uexküll, and Helmuth Plessner in relation, of course, to the highly influential philosophical projects of Husserl, Heidegger, Weber, Cassirer, and Simmel (but also Bergson in the French tradition) unfolding in full force. This remarkably complex terrain is oftentimes obscured by dismissive generalizations, under such names as *Naturphilosophie* or *Lebensphilosophie*, which are retrospectively marred by restrictive associations with Nazi atrocities having been conceived and committed in the name of an *orthology* of human nature. What interests me here is a certain materialist understanding—a real historical materialism, if we can disengage this notion from its Marxist language—that reiterates (while reconfiguring) some crucial elements of sentient Enlightenment thinking that had meanwhile been suppressed by a nineteenth-century metaphysics of rationalism and positivism.

Of those thinkers, Helmuth Plessner (1892–1985) may provide the most lucid unfolding of this nexus. Not incidentally, upon his return to Germany from exile in 1951, after miraculous survival in the Dutch underground during the war, Plessner was invited by Horkheimer and Adorno to participate in the postwar Frankfurt School, signaling their recognition of his formidable oeuvre in biology, anthropology, and sociology since the early 1920s. At that point, Plessner was already famous for his theory of ex-centric positionality (*exzentrische Positionalität*) developed in his seminal work *Die Stufen des Organischen und der Mensch* (Levels of the Organic and the Human), published in 1928, the same year as Benjamin's *One Way Street*. Plessner's idea of an organically present spatial eccentricity, although conceived as a mark of distinction pertinent specifically to the *human/animal*, is nonetheless conversant with Uexküll's more general (and nowadays better known) notion of onto-bio-environment (*Umwelt*) developed six years later in his *Foray into the World of Animals and Humans* (1934), which contested the general proclivity at the time to imagine living-being in machine terms. The fact that certain sensory processes might be deemed to be the work of "elementary machine operators"—the very constitution of the cellular function—does not mean that the organism in its biological totality operates with the "logic" of a machine.

Uexküll, who may be said to have invented biosemiotics, was groundbreaking in expanding the basic notion of how all living-being exists first and foremost in a world of its own (*Eigenwelt*): a world that it makes its own as primary requirement for signification (what the existentialists would eventually call *pour-soi*), so that the very process of producing and attributing meaning would take place. Without "meaning"—which signifies here nothing more than a basic framework of distinction, evaluation, and communication—no living-being can live, even in the simplest biological sense, which makes it all the more remarkable that the *human/animal* is what it is and knows what it is as a living-being specifically in *knowing* that it must create/give meaning to what it also *knows* (in interminable and perhaps even indeterminable ways) to be meaningless.

In light of this, Plessner points to a specific displacement within the category of *Umwelt*, which comes about with the natural-historical development of the *human/animal*. This displacement does not compromise the fundamental parameters of Uexküll's *Umwelt* as it pertains to all living-being; on the contrary, it enhances its nuances.[102] For no proper environment—in the sense of "a world of one's own"—can be signified (given meaning) without some notion of limits, boundaries, or space markers of what are the environs of self and other, which is also to say that, in the last instance, *Umwelt* and *Eigenwelt* are not contesting or contrasting notions.

As Uexküll makes clear, every organism creates and reshapes its own *Umwelt* in the process of organizing itself in its encounter with the world (the other) and, from this standpoint, organisms have singularly different *Umwelten* even when they might be sharing the same environment. In this sense, the notion of what is "one's own" is hardly a tautological or self-referential category. Simply put, "one's own" (*Eigenwelt*) is always "one's own *environment*" (*Umwelt*)—a space of self defined by markers of encounter between self and other, self and world. These markers may be either hard and uncompromisable or nebulous, ambiguous, and contested. Often what is one's own extends into what is the other's, and a basic antagonism is always in place even though the psyche's recognition of what is one's own can never admit anything otherwise. This is not a statement driven by a human(ist) model, but it is pertinent to the basic parameters of living-being. In fact, psychic recognition in the *human/animal* is signified precisely by contesting limits and boundaries, and even more, as an outcome of this contestation, by driving *human-being* toward an *Umwelt* of impermanence, a proper environment where boundaries, limits, or spatial markers are constantly fluctuating, often to a perilous degree.

Plessner's particular attention to human animality, as opposed to Uexküll, whose concern is grounded primarily on the study of insects, may explain why in today's "posthumanist" universe his work might seem old-fashioned and has not been equally translated. But epistemologically speaking, the implications of Plessner's work go beyond a strict anthropology. Even if the idea of ex-centric positionality is configured on the basis of certain anthropological assertions that have become outdated—the primacy of the biped field of vision, for example—what I retain is the emphasis on what can be called a sort of border ontology, where subject and object or self and world (or environment) are never quite consistently the same at all times, therefore barring a hard ontological center that, even if just instinctually, remains a sovereign point of self-reference. Even the emergence of language in the *human/animal* cannot really be understood as a bio-ontological development in a literal sense: "Speech intrinsically tends toward the signaling [*Zeichenbegung*] of meaning. Language can 'arise'—if indeed it can—not out of the human but with the human" (*Conditio humana*, 179). In other words, whatever "the human" might be it is both "external" and plural, indeed interactive, a relation with otherness that is nonetheless immanent, intrinsic nature: a paradoxical nature, to say the least. It is also, for the same reason, an intrinsically exilic nature, if I may be allowed a loose use of the term: the nature of an animal that Plessner (invoking Herder) calls "invalid relative to its highest capacities" by virtue of being "biologically nowhere at home" (183), thereby needing and always seeking to *create forms of environment*—in the strictest sense of *poiēsis*—with alternating consequences of openness to the world and mastery of the world, both of which are enabling and debilitating at the same time.

In this respect, however we might determine what is the "self" domain in the *human/animal*, it is impossible to fully separate the "self" from what might be deemed to be its environment, not merely because the *human/animal* inhabits an *Umwelt* like every other living being, but rather because this *Umwelt* is constantly mutable and forever alterable, even if to an utterly catastrophic degree. That's what enables Plessner to say that *human-being* "encounters boundaries but not limits."[103] The difference is essential, for in the gap between the two terms—or what might be two different significations of the same notion—exists this peculiar natural history that enables the *human/animal* to create (and, just as well, to destroy) itself as a new species, whether according to Benjamin's previous quotation or, as we saw earlier, according to Marx's sense-determined *Gattungswesen*, which is in that respect hardly generic, or to Fanon's argument in reference to colonized populations as a historical species that must disappear so that a new humanity can create itself.

This gap is also where the specific interplay between psyche and society takes place, which enables this specific form of living-being to attain what we call historical consciousness. History, which, as Plessner argues, includes all the elements that claim to be beyond history (all sorts of eschatology, in short), can also be understood as the domain where the *human/animal* engages with the consequences of the boundlessness that characterizes its border-nature: "This boundlessness of the human being, anchored in his specific life structure though he may be, allows us to speak of the *homo absconditus*, the man who knows the limits of his boundlessness yet grasps himself as unfathomable. Open to himself and to the world, he recognizes his own concealment" (501). And as he elaborates later on:

> The concealment of man from himself as well as from his fellow men—*homo absconditus*—is the somber side of his openness to the world. He can never discover himself completely in his actions—only his shadow which precedes him and remains behind him, an imprint, a clue to himself. Therefore, man has a history. He makes it and it makes him. His activities, forced on him because they make possible his mode of life, at the same time disclose to him and conceal from him the interpretation of events, which not only depend on some initial constellation of circumstances, but also on their effects which are open to an incalculable future. (503)

Openness to the world and self-concealment exist in the order of *co-incidence*, which means that neither is ever fully constituted and final. It is in the movement between them, the oscillation in the gap between boundary and (no) limit, where *human-being* occurs without ever achieving resolution. In the face of this inherent existential unlimitedness, self-limitation is the very first act toward autonomy, as the Greek tragic poets understood so long ago, and yet the overcoming of self-concealment remained even then an inordinate obstacle (what in the tragedies is coded as hubris).

For Plessner, this incapacity for self-transparency—the opaqueness of being—is precisely what structures the openness to the world as an existential condition. Not knowing exactly where one's limits are enables a continuous seeking of what is other. It matters not whether this often proves to be catastrophic for either self or other or both—that's a different discussion. More relevant here is how Plessner translates this ontological framework into the social and political sphere in a way that enhances Aristotle's *zōon politikon*. He makes an explicit reference to this Aristotelian notion in connection with his theory of ex-centric positionality in the early text *Der Mensch als Lebewesen* (1924) in order to elaborate an argument for how the *human/animal* lives not just "naturally" but by conducting or driving life in a certain direction, sometimes even against life itself. From this standpoint, seeking the other ontologically is reconfigured in terms of what Plessner calls the "duty for politics," whereby politics does not merely signify the sphere of power conflict but also the sphere of trust and engagement with what is other, foreign, or strange.[104] Here, the unlimitedness of the world that makes the *human/animal*— but equally, the unlimitedness of the world that the *human/animal* makes—becomes the sufficient condition for an ever-open horizon of alternative possibility, of *poietic* creation (for better or worse, but, I repeat, calculating an ethical measure is not our concern here).

In this respect, the *human/animal* is never a priori limited to one species, for it (re)invents itself in the very social-historical process that it creates—whereby, then, "it" might express itself in a variety of generic names, whether *anthropos*, man, humankind, human being, humanity, human animal, posthuman, cyborg, and so forth. Insofar as these names, generic though their claims may be, produce marks of difference (as in the way they encrypt or deny their gendering, for example), their specific significations no doubt matter a great deal. But, in effect, these too are no more than different instances of historical ontology in a trajectory that has no structural logic, no generic species. "As historical being, [the human] is something more, or very often something less, than its physical nature, because to be human does not only mean to belong to humankind but to find oneself facing an opportunity that anyone might just as well seize or miss" (*Conditio humana*, 140). This too is a mark of the ex-centric positionality of this animal that always seems to struggle with but never achieves sovereignty of being, not even according to the most elementary demands of survival and self-preservation; an animal where self and being belong to each other as mutual outsides (*Aussersichsein*); an animal that for this very reason objectifies itself without limit and yet never fully knows itself even as distinct object; an animal that shares itself with the world (*Mitwelt*) without ever quite knowing how to avoid destroying this world—in effect, an undecidable animal that lives not by some natural unfolding of its being but precisely by making decisions (sometimes arbitrary) about being and often against being, the only animal whose sense of identity might involve *identicide*.[105]

This inherent undecidability at the level of animality, which for that reason enables and demands ontological decision, opens *human-being* to the political at an ontological level in a way that reiterates Aristotle's notion of "the political animal" beyond the definitional description of the animal that invents and lives in the polis. No doubt, such openness to catastrophic instability, which characterizes this political animal that challenges even the categorical integrity of its own species, can easily confirm adherence to some Hobbesian politics of statist sovereignty, as both Arnold Gehlen and Carl Schmitt argued in response to Plessner as Weimar contemporaries. Yet, there is no a priori ground for one to necessarily assume this position; Gehlen and Schmitt merely make a political decision. In fact, the contrary can be argued just as well, and it is much closer to Plessner's political insight. The ontological undecidability that makes this animal political in its very nature, as it were, is perfectly suited to a radical democratic politics, an anarchist politics as I elaborate in the next essay. It all comes down to whether philosophical anthropology nowadays can assume the risk of the question of what is human without falling back to either old humanist certainties or newfangled presumptions to dispense with the human altogether.[106]

A DIGRESSION ON THE DIGRESSION OF THE ANIMAL

I understand the importance of philosophical inquiries into the notion of the animal in twenty-first-century thought, at whose forefront I would place Jacques Derrida's *The Animal That Therefore I Am* (2006), Giorgio Agamben's *The Open: Man and Animal* (2002), Cary Wolfe's *Zoontologies* (2003), and Donna Haraway's *When Species Meet* (2008). There is an explosion of writing on this issue, but, at the risk of a certain simplification in order to move further, this writing rarely avoids, in the last instance, the determinant encounter with the long line of thought in the "Western" tradition, from Plato and Aristotle to Aquinas and Descartes to Kant and Wittgenstein.[107] And while it is inarguable that traditional philosophy contemplates the animal within the framework of an avowed anthropocentrism, the tenet of much of this recent work, assumed to exemplify posthumanist thinking, is no less anthropocentric, whatever might be its claims, its pretensions, or indeed its bona fide philosophical ruptures and insightful contributions. The meaning of anthropocentrism need not necessarily be reduced to humanity's epistemological tyranny over all other natural being or living being. But even if it were, the self-ascribed posthumanist deconstructions of the deadly privileging of anthropic being over all other living being—deconstructions that, of course, I applaud—is performed by and in the name (not to mention benefit) of what sort of being? What is the being that does the thinking about the vicissitudes of being (and beings)?

Rhetorical questions, of course. Human beings are conducting this thinking, and indeed we're talking about radical interrogative thinking—*poiētic* thinking, that is to say, not just thinking analytically in/through concepts but thinking creatively in/through phantasms. This specific difficulty in outmaneuvering the phantasmatic anthropocentrism thereby denied in posthumanist analysis is very much the point of my inquiry here. Moreover, I very much abide by how Zakiyyah Iman Jackson has made this point succinctly in similar terms, but from the standpoint of how easily critical discourses animalize what she calls "black(ened)" bodies (instead of interrogating the specific ways in which they are *abjectly humanized*), and furthermore how easily the established critique even of racist structures slides into a general critique of anthropocentrism and an uncritical embrace of animals:

> A critique of anthropocentrism is not necessarily a critique of liberal humanism.... Many critics of anthropocentrism have mistakenly perceived that the problem of our time is anthropocentrism rather than a failed praxis of being. Such critics of anthropocentrism often proceed by humanizing animals in the form of rights, welfare, and protections without questioning how advocates are constructing themselves in the process.... At present, animal studies scholarship tends to presume a humanity that is secure within the logic of liberal humanism rather than engage with a humanity that is often cast as debatable or contingent. (*Becoming Human*, 15–16)

From this position, Jackson derives a two-pronged conclusion: First, discourses of exclusion and denied humanity are inadequate to address the conditions of blackness "because the African's humanity is not denied but appropriated, inverted, and ultimately plasticized in the methodology of abjecting animality" (23). This becomes essential, as a disguised or repressed element, to the imaginary of universal humanity: "black abjection is transposing recognition and an inclusion that marks itself as exclusion" (23). Second, "blackness is not so much derived *from* a discourse on nonhuman animals—rather the discourse on 'the animal' is formed through enslavement and the colonial encounter encompassing both *human and nonhuman* forms of life" (23). Therefore, in what is surely a reconfiguration of Derrida's foreclosure of the human-animal continuum, Jackson argues that "the animalizations of humans and animals have contiguous and intersecting histories rather than encompassing a single narrative on 'animality' " (23).

Going further, Jackson makes a key historical point regarding "Western" philosophy's record on this matter. Despite a somewhat conventional miscasting of Aristotle as privileging the human as the rational animal—this is never the case in Greek, as *logos* has nothing to do with reason in the sense understood by the later European tradition—nonetheless, she acknowledges that in Aristotelian thinking "humanity and animality are not mutually exclusive terms," which, she adds, prevails in the early instances of European humanism until the modern "logic of conquest, slavery, and colonialism produced a linear and relational concept of human animality" (26). In other words, Jackson reiterates Wynter's understanding of a radical shift in the European humanist imaginary that leads to and is derived from the Spanish conquest of the Americas. The presumed internal continuity of Western philosophy, which is tacitly invoked even by detractors (whether consciously or not) is thus disrupted by an indisputable *historical* ground, according to which " 'Being human' provided a vehicle for reinforcing a striated conception of human species. Thus, the extension and recognition of shared humanity across racial lines is neither 'denied' nor mutual, reciprocal human recognition; rather, it is more accurately deemed bestializing humanization and inverted recognition. Instead of denying humanity, black people are humanized, but this humanity is burdened with the specter of abject animality" (27).

I am quoting Jackson extensively because her counterargument troubles both the general account of how philosophy has dealt with the human-animal equation or distinction and specifically how Derrida, in his attempt to criticize this account, also falls prey to the convenience of this philosophy's inveterate problem-method of recognition. Significantly, even though it had already been an important part of Derrida's work, in this case the problematic of race is entirely missing from his meditation of the human-animal relation.

To his credit, even if not extending himself to how intricate the relation between humanization and animalization really is, Derrida acknowledges that thinking about the animal is constitutively impossible for philosophy and belongs instead to poetic thinking.[108] This is not because poetry is any less anthropocentric than philosophy but because, compared to philosophical thinking, poetic thinking is less repressed about expressing its animality. Burdened, alas, by Platonism's hatred of the sensuous (*aesthētikon*) and with the backdrop of a basic Aristotelian naturalism, modern Western philosophy might be said to have obliterated, in its uninterrogated adoption of Aristotle's *zōon logon ekhon*, the determinant force of *zōon*. As a result, the trajectory of Western philosophy since Plato would come to attribute all sense of the living substance (*zōon*) to the possession of *logos*—a word that, I repeat, cannot be reduced to signifying reason or language as indication of rational thought, as traditional humanism has always had it. Rather, if we care at all about the social imaginary that invented it, *logos* must be reconfigured to retain its signification of language per se: that is, *language as an animal virtue*.[109]

It is the deconstruction of this precedent anthropocentric trajectory that Derrida signifies in his ingenious de-Cartesian title *L'animal que donc je suis*: the animal that therefore I am [is] the animal that therefore I follow. In this double gesture of *suis* the Cartesian authority of the "I" is irreparably disjointed. It is only by virtue of this disjoining that a discourse about the animal can even become possible: "the most *chimerical* discourse I have ever attempted" (D, 23). This is because a discourse about the animal is paradoxically both an *autobiographical* discourse (a discourse about the human) and yet a *hetero-graphical* discourse (a discourse about the other—indeed the otherness of authorial life, animality as such—as limit of the human). There is merit in Derrida's naming the human "the autobiographical animal" in opposition to the usual naming: the animal in possession of *logos*. Following this trajectory, Derrida entertains the possibility of contemplating the animal, not as the being who cannot speak because it has no *logos*, but as the being who does not *respond* to *logos*. To say "respond" is certainly not to say "react." It pertains to the game of interpellation that induces in one a sense of political being: in other words, not mere reaction to being called by name, as one could whistle one's dog into obedience. Evading this specific game of interpellation is not only indicated in the incapacity to respond to *logos* but in the incapacity to position oneself as an "I." Interpellation is prerogative to autobiography, for if you do not respond to being called upon politically, you have no calling to narrate yourself, to write yourself in your name, as Fanon conducted so brilliantly in *Black Skin, White Masks*. It is in this sense that "power over the animal is the essence of the 'I' or the 'person,' the essence of the human" (D, 93).

Insofar as traditional philosophy since Plato is engaged, in some form or another, in the contemplation/expression of an "I" under the authority of *zōon logon ekhon*, it has failed its task in relation to the animal. Derrida equates, in this respect, the philosophical aspirations of Cartesian rationalism with Kantian transcendentalism, Heideggerian ontology, Levinasian ethics, or Lacanian theories of the unconscious (D, 89–90). He is correct to claim that no philosopher who takes up the question of animality as an actual philosophical problem has ever engaged with the peculiar designation of the general-singular—*the* animal. This singular name, which simultaneously abolishes any bona fide singularity as it renders generality vacuous, is a cipher for how the autobiographical animal (the human) registers its authorial presence. The unexamined false singularity of *the* animal—which is another way of saying that animals are deprived of an "I"—dovetails with the conviction that whoever says "I" is not an animal. In so many words: the professed (false) singularity of the animal is possible only because of the authorial singularity of the human.

From my standpoint, this is the very same equation that suppresses the animal-in-the-human, paradoxically by transferring the singular essence of the human to what is conjured, in singular grammar but nonetheless generically, as other-than-human. And not only so, if we consider again blackness as a corrosive element in the entire human-animal equation. To quote Zakiyyah Jackson once more: "Recognition of personhood and humanity does not annul the animalization of blackness. Rather, it reconfigures discourses that have historically bestialized blackness.... Animalization is not incompatible with humanization: what is commonly deemed dehumanization is more accurately interpreted as the violence of humanization or the burden of inclusion into a racially hierarchized universal humanity" (*Becoming Human*, 18). Derrida is unusually explicit on this philosophical matter, foregrounding Kant as the epitome of this long trajectory: "The Kantian has nothing but hatred for the animality of the human. It is even his 'taboo' in all senses of the term, and it begins as a sacred injunction against impurity" (D, 103).

Derrida engages the calamity of unresponsiveness before the animal by conjuring what he calls a "chimerical word" to counter the animal's false generic singularity: *l'animot* echoes the repressed plurality (*animaux*) while registering at the same time the power of the singular-generic animal as the animating word—the "living word" would be its literal rendering—of humanity's authorial differentiation. The autobiographical gesture, being at some level a gesture of immunity against nature's obliterating inevitability (death), is always threatened, Derrida correctly argues, by an autoimmunity condition, by producing an idiomatic death process that I have called, on multiple occasions, *identicide*—for me an essential characteristic of the human, which outmaneuvers the basic (and rather banal) rubric of mortality as generically intrinsic to all animal life.

In this respect, I would propose here a divergence from Derrida's thinking, though very much in the sense that I am within and I follow from (*je suis*) Derrida's thinking. The consequence of this sort of meditation, as far as I'm concerned, is the reverse: in effect, only humanity may be said to have a generic-singular, a sui generis, animality (*Gattungswesen*—generic essence/specific being). Only the animal that, despite its own sense of itself, is *as such* an animal, yet is also *as such* like no other animal, can be animal in a singular sense. This is the case even more if we consider that the plurality of living creatures to which *human-being* belongs, but from which it is extracted in order to constitute its singularity, nullifies animality as such: that is, the condition of being content to exist in the self-generating singularity of one's species environment, one's absolute uninterrogated specificity. The only way we can perhaps speak of a common *physis* between the one animal that generalizes all singularity and the multiplicity of animals that, in their unresponsiveness to *logos*, fall prey to generalized singularity is the category of the living being as a mortal being: what Derrida suggestively calls *vivants à mort*, mortal living beings, living-in-order-to-die beings. In the end, the important step to take—which Derrida does not—is from *l'animot* to *l'animort*: to the animated death substance that *human-being*, as living being constituted by its knowledge of death, enacts at its most radical core of self-constitutive imagination. Dying is in this sense inextricable from living, and this has nothing to do not only with Heidegger's *Sein zum Tod* or Freud's death drive, but also cybernetic discourses of expiration or obsolescence. Certainly, the existential necessity of obsolescence in robots, whether actually produced or fictionally created in various literary forms, cannot be equated with the finitude of living being. The liquid carbon materiality of living being truly decays and is recirculated, while the obsolete machine's materiality is preserved, even in landfills.

There is yet another word to be said. Despite marking philosophy's inadequacy before the animal—or perhaps, because this inadequacy makes philosophy unresponsive to the living being's death-animating substance—Derrida cannot move onward to an affirmative assessment of *human/animal*, whereby mortality as mere fact of living would not serve as decisive *archē* but as just one instance in the amorphous pool of all those elements of *physis* that make one a living being, an animal—human or otherwise. This lapse is perhaps Derrida's own moment of autoimmunity in his discourse, the guardian angel's identicidal shadow. The animal, for Derrida, remains singular despite his *animot* because it seems to settle on the most unsettling position possible (because undeconstructible): the absolute Other. Derrida's consistent reluctance to deconstruct absolute alterity renders an otherwise sumptuous meditation on the animal impertinent to the exigency of characterizing the *human/animal* in affirmative terms, a risk I consider essential to rethinking humanism or, which is the same project, to reanimating the mutable condition of *human-being*.[110]

Donna Haraway has some sharp things to say about Derrida's reluctance, even if ultimately her own position too stands on an ontological turn. From her standpoint, the matter falters at the original assertion of the animal's incapacity to respond. The philosophical undertaking from the standpoint of the question "what if the animal responded?" should be reconfigured from the standpoint of the conditional affirmation "as if the animal responded" in order to reach the speculative question "what if the philosopher responded" to the animal? All instances are adeptly performative, and just as well—the conditional "if" marking the shared rules of the game is quintessentially performative and granted in all instances by commitment to the unconditional. The most fruitful kernel of this dissenting intersection between Derrida and Haraway lies there: precisely on how each one configures the unconditional—animal? human? human/animal?

Haraway's ironic reversal of Derrida's question redraws the ground of argument around the problematic singularity, not of *the* animal or *the* human as such, but of the disjunctive relation human vs. animal, an opposition that usually turns animality (even when pertinent to the human) into absolute alterity. Haraway proposes to turn the traditional philosophical position of animality as alterity into the affirmative gesture of what she calls, working off of Derridean naming but also echoing the language of radical antiglobalization ecologists, *autre-mondialisation*. This kind of alternative worlding, this other-worlding, is hardly otherworldly. Rather, it extends the material undoing of the metaphysics of human exceptionalist world-making by breaking the closure of human *Weltbildung* and opening up a meditation on alterity within the parameters of worldliness. Haraway's contribution is to remove the singularity of the interspecies relation, and to speak instead, ontologically, of interspecies being, of species as companion entities: "Companion species is my awkward term for a not-humanism in which species of all sorts are in question. Companion species is a permanently undecidable category, a category-in-question that insists on the relation as the smallest unit of being and of analysis.... Singular and plural, species resonate with tones of logical types, of the relentlessly specific.... Species, like the body are internally oxymoronic, full of their own others, full of messmates, of companions. Every species is a multispecies crowd."[111] Haraway configures Derrida's philosopher standing naked before the animal as a missed opportunity of other-worlding, an inability to engage the matter from a companion species position. She rejects the singularity argument altogether: both the generic-singular and the autobiographical singular are inadequate categorizations still under the pall of ontotheology. Instead, she proposes what she calls "risky worldings," yet another configuration of her *autre-mondialisation*. Achieving a sense of animality—"becoming animal" in her words—means to discover "the rich multiplicities and topologies of a heterogeneously and nonteleologically connected world" (27).

While as a retort, or an alternative ontology, this argument is noteworthy, there is an ease here that is certainly unaccounted for. It is ironic that *real* companionship between humans and animals flourished in epochs before humanism was deconstructed, theoretically but also technologically. "Companion species" was not articulated then as a concept because it was lived as a reality. It is ironic even further that moral and political concerns about animals, which generate discourses of animal rights (merely duplicating human rights—how this irony is lost in the eyes of animal-rights activists is utterly befuddling to me), develop precisely at the point when this companionship is rendered artificial: imposed by new discursive practices that respond to the—largely technological—disruption of sharing creaturely life and modes of living that go back eons.

Certainly, in hunter-gatherer societies no relation to an animal would be conceivable under the notion "companion species," and yet even when the animal is the necessary object of the hunt, even when an animal exists in order to be killed out of existential necessity, the rubric of relation is one of mutual animality. The precariousness of a hunter's life, the ease with which in such a world you may pass the threshold of death at any moment, like any animal, underlines the horizon of immanence that intersects with every moment of life. In this universe, hunter and hunt are one, which is not to say collapsed into one, but one in a tandem of living (and dying) being. Obviously, a hunter is always also potential hunt, a lump of protein in someone else's appetites, and this animal reciprocity cannot be overcome, which is why the hunter conducts funereal rites for the animal he kills. The gesture acknowledges the fact that the act of hunting removes a piece of the universe for which the universe must be compensated, even if by symbolic ritual. But this act of symbolic logic is nothing more than an expression of the specific animality of the human, certainly not an indication of "man's superiority" of mind, brain, or whatever else. On the contrary, "man's superiority" registers its perversion in that, in the course of time, hunting turns into sport and this sense of immanence and reciprocity is lost—"superiority" here clearly marking the very delusion (and loss of sense of animality) that animates a way of being which fuels the catastrophe of the planet.

In the end, one does not resolve the singularity of traditional humanist species-being by sheer multiplication or even mere *othering*, by substituting one ontological other by another. "Becoming animal" in Haraway's sense is tantamount to disregarding (forgetting?) that *one is animal already*, and thus renders "animal" yet again a sort of redemptive prosthesis. By the same gesture, effacing the human in a multispecies crowd ends up effacing the animality of the human.[112]

Although her critique of Derrida is warranted, Haraway's long-term antihumanism carries with it a whole set of limitations. It's interesting that Haraway disavows being a posthumanist (19) because this too is another identitary categorization and speaks instead of belonging to a posthumanities, which she explicitly cites as "another word for 'after monotheism' " (245). Here, there is indeed something revealing about the explicit distinction between posthumanism and posthumanities, on the one hand, and the association of posthumanities with postmonotheism, on the other.[113] The work of posthumanities, in these terms, would consist of breaking down both singularity and alterity as determinant conditions.

Certainly, alterity as *physis* is very much implicated in a monotheistic logic. It is indeed a singular notion; it belongs to the logic of the One, as do all absolute notions. Even, let us say, in the archaic imaginary of Hesiod or Anaximander, where *chaos* might be translated as abyssal alterity, it is nonetheless inconceivable for *chaos* not to be implicated with the *kosmos* that emerges from it, albeit discontinuously and groundlessly. In the world of human institution, or even living being more generally, the absoluteness of alterity is a perverse equation whose solution is absolved of any reality. We are not speaking of brutal natural externality, say, the effect of gravity or the annihilating power of fire. We are speaking of absolute alterity residing in living substance, in the realm of animal. There is nothing absolutely other in the realm of living being. Even death cannot be deemed to be absolutely other, unless we were to divorce it from the realm of living, an impossibility that, on the one hand, Derrida articulates perfectly (*vivants à mort*) and, on the other hand, rescinds in his quest for absolute alterity in animality. In the end, alterity within living being is only phenomenologically conjured to be absolute; it only appears to be absolute. It is *imagined* as absolute because alterity's *all too familiar reality*—its worldly proximity—is intolerable. One might go so far as to say that precisely because alterity is not absolute as pure human *physis*, precisely because it is not conveniently determined by its own rules and thereby does not escape the *kosmos* but is rather internal, partial—partial to us, part of us, and therefore very much our own—that *it must be made absolute*, so that we can be rid of our responsibility for it, so that we can then submit to its regal externality, its determining force.

Therefore, despite the philosophical merits of contemplating the significance of the animal per se and whatever the inventiveness of the techniques of such contemplations, the process can never be anything other than the contemplation of the question I posed at the outset, the definitive question, whose affirmative content can never overcome its essence as a question and whose multivariant answers cannot but rebound back to the interrogative domain: the question "what is human?" This interrogative domain, I repeat, is the framework of *zōon politikon*, the entwinement/intersection of *physis/nomos* that enables us to consider how human animality opens the way to the political.

How animals have been captured, raised, bought and sold, employed, exhibited, domesticated, trained, sacrificed, slaughtered, and consumed is—and will always be—a matter of human history and the politics it entails, *the only history there is because it entails a politics*. It is almost banal—but how horrifying that it is so!—to say that this same list of verbs has been applicable to the treatment of humans throughout this said history and continues to be. Singularly indicative, but not often invoked, is that the very institution of the zoo was derived from the construction of exhibition parks in the mid-1870s, themselves direct by-products of European colonialism, that presented peoples from various parts of the world (Laplanders, Sudanese, Inuit, or Singhalese) in controlled existence environments that presumably reproduced their "natural" conditions.[114]

I consider history here neither mere representation of living and dying in the world, which would be apt to every living being, every living-in-order-to-die being, nor the representation of creating and destroying the world, which is the exclusive property of the human being. History has meaning precisely in that the representation of living and dying, creating and destroying, is open to question, rendered political. This entails, at the very least, that besides being a domain of action, of creation/destruction, history is always and at the same time an object of reflection—both action and reflection taking place in a sphere of contention. History's meaning then is subject to judgment, and in this specific sense—even when there is no judgment, even when there is ignorance or deliberate denial of its significance—history is the determining force of how we signify living and dying in the world, creating and destroying the world.

I say this because the discussion of the animal as it pertains to the human can be conducted with neither the naïve expectation that it will reach some sort of transcendental knowledge of what an animal actually *is*—other than the simple, but oh so complex, matter of living being, living-in-order-to-die being—nor the spurious intention, philosophically speaking, that by contrast the discussion of the animal elucidates the truth of what the human animal actually is. The first will lead us to accounts of animality inevitably drawn from the position animals have had in history (once again, unavoidably, accounts of their encounters with humans, within the world of the humans). The second will be implicated in the classificatory paradox of the name "human animal," which cannot obtain an unequivocal truth by definition: because the human *animal* is indeed an animal like any animal (within, of course, the specific zoological classification that pertains to it), yet, insofar as it is the *human* animal, it is like no other animal on the planet. It is in this respect, as mark of this constitutive disjunction (which after all makes an animal political), that I write it as *human/animal*.

Let us consider a final point: The disjunction *human/animal* might be used to address Agamben's thesis, contra the traditional schema, that what characterizes the human is not merely the sum total of animality plus some other, excessive, superimposed, and perhaps even supernatural, order: spirituality, reason, divinity, etc.

> If the caesura between the human and the animal passes first of all within man, then it is the very question of man—and of "humanism"—that must be posed in a new way. In our culture, man has always been thought of as the articulation and the conjunction of a body and a soul, of a living thing and a *logos*, of a natural (or animal) element and a supernatural or social or divine element. We must learn instead to think of man as what results from the incongruity of these two elements, and investigate not the metaphysical mystery of conjunction, but rather the practical and political mystery of separation.[115]

Although, like Agamben, I too recognize the *human/animal* as a disjunction, I disagree that this implies a separation, because the two elements of disjunction (as Agamben later admits too) remain always in *co-incidence*. The human *is* an animal; animality is an undeconstructible condition of *human-being*. However, what makes this animal human, as opposed to canine or reptilian, is very much the proposed denial of its animality, or the striving to overcome its animality (which is, in effect, a denial). A concurrent description could be what Sloterdijk calls "the chronic animalian immaturity of the human," which goes "so far as to suggest that man is the being in which being an animal is separate from remaining an animal" (S, 20)—as long as we don't take seriously the word "immaturity."

One crucial form this impossible denial and yet impossible striving to overcome this separation takes is to conduct "objective" inquiries as to the animal, whether they are manifested in terms of the classificatory investigation of biology, the philosophical categorization of ontology, or the aestheticist preoccupations of so-called animal studies. This is the work of what Agamben calls the "anthropological machine." However, although he is right to want to dismantle the anthropological machine, Agamben is wrong to attribute to it ontological primacy. Even if the anthropological machine, at its most abstract, is humanity's putting into practice the specific anthropomorphic designs of an ultimately monotheistic imaginary—to make the world according to its own image and likeness—any anthropological machine nonetheless signifies a social-historical condition. And even if we disagree about the specifics of this condition (which society or societies? which history or histories?) or even if, moreover, we might agree that the anthropological machine is there from the outset, from the first human societies on the planet, still this does not exempt it from being a social-historical condition.

Pierre Clastres duly points out that the self-ascribed names of tribes in the Amazon (Guayaki, Yanomami, Guarani)—but also the Eskimos who call themselves Inuit—all mean human in some fashion or other. The differences in the social imaginaries between those societies and the contemporary ones are enormous, but this does not preclude their own "anthropological machine"; it's just that in their case their animality is not rejected or repressed.[116] In other words, there is nothing ontological about the anthropological machine, unless the ontological domain of the human is history itself. This would make for a peculiar ontology: a framework of self-cognition where *on* (the Greek word for living being) is by definition self-authorizing and interminably mutable (self-altering)—hence, something that, in self-induced fashion, is always more than itself and other than itself. In this sense, conditions of surplus and alterity would be self-emergent of/in *human-being*, never external to this being, even if they are invariably externalized.[117]

Strangely, Agamben not only ignores this surplus of mutability but also reiterates a traditional anthropological purview according to which in "the becoming human of the living being [ontology] is realized" (79). Yet, if we are going to be serious about it, ontology realizes nothing. However we might account for its various meanings, ontology cannot realize or actualize anything, cannot be the cause or source of anything, other than a whole lot of philosophical propositions about what is essential to being. The very contradictory multiplicity of such propositions is itself the supreme evidence that there is nothing essential to being. If ontology actualizes anything at all, if it brings reality to anything, this would be (the) nothing. The nonessential character of being, the nonmeaning of being, is precisely what was posited by the philosophy that preceded the birth of philosophy—if the latter can be attributed to Plato and the former continue to be called pre-Socratic. This is the only ontology that is not ontotheology because it recognizes mutability as the basic force of the cosmos.

In another register, these conditions of self-emergent surplus and alterity could also be conceived in terms of Heidegger's "world-image forming" (*weltbildend*) capacity of the human, a capacity that automatically characterizes "being-in-the-world" as a figure that presupposes and ensures the inseparability between being and the world. I acknowledge, of course, the lurking danger of collapsing the notions of human and world, dangerous because it leaves the politics of world-making uninterrogated. So, in using and addressing this relation, we must account for the fact that world-building is always simultaneously world-destroying and can never be tantamount to the historical mission of a people, as Heidegger famously announced. In fact, in the act of world-imagining we have to be able to imagine the possibility of total extinction—of humanity, of the nature of the world, of planetary being itself. This is not a fantasy. It is already a reality in the sense that it is technologically feasible: the self-annihilation of humanity is perfectly possible here and now and so is, in physical, material terms (though we know not the full extent), the annihilation of the planet Earth. This annihilation is, as of this time in history, inherent in world-building; otherwise the notion is dangerously privileged and instrumentalized.

THREE DEFINITIVE TROPES OF HUMAN ANIMALITY: *PSYCHĒ, PAIDEIA, PHILIA*

In his late paper "Analysis Terminable and Interminable" (1937), Sigmund Freud, not altogether in jest, identifies three impossible professions: psychoanalysis, pedagogy, and politics. Let us ignore the matter of profession, so as not to get stuck on issues of technique, and simply call them practices. These practices are impossible because they are interminable. All three claim as their end (aim) to undo the entrenched and unquestioned conditions that are accepted as ends (terminations), in the sense that they seek perpetual transformation, and indeed, to be precise, transformation conducted from within, as an intrinsically creative process, a process of self-alteration. It is only in this respect—as self-analysis—that psychoanalysis can be said to be interminable, not because the master analyst has decided to defer its termination.[118]

I find these three domains useful in elucidating further in what terms the question "what is human?" is, as such, the platform of the signification of the human. As a question that is itself the signifier of the answers it demands and generates, it is likewise impossible and interminable. The question itself is exemplary of the *poiētic* praxis that characterizes the *human/animal*: the creative transformative substance that entwines psychic and social-historical realities and, without abolishing their contradiction, enacts them as ontological dimensions of human animality.

I anticipate that misunderstandings may possibly arise about the naming of these three domains (*psychē, paideia, philia*), so let me offer a few preliminary clarifying remarks. First of all, although identified by Greek words, the domains should not be considered Hellenic in nature. That there is a specific social imaginary which, in this case, animates my thinking about these domains, and that this social imaginary is an ancient Greek one should serve here as just that: to remind us that these notions, these very names, were created by human beings with a specific history, a history that may (but does not necessarily have to) be considered relevant to our own history today—to our making history. In short, though these words do have a specific meaning in an ancient Greek world (this already being a statement entirely lacking in rigor, but let us move on), they should not be read as Greek concepts per se in this discussion, that is, as ready-made meanings applied to a situation.

Second, and more important, these three notions are not equivalent. *Paideia* and *philia* certainly belong to the realm of society. They are in the simplest sense social-historical institutions: they emerge from a certain *nomos*. *Psychē*, on the other hand, belongs to a certain *physis*, which may not survive without a *nomos* but certainly "precedes" *nomos*—if we can use this verb without attaching ourselves to strict chronological or topological structures and think instead of *psychē* as a sort of *co-incident* (that is to say, nonderivative) substratum of *nomos*. To say that *psychē* does not survive without *nomos* pressures us to consider that what pertains to this domain adheres to particular social-historical forms, or if you will, social-imaginary institutions, and that, in this respect at least, it comes to meet the demands of the other two explicitly social-imaginary domains (*paideia, philia*). At the same time, in order for the latter two domains to perform the work I am considering, a specific psychic component is essential—a certain creative element of the radical imagination of the *human/animal*. In short, though not strictly equivalent, the three categories are in a substantial sense intertwined in a shared path of interrogation.

Finally, in respect to the Freudian triptych I began with, while *psychē* and *paideia* correspond directly to psychoanalysis and pedagogy respectively, this cannot be easily said of *philia* in relation to politics. Here, an extended argument is being made, an interpretive argument, that enters the domain of political anthropology with a claim, again, about a certain *physis* that inhabits the making of a certain *nomos*. To the extent we can argue, contrary to the overwrought post-Schmittian convention, that friendship and *not* enmity is the ground of the political, we may make possible a primary understanding of the political that would not be based on the be-all and end-all of sovereignty. The extensive unfolding of this argument in all its implications is the essay on democracy's anarchy that follows in this book. Here, the stakes remain essentially anthropological, even if as I asserted at the outset, the impetus is to consider *human-being*, in the last instance, as a condition of political life, of political animality.

These three impossible and interminable domains of practice, which I lay out here after a long trajectory that began with the call to rethink humanism, are meant as directions toward a resignification of the *human/animal* against the conventional parameters of humanism. There could be others, of course—like the matter of vestment, as Jacques Derrida theorizes in relation to the singularity of the animal, or the privilege of laughter, as Henri Bergson famously argued. Perhaps even the notion of labor, as Hannah Arendt has forcefully foregrounded in *The Human Condition*, even if the Marxist shadow that haunts her argument (and cannot be overcome) is still there to remind us that the category of labor is a product of capital and not an anthropological given. In any case, the risk one assumes in rethinking humanism against the grain of both humanism and posthumanism demands that one posits (in the sense of *affirms*) some such specific domains that are predicated on the fact that the question "what is human?" remains open, even while they denote the horizon whereby the animality of the human is exercised or performed in indefinite processes of humanization.

1. *Psychē*

Since Aristotle's *Peri Psychēs* (*De Anima*), an option has been available to determine the animal not by physiology but by the living substance that animates it: the psyche. And although the translation of the Greek *psychē* to the Latin *anima* is problematic to say the least (particularly as it becomes interpolated by Christian thought and turns into the "soul"), what determines the *human/animal* as specifically human resides in this animating psychic substance. This substance is certainly not reducible to the mind or, worse, the faculty of reason. An elementary account of how human beings operate in relation to their environment demonstrates them to be quintessentially unreasonable. Nor is it the capacity for language, if by that we don't refer to complex semiotic structures but to the foundational function of language: communication. All animals—well, all beings, including flora and mycelium—communicate with their environment and the overwhelming majority of animals act reasonably. But human beings don't act reasonably and often fail to communicate, and this has to do with neither the discontents of civilization nor any sort of organic mishap but with their psychic constitution.

Aristotle introduced us to the notion that all animals (living beings) possess a psyche, but only in the *human/animal* is the psyche essentially phantasmatic capacity—phantasmatic capacity for knowledge, for thought: "The psyche never thinks without a phantasm" (*oudepote noei aneu phantasmatos ē psychē* in *De Anima*, Book III, 431a 17-18). The importance of denoting *nous* here is as crucial as the importance of *phantasma*. Whatever it might consist of physiologically, the mind is essentially powered by fantasy; it thinks by way and by virtue of fantasy. Not fantasy in the strict Freudian sense, although Freud's understanding of the thought-power of the dream-work is very much part of this trajectory, as is his commitment to deciphering the underlying phantasmatic link between dream-thoughts and human sexuality, despite obviously the patriarchal inadequacy in his interpretation. Rather, I mean fantasy as the capacity to imagine (indeed, to build and populate) worlds—and encounters between worlds—that do not exist, or do not yet exist, since this phantasmatic capacity is perfectly amenable to becoming a reality.

There is a famous passage in *Capital* where Marx discusses labor as an indication of how human nature is a self-transformative quality, a mutable nature that goes against nature-as-essence. Labor works upon nature and in the process transforms human nature. This is very much in tune with the argument already made in the 1844 Manuscripts about *Gattungswesen*, which we have already examined, and stands apart, in its abstraction, from the more calculative writing on economics that forms the purpose of *Capital*. But a particular phrase takes the *Gattungswesen* argument even further and perfectly addresses the psychic component of nature in a way rarely seen in Marx, apart from his argument on commodity fetishism: "A spider conducts operations that resemble those of a weaver, and a bee puts to shame many an architect in the construction of her cells. But what distinguishes the worst architect from the best of bees is that the architect raises his structure in his imagination [*Vorstellung*] before he constructs it in wax. At the end of every labor-process, we get a result that was already available to the worker at the outset."[119] The passage is often remarked upon in the general account of mechanistic calculation and materialist determination in order to underline the sort of Marxist rationalism that marks the humanist privilege of reason overlaying action. In other words, humans think before they act; they actualize a priori conceived blueprints, while other animals follow their instincts. But the passage says nothing about reason or even conception in the abstract rationalist sense. If there is a moment prior to action, this belongs to the psyche's atemporal capacity to bring forth not a thought but an image—in our language here, a phantasm. The architect is not a machine to generate blueprints, but an animal that lives by seeking out the phantasms (and indeed the fantasies) that it creates. Precisely what Aristotle says as well: the *human/animal* is a quintessentially phantasmatic animal. *Vorstellung* is the word that Freud also privileges when he seeks to describe how the psyche thinks, for the psyche knows no reason and no calculus. Somewhere beyond the stimulus-response relation to what is other, according to which all living beings create and engage with their world(s), the *human/animal* enacts a capacity to other what exists *before* it comes into contact with this otherness. It is precisely in that sense, to return to Marx, that the *human/animal* is constantly transforming (othering) its nature.

One of the obvious ways to understand this phantasmatic capacity characterizing the *human/animal* is to trace it in its sexuality. Human sexuality is essentially animated by fantasy, which defunctionalizes the sexual act by privileging pleasure for its own sake and unhinging it from the compulsion for reproduction. In fact, the very concept "sexuality" is incomprehensible outside the purview of human animality, whether we adhere to Foucault's persuasive insistence that sexuality is a social-historical concept (and thereby not even pertinent to "humanity" as such) or whether we choose to remain in the psycho-zoological realm of judgment. The second does make the argument more challenging, especially in light of the voluminous discussion in recent years about the sexual practices of various animals that seem to deviate from the necessity of reproduction. The scholarship on this matter is huge—before we even account for the popular obsession with titillating details—and can be said to have been spearheaded by primatologist Frans de Waal's book *Bonobo, the Forgotten Ape* (1997), which, like most of his influential work, argues for primates' capacity for mutual pleasure based on empathic relations. And there is a whole slew of work that examines all kinds of examples of same-sex acts in various animals from bonobos and bison to dolphins, penguins, or black swans.

What this work is still striving to establish is animal parallels to the human and, though obviously I speak here as an amateur, it is precisely this striving that proves human exclusivity. Moreover, to name same-sex acts among other animals "homosexuality in animals," as is often thoughtlessly articulated, is an extraordinary deauthorization of most of what is powerful and subversive in queer thought and queer politics. In the end, a whole lot of variables—as, for example, the difference of behavior in captivity as opposed to natural habitat—are left unexamined or remain in the realm of speculation, while the discussion of unreproductive sexual acts in animals slides into a discussion of pleasure much too easily, without differentiating pure sense-pleasure from fantasy-induced pleasure. Yet, even when the primary pleasure of human sexuality is invested in reproduction, as for example in conditions of socialized compulsion under imposed norms (the rules of certain religions, cults, or sects; the nationalist imperative to populate *terra patria*), it is the *phantasmatic* investment in those particular social-imaginary institutions that enables this pleasure, not some functional animal need for the preservation of the species. Conversely, even in those cases, as in certain primates, when masturbatory activity is observed among animals, the only zoological inference we can make is that this "deviation"—for that is precisely how such activity is configured in a world of functional reproduction—is animated, as it were, by sensuous organ pleasure and not by defunctionalized fantasy. Otherwise, chimpanzees, not humans, would have invented pornography.[120]

In broader terms, the human psyche mobilizes what essentially preserves it (and thus preserves the human) in its capacity for a defunctionalized imagination, unbridled and unlimited, apart from the limits that the psyche itself learns to imagine and to institute. The psyche's quest for meaning as a survival response to an environment in which the *human/animal* is biologically inept is the primary animating substance of *human-being* and constitutes the necessity of this learning. Loosely speaking, on the basis of its psychically animated radical imagination, the *human/animal* can even become something that it is not. No other animal can do this. A human can become just as much a dog or an extraterrestrial being, and this can happen either by adventurous volition or brutal violence at the hands (and the imagination) of another human. Of course, any moral community would reject such becoming as utterly mad. But from the standpoint of *physis* in a strict sense, the *human/animal* indeed appears quite mad, precisely because a human being can indeed become a dog or an extraterrestrial despite its physiology in a world self-created as the "human" world of a dog or a space alien, or, more seriously, because a human being can reduce another human being to a brutality that, by the natural standards any other animal, would be impossible (except in the hands of humans) or, in the end, because the *human/animal* is physiologically unfit for life *qua animal*—at least, a "natural" life outside the realm of society in whose imaginary anything and everything is possible, including the total destruction of society and of nature as such. Of course, the *human/animal* has managed to overcome this constitutive unfitness by creating the capacity for the complex institution of society, a capacity, let us note, that emerges from the same imaginary space as does its "madness" in a vicious circle that indeed can know no end.[121]

Without its capacity to imagine and institute (other) worlds, the *human/animal* would have ceased to exist as a living species. All language, reason, culture, and so forth are manifestations of this quest to signify and institute what in psychoanalytic terms are processes of sublimation that enable and enact this learning. Sublimation, as I have argued elsewhere, has a politics; it is not an organic or ontogenetic process, but a social-historical process.[122] Hence, the excess of the alleged desublimation of our era, in Herbert Marcuse's famous terms, is not some sort of psychic loosening. But neither is it some extraordinarily devious plan for power by societies of control, as Deleuze has duly named them. In fact, it is not at all desublimation, strictly speaking. It is bona fide sublimation toward structures, practices, and institutions that dehumanize *human-being* by investing in objects that in fact suppress the transformative power of the imagination and turn it into mere conformity while—this just becomes a matter of course—depriving the psyche of pleasure.

A precise, hence unsettling, description of this process can be found in Michel Houellebecq's early novels, especially *The Elementary Particles* (1998) and *The Possibility of an Island* (2005), where this debilitating, desexualizing sublimation goes hand in hand with the project of cloning sexless beings—which, in addition to everything else, dismantles the very problematic of sexual difference. Although these beings are created by humans, they are not human at all—most importantly, though not exclusively, because they are sexless.

What really matters in these novels is not the problematic significance of genetic cloning but the remarkably self-destructive lineage that the imaginary of genetic engineering cannot escape from. The capacity of humanity to create its own destruction is the mark of *human-being*; it is an elemental dynamic of the human imagination. Only under this rubric can we make sense of the Freudian category of the death drive in anthropological terms. If there is indeed an instinct "beyond the pleasure principle," this would have to be due to a psyche that finds pleasure in its own undoing, which is tantamount to the undoing of everyone and everything around it, the destruction of the living environment itself. From this broader horizon there is no beyond the pleasure principle. Like metaphysics itself, whatever is beyond belongs to the realm from which it presumably departs. The *human/animal* creates indefinite variants of beyond-the-human as elementary particles of *human-being*, going so far as to develop what is unfathomable for every other animal: a death instinct. Far from this being a culmination of Derrida's notion of *vivants à mort*—"living-in-order-to-die beings"—which marks the undeniable limit of life's mortality common to all, the death instinct signifies in fact the denial of mortality as an element of living being.

The implications of this elemental dynamic have produced tremendous self-occultation. In contemporary neoliberal societies of control, it may have become no longer possible to disentangle antihumanism from misanthropy. It has certainly become difficult to determine whether misanthropy is a symptom or an ideological effect. Much of Houellebecq's literature (indeed, like the philosophical ruminations of John Gray in *Straw Dogs*) draws its power from a misanthropic imagination, which, as far as both Houellebecq and Gray are concerned, includes a large part of traditional humanist ideologies.[123] In *The Elementary Particles* the target is the entire framework of the 1960s generation, its utopianism and its sexual revolution, its investment in the desirability of humanity's emancipation from the worst of itself that ironically becomes the driving force of a commodified ideal. Juxtaposed to this bankrupt mode of commodified life is a vision of mechanical purity, the possibility of genetically engineering this emancipation. The book abounds with irony, right next to its savage sarcasm against left humanism, but this cannot disguise its borrowing from a well-trodden tradition of dystopian science fiction, which can easily be said to reside in the same left-humanist framework of meaning. *The Possibility of an Island* is in many ways an elaboration of the argument of engineered desexualization as an extension (even if the underside) of Enlightenment-driven emancipation. The dystopian actuality of a genetically engineered world is now the impetus of a narrative retrospection that nods toward a possible critique, but in the end dehumanization still reigns all around in both domains, naïve utopian humanism and (ultimately equally naïve) dystopian antihumanism. Houellebecq's writing is profoundly ambivalent—hence the befuddled vehemence of his detractors—so it's difficult to determine what can be distilled from his relentless misanthropy, especially without in-depth textual analysis. Yet I take from it an obvious lesson: not only is dehumanization one of the principal characteristics of the human imagination, but the very need to overcome the human is often animated by a psychic investment in misanthropy.

More severe than Houellebecq's early novels are Lars von Trier's films, especially his *Antichrist* (2009), which might be said to follow (and surpass) in misanthropic horror his *Breaking the Waves* (1996). This is not the context to discuss the overwrought Christian metaphysics of pain that authorize the imagination of both films or to go into detail on how the destructive psychic fury can be considered, psychoanalytically, as an exercise in the aesthetics of the death drive. Much of what is misanthropic in *Antichrist* is predicated on an explicit aversion to any sort of affirming eroticism—an eroticism animated by a sense of wonder in one's encounter with the other, whose risk resides precisely in engaging so profoundly with the other that one's own internal otherness might emerge as a (self-)altering force. What is staged as erotic in the film is explicitly the destruction of the erotic—and the filmmaker is perfectly aware of the significance of this staging. This destruction of the erotic hinges on what is given as inevitable manifestation: the complex architecture of mutual self-destruction of the most elemental aspects of *human-being*. The easily presumed explanation, perfectly supported psychoanalytically, that the characters' constitutive alienation (both social and psychic) incapacitates them as to any sort of real erotic entwinement, thereby producing the abject sexuality the film exposes and (why not say it?) celebrates, is surely not an adequate response to an elemental set of questions: Is this incapacitation/destruction/dehumanization necessary? Is it inevitable? Why?

There is an alarming trend in many contemporary artistic and theoretical representations of inner torment in neoliberal societies of control to either foreground the negative and the death-driven (presumably under the force of desired expiation) or to belittle the faithless and the truly tragic (arguably propelled by a cultivated aversion to things pagan). Of course, how could one not embrace the negative, especially when bombarded daily by the insidiously vapid society of "Have a nice day!" (to take one of the most insufferable variants of American expression)? The extraordinary nihilism of rioting youth in various cities and contexts worldwide in recent years, which is animated by unmitigated rage toward all instituted principles—the purity of this rage is truly rare in social-historical situations—is an understandable (and I think warranted) example of a kind of mass actualization of the negative. And yet, figuring out how to creatively imagine new and unprecedented venues of affirmation, precisely in this social-historical juncture in which affirmation has been rendered grotesque to the point of utter paralysis, is one of the supreme callings of our time.

"Affirmation" is a word I use provocatively. I understand its limits. But I'm trying to lay open the secret comfort found in adoring the negative, a comfort that is conformist in the ultimate sense. I'm certainly not disavowing the critical force of negation—to the contrary. If critique—since Hegel at least, being the epitome of negation—is to be properly engaged (*engagé*) and not remain in some sort of cerebral neutrality worthy of the worst of liberal objectivity, then it must be invested in making and taking *positions*, in making arguments *for* and not simply against, in breaking open the occluding obstacles of alleged balance, in underlining *poiēsis* instead of catastrophe. Even the most Beckettian gesture of devastation and incapacity points precisely to this position: *I can't go on . . . I'll go on*. Even the most aporetic brutality in the abyssal sphere of art does not have to disintegrate to dehumanized *pathos*. This is what separates, for example, Heiner Müller from Lars von Trier or Sarah Kane—whose extraordinary artistry, in both cases, is surely not to be disputed, but should it be fetishized? The difference may lie in how both Trier and Kane, unlike Müller, have not managed to extricate themselves from the burden of a Christian metaphysics of pain. (This may also be what differentiates the films of Michael Haneke, where the extraordinary violence is utterly devoid of metaphysics.) Having said that, Trier's *Melancholia* (2011) signified an instance of abandoning this metaphysics of pain, much as one might say misanthropy is abandoned in Houellebecq's *The Map and the Territory* (2011) or turns into productive cultural critique in *Submission* (2015), subversively anticapitalist in the melancholia of *Serotonin* (2019)—where the old European bourgeois world is literally "dying of grief"—or, even further, affirmatively nihilistic in a tragic, indeed humanist, sense in his most recent *Anéantir* (2022), whose concluding account of the end of human life in a world that kills life with banality is simply breathtaking. Perhaps these are instances when the world broke through the artist's self-enclosure in the sense that, on this turning point at the outset of the twenty-first century, the collapse of the liberal dream, savaged by its own markets, and the urgent confrontation that this brought out into the streets and squares of the world, propelled, even if unconsciously, an aesthetic orientation away from the self-satisfied adoration of the metaphysics of catastrophe.

I am calling on affirmation not to void negation but to liberate negation from its debilitating simulacrum. This, too, is the crux of rethinking humanism and *human-being*. And it is to be conducted precisely by returning to the configuration of the psyche its instituting power, the creative capacity of the radical imagination.[124] This is why, to my mind, discourses that see the human penchant for planetary destruction—or simply, the desire of the *human/animal* to annihilate its own environment—as an elaboration of the death drive are ultimately inadequate, especially when they insist on this matter as some sort of psychopathology. There is no psychopathology in the *human/animal's* desire for (self-) destruction, any more than its radical capacity for poietic creation is some sort of sublime privilege. Both are in essence of the same order and are projected from the same source: the permutations of the psyche. Like *physis*, *psychē* has no normative a priori value—there is no nature to the psyche. There is neither *archē* nor *telos*, there is only *nomos*, which is to say simply the relational field of interdependent being. How we can come to imagine affirmative ways to elaborate this relational field, so that all forces who deny it, wage war against it, and seek to annihilate it in the name of some sort of human(ist) singular privilege can be overturned, is the gravest and most urgent task of *human-being* at this juncture of our planetary time.

2. Paideia

The sublimatory quest of the psyche to signify and institute cannot possibly repeat itself automatically and identically. Whatever it signifies and institutes becomes itself a force that rebounds and acts upon the process of signification and institution. But even then there is no sequence. The signifying and instituting imagination may be unbridled and defunctionalized but does not exist in a vacuum, in the void of its windowless solipsism. The instituted is simultaneously an instituting ground—this simultaneity is undeconstructible—but this does not mean tautological circularity, mere reproduction of the institution. Precisely because the psychic dimension is defunctionalized there can never be purely functional reproduction, the simple reinstitution of the same—aspirations of both heteronormativity and human cloning notwithstanding. Both the instituting and the instituted are open to self-alteration, and this itself is the ground of the socialhistorical domain that counters and complements the domain of the psyche.

Crucial in the assessment of the psyche in the *human/animal* is the process of learning. Here too—and this is so obvious as to be banal—human learning can never be reduced to the functional reproduction of the same, of what is known. Principally this is because the whole dimension of learning hinges on two realizations that occur in the earliest phases of life: the fact that nothing can be known exhaustively and the fact that behind whatever becomes known exists something or other that resists being known. Thus the process of learning is always haunted by an experience of inadequacy versus the field of learning at the very same moment of experiencing the inordinate pleasure of discovery or understanding. This intrinsically contrasting double experience continuously reiterates to the psyche a discrepancy with the world that the psyche can never efface. In this sense, from the standpoint of the psyche, learning is completely irrelevant to mastery. At best, it can be described as an incessant process of creating meaning out of meaninglessness where meaning is indeed created but meaninglessness is never abolished. That is why human learning is primarily phantasmatic before it is ever codified as calculative, before it is measured by and as *logos* and *technē*. And the desire for the abolition of meaninglessness is one of the most powerful and stubborn phantasms in the *human/animal*.

In fact, not only is human learning ultimately incalculable and veritably unlimited, but its phantasmatic "quality" suggests that it is not strictly bound to one's encounter with the world, that it exceeds experience. Characteristically, Aristotle considers mere experience inadequate learning, in relation to the learning achieved by art, because one cannot teach out of experience alone, and to teach is to be an artist (*Metaphysics*, 1:981b 10). To say that human learning exceeds experience is ultimately to say that it defies full account: human learning may be (and is often) instrumental but it can never be instrumentalized. Castoriadis hits it right on the mark when he says that "the astonishing thing in the human being is not that it learns but that it doesn't."[125] This fact is only pertinent to the human; it cannot be said of any other animal. (I am certainly not speaking of training animals within their specific natural parameters.) In effect, Castoriadis points to a radical difference in animality: the only animal whose encounter with the world does not necessitate *learning how to encounter the world* is the human. Not learning is an element of human learning, a preposterous notion within the strict boundaries of both natural and mechanical logic.

In an instrumental sphere of meaning, whereby living being depends on learning how to encounter the world, not learning is tantamount to not living, to not surviving. However, humanity's preposterous penchant for not learning has never been a threat to its survival, at least in any kind of direct determination or necessity. On the contrary, it is a mark of the intrinsically conflictual character of the human psyche and its consistently ambivalent relation to all that it perceives as other to it, which would include *physis* itself. Thereby all human learning takes place in the terrain of antagonism that organizes human life, which we call society, and insofar as it involves the development of practices that simultaneously express and address this conflictual terrain in conscious action, all learning, at some level or other, implies a politics. The recognition that learning implies a politics was already fully signified in what the Greeks called *paideia*.

As example of its social-historical function, it has been a classic thesis of traditional humanism to name *paideia* as one of its nuclear principles. The referent, however, was restricted: it was essentially *paideia* as a Platonic idea, the Socratic model of submission to the master interrogator of the truth, the philosopher. In essence, this does not change in the trajectory of Enlightenment thinking, whether it is Locke's view of education working upon a tabula rasa or Rousseau's marvelous tutorial fictions in *Emile*. By the same token, this model also animates the colonialist *mission civilisatrice*, which, as Franz Kafka inimitably showed in his *Report to an Academy*, is closely kin to animal training, to a sort of zoological socialization. As radical educators, however—and I presume that we recognize and share this aspiration, even if we may disagree on the terms—we would reject this model of *paideia*, if nothing else because it shields the most essential pedagogical element: that knowledge is not extracted and imparted out of some complete and preexisting pool, but is continuously—that is to say, interminably—made and unmade, created and interrogated. It is therefore never possessed singularly and exclusively by any one person, any one culture, or any one history, because every such person, culture, or history is as much an object as it is a subject of knowledge. I am certainly not arguing anything novel, at least, nothing more than Paulo Freire's radical pedagogy put forth decades ago: learning and teaching are intertwined at the psychosocial core of a *human/animal*.

It makes perfect sense that in his understanding of *paideia*, Plato ignores the philosophical lesson of tragedy. In the famous ode to *anthropos* in *Antigone*, Sophocles defines the extraordinary force of human beings—*ouden deinoteron pelei*—as the capacity to teach themselves (*edidaxato*) the very things that surround them and act upon them. Castoriadis has drawn attention to this essential paradox, which is nonetheless hardly illogical.[126] To teach yourself means that you know something (in order to teach it) that your self doesn't quite know (in order to learn it). In other words, you embody simultaneously both a capacity and a lack in regard to the same field, to the same process. This cannot be sufficiently reduced to theories of split subjectivity, Freudian or otherwise. In fact, the split is a matter of an internal *co-incidence* of one being both subject and object of one's knowledge.[127]

This paradoxical mode of self-teaching, which I consider the basis of all pedagogical relations and present simultaneously in both positions (teacher and student), points to a threefold epistemology that makes pedagogy, emergent as it is out of the psychic substance, the primary social-historical *anima* of the human: (1) self-knowledge alters and transforms—it does not confirm behavior or conform to necessary instinctual or mechanical patterns; (2) in recognizing oneself as an object of knowledge, the knowing subject recognizes that it is not absolutely sovereign, but rather itself subjected to interrogation, to the quest for (further, new, or other) knowledge; (3) the process of self-knowledge, and therefore of teaching and learning, is interminable as long as humans are alive, for both its source and its aim is the perpetual capacity of the *human/animal* to alter itself and its relation to its environment. In this particular sense, the reconsideration of *human-being* I am proposing—which comes together with a reconsideration of the epistemology of humanism—turns on the question of how we reconfigure the politics of *poiein*.[128]

Such pedagogical epistemology extricates us from the long and burdensome weight of *paideia* as *humanitas*, which characterizes traditional humanism all the way through the trajectory of Christianity to Heideggerian ontology. Cast as the politics of *poiein*, this epistemology points to an antithetical strain in this trajectory: the work of Giambattista Vico and its legacy. Indicatively neglected in this discussion, except for the long-term commitment to it by Edward Said (and subsequently Paul Bové, who reaches toward Vico imperatively in his *Poetry Against Torture*), Vico's conceptualization of *paideia* (the proper translation here would indeed be *scienzia*) points precisely to the pedagogical dialectics of being simultaneously subject and object of learning. It is surely not a coincidence that in one of his earliest meditations, perhaps his very first interrogation of the notion of humanism via an examination of Vico, Said underlines explicitly this radical epistemology of autodidacticism.[129] Not yet aware of the high stakes of his later configuration of "nonhumanist humanism," Said is already showing the groundlessness of the sort of historical *poiēsis* that embroils the *human/animal* in an incessant demand for emancipation from its inherited parameters, regardless of utilitarian calculation and irrelevant to the logic of consequence, even if this may lead to destruction. The epistemology of autodidacticism —which, I reiterate, emerges out of the most elemental aspects of the *human/animal* psyche—resides thus at the core of humanity's *poiētic* capacity as the undecidable figure of creation/destruction beyond any restrictions of instrumental reason.

A great deal can be said in this regard about the significance of autodidacticism in the tradition of black radicalism in postwar American politics. *The Autobiography of Malcolm X* is characteristically seen as the source text in this configuration—of course, harkening back to the textual self-making of Frederick Douglass and the slave narrative itself as specific socio-ontological genre.[130] For all of Alex Haley's questionable editorial interventions, the fact is, as Manning Marable argues in his biographical tour de force, that Malcolm's life is symptomatic of continuous self-invention: the sort of self-fictionalization that brings to the forefront and makes utterly palpable (to oneself but also the community) the hardcore reality experienced on the very body and soul of black people in America. This gesture is simultaneously didactic and autodidactic—the second pertaining not only to the authorial self but just as well to all those who recognize themselves in this experience. And it is not simply a matter of self-learning, of inventing forms and selves of learning as an obvious response to institutionalized lack and refusal, to being excluded from the venues of learning including literacy itself, but it is also, in the very same gesture, a matter of *unlearning*, an abolition of inscribed patterns of self and form that shape and sustain this exclusion.

Even if not granted equal iconic status, the cases (and autobiographical registers) of George Jackson (*Soledad Brother*, 1970) and Huey Newton (*Revolutionary Suicide*, 1973) in this same period bear the full range of this gesture, deploying a similar strategy of autodidactic self-invention, of self-fictionalization as expression of a recognizable communal reality. One of the crucial dimensions of Black Panther power was the confidence drawn from the capacity and realization of autodidacticism as method of both life and learning, particularly in relation to conditions of incarceration that, given the arguments that both Malcolm and the Panthers (or Fanon, for that matter) made so incisively, are not reducible to one's life literally behind bars but pertain generally to one's daily life in a racist world.

High on the shelf of such iterations of Black Panther ways of self-learning in-and-through incarceration—which should really be articulated as the Black Panther genre of *human-being*—is Albert Woodfox's *Solitary* (2019), his account of being in solitary confinement for *forty-three years* precisely because he was a Panther in the famous story of the Angola 3. Following Jackson and Newton, but really standing next to Malcolm above all else, Woodfox chronicles the process of creating consciousness out of annihilating conditions of incarceration, whose aim is not only to brutalize your body but to kill your very soul, as a daily struggle of transformation in the ultimate sense—a sort of continuous metamorphotic existence that alters everything in your inner world but also, even if in part, the world of everyone around you, the prison itself. At one point, Woodfox defines consciousness-raising as simply the moment when something you thus far deemed tolerable you now consider intolerable and act on this basis. A moment (and a phrasing) of poetry indeed, of *poiēsis*, in the Greek sense, that Cornel West cites at almost every occasion he speaks as the essential way of being black: the music and the poetry that emerges as so much hardcore biosubstance from the enslaved body through the voice in the form of song or breath blowing into a saxophone. What Woodfox denotes so succinctly as the mark of autopoietic consciousness is precisely the moment of creative unlearning that is always embedded in self-learning. Woodfox became a Panther in prison by unlearning his petty criminal ways (as Malcolm did in order to go on and become a Muslim), and he never saw Black Panther society in action, but he epitomizes its collective spirit, remaining a Panther in the suspension of prison isolation long after the organization folded in defeat. His personal account must be read alongside the social history of the Black Panther movement in Oakland, Chicago, and other cities, which stands as one of the brightest moments of radical communal autonomy and self-organization in American history, authorized by and authorizing in turn a spectacular instance of autodidactic autopoietic pedagogy. In this specific sense of autoconstituent power, Black Panther history needs to register as a unique contribution to the history of radical democracy, as trenchant and significant to the radical tradition as the glory of workers' councils.

Autobiographical writing in the black tradition, which I am reading here expressly as an autodidactic gesture, surely exceeds the limits of Derrida's claim that the human is the autobiographical animal in a generic sense. Ultimately Derrida's claim does not depart from Kant's definition of the human as the animal that can say "I" even while, in order to criticize Kant, Derrida transposes this capacity into the realm of writing, with all the deconstructive significance he has attributed to writing from the outset. This specific autobiographical-autodidactic gesture I am describing through examples of the radical black tradition as one of the key elements of the *human/animal* is instead better understood in relation to what Sylvia Wynter has called autopoietic being in her reworking, specifically in the terms of this tradition, of Maturana and Varela's biosociological argument in *Autopoiesis and Cognition*, published in the same period (1972).

Humanism, Human/Animal, Human-Being 107

As a structural consequence of the initial closure of autopoiesis, Maturana and Varela posit that, as an autopoietic organism, human society is conservative by default and ultimately tends toward totalitarian organization, whereby all significations are (re)circulating inside it as light inside a black hole. The image does well in encapsulating the sort of society that does not achieve its order of closure necessarily by overt violence but by very efficient semantic mechanisms of manufacturing consent. Once they posit this default position in social organization, Maturana and Varela go on to consider the operations of such closure from the standpoint of organisms (individuals) who are thereby debilitated by it: "A human being that through his interactions with other human beings participates in interactions proper to their social system in a manner that does not involve his autopoiesis as a constitutive feature of it, is being used by the social system but is not one of its members. If the human being cannot escape from this situation because his life is at stake, he is under social abuse."[131]

Let us read this from the standpoint of Wynter's translation of it into her remarkable epistemological reconfiguration of humanism: An African slave or an indigenous American locked into the plantation/*encomienda* system may be useful, or even necessary, to a society's autopoiesis but carries no autopoietic capacity for themselves. Indeed, making one a slave is tantamount to depriving one of autopoiesis, and a society based on slavery is autopoietic only to the degree that it institutes itself as a slave society and makes necessary the reproduction of the social-imaginary institution of the plantation economy and of slavery.

If we follow Maturana and Varela's terms strictly, the imaginary of this society is deinstituted only when enough slaves—in their language, "socially abused individuals"—become dissidents so that the system can no longer contain their newly acquired and articulated autopoietic capacities. After the system's initial reaction to neutralize and expel such dissident elements—what the Chilean biologists call "uncoupling" from the structures and properties of a society's process of autopoiesis—the only option for the social system is either to reinstitute itself differently (by another sort of autopoiesis) or to collapse before the institution of a powerful autopoietic alternative. Because in society's default totalitarian mode of full closure no socially abused organism can become autopoietic by inheritance (by some sort of natural reproduction), the operative mode of a dissident's newly articulated autopoiesis requires a leap and is thus by definition autodidactic.

For Maturana and Varela, the ultimate manifestation of such a "product of human art" is "an artificial society that accepts every human being as not dispensable. Such a society is necessarily a non-hierarchical society for which all relations of order are constitutively transitory and circumstantial to the creations of relations that continuously negate the institutionalization of human abuse. Such society is in essence an anarchist society" (xxix–xxx)—that is to say, a radical democratic society, as the next essay in this book develops explicitly. Such a society or even simply community is also rare, historically speaking, and in every way against the grain of the heteronomous imaginary that the autopoiesis of almost all human societies in history leads to by default. Therefore, autopoiesis does not entail autonomy by formal definition, unless we think of autonomy mechanically, as automation. But *autodidactic poiēsis* is indeed essential to autonomy, even if rarely achieved.

Maturana and Varela never use the word "slave" in their analysis; this is my own attempt to make their argument more tangible following Wynter's groundbreaking appropriation of their thinking and the examples of autodidactic autonomy that the radical black tradition is rife with. The two Chileans speak as biologists with extension into cognitive science, so they miss out on the nuances that Wynter sees in reconfiguring their thinking in the specific social-historical situation that concerns her. Because, as the entire history of radical black American thought has shown, the leap in the slave's autopoiesis involves the added dimension of species transformation and all the complications this entails, which includes the question of whether it is indeed feasible at all. To the degree that slaves in the plantation system were not considered human but were evaluated (literally, measured) alongside domesticated animals—with all other analogies to this extent noted, from the configurations of indigenous Americans in the Sepúlveda/Las Casas debate to Fanon's notion of colonized people as a species—self-making cannot just be contained in a mere autobiographical gesture, in merely saying "I," in signing one's name. Whose name?

The very question opens an ontological chasm. From the standpoint of this chasm, this specific gesture of autopoiesis cannot signify anything short of ontological alteration. Not just self-alteration, which I have always argued to be essential in every condition of autonomy. Even if self-alteration is indeed a self-authorizing act, because its first precondition is not making and altering a self but the very act of becoming human, of learning how to become and be human. Here, the stakes are higher and elemental, so we can understand better how heavy the notion of autodidacticism is in the black tradition. The gravity of this notion, as essential to a radical democratic *paideia* as anything, is to be found in this specific social-historical distillation.[132]

As a postscript, let me reiterate something obvious by returning to a classic figure in modern literature. What I'm espousing here is the exact opposite to the caricature figure of the Autodidact in Jean-Paul Sartre's classic existentialist novel *Nausea* (1938). For Sartre, the Autodidact epitomizes what, according to Roquentin, the novel's protagonist, is the most despicable element of humanist ideology. This is before Sartre is forced to declare, in response to critics, what in retrospect is deemed to have been self-evident in his philosophical system all along: that "existentialism is a humanism." In the novel, the character named Autodidact declares, with ample pomp, that he has embarked on the ultimate project of mastering all knowledge—or, more precisely, all knowledge produced by *great men*—by reading alphabetically through the entries of the *Encyclopedia*. He thereby reproduces the theological aspiration for absolute knowledge in the most grotesque deformation of the lexicographic Enlightenment *paideia* into ontotheology.

In *Nausea*, Autodidact is a catachresis of a name, a would-be ironic naming except that this particular novel seriously lacks in irony. For, Autodidact has no self—to learn from or to interrogate. And instead of fashioning a self from nothing—say, as Frederick Douglass or Malcolm X—he learns from an established body of knowledge, and he learns in uninterrogated and arbitrary fashion—precisely *not* in autodidactic terms. He merely assimilates, and is thereby assimilated into, received knowledge. Sartre's Autodidact could just as well be working his way through Flaubert's *Dictionnaire des idées reçues* in alphabetical order, except that he is even more heteronomously unlearned than are Flaubert's quintessential heroes of *l'idée reçue*, Messieurs Bouvard and Pécuchet. At least Flaubert's amiably ridiculous heroes, even if propelled by the sheer idiocy they share with glee, take on the world's inherited structures empowered by the irrepressible daring of a mad friendship. And this is precisely what makes Flaubert's fictional imagination more radical than Sartre's was purported to be one hundred years later.

3. Philia

One of Aristotle's key differences from Plato is not that he identifies the human as "the language-bearing animal" (*zōon logon ekhon*, translated thoughtlessly as "the rational animal")—this Plato would equally espouse—but as "the political animal" (*zōon politikon*). With this peculiar naming, Aristotle inaugurates what may be called a political anthropology, not in the way this is signified as a subfield in the discipline of anthropology to refer to the culture of political bodies or modes of rule, but as a field of inquiry where *physis* and *nomos* permeate each other without ever being reducible to each other in a specific historical nature or general natural law.

The precise phrasing of this well-known argument is quite suggestive and worth a second look:

> Of the community [*koinōnia*] composed of several villages, most perfect [*teleios*] is the city. It has already achieved, as the story goes [*epos eipein*], the limit of self-sufficiency [*peras autarkeias*], and thus, though it comes to be for the sake of life [*ginomenē men oun tou zēn*], it exists for the good life [*ousa de tou eu zēn*]. Hence, every city exists by nature [*pasa polis physei estin*] insofar as the first communities have come to exist. For the city is the completion/end [*telos*] of those communities, as nature is a completion/end [*physis telos estin*], since everything by coming-into-being tends toward completion/end.... As completion/end is the best for each thing, [for the city] self-sufficiency is both completion/end and the best. From this, it is apparent [*phaneron*] that the polis exists by nature and the human is by nature a political animal [*physei hē polis esti, kai o anthrōpos physei politikon zōon*]. (*Politics*, 1252b 30–1253a 4)

The mobilizing (and yet multivalent) hinge in this passage is the signifying qualifier *physei* ("by nature"). Crucial to this signification is the thread of Aristotelian entelechy, whereby the perfectibility (*teleion*) inherent in a thing is tantamount to its finitude (*telos*). Equally significant to the qualifier *physei* is the condition of living being (*zēn*), whose *telos*, however, is specifically determined to be the work of human perfectibility: the good life (*eu zēn*), released, in this case, from its Platonic adherence to the work of philosophy per se. In the trajectory from *zēn* to *eu zēn* we see the particular dimension of humanization in whose terms, one may say, Aristotle names the *human/animal* substance as the surplus of the singular animal that Derrida critiques. *Human-being* can come to be considered a condition—and become *humanity*—because its being is animated by a communal bond. Yet not just any notion of community or society (Aristotle's *koinōnia* signifies either word). A great number of species are demonstrably social animals, although to be strict about it, this is a catachrestic use of the notion "society" because the collectivity of the herd or the hive does not produce (and reproduce itself as and through) phantasmatic institutions. A beehive sports a splendorous and highly efficient architecture, but bees do not spend their time in the service of phantasms that will build them rocket ships or extermination camps. In any case, however we are to determine what "society" signifies, one thing is certain: only the society of *human-being* is political, and that's what determines this animal's life.[133]

For Aristotle, the humanization of the *human/animal* is achieved not by reference to the natural capacity for society in the conventional sense of "natural"— whereby "natural" signifies the means of the physical universe—but by virtue of a social-historical determination of humans belonging to a polis. Aristotle does consider the existence of the polis a natural event (*pasa polis physei estin*), but only in the sense that it bears the entelechy of communal association, indeed the perfectibility of the human/animal's social bond. Note that, as Greek texts tell us over and over, to become *apolis*, to be exiled from the city, is tantamount to death—in fact worse than death, because one lives a life not worth living, a life of utter inhumanity or, as Aristotle, quoting Homer, says: "clanless, lawless, hearthless" (*Politics*, 1253a7). The polis first and foremost is not an actual place; it is an existential entity. Thucydides speaks of the Athenians or the Corinthians, not of Athens or Corinth, and he quotes the general Nicias reminding the men of an old warrior code: "remember you are at once a city wherever you sit down" (7.77). The polis is this conflictual, interrogative sharing, whose "place" exists in the social imaginary itself, even if narratives of autochthony, of being *native* to specific geographical coordinates, are inevitable processes of occluding this imaginary.

Even though in Aristotle's mind the city's communal bond may be a potentiality inherent in the nature of the thing, its achievement/completion (its *teleiopoiēsis*) is a historical institution of a particular social imaginary. Because we are not Aristotelians to get hung up on entelechy, we can understand that there is nothing in the emergence of the polis that was predetermined or *had to happen* or is, for that matter, the manifestation of the perfectibility of community as such. We can thus concur, as historical thinkers outside the demand for entelechy, that the polis is a historical institution of a particular social imaginary and only in that sense, as a historical occurrence, a manifestation of the capacity of *human-being*, a concretization of its imagination. To be precise, what in this case animates *human-being*, insofar as it enables the institution of the polis, is predicated on sharing a communal interrogation and authorization of the law, whose ultimate consequence, actualized in the democratic polis, is to constitute a social bond that counters even the natural bonds of kinship. In this specific sense, *zōon politikon* does not pertain to a natural condition of *zōon* as such, and about this Aristotle is unequivocal. The specific form of living being (*eu zēn*) that Aristotle recognizes to be the nature of the polis qualifies the matter of nature in living being in reverse: it is the *politikon* that bespeaks the nature of the human *zōon*, not the bare *zōon* as such.

On this basis alone Agamben's famous claim of *zoē* as "natural" in opposition to *bios*, which he identifies with the political, is shown to be a contrivance. I am certainly not the first person to say so, and this is not the place to get embroiled in the details, including Roberto Esposito's notable correction.[134] Among other things, Agamben's general tendency to project Roman juridical thinking backward to things Greek and from there on to draw, retroactively, a transhistorical passage forward to the contemporary loses track of Foucault's grave reminder that life does not become a "bare" concept with its very own discourse (biology) until the nineteenth century, with the concurrent construction of zoology as a subcategory of classification. In a way that is so elementary as to befuddle any sort of elaboration, human life has always been a political matter since society was instituted and this takes us to the earliest traces of human history. Foucault's notion of biopower is directly implicated in matters of living substance (*zōon*), and there is indeed something unfortunate about how the name biopolitics is invoked to efface the fact that in the Greek imaginary the semantic distinction between the two words for life (*bios*, *zoē*) was never determined politically. In this sense, Brooke Holmes is perfectly accurate to name *bios* a post-biopolitical concept. This anachronistic signification not only occludes the complexities of invoking the lexical power of Greek terms in the various registers of modernity, reproducing thus the oldest and most traditional of humanist tendencies, but in effect depoliticizes the long-term historical process that consistently turns human life into a commodity of power. Moreover, the analysis of the contemporary conditions in global capitalism that have introduced biopower into politics is further weakened, on the one hand, by disregarding the precise historical dialectics of discontinuity that Foucault has provided us and, on the other, by conjuring a false Aristotelian authority where there is none.

Instead, Aristotle's famous characterization of *zōon politikon* gestures toward a physical nature exceeded—while surely permeated and configured—by the political. The notion itself yields an uncannily precise expression of a key element in the Greek imaginary since the earliest vestiges of pre-Socratic thinking: namely, the intersection of *physis* with *nomos*, where both permeate each other without ever being reducible to each other. No doubt the specific content of *nomos* operating in this case is the gradual configuration of the polis as a communal form that interrogates the sources of law beyond the terms that are ritualistically instituted by custom and kinship. The democratic polis is surely the sublime, if precarious, form of this configuration, and it would be difficult to imagine how Aristotle could have come to the term *zōon politikon* without the historical actualization of democracy. The great American political theorist Sheldon Wolin put it succinctly, "there is an extraordinary element in this characterization" because there had to have existed "a powerful, undeniable experience of politicalness, an actual practice sufficiently widespread to justify claiming it not simply as a human possibility but as the teleological principle of human nature itself. What was captured, *a posteriori*, by Aristotle's formula was the revolution in the political accomplished by Athenian citizen democracy of the fifth century."[135] The revolution of the political may be otherwise configured to be a revolution of the natural. As Wolin himself and many other thinkers of radical democracy recognize, this palpable and fully actualized political mode of living being (*zōon*) leans on the very processes of subjectification, configuring the sort of subjectivity whose nature is interrogative and transgressive while being, at the same time, collaborative and collective against previous structures of communal hierarchy. The analogy in contemporary terms would be what Etienne Balibar has famously argued to be the "becoming-citizen of the subject" (*le devenir citoyen du sujet*), which is always codetermined, in palindrome fashion as it were, by the "becoming-subject of the citizen" (*le devenir-sujet du citoyen*).[136]

What does Aristotle's anthropological formulation entail in specific terms? For a thinker like Aristotle, who is formed by the traditions of Athenian democracy, even if his own experience coincides with democracy's suicide, the imaginary of the polis from which he draws his anthropology is specifically instituted against kinship structures. This was the most radical significance of the Cleisthenes reforms (507 BCE) that reconfigured the political parameters of Athens against a deeply ensconced politics of kinship according to tribal organization. It is precisely why, unlike Plato (who was after all terrified of democracy), Aristotle is the first philosopher to investigate the unraveling of kinship that Athenian tragedians inimitably staged as first order interrogation arising from the specific political demands of a city at war. While Aristotle's assessment of tragedy in the *Poetics* is tainted by experiencing tragedy's increasing political irrelevance in his own time, his much discussed meditation on how friendship exceeds kinship (configured as an ethics but by all accounts retaining the tragic dimension) elucidates what is, for me, the third crucial component or animating substance of being human. It is the peculiar capacity for friendship (*philia*) that makes the human being a political animal: *zōon politikon*.

This is not contradicted or compromised by the existential (and thus primarily ethical) terms that Aristotle repeatedly reserves for his definitions of friendship because he never ceases to have the polis in mind. For example, the well-known statement "for, without friends no one would choose to live, though he had all other goods" must be juxtaposed with what follows a few lines further down: "friendship seems to hold cities together" (*Nichomachean Ethics*, Book VIII, 1155a). What is existential (ethical) and what is social (political) are one and the same process in the realm of living, and this is an essential indication of the tragic imaginary that permeates all matters of life. So, although a strict Aristotelian in discussing friendship might often choose to remain in the realm of ethics, the tragic ethos of Athenian democracy itself demands that we bring into the content of *zōon politikon* the dynamics of *philia*, for whether it is ethical, philosophical or simply erotic, *philia*—in Aristotle's language, "the deliberate decision to live together" (*hē gar tou syzēn prohairesis philia*—*Politics*, 1280b 38-39)—is an essential signification in the imaginary institution of the polis.[137]

I realize that in explicitly placing friendship at the crux of what is political I am departing not only from strictly philosophical Aristotelianism but, in contemporary terms, also from Carl Schmitt's well-known thesis that hinges the concept of the political on the existence of the enemy. In staking out this divergence from Schmitt, I certainly don't mean to suggest that we abolish the friend/enemy distinction. Rather, I suggest we reconsider the institution of friendship—a socialimaginary institution permeated by all kinds of historical specifics—within the polemical framework that Schmitt requires for the assessment of what constitutes the political. The biggest problem that friendship poses for Schmitt is that it blurs those categorical boundaries necessary for the clarity of the political, a clarity dependent on the distinct drawing of the lines of conflict. While friendship is hardly incompatible with conflict as such, it does indeed—as an anthropological notion that crosses social and cultural particularities—blur the boundaries of kinship. In the Greek language *philia* pertains both to kin and nonkin relations (as well as erotic and nonerotic relations), perhaps as an overarching category of communal association that definitely exceeds the rules and consequences of family institutions. For this reason, despite historical exigencies that gesture in this direction, in the last instance friendship cannot be reduced to the discourse of fraternization.

Unavoidably, this brings us directly into the terrain of Derrida's meditation on the full range of such intersections, both in Greek and in modern terms, both in light of friendship's relation to kinship and to enmity. I cannot discuss the full import of Derrida's *Politics of Friendship* here, but I do want to stress a couple of points that elucidate, as much as they complicate, the contours of this problematic. It's fair to say that this particular meditation on friendship inaugurates Derrida's extensive discussion of democracy in the late period of his work, which does, genealogically speaking, lean on previous discussions of racism, hospitality, and justice that are in turn also linked to his long-term ruminations on ontological matters, especially pertinent to the questions of death and mourning. An examination of the Greek elements in this long trajectory deserves its own extensive account. For our purposes, two specific assertions by Derrida are useful: (1) *philia* is animated by an *eros* that undoes kinship and exceeds mere fraternization; (2) friendship cannot remain confined to its determination as other to enmity, indeed as *politically inferior* to enmity.

I proceed in reverse order. It is Derrida's excavation of the agonistic dynamics of *philia* in the Greek imaginary as counterposition to the Schmittian thesis that makes his argument so valuable. The extensive examination of difference between war (*polemos*) and civil insurrection or revolution (*stasis*) in the Greek imaginary enables us to understand that war among friends or, by virtue of the ambiguity of *philia*, war among kin (thereby, civil war), even if socially considered to be an affliction, is nonetheless perfectly possible and in fact (though Derrida does not explore this further) appears to be an intrinsic element of democracy, ever present as democracy's sign of instability. In other words, friendship and enmity are not strictly oppositional: "the two concepts (friend/enemy) intersect and ceaselessly change places."[138] This realization underlines the understanding that friendship is conflictual and agonistic in itself, which is hardly surprising to anyone who takes the Greek imaginary seriously but is often elided under modern liberal compulsions toward consensus or Christian remnants of wishes for brotherly love.[139]

A look at Aristotle's ambiguities here is essential again. In the famous opening of Book VIII of *Nicomachean Ethics*, Aristotle establishes a curious relation between friendship and justice that shows how friendship is political through and through:

> Friendship seems to hold cities together [*eoike de kai tis poleis synechein ē philia*] and lawmakers mind it more than justice; for concord [*omonoia*] seems most like friendship and this they aim at most of all, while *stasis*, as it is enmity [*echthran ousan*], they most seek to banish. And when men are friends, justice is no longer necessary [*kai philōn men ontōn ouden dei dikaiosynēs*], while being just demands adherence to friendship [*dikaioi d'ontes prosdeontai philias*]. Indeed, the highest form of being just seems to involve an element of friendship [*kai tōn dikaiōn to malista philikon einai dokei*]. (1155a 23-27)

The most striking thing in this statement is Aristotle's establishment of a tension between friendship and justice, where the first seems essential to the second, but also impervious to it. The very existence of friendship may be said to achieve justice, while justice as such cannot achieve its highest form without engaging friendship. Simply put, justice requires friendship in order to be fully achieved, while friendship is justice in itself. The tension then is not a matter of opposition but of asymmetrical relation; the opposition in this passage is between *philia* (friendship) and *stasis* (internal strife). The latter is enmity insofar as it is opposed to friendship, but not enmity *as such* because, after all, it is an internal affair—an affair between erstwhile friends. I discuss *stasis* elsewhere, and this is not the context to elaborate on it, but there is no doubt that the politics of friendship cannot consider *stasis* alien (or enemy) territory.[140] As alternative relation to pure kinship, friendship is not determined by what challenges it existentially—enmity—since it already establishes an elsewhere in the most essential of *political* terrains: justice between equals, an *anarchic* justice that does not require the friend/enemy distinction to achieve its authorization.

And this brings us to the former of the two Derridean assertions I noted, the question of *eros*. Derrida's impulse is ultimately to question the unexamined coexistence of the French revolutionary calling for *egalité* and *fraternité* within the terms established by the Greek social-imaginary institution of *philia*. *Liberté* is, in this respect, assumed as groundwork. Without it nothing happens at all, but this radical condition cannot be configured as a prerequisite that occurs at the anthropological level of society. Although Derrida is correct to seek the origins of democracy's radical invocation of freedom in the existence of autochthonous natural being (evident in Aristotle's notion of *zōon politikon*), he is stretching the argument by establishing a direct (social but also semantic) correlation between the archaic aristocratic privilege of equality as freedom by birth (*isogonia*) with the freedom achieved by equality before the law (*isonomia*), as this culminates institutionally in Cleisthenes's reforms. In fact, the exact opposite may be said to have taken place: *isonomia* is instituted precisely in order to break down the regime of *isogonia*, even if it emerges within the semantic framework of said aristocratic equivalence.

Specifically, *isonomia* enacts a new politics that gives every man the equal capacity to share in communal rule in order to replace the rotation of rule among those few who, as equal by birth, claim a natural right to ruling. Here, replacement does not mean substitution but revolution. No doubt one can say that the operative principle in both cases is the notion of *ison*: equal in capacity. It is. Yet, the shift from being equal in capacity by birth (*physis*) to being equal in capacity by law (*nomos*) is an epistemic shift of grand proportions, a shift that exemplifies the revolutionary event of the institution of democracy. In other words, if the aristocratic equality of warrior tribes is recognized in retrospect as the generative imaginary element of what later becomes democracy—that is, the equality of all warriors, regardless of tribe and regardless of whether they are the best or not—this can never mean to establish a direct and necessary determination. Democratic equality is a political *nomos* and not a social *physis*.[141]

For this reason, although *philia* is an essential principle in the democratic imaginary—Derrida asserts that democracy without friendship is impossible[142]—it thereby exceeds the institution of fraternization, which is traditionally a tribal institution, the band of brother warriors, as the Homeric epics show, that becomes the basis of aristocratic rule in Greece, but it is also the operative principle in all archaic tribal societies under the signature of a patriarchal imaginary. The known exceptions to this gendering are codified as exceptional only because of the vast partiality of the archaic record. In the Greek world, which I know best, these few exceptional instances are too powerful to be read in the margins. For instance, the Sapphic fragments are incomparable expressions of *philia*, as is from another standpoint, within the family structure but also simultaneously against its patriarchal restrictions, the relation of Antigone to Polynices. A great deal has been made of the verses *outoi synechthein alla symphilein ephyn* (*Antigone* l. 523): "it is in my nature not to share in hating but to share in loving," which can also be translated as "I was not born to partake of enmity but of friendship," since the verb form *ephyn* signifies both the product of *physis* (nature) and the fact of springing forth, sprouting (*phyein*), therefore, being born. The phrase may be said to resound the cosmological universe of Empedocles in that the infinitives *synechthein-symphilein* bear a foundational (natural) opposition between enemy and friend (*echthros-philos*). However, let us note the qualifier *syn*: one never engages in friendship or in enmity alone; one comes together with an other in order to constitute the position of enemy or friend; one participates in or shares enmity and friendship both.

This verse in *Antigone* registers an opposition between two kinds of communities: one based on the friend/enemy distinction (*synechthein*), and another based on the entwined nature of otherwise separate persons (*symphilein*)—what Nietzsche in the idiom of Zarathustra names "to die in common through separation." In the first case, *philia* registers a divergence from the constitutive social cohesion enabled and enacted by clear-cut enmity. This is the basis of Kreon's charge of Antigone's treasonous differentiation. Accordingly, *philia* itself becomes recognizable as *an object of enmity*; by *symphilein* with a traitor, Antigone herself becomes a traitor, an enemy of the polis. In contrast, Antigone argues from her standpoint against any sort of natural *synechthein*, which is precisely unnatural insofar as it is symptomatic of an internal division of the political body enabled and enacted by a singular *archē* that flourishes on the symptoms of civil war (*stasis*). That is to say, what for Kreon (who might be said to follow a Schmittian logic) signifies the distilled capacity of the sovereign state, for Antigone is rather the tyrannical depoliticization of the *dēmos*. Antigone's own slippage into the hubristic terrain of *monos phronein*, in that she too acts alone and against all, does not nullify her valid opposition to the *monarchical* logic that can only express itself as the logic of enmity, outside and against the capacity for friendship.[143]

I cannot but recall here the exhortation by Etienne de la Boétie in his "Discourse on Voluntary Servitude" (1549) that friendship constitutively mobilizes resistance to tyranny even if, at the same time, it is the very thing that humans voluntarily sacrifice in their perverse desire to relinquish their autonomy, to submit to external authority.[144] Reiterating Xenophon, La Boétie argues that a tyrant can have no friends by definition because, in the last instance, he rules alone. But even on such occasions where he may resort to conspiratorial oligarchic alliances, these remain within the command-obedience structure with power shifting according to the permutations of self-interest: "When the wicked assemble, there is a plot, not companionship. They do not provide for one another, but fear one another. They are not friends but accomplices."[145] The difference is categorical. A monarchic or oligarchic structure operates exclusively on the basis of the friend/enemy distinction. (Democracy has enemies too, but they do not determine its existence—certainly not exclusively or as primary cause—because the existential core of democracy is itself. It rises and falls on its own in/capacity.) In the order of this distinction, the enemy takes precedence and has the upper hand of determination. So whatever friendships may be formed in this context, they are subordinate to the order of the distinction. They come to be in order to defeat an enemy and are themselves defeated by their very achievement. They are teleological and instrumental. They are mere means; when the end is achieved, they are rendered irrelevant. This is why such relations are not actual relations between friends but associations between accomplices, forms of alliance. They are at once subject to and products of power, thereby significations not of equal sharing and mutual overcoming of self but of calculation based on self-interest; hence, the commonplace qualification of corruption: "he has powerful friends"—in Washington, on Wall Street, or what have you.

One may well ask: Is friendship as such impervious to corruption? Isn't there an exclusivity bred in such intimacy that might lead to the pursuit of interests against the community? Isn't there in such exclusive intimacy a temptation to oligarchic desire? These questions are legitimate, and indeed denying them actually confirms them. Innumerable historical examples testify to friendships trading their power for their subjugation to power. This is the tragedy of the heteronomous impulse, and there is nothing like La Boétie's discourse on voluntary servitude to call it like it is. By the same token, however, friendship is the mode of a mutual overcoming of self that dismantles both the "natural" order of kinship and the "artificial" alliance on the basis of self-interest that characterize hierarchical modes of society—which is to say, in my terms, modes that depoliticize society. This isn't to argue that friendship is constituted outside power or that it bears no power. To the contrary, it is essential to democratic power with all the elements that this involves. Just like in democracy, in friendship there is nothing determined or determinant a priori, and nothing that guarantees it in perpetuity, nothing eternal. Like democracy, friendship opens one to exceeding risk, including the possibility that it might slide into a relation of mere oligarchic alliance or even enmity. Just as we would insist that the politics of friendship can never be reduced to fraternization (that is, to masculinist or Christianized ethics), we would have to accept, in friendship, the condition of possibility for intrinsic deconstitution, where the logic of the friend/enemy distinction returns to take over the field of political meaning.

The sustenance of friendship, therefore, is predicated on a mutual decision to perpetuate its reimagining and the reinstitution of its terrain. There is no organic sustenance to friendship; its nature is political. This peculiar condition, among other things, drives my own decision to name friendship as the key element of *zōon politikon*, from a certain standpoint even more primary than citizenship, precisely because it refers back to a *physis* and not to a *nomos*, to matters of living (life) and not merely acting (in society). This pertains to the sort of political *physis* that tends toward *nomos* and may even determine the institution of society but is never subordinate to or derivative of the institution. Antigone's claim of *symphilein* is intrinsic to her *nomos*; it determines her politics. It is true that in this passage *symphilein* is contrasted to *synechthein*, almost as a matter of existential decision. But neither this instance nor any other until Carl Schmitt theorizes his assertion—which, let us recall, pertains to a specific social-historical condition, regardless of subsequent universalizations—sets up friendship as derivative of enmity. Even in constitutively polemical societies as the Greek ones were (as archaic societies tend to be by rule), the psychosocial institution of friendship participates in the social-historical conditions of enmity without, however, being dependent on it.

NO MORE ARTIFICIAL ANTHROPISMS

When I began writing this section in 2019, multiple fires were blazing through the Amazonian rainforest with inextinguishable force, a network whose expanse at one point was equivalent to the width of the continent of Europe from Lisbon to Kiev, making altogether tangible the assessment that the region is at the tipping point of irreversibly switching from canopy forest formation to open grassland, from rainforest to savannah. In 2019 alone, "the year the world burned"[146] (well, until 2020 and then 2021, 2022, 2023—the timeline is ongoing), the Amazonian rainforest suffered more than 73,000 fires, an 84% increase from the year before. In the same year, the typical worldwide summer fest of wildfires included, in addition to what by now has become routine in California, which experienced the worst drought situation in 1,200 years, the biggest fire ever to assault the forests of Siberia, burning an area of more than 11,000 square miles, and, of course, the inconceivable horror of the bushfires in Australia, in which fifteen million acres of land burned and three billion animals were killed or irreparably disrupted, with no precise sense as to possible species extinction in the continent's native flora and fauna. Less than a year later, in the autumn of 2020, the Pacific Northwest wildfires burned 80% of Oregon's forests in just a few days. Even further, in 2021, most of the planet's unburned forests, almost 100,000 square miles from California to Siberia and from the Mediterranean to southern Africa went up in flames under scorching temperatures that broke all records. And in the summer of 2023, after wild fires burned twenty-seven million acres of Canada's forests, covering half the United States with thick smoke for two weeks, the month of July registered the hottest period in Earth's history in 100,000 years. A new meteorological term has been invented: the heat dome, which, like its kin opposite the polar vortex, has become the new norm in a planetary atmospheric ecosystem that is collapsing from the stratosphere down to the deepest ocean floor.

While vast and catastrophic forest fires have horrifically become routine events of climate change, linked to dry conditions from planetary temperature rise to whose further rise they contribute in an abyssal cause-and-effect turnaround, in many cases, including both the Amazon and Australia, the hand of land speculators, extraction companies, and corrupt governments is demonstrably the cause. Of course, the two conditions are the same. Climate change is a misnomer. It is surely not a natural shift, or simply even a natural disaster, despite the fact that in the vast expanse of geological time going backward the planet has had substantial phases of heating and cooling that are unfathomable to the human mind.

Fifty-six million years ago the planet warmed 5-8 degrees Celsius after expelling 5,000 gigatons of carbon over a period of 5,000 years. It took the planet 150,000 years to cool off back to its previous temperatures. Geologists call this the Paleocene-Eocene Thermal Maximum, which they identify significantly not as an epoch but as an event. It is hardly unique in geological history. Thirty-eight million years prior to this event, the planet had also warmed up around 8 degrees Celsius because of extraordinary carbon dioxide emissions that depleted half the oxygen of the seas. (For comparison, we are now confronting oxygen decrease in the oceans at roughly 2%.) This is called the Cretaceous Oceanic Anoxic Event 2, and it lasted half a million years. I am only mentioning two out of a number of such events, which themselves are but little dots buried in the chasms of geological time, often just mere particles of epochs that are themselves organized, mapped, and named by geologists according to a whole lot of factors way beyond the scope of these events, which may have caused mass extinctions of life forms but, geologically speaking, are rather insignificant.[147]

In fact, geological history in its unfathomable expanse makes *all* human perspectives ridiculous. It certainly makes me wonder whether the text you are now reading was ever worth writing. And while there is certainly merit in thinking of the human in both a zoological and a social-historical framework—even more so, in the sense that whatever is zoological about the human cannot be disengaged from the social-historical, which, in this infinitesimal parenthesis to geology, is unquestionably significant and determinant of how and why we live our life in its minutest detail—nonetheless, elevating the human to any sort of geological scale is absurd. To say the least—because in fact it is testament to the arrogance of this animal that sees nature not as its context but as its object to make and unmake as it pleases.

And yet we are surrounded by the clamor that we are currently undergoing the age of the Anthropocene, since the Dutch Nobelist atmospheric chemist Paul J. Crutzen introduced and popularized the term in a series of articles and announcements starting at the dawn of the millennium.[148] The basic argument for the Anthropocene is conducted in geological terms but is derived from the discourse of atmospheric chemistry and centers on the fact that the extensive production of chlorofluorocarbon emissions by human activity (in essence, the extraction and burning of fossil fuels) has altered significantly the planet's environment, both on the ground and in the atmosphere. Dating the onset of the Anthropocene varies. It is usually thought to coincide with the invention of the steam engine and the Industrial Revolution more than two hundred years ago. Some thinkers extend it either backward to 1492 and beyond, with the conquest of the Americas, which precipitated mineral extraction, slave labor, and intercontinental exchange of flora and fauna at an unprecedented scale, or forward to 1945, with the invention of the atomic bomb and the onset of the nuclear age. There have also been suggestions that the Anthropocene must be defined in terms of the trajectory of *Homo sapiens* on the planet and its interference with Earth's biosphere since the first days of agriculture. But even then, if we consider that geological measurements of epochs come with a plus or minus fifty-thousand-year margin of error, the very assessment of the Anthropocene signifies a radical reconfiguration of the entire framework of geology, nullifying the depth complexity of stratigraphic evidence and reconfiguring geotemporal order to such a point that the epistemological structure of geology as a science is alienated beyond recognition.[149]

There is a counterperspective that takes the Anthropocene as a geological epoch that has not yet happened. Or more precisely, it identifies it as happening now only to the degree that it sets into motion an irreversible future. What is currently already traceable as global warming is catastrophic to the extent that it stands to determine Earth's climate for the next 100,000 years, derailing the projected next ice age by a margin of between 50,000 and 500,000 years. Now, this is a proper geological scale, except for the uncanny aspect of its being qualified not as something that belongs to Planet Earth's sedimented history, to its already being physically what it is, but to its becoming something else. Key here is David Archer's argument that the current use and certain depletion of Earth's carbon fuel deposits is creating, as we speak, future carbon deposits that will become the archaeological evidence of geological activity by an animal species millions of years after it will have been extinguished.[150] This may in fact be the most insightful argument regarding the Anthropocene, but because it is not archaeological in the way that geology is structured by definition and is rather oriented toward an imaginative terrain, it belongs to the realm of the humanities and not of science strictly speaking.

Of course, that's neither here nor there. What is properly scientific, after all? Or, what is properly humanistic, after all? These are contested and surely intersecting domains. In the end, the strictly scientific status of the Anthropocene is fully open to debate, no matter that a range of scientists, including geologists, are actively engaged with the idea.[151] Discrediting it straight out, however, runs the risk of arming further the arsenal of climate change denial, most of which is mobilized (and funded) by the petrochemical and extraction industries and their political servants. There is, alas, another ally to this doubt that comes from certain radical ecology circles that scoff at the significance of the human factor relative to planetary magnitude. Such arguments, forwarded by James Lovelock and the purveyors of the Gaia hypothesis or bona fide misanthropists like John Gray, look forward to the innate mechanism of self-protection that Planet Earth is already mobilizing by making life conditions of humans intolerable until their guaranteed eventual extinction will thankfully return the planet to its intrinsic physical self-balance. In this respect, perhaps, the singular utility of the Anthropocene concept is polemical, serving above all the needs of climate change activism, including the intellectual work that might serve as a platform for activist practices. It's not surprising, in this regard, that the term has great purchase in the humanistic social sciences, in certain strands of anthropology, environmental studies, and ecocriticism. This is why it is appropriate for us to consider it here at the tail end of an argument about the significance of human animality and the peculiarity of *human-being*.

To be sure, I take for granted and without the least doubt that the planet is endangered by the way of life of the *human/animal*. The very fact that all life on this planet can be irreparably altered by nuclear catastrophe is enough to seal the point. And the further fact that such a nuclear catastrophe would not be an aberration but a mere extension of a way of life already in place for some centuries before nuclear power was even invented takes this matter out of the narrow orbit of a singular event and into deeply imbedded diachronic structures and institutions of social organization. No discussion of planetary environmental calamity can be disengaged from the specific psychosocial imagination that creates and sustains the techno-economic power of what we call capitalism in all its variants, historically actualized or potentially imagined. Which is why John McGuire is correct to stigmatize what he calls "technophilic solutionism" when in facing certain climatic catastrophe some respond by noting doors of opportunity and inventiveness, like new agricultural lands opening under the melting ice to counteract the uninhabitable scorched earth of equatorial regions. The very image is the epitome of colonial perversion, as part of a capitalist logic in which "climate change is treated like a cinematic MacGuffin—a convenient plot device within our civilizational narrative, whereby the loss of biodiversity awakens human ingenuity to overcome all planetary boundaries" (McGuire, 129-30).

In these terms, planetary environmental catastrophe can neither be considered in itself, say, as a matter of nature disengaged from history, nor, on the other hand, considered as an extension of mere *human-being*, which is what the category "Anthropocene" ultimately does, regardless how one might date its emergence.[152] For to deal in matters of history—which is always history of societies—means that whatever the ontological domain (be it anthropic or geological) is, it is always temporal and heterogeneous, not reducible to an essence. This is the underlying methodological supposition throughout this essay.

From this standpoint the Anthropocene has no real geological meaning—nor an ontological one, for that matter. It is part of an ontological inquiry, and therefore belongs here only to the extent that it is conceptualized within a broader historical formation in the course of human existence. In these terms, the historical form that gives rise to the Anthropocene as an event and surely as an interpretive framework is nothing less than capitalism, pure and simple. This seems a no-brainer to me, and there is a trail of important arguments that spell it out, most influential of which is Naomi Klein's *This Changes Everything: Capitalism vs. the Climate* (2014).[153] Nonetheless, this position remains hotly contested, because even though the Anthropocene may not be entirely coherent as a geological notion, it has set in motion an epistemological framework with its own projections as to what politics it necessitates. From this perspective, some people argue that just as capitalism may not be the cause of the Anthropocene but instead an enabler of its acceleration, the abolition of capitalism will not avert planetary catastrophe.

The most vocal and celebrated thinker disputing an exclusive association between climate and capitalism is Dipesh Chakrabarty, who has become a formidable figure in this discussion since the publication of his influential essay "The Climate of History" (2009) and an array of elaborations, still ongoing. Key to Chakrabarty's intervention is that he speaks as a historian, and it is history as the existential epitome of the *human/animal* that concerns him the most. Yet, strangely, the arena of history has become nebulous in this discussion for both Chakrabarty and his critics, since they are all drawn swiftly into the gravitational orbit of the Anthropocene framework, thereby strengthening it as a *metaphysical* structure that thrives on apocalyptic discourses very much against the grain of its quintessentially *physical* meaning.

Chakrabarty rightly points to an extraordinary difference in temporal scale between the politics of climate change and anticapitalist politics, for the politics of climate change is conducted in the present *for* the future in a way that is concrete (even if unfathomable), unlike, say, the messianic politics of communist revolution, whose deferred future remains inevitably abstract. From this same standpoint one can equally argue that the politics of climate change is difficult to entwine with an anticapitalist politics of democracy, for democracy is *always* a politics of the present, regardless of what might be its own utopian future vision or its constitutional/legal ancestry. While the complicity between capitalism and climatic catastrophe is indisputable, what is valuable in Chakrabarty's position is precisely this matter of scale and the disjunction this produces in our inherited parameters of how politics comes to signify *human-being*, including the time and space of action, the permutations of desire and of vision, and the reflection all this has on matters of daily living.[154]

Keeping the focus on this salient matter of scale, whereby what is historical and what is ontological about *human-being* is profoundly problematized, I will purposely forgo further discussion on the political question of capitalism as catalyst of/to *human-being*, including the notorious critique of climate change activism as a First World luxury that deprives (yet again) poorer societies of the equal right to prosperity. These questions will be extensively explored in the essay that follows, since they are hardcore political questions that pertain foremost to the problematic of democracy. Here I will focus in turn on the epistemological dimensions that derail conventional historical arguments as to whatever the Anthropocene is made to signify, and I will do so in two directions.

First is the problem that Srinivas Aravamudan, in a series of brilliant essays on environmental criticism late in life before his unfortunate passing, identified as "catachronism": specifically, "the inversion of anachronism [which] characterizes the backlash of the Anthropocene as post-human nomenclature" especially insofar as "similar to anachronism that reimagines the past in terms of the present, catachronism re-characterizes the past and the present in terms of a future proclaimed as determinate but, of course, not fully realized."[155] The emphasis here should be placed on the tension between "determinate" and "not fully realized"—that is to say, the peculiar notion of something that has not happened (and in this sense does not exist) carrying the full force of real material determination on what exists and what will presumably continue or come to exist. Aravamudan immediately points to what he sharply calls "the theological grasp of time" (8) that underlies this notion, which celebrates catastrophe as "a catachronistic history that inexorably begins to reverse the Enlightenment" (9), by reminding us that, more than anything, catastrophology has become so prominent because it is "oddly comforting" (10).

Not so oddly, I would add, and I imagine very well he would have agreed, because this whole discursive machine, of which the Anthropocene as a name is both a sign and a symptom, is predicated on *naturalized* narrations of "the general story of human misery, exploitation, and damage over history" (11). Perhaps not oddly but surely comforting nonetheless, because this image of catastrophe—no matter its indisputable reality—is a narcissistic extension of what human beings do, in the most banal sense of this phrase. Hence the reason why catastrophology has fostered such antihumanist vehemence, which is the immediate second order of humanist narcissism disguised as self-critique. All proclaimed adoration of other sentient life from the privileged standpoint of the human as antihuman lament for its violation by the hands of humans is part of this narcissism complex at the very least because only humans can be antihuman, for the psychic benefit of being human ad absurdum: "Anthropogenic climate change is another paradoxical corrective to our anthropocentrism" (13).

Aravamudan thus presents a radical challenge to Chakrabarty and his followers, and one can only regret that his untimely death prevented us from having the full force of such a debate. Aravamudan's position resonates with me especially because of his relentless attention to how arguments about history can so easily shift into arguments about nature, an intellectual sensitivity that we all owe to the best of Marx. "The move from history to geology with the application of the concept of the Anthropocene shifts a social science of life evolving over time (and within a lived environment) to a natural science of species death, discovered afterward as a geological stratum of so many fossils of life once lived" (12). Wonderfully phrased and utterly succinct. The shift Aravamudan describes not only naturalizes history—"re-enchanting nature against the Enlightenment" he says later on (15)—but also occludes (and indeed *occults*) any radical attempt to reconfigure the terrain of ontology away from the ubiquitous desire to turn it into metaphysics. It is this metaphysical desire that attaches ontology to the apocalyptic imagination and turns discussions of being and of nature into discussions about ends—well, indeed, *the* end. Which is itself epistemically fraudulent, because it silences the history of endings of innumerable societies and populations, which capitalism (and its substructures: imperialism, colonial and settler conquest, financial ruination, indebted life, technology-and-commodity-driven deformation of subjectivities, etc.) has precipitated at an unprecedented scale.

As I said earlier, the Anthropocene discussion is fully permeated by theological desire; Aravamudan confirms this by saying "the Anthropocene is a negative theology of messianicity" (24). But what is particularly dire in this observation is how this theological discussion claims to possess the future as an always already determined formation. From a political standpoint, this is politics of eschatology, a politics of ends without means, and worse, a politics that loses sight of the fact that "endings are also mutations" (25)—indeed, in essence beginnings, very much in Said's sense of the term. A profound reminder, for even a politics of reversal of such a projected end, as is climate change activism at its best, cannot possibly achieve its aspiration if it remains a politics based on ontological certainty, human or planetary, self or other. Gayatri Spivak has phrased it beautifully and it deserves to be repeated: "The planet is in the species of alterity, belonging to another system, and yet we inhabit it.... If we imagine ourselves as planetary creatures, alterity remains underived from us, it is not our dialectical negation."[156]

The second significant questioning of the Anthropocene epistemology comes from the standpoint of black studies, and if Aravamudan's critique unmasks the Anthropocene as a theological discursive formation that turns history into nature, this critique points to the Anthropocene's profound historical failure as a political perspective. It thus addresses, even if not directly, the arguments Chakrabarty makes about climate change as a whole other way of historical thinking by pointing to a stunning denial of essential aspects of human history in the last five hundred years, namely the nexus of planetary conquest, extraction of the Earth's material wealth, slave labor, and reification of human bodies that starts with the Spanish conquest of the Americas and persists unabated to this day. From this perspective, any doubt as to whether climate change politics is beyond capitalism is rendered nonsensical at best, ahistorical and indeed racist at worst.[157] The work in this direction is huge, complex, and still evolving to give a full account of it here. It partakes of a number of concurrent debates on blackness, Afropessimism, the ontology of the slave, mineral extraction capitalism, as well as the worldwide symbolic significance of the Americas, which do not address Anthropocene politics per se. Yet, much of the formidable work of thinkers I admire—Hortense Spillers, Cornel West, Saidiya Hartman, R. A. Judy, Fred Moten, Achille Mbembe, and a host of other younger interlocutors, as well as, of course, Sylvia Wynter, whose astonishing conceptualizations from decades ago still preside—is essential not only to this specific section but to my problematic overall, extending in many ways (but also going beyond) the arguments made by the anticolonial humanists of the 1930s-1960s.

Judging from Wynter's perspective, there is a certain libidinal economy of geology that capitalism holds dear at the deepest folds of its core. The desire for extraction, initially of gold and later of coal and oil, that fuels the settler conquest of the Americas is tantamount to the liquidation of human bodies, initially indigenous Americans and soon thereafter African slaves. The equation must be understood in the strictest possible material terms: bodies and minerals become one and the same, and both serve their mutual liquidation into capital through a process of unfathomable brutality, where to speak of dehumanization, even if accurate, is hardly adequate. Instead, what we cannot afford to lose sight of is that geology and biology are disciplines which develop their language—their very scientific stature—precisely in these conditions and as beneficiaries of gigantic enterprises of liquidating earthly matter, mineral and human both, at once and indistinguishably. Biopolitics is, in this sense, always a geophysics of both power (the political) and being (the ontological) without measure. "Geology is a relation of power and continues to constitute racialized relations of power, in its incarnation of the Anthropocene and its material manifestations in mining, petrochemical sites and corridors, and their toxic legacies—all over a world that resolutely cuts exposure along color lines."[158]

In this context, unlike in discourses of posthumanism, the inhuman achieves far more significant meaning than its mere antithesis to the human, for it is materially *co-incident* with the inhumane. And this takes place at a world-making scale—"world making as a geophysics of being" (Yusoff, 13)—where *human-being* is engaged in a creative enterprise through an unfathomable destruction of what is earthly, human, and inhuman alike. This engagement is racialized with such vehemence that whatever was deemed to be humanist about it was de facto implicated in the tearing apart of any ontological integrity of *human-being*. The contradiction was occulted beyond recognition, so that, say, the humanist desire of Bartolomé de Las Casas in the sixteenth century to save the Amerindians by pronouncing them children of God delivered them even more insidiously into their complete subjugation and ultimate annihilation of their history and culture. This new geophysics of being upon which the Anthropocene dates its historical trajectory was always instrumental and, on this basis, *human-being* itself has been (thus far) irreparably rent asunder by a racial differentiation that made some humans fodder in the entwinement of the inhuman with the inhumane: "The color line of the colonized was not merely a consequence of structures of colonial power or a marginal effect of those structures: it was/is a means to operationalize extraction (therefore race should be considered foundational rather than as periphery of the production of those structures and of global space)" (33).

From this standpoint, the Anthropocene argument that sees environmental activism as independent or transcendent of anticapitalism becomes scandalous. The specific mineral extraction and plantation systems that emerge with the conquest of the Americas are neither external to capitalism, by being presumed to historically precede it, nor anomalous relative to capitalism's central signification of unattached global circulation of money. Here Wynter is again right on the mark, with a nod to C. R. L. James's understanding of the Haitian revolution:

> Both the hegemony of the Western bourgeoisie and of capitalism were in their origin based mainly on New World land, the forced labor of the Indian, and the conversion of man—the black man—into a commodity. The later large-scale dehumanization of the European proletariat *followed* on and *did not precede* the

total negation of the black as human. Capitalism as a system therefore required the negation of the black as human. Far from being an anomaly in the rational system of capitalism, black slavery was *rationally* central to capitalism as a system.[159]

Why the epistemology of the Anthropocene is predicated on futurity thus emerges in sharp relief. Blind to this racialized production of the *co-incidence* of the inhuman with the inhumane, the Anthropocene logic negates extinctions of being that have already taken place, extinctions, moreover, that are essential to the machinery of future extinctions that the Anthropocene announces. This logic is thus ahistorical not only in the sense that it continues to suppress the history of violence in how *Anthropos* has come to be categorized as integral ontology, thus recirculating the effacement of difference in the universal, but also in the sense that it projects an integral futurity under the sign of the planet it purports to save without doing anything to save the planet's genocidal history from oblivion.

From this perspective, the Anthropocene as a concept/name/categorization is yet another instance of *coding the human* according to how Wynter, following Fanon, has elaborated as "the sociogenic principle": in this case, a coding instance that perpetuates the convenient disavowal of *human-being* as a social formation with different species content, with different anthropo-ontological situations, in the name of yet another iteration of the human as a natural principle. This disavowal involves the obliteration of a genocidal history internal to *human-being* to such an extent that it has become part of its code—Wynter would say its ontogenic (neural) code, though sociogenically created. The genocidal history of what is thereby repressed in the bioeconomy of modern (liberal/capitalist) humanism, with the conquest of the Americas as its departure point, is a powerfully determinant sociogenic principle that continues to fuel a vast reproduction of human practices across societies and cultures on a planetary scale, which certainly include, as Wynter says (in ways similar to Castoriadis), elaborate mechanisms of self-occultation. Fanon's notion of colonization as a specific mode of production of human species belongs to this trajectory. His militant call for the disappearance of this means of production, as well as the species it has brought forth, is very much a call against such self-occultation, which is why it exceeds the event of mere political decolonization in the name of national independence.

As political as this thinking is, its radical impetus fails to register as long as one considers the political as superstructure to the ontological. Fanon's incomparably pointed reiteration of the fact that all humans wear cultural masks, which effectively mediate and indeed override their biological skins, is not just an indictment of the brutal psychological states created by racism. By foregrounding the psychosexual inner workings of racism, Fanon goes even further to stage a radical ontological argument, for the sociogenic principle is not just a referent to social constructions but produces actual modes of living being down to the neural core.

This is the key to Wynter's powerful argument about both humanism and *human-being*. Following, alongside Fanon, the early work of renown cognitive philosopher David Chalmers, Wynter conducts an idiosyncratic, baroque, but nonetheless formidable argument about the neuro-ontological dimensions of the sociogenic principle "as the information-encoding organizational principle of each culture's criterion of being/nonbeing,"[160] dismantling thus both traditional humanism's occulted cultural universals and traditional ontology's uninterrogated certainties (whether scientific or theological) about the biological integrity of living-being. In this sense, although she never quite phrases it this way, Wynter is fully engaged with the problematic of the *human-animal* as a political entity following how it was first articulated by Aristotle's *zōon politikon*, where politics indeed "institutes a regime of *being*."[161]

Since his groundbreaking work *The Conscious Mind* (1996), Chalmers has notoriously argued that human consciousness is autonomous from physical (biological) operation, despite the brain being and functioning like any other physical organ. Of course, to the degree that the brain is a physical organ of the body, some sort of proposition of a mind/brain split has occupied thinkers since antiquity. But Chalmers goes far enough to argue that the phantasms of the mind, along with their immense and complex affective states, not only are autonomously created by consciousness and are not reducible to the electromagnetic work of brain synapses, but also produce such synapses as instruments of actualization of mental states in the physical body. By analogy—which Wynter radically exploits—Fanon dares to describe the experience of racism as a sort of neurologically effected genetic mutation: "The black man who has lived in France for a length of time returns [to his native land] radically changed. To express it in genetic terms, his phenotype undergoes a definitive, an absolute, mutation" (BSWM, 19).

Wynter reads Chalmers armed with Fanon. She goes on to argue that when it comes to *human-being*, the genetically programmed processes of ontogenesis present in all living being take place alongside with—and are directly transformed by—symbolically encoded processes of sociogenesis. The neurophysiological mechanisms of the brain may have their own biochemical dimensions, without which they are not operative, but the conditions of living/knowing that they produce are never mere extensions of biochemistry, for biochemistry itself ultimately operates in the service of code-producing systems of affect/meaning. Here, "code" is entirely translatable to mechanisms of neurotransmission, with effects going in both directions, where affect/meaning will produce neural impulses and yet also be the recipient of neural impulses in order to translate them into affect/meaning within the specific sociogenic signifying systems pertinent to every human. I quote Wynter channeling Chalmers, with Fanon very much in the background:

> The always already socialized, and therefore symbolically coded, orders of consciousness through which we experience ourselves as this or that mode of the human have to be seen as an expression of mutation in the processes of evolution, one by means of which a new level of existence, *discontinuous with evolution*, is brought into existence or, rather, brings itself into existence. Therefore, [this is] a level whose self-instituting modes of being will respond to and know its order of reality, *not* in the species-specific terms of its genome, of its genomic principle, but in the genre-specific terms of a narratively prescribed master code or sociogenic principle.[162]

This is a remarkably Castoriadian phrasing to my ear, and it might be useful here to remember Castoriadis's understanding of how sublimation, as an essential process of an individual's socialization, is always tantamount to humanization.[163] That is to say, society is not some by-product of human existence but its necessary bio-ontological condition. Aristotle's *zōon politikon* signifies this point precisely. There is no *human-being* as biocentric being—that is the central premise throughout this essay. Human animality itself is comprehensible only as a complex process of hybrid ontogenic/sociogenic entwinement where biological and/or zoological components are mere ciphers, themselves subjected to time and therefore uninterpretable as constants. Although never exhaustively answerable, the question of "what is human?" is a function of what is *humanized* and of how this "what" *comes to be humanized*, which always includes the "what" and "how" process by which it (or part of it) is indeed *dehumanized*. What is human is thus always something that *becomes* human, even in cases where its evident humanity is ontologically assaulted.

In this sense my argument converges with Zakiyyah Iman Jackson's, for whom the ease with which blackness is associated with dehumanization and animality paradoxically serves not only the logic of exclusion of blackness from the parameters of the human but substantiates an a priori humanity in which blackness would eventually be absorbed and nullified in some reparative restoration. Instead, Jackson's insistence that racism produces a specific mode of humanization that gives meaning to blackness, albeit abject, also understands, in ways similar to Fanon and Wynter, that racism works on the neural black body in epigenetic fashion: "environmental and social processes have the ability to modulate gene expression without changing the underlying structure of DNA" (*Becoming Human*, 200). Epigenetic scientists contest the exclusive relation between DNA and phenotype by proposing a flexible system of interactive factors, in which what is external (the sociogenic principle) and what is internal (the body's genetic structure) are entwined in such a way that what is "self" and what is "environment" is no longer categorically divided. Epigenetics examines how environments and social structures "come into the body" and how this interactive entwinement modulates the genomic structure in such a way that we can no longer simply say that experiences of the violence of poverty or racism or misogyny are secondary psychological factors but rather entirely and physiologically incorporated. In Jackson's terms, they are part of the ongoing, though mutable, humanization of the species.

Jackson correctly also warns, however, that despite its enabling displacement of simply biocentric notions of being, epigenetics inheres a danger that is strangely complicit to liberalism's modes of subjugation. If one takes for granted that biology is "made" rather than given, then the paradigm can easily revert to a politics of will and choice, which ironically buttresses claims of the *unwillingness* of the poor (say, "welfare mothers") to overcome their situations (208-12). The acrobatic position of epigenetics between the physiological and the psychosociological is its main weakness. Namely, if we are to be serious about the physiological transformations of bodies because of psychosocial factors, then we cannot revert to mere sociological categories when we are striving to imagine therapeutic solutions. One category does not substitute for the other; both must be pursued at one and the same time in their proper domains.

Processes of being humanized/dehumanized, which often are simultaneous strains of the same action, ultimately presuppose an integral notion of the human according to different social imaginaries, but that is no more than a specific sociogenic reality. Even in its remarkable plurality through various histories and societies of *human-being* on this planet, humanism is a precise example of such a sociogenic reality, even when its purpose has been to conceal this sociogenesis and present itself as metaphysical (natural) ontology. Indeed, the manifestation of the human as an inexhaustible question is best perceptible when sociogenesis is unconcealed. It is at this point that whatever about *human-being* is categorized as ontological can be understood to be a matter of *poiēsis*, indeed autopoiesis as we have seen, which, to remember Maturana and Varela's groundbreaking thesis, is the basis of all organic life regardless. This should put to rest both the arrogance of discourses of the self and the fetishism of discourses of the other in equal measure. Autopoiesis is a process of self-othering, which, by all accounts of microphysics we know so far, seems to be the operative principle of the universe. Autopoiesis is thus fully meaningful in a fundamental context of symbiosis, where no organism is anything other than an other to itself in a complex network of sibling others, even when in certain circumstances or proportions these sibling others become adversaries or even more, at the limit, existential enemies.

Notwithstanding the obvious limitations of the Anthropocene discourse, the factuality of climate change and of planetary precariousness overall has brought forth more acutely the symbiotic basis of all being. The Covid-19 pandemic that swept the planet was a crystal-clear demonstration of how even the most ironclad institutions of *human-being*—society, economy, politics—prove inadequate in their capacity to safeguard the delusional presumption as to the integrity of the human. The pandemic showed that even planetary microorganisms take advantage of the overwrought mechanisms that buttress this presumption. Entire state health systems, already gutted by profit-making arrogance, collapsed; governments were rendered pathetically incapacitated; populations went into paranoid hypergear or reveled in festivals of denial; and even the global machinery of capitalist commodity flow—whose auto-consuming (cannibalistic) practices had opened these new eco-bio-spaces in the first place—was brought to a halt, even if momentarily, by this new planetary cohabitation.

Of course, it is common knowledge that in the first instance human bodies are nothing without being microbial hosts, as are all bodies, all living matter on this earth, in an extraordinary chain of symbiosis that humans alone sought to disregard in full consciousness of its fact—a fact, I repeat, as fundamental to the universe as nothing else. As the inimitable Eugenia Bone puts it, "my body is a renter of matter that has been elsewhere before."[164] The comment resonates strikingly with Gayatri Spivak's often quoted phrase that "the planet belongs to another system and yet we inhabit it, on loan" (*Death of a Discipline*, 72)—the minutest micro and most unbounded macro invoking here together and at once the organic nonintegrity of the human: *human-being* as a threshold of alterities permeating it from all aspects of universal time and space.

At this closing juncture, it may be important to reiterate that discourses which revel in the disintegration of the category of the human continue to be riveted by the very thing they wish to deny, at the very least because of the obvious and insurmountable fact that all discourses are human-made—as instances of *human-being* registering itself, even if against itself. Humans are enamored of their own denial; it is a mark of their ontological arrogance, even if this is always sociogenically manifested. As we have already discussed, new obsessions about AI claim that superintelligence machines will ultimately become incomprehensible to humans, by which researchers mean that machines will become un(re)programmable, impossible to tame or control by algorithms alone. The assumption here is that the capacity of superintelligence to produce its own algorithmic ranges and patterns will ultimately exceed not only its programming but the means programmers have at their disposal to algorithmically communicate (and compete) with the machine. Within the AI universe of mind this makes total sense; it is a mere extrapolation of an already existing logic and already existing frameworks of logic—technics. The researchers mean to warn humanity of their own emerging incapacity as they create all the more capacious machines.[165] But this assumes that AI technicians are the equivalent of humans as a whole, denying the simple fact that, although humans have created algorithms—on the one hand, to explain and, on the other hand, to intervene and manipulate "nature"—they also think and do whatever they may think and do beyond algorithms and without algorithms. The very framework of computational thinking, however, disputes this simple fact, so that we see instances when Mo Gawdat, ex-Google CEO, will state in perfectly cavalier fashion that "human ingenuity is algorithmic" based on the definition of creativity as the clearing out of tried solutions until the one that has not been tried emerges—a truly impoverished way of thinking.[166] In the simplest terms, we are talking of nothing less than the assumption that humans are the original machine and therefore creating their own machines is a way of appeasing the universe. We have not moved far from the creation of the first totem pole.

Thinking from this long-term anthropological perspective might enable a certain distance from the rush to embrace whatever newfangled thing technology serves, which, let us not forget, has a money-making machine bubbling beneath it. I was struck by a phrase in James Lovelock's last book, launched on his hundredth birthday, on what he calls the Novacene: "Live cyborgs will emerge from the womb of the Anthropocene. We can almost be certain that an electronic life form such as a cyborg could never emerge by chance from the inorganic components of the earth before the Anthropocene."[167] The ease with which Lovelock accepts and underscores a geological age created by human naming in whose context Artificial Intelligence will presumably reign as a by-product of *human-being* is astonishing, all the more so when the whole point of his argument—of his entire body of work—has been to diminish the significance of the human. Equally astonishing is the ease with which he establishes a genetic parentage between humans and cyborgs who "are a product of the same evolutionary processes that created us" (118), albeit "more sophisticated descendants" (107).

My use of "genetic" is quite literal; one could say "generative," but why bother? Lovelock paints a seamless picture of ancestry, moving from the Darwinian model of evolution as natural selection and adaptation to what he calls "much faster intentional selection" (84), which he attributes to the evolution of humans who then intentionally pass it on to machines where intentionality in effect becomes equated with programmability. The ultimate unfolding of this process is the projected capacity of machines to generate themselves—not merely to program themselves but to create themselves beyond the capacity of human programming, beyond the purview of human intelligence. AI thus *inherits* an evolutionary capacity of *human-being*, the capacity for autonomy. It is quite interesting in terms of the argument I have been making here in the previous sections that for Lovelock the key element of this autonomy is self-learning. His primary example is Alpha Zero, a computer generated by the chess master computer AlphaGo in what appears to be, by analogy, a sort of intentional mechanical mitosis. Having beaten all human chess players, AlphaGo created another computer mate to play with. It turned out that Alpha Zero became an even more powerful machine that operated—always speaking within the purview of playing chess—not only at unfathomable speeds in terms of programmed algorithms and synthesizing memory but also with a capacity that Lovelock calls "some AI form of intuition" (80). An autopoietic, autodidactic machine that, moreover, teaches itself to think intuitively, is the epitome of human autonomy—one might say, just as well, the epitome of humanization.

Questions abound all over Lovelock's argument. Does it matter that the Anthropocene, a discourse entirely authorized by the future, is by virtue of this projection of replacement already extinct from the standpoint of the future? Does it matter that the Anthropocene was invented in the name of Earth—indeed, of saving the Earth by striking the alarm of global warming—yet to displace Earth's own geological history by virtue of elevating humanity to geological status? Is the nominal Novacene really new, in this respect? Can there ever be anything new, in this sense of beyond-the-human, if we understand *human-being* as an ever-mutating ontological horizon and not as some biological given? How long will this game of aspiring geological or technological names be used as shield for this indomitable ontological horizon? Have we not had enough already with antihuman apocalyptic desire? With catastrophe as a way out of our existential enigma? How many more artificial anthropisms can we take? Is there no end to our desire for denial of the human as yet another human act?

Lovelock's basic contradiction resides less in his argument and more in his attitude. His machine fetishism in welcoming the Novacene curiously reveals that his previous ecological grandeur, articulated as the Gaia hypothesis, is indeed also a machine logic. Above all, despite his rapturous overtures to intuition, Lovelock worships the principle of self-regulation. In this sense, he remains not only enthralled by the imaginary of liberalism, to which self-regulation is an epistemic cornerstone, but by this token he enacts a by-product of capitalist market thought, no different than Adam Smith's pinheads. At the same time, his insistence on Gaia's cosmic uniqueness, in which *human-being* (and the planet's entire evolutionary process) is a happy accident of cosmic chemistry, fuels an antihumanist sentiment predicated exclusively on the hypothesis that humanity is a unique occurrence in the universe. This is about as monohumanist as one gets, and it serves to show how humanist orthodoxy very much includes all its alleged overcomings—in Lovelock's specific terms, whether by planetary destruction by humans or planetary survival via the coveted sovereignty of Artificial Intelligence. In underlining these contradictions I hardly mean to diminish Lovelock's inventive mind or his extraordinary achievements in a rich century of life on this earth, but to clarify how his futurist ruminations are rather typical of classical modernity: well rooted in eighteenth-century British Enlightenment adorations of rationalist technoscience, reconfigured so that a certain kind of anthropological mathematics is elevated from the historical purview of this island in the northern seas to the entire cosmos.[168]

Of course, one might argue instead that Lovelock is perfectly antihumanist in that his entire cosmological model is info-cybernetic to the core. This includes *human-being*, which becomes no more than a specific modality of the universe conveying information in biochemical fashion: "I can't help wondering whether, when the cyborgs are the dominant species... they will discover a proof of my own view that the bit is the fundamental particle from which the universe is formed" (89). But by considering the information bit fundamental cosmic matter, akin to energy or gravity, Lovelock shuts down any biotic significance to the Earth—perhaps even the Universe—and trades the autopoietic for the automated.[169] Even hardcore geneticists or neuroscientists, for whom cellular or neurological transmission of information is essential, would not quite put it this way. And a number of them, though they work with information in trying to understand things better, experience no scientific or theoretical need to posit as primary reference frameworks models of calculation and memory storage, that is to say, computer models.[170] In the end, this a moot point. The concept of information is a human invention: it is a hermeneutical model, a language to explain the workings of the universe, like mathematics or physics or religion. To project it onto the universe as its essence is no different than creating a god—a perfectly theologizing gesture, one of the most amazing tendencies and capacities of the *human/animal* but hardly new and unlikely to ever cease.

Along these same lines of motivation, like Lovelock, David Chalmers himself has recently embraced the simulation hypothesis: namely, the altogether literal *reality* of virtual reality experience.[171] Anchoring himself on one of the foundational philosophical quandaries since Descartes—namely, the impossibility of discerning the authenticity of whatever is external to our being—Chalmers goes all in on the aporia of never fully knowing whether we are in or out of a simulation, very much à la *Matrix* but with a counterconclusion, to argue that, from the standpoint of consciousness, virtual reality immersion is perfectly real. Philosophically speaking, the argument is cogent, of course, and charmingly written even if contorted. On the basis of being certain as to the uncertainty of determining whether we are living in a virtual world or not, Chalmers produces what I would call a relativist realism, which is no less a child of reason than any other human phantasm ever created by rational analytical thinking. Curiously, the contradiction of using uncertainty to vitalize yet another certainty—once again, a perfectly theological desire—is never examined.

So, although since reading Aristotle's own words I too recognize that "no mind thinks without phantasms," and moreover that whatever belongs to the realm of the psyche—which is to say, everything human—is perfectly and always real, at the very least because one way or another it affects real men and women in real material world conditions, nonetheless I do not see in Chalmers's technophilosophy (his own term) anything other than a present-time social-imaginary activation of what has always been existential to *human-being*: the desire to enact—to *realize* (both literally and in a theatrical sense)—one's dream world. Indeed, we have not moved far from the first engravings in the caves of Lascaux, and this is not at all a disparaging thing. On the contrary, it confirms the human psyche's indomitable capacity to intervene and alter its living environment. What I still do find disparaging, after all these years and all these pages of writing and rewriting thoughts about the existential contortions of *human-being*, is the libidinal investment in disavowing human animality for yet another techno-overcoming: an algorithmic substitution for the ineffable, the incomplete, the infinite—*apeiron* in Greek reminds us that infinite means incomplete.

To be sure, I understand the psyche's motivation: it is the very same denial of finitude that is the way of all living matter but is refused only by humans, the denial of death. As desire, this cannot be faulted or criticized. But as denial, it is yet another way toward delusion, toward the very virtuality of being it denies by use of reason. Such are, in the end, the peculiarities of the *human/animal*, this most unreasonable of creatures. We've come around, yet again, to the point that the long adventure of this text has been encountering throughout: the sort of desire we call "antihumanism" is part of the trajectory of humanism, of the human propensity to authorize what is beyond-the-human, which is itself no more than the phantasmatic capacity to externalize everything that the inner psyche—*the animal substance*—confers to what it calls "the world" in an infinite number of languages and nonlanguages, constantly building worlds in the world even as it is forced to consider that it is no more than mere matter in the midst of matter.

CHAPTER 2

Democracy's Anarchy

Anarchy Is the Archē of Democracy—Archē and Finitude—Democracy Is the Regime of the Living—The Constituent Violence of Democracy: The Liberal Enclosure—The Constituent Violence of Democracy: The Anarchist Opening—Democracy Is a Tragic Regime—No Democracy Without Dissent—Surplus Over Nothing—Notes on Left Governmentality

—for Andreas, to whom it belongs

I confess that my title bears a certain equivocation, even if accidentally. In the requisite logistical correspondence about the presentation of an early version of this argument, I was surprised to realize that my original title "Democracy's Anarchy" had become "Anarchy's Democracy." In checking the details of the exchange, I discovered that the mistake—if indeed it is one—was mine. I had carelessly enacted the reversal. In effect, the occurrence is trivial. The beauty of language, however, does not allow me to settle on this simple recognition. What emerged from this triviality was an opening to a certain equivocal terrain that underlies my inquiry which would have been otherwise unperceived.

The English language specifically is very helpful here. In colloquial English, the apostrophe that marks the possessive case, whereby one term is always formally subordinate to another, also delineates the exact opposite: it marks the verb of equivalence. So, if my initial thought was to investigate democracy's anarchy, whereby the primary object of examination is presumably democracy, its reversal (where anarchy would be presumed as primary object) implies neither a cancellation of the relation nor a departure onto an entirely different order. Rather, it reveals the underlying equivalence that was after all already there, grammatically present and signified as such.

The proposition "democracy *is* anarchy" works precisely because the subject and object of the sentence are not enthroned in their positions. Obviously, the logic for this is not grammatical; it pertains to the content of the proposition. What mobilizes this particular subject/object relation, what lends it equivalence and equivocation, what renders it into a relation that abolishes the hierarchy of one term over another, is a *political* matter. My broader argument is predicated on this specific political understanding that renders the subject/object relation undecidable and conceptualizes not merely the abolition of hierarchy but the interrogation and deconstitution of *archē* to be the core signification of democracy.

However we might ultimately determine what is political leans on an argument about rule and, more precisely, on what legitimizes rule: how, in other words, we are to configure the relation between rule and law (*archē* and *nomos*)—a configuration that is neither self-evident nor adequately descriptive but is itself subjected to and expressive of a certain politics. This is a politics that explodes the presumed certainty of the meaning of *archē*—which, as we shall see, is hardly certain even in its original ancient Greek parameters—thereby rendering democracy the specific political regime (or, some would say, the regime that exemplifies the political) that plunges the relation between rule and law into permanent contestation. One of the most contentious dimensions in this configuration is the issue of violence as a mode of political action—indeed, the issue of violence as legitimate or illegitimate mode of political action. According to this argument, violence as political action would thus pertain both to rule and to law, for and against either or both. I will address this specific point in due time, but meanwhile let me clear the board with some preliminary assertions.

In the rubric I construct here, I deliberately disregard exhaustive or systematic theories of democracy, particularly those focused on its voluminous and complex procedural characteristics, and especially those that don't find problematic the irreparable metaphysics of representation in modern democracy. I'm interested instead in what can be called "radical democracy," which is at best a political attitude toward a practical politics that may come to be but just as easily may not. This attitude is implicated in a tragic sense of life, which has nothing to do with any sort of catastrophic way of being, but rather with learning how to live with the absence of external norms and guarantees in a cosmologically unprotected universe. Although tragedy as a literary form is of great interest to me, on this occasion I am not concerned with tragedy per se, except to the degree that it was once a manifestation of a politics made and lived in the absence of external norms and guarantees. Furthermore, this inquiry deliberately advocates a methodology of generalization, which is itself a political position against the grain of conventional academic practices in pedagogy and the production of knowledge. In this respect, although historical precision is invaluable and always in play, an occasional decontextualization of concepts is warranted in order to break down closed boundaries of reading.

Arguably, to generalize about democracy might be one of the most impossible of tasks. Yet we do it all the time, despite the tireless historical work that elucidates the profound multiplicities, diversifications, and contradictions of this political form since the Age of Revolution. Moreover, as many argue quite aggressively, even to think about democracy these days may be a worthless gesture, banal in light of one's intellectual demands, wasteful in terms of one's scholarly time.[1] To think of *radical democracy* may seem even worse: at once irrelevant and rarefied, utopian at best, decadent at worst. The word "democracy" itself is crying to be let go of, burdened with so much politicized filth, mass media designification, popularized emptiness, not to mention the vociferous banalities by armies of experts waddling in the term's self-fashioned and self-serving conceptual void. It is clear to me that any attempt to think in terms of democracy with the intent of interrogating and yet enhancing its meaning cannot altogether rid itself of this overburdened terrain; many would argue vehemently that whatever a thinker's skills may be, the attempt is hopelessly compromised.

So I have already put myself in a bind. For how does one argue in favor of generalization as a radical gesture regarding a subject that, despite its being researched in inordinate detail, is always already thoughtlessly generalized? Moreover, how does one argue in favor of the radical emancipatory (and even insurrectionary) significance of a name that has been used to justify the most horrifically oppressive and destructive state politics worldwide? There is something untenable about this task, as untenable as is the coincidence between the name of democracy and what democracy historically has enacted in its name, but the untenable element (and the politics it demands) is one of the central motifs of this inquiry.

In the end, what galvanized my motivation to pursue this task in this fashion was a fortuitous textual encounter in the casual reading of Rüdiger Safranski's commendable biography *Martin Heidegger: Between Good and Evil*. In sinuous style,

Safranski describes the early months of 1933, when the Nazis have just ascended to power, as an atmosphere of delirious mass intoxication, animated by not merely the widespread "impression of resolution and brutality" but a profound "yearning for non-political politics [since] 'politics' was seen as a betrayal of the values of 'true' life, family happiness, spirit, loyalty, courage." Safranski documents the extensive investment in this euphoria by citing numerous expressions of the educated German bourgeoisie, including Jewish academics otherwise aware of the coming danger (though certainly not of its magnitude). His most telling citation, however, is of the renowned journalist Sebastian Haffner, who escaped to London in 1938 in order to save his Jewish wife: "It was—there is no other way of putting it—a widespread feeling of deliverance, of liberation from democracy."[2] Safranski elaborates on how this "sense of relief in the demise of democracy" was shared even by self-identified adherents of republicanism, who envisioned, in utter perversion, a "people's rule without political parties." What Safranski later calls, in reference to Heidegger, "a philosophical somersault into primitivity" is expressly linked to this overthrow of the weight of democracy from society's shoulders, which is the most perverse gesture of a highly politicized ideology that annihilates politics, an ideology that thoroughly depoliticizes society in the very ritual travesty of its ceremonial aesthetics of Führer adoration.[3] A similar affect can be seen in the politics of originally Tea Party and later Trumpist shenanigans in the United States—a con-game politics that has taken over the quintessential party of elite politics, the Republican Party—whose stupefying intoxication consists in the total mobilization of a depoliticized citizenry to withdraw all investment in government, as if government happens elsewhere, in another planet by another species or by evil aliens.

Of course, the content of terms is always historical and never eternal. If the name "democracy" is discredited or nullified, it is for historical reasons that are as such finite and provisional. The hatred of democracy, as Jacques Rancière has aptly identified it, has nowadays become fashionable for a self-ascribed antithetical lifestyle (sometimes fueled by generally anti-Western sentiment, but not exclusively), whose ideology may in fact be plural and heterogeneous but whose logic is singularly perverse: "There is only one good democracy, the one that suppresses (*réprimer*) the catastrophe waged by democratic civilization." And later on: "A good democratic government is one capable of mastering (*maîtriser*) the evil quite simply called democratic life."[4] Revealed in this logic is obviously a certain trouble in the naming, not only because the invocation of democracy as impetus for the charge is, in this case, patently deceiving but also because what is attacked as the fault of democracy is the very thing that is waged undemocratically in its name. Rancière calls this "the democratic paradox" and goes even further to argue that it is the paradox of politics itself, which only democracy can disclose.

As he sees it, the hatred of democracy consists in a double gesture: a de facto adoration of the authority of the liberal state while pretending to critique liberalism for the destruction that liberal politics enacts because allegedly it cannot rein in its excesses. Yet the reality of the matter is that the alleged destruction, the "catastrophe of democratic civilization," is waged not by what are self-fashioned as democracies but by what are in actuality liberal oligarchies. From a certain angle, this so-called critique of democracy is but a feeble elaboration of a Schmittian fetish for law and order. In any case, it has nothing to do with democracy, because either side of the equation—both the subject and the object of hatred—is unwilling to invest in the imaginary of democracy, perhaps even—to be blunt—because either side is fearful of the inordinate demands democracy places on one's living being, demands that are, I argue, the makings of a tragic life. Notice that, as Rancière puts it, the target of this hatred is "democratic life" which, according to this perverse schema, must be dismantled in order for so-called democratic politics to flourish. Here we have a travesty of naming, not just of the name "democracy" but also of the name "politics." For, a politics that aims beyond or gets around life—a politics that has no life—is the most profound constitution of a depoliticized people, that is to say, a servile people.

As a way of encapsulating the circuitous trajectory of what follows, even if this might give the game away (but this is not a detective story in the least), let me clarify from the outset that my overall argument follows from three presuppositions:

1. Philosophically speaking, democracy is a historical manifestation of self-organized politics that rests on no foundation other than its own self-authorization, which, being occasional and provisional, has no antecedent and therefore is abyssal. Democracy is groundless. All its otherwise presumed grounds—the equal sharing of power, the freedom to speak with impunity, the constitutional safeguard, even its most cherished and incontrovertible *subject* ("the people")—are its symptoms, its creations, its creatures. The people—this bizarre singular-plural subject that only has meaning as subject in democracy and nowhere else—does not exist except in the very act of coming to be in democratic action, the primary component of which

is not the electoral act (that is a secondary symptom) but the impersonal collective assembly in the public space, which becomes public by virtue of this act. There is no ground to democracy, there is no ground beneath democracy, there is no ground to stand on in democracy, except this provisional coming-to-be, coming-together-to-be, because of and in order to equally share power. For this reason, democracy does not derive from norms of any kind—even if it goes on to produce them (but again provisionally)—and provides no guarantees. From this standpoint, the term "radical democracy" is a pleonasm, much as "liberal democracy" is a pseudonym, for democracy is always radical since there is nothing external to it that gives it meaning; it is its own self-generation and self-definition.

2. Politically speaking, democracy requires an imaginary of rule without *archē* or *telos*—a literally anarchic imaginary that disengages itself from traditional parameters of the command-obedience structure. This is not to say that democracy entails no rule. On the contrary, it engages in the paradoxical practice of anarchic rule, or rule shared by all (even those in opposition), so that the traditional division of power between rulers and ruled is destabilized. I am referring here to Aristotle's famous notion in *Politics* that no ruler can rule without learning and knowing what it means to be ruled. This means right away that those who are ruled or governed are not the others of government—they *are* the government. Indeed, in democracy the subject-position of the governed is a position of power—equal power with those who govern, since those who govern only happen to govern at this juncture and do so only because they are authorized by those who at this juncture are governed, who can easily recall them (and must recall them, if the governed feel that their authorization is usurped). In democracy the governed are always in a position of governing power. This is what makes democracy unlike any other mode of politics ever invented on this planet. Power (*kratos*) is recognized to be shared by all equally and can never become self-sufficient or transcendental. The term "democracy," in this respect, resides between the terms "autonomy" and "anarchy"—so long as the *auto* in the first never turns into *archē*. Likewise, anarchy as a mode of rule is what keeps democracy democratic.

3. Ethically speaking, there is nothing good or bad about democracy; all moral imperatives are foreign, perhaps even contrary, to democracy. Democracy has no morality. It is not a good—it is even beyond the notion of the common good, which is an instrumental, a utilitarian logic. Democratic politics operates in an ethical realm without categorical imperatives, a priori principles or transcendental

guarantees, and is thereby constitutively perilous and precarious. It derives from, creates, and sustains a politics of conflict, of contention and contestation, a politics of dissent. Contrary to whatever liberalism argues, the cornerstone of democracy is not consensus but dissent. You can still have democracy without consensus, but you have no democracy without dissent. Therefore, divisiveness is not a negative or politically disempowering principle in the democratic imaginary. On the contrary, it underlies the requisite resistance to uniformity; it animates the heterogeneity necessary to withstand a debilitating stability (or status quo) of political agency. For this reason, the only ethics of democracy–the ethics that democracy creates, not the ethics that create democracy (there is no such thing)–is an ethics of decision, of responsibility and accountability for the political decision, no matter what that is, and in light of the provisional and conflictual situation on which decisions must be taken. Democracy thus involves a tragic imaginary, as we know from Athenian history. It enacts a politics of tragic life that sometimes is driven to folly without heroic salvation, yet always demands lucidity in conditions of total uncertainty.

To be sure, democracy is politics of high risk. It is not easy politics, it is not even necessarily good politics or wise politics, but it is free politics, an autonomous politics, the only autonomous politics there is.

ANARCHY IS THE *ARCHĒ* OF DEMOCRACY

To begin with, elucidating the tragic element demands a way of thinking the political, which at a primary level, even before democracy itself emerges, is a matter of understanding the peculiar social imaginary of the polis. To speak of a social imaginary is to consider matters, beyond mere social organization, on the basis of prevalent significations that make sensible a society's creation of a proper world, the vision or notion of its own cosmos. In this respect, my contention is that for the Greek cities from the seventh to the fifth century BCE, more than *logos*, the key signification is *archē*, and it is to this that I devote the first part of my discussion.

Let us look at a well-known assertion in Aristotle's *Politics*: "There is a sort of rule [*archē*] pertaining to those similar in birth and free–this we call political rule–where the ruler learns by being ruled [*ēn dei ton archonta archomenon mathein*]"

(*Politics*, Book III, 1277b, 8-10). This phrase encapsulates not only the paradox of democracy, but the deeper significance of what it means for a society to constitute *on its own and for itself* a mode of political life without fixed norms and without guarantees. This mode of life is political par excellence, and democracy is its name. It is a mode that animates political life as such: the essence of *human-being* as *zōon politikon*. If the human animal is a political animal, it is because it refuses to consider the *archē* of things as natural and subjects it to interrogation.

We must not forget that *archē* means both origin and rule, much in the sense that, in the English language, we understand rule to pertain both to matters of governance and to matters of principle, indeed first principles, the essential rules of the game, of proposition, of foundation, of order. The ruler, after all, is a primary figure (even in cases articulated as *primus inter pares*), the premier in a constitutive mechanism of ruling that presupposes him to be the primary guardian of the set of rules he represents. In any archaic configuration of power, the *archon* not only commands authority over the domain of rules that govern a society; he also embodies the point of departure of whatever trajectory such rules are to have in their implementation, whether they are to be enforced in principle or not, safeguarded for future generations (of rulers and ruled), or dismantled in favor of another course of rule, another beginning. Such is obviously the essence of the figure of the *patriarch*, which is why even when the primordial parricide takes place, according, let us say, to Freud's tales—when, in fact, the singular origin of principle and rule is to be multiplied and distributed (in Freud's analysis, institutionalized) in the hands of the many murderous sons—the patriarchic order is hardly abolished. On the contrary, in its multiplication, the authorial origin is consolidated.

But when Aristotle demands that the *archon* must also be *archomenos* something else entirely takes place. The singular notion of *archē* is deconstituted by a corresponding alterity. In order to know how to rule, one must know how to be ruled: this is the quintessential element of autonomy. Knowledge of being ruled does not mean mere experiential accounting from the standpoint of the (always) ruled. In a direct sense, it means knowing the other side of rule, enabling an affirmative investment in the object of rule from a subject-position that is not consumed in the typical objectification suffered by those ruled. In this respect, being ruled provides the sort of knowledge—achieved explicitly as a result of learning (*mathein*)—that relativizes a ruler's presumed monopoly over the authority to determine what rule means and, in effect, abolishes the presumed epistemic distinction between rulers and ruled in producing a subject of authority, of power, in the double sense.[5] Aristotle's phrasing is perfectly apt: "the rule of the free is known [*epistasthai*] from both sides" (1227b, 16–17).

This *co-incidence* can be considered from two standpoints. On the one hand, the ruled authorize their own position as ruled; that is, they are not ruled in the simple sense of submitting to the authority of the ruler, an authority predicated on the assumption that the ruler is also the origin of rule. They are ruled by virtue of their own decision to be ruled, which means they are the ones who pose the questions (and give meaning to the questions): who rules, why, and how? This is the very mode of interrogating the rule of law, and this is why this notion has nothing to do with the debilitating paradox of "voluntary servitude" that Etienne de la Boétie so brilliantly exposed several centuries ago, which nonetheless continues to characterize most of today's societies of consensus. The ruled who hold the reins of interrogation over the signifying framework of rule can never become servile by definition; they are motivated by a principle of self-limitation that safeguards their autonomy, their self-determination. That is why in the Athenian polis slaves are not ruled, strictly speaking; they just execute commands. For this reason police work was assigned to slaves, the famous Scythian archers, who, of course, were paid for their services.[6] And it is similar in the case of women and children, whose existence within the *oikos* bears its own economy. As Hannah Arendt has famously argued, Athenian democracy makes the realm of the political independent of the social; the necessity of entwining these two domains is a problem of modernity. Whatever the conditions of power within the *oikos* and the specific variations of patriarchic society pertinent to the Greeks, *archē* in the political sense exists only in the public space of male citizens. All others are outside the realm of ruling, not only because to be ruled means to participate in ruling but also because ruling does not mean issuing commands within a hierarchical structure. Rather, ruling becomes a condition shared by the free and the equal, which is as such *political rule (politikē arkhē)*. Aristotle is unequivocal on this. By this logic, a ruler who has never known how to be ruled—*a ruler who has not known the autonomy of being ruled*—cannot possibly rule without abusing autonomy in favor of ruling in its name. Aristotle's injunction against such a ruler opens the way toward considering the project of autonomy as an interminable exercise of self-rule even in the political domain of being ruled.

On the other hand, Aristotle's configuration of *archē* also subverts the signification of ruler as primordial authority, which is why it is pertinent only to democracy and not monarchy. If, concurrently to rule, *archē* signifies origin, the requisite knowledge of *archomenos* forbids the ruler's singular occupation of the origin of authority, thus introducing a difference at the origin, a foundational *différance*. As *archomenos*, a ruler can never claim to be the first and only. At most, he can acknowledge the position of *archon* as a transitory moment in the process of ruling, which is a process whose ultimate beginning is unknown and irrelevant and whose ultimate endpoint is incomprehensible as such—a process undertaken by society as a whole, provided that society recognizes and enacts its autonomy.[7] For an *archon* to recognize the *archomenos* as a subject position means to recognize an alterity within, which by traditional logic is impossible. What makes this possible—the capacity for *self-alteration*—is even more far-fetched, logically speaking. It signifies a process by which alterity is internally produced, dissolving the very thing that enables it, the very thing whose existence derives meaning from being altered, *from othering itself.*[8]

If knowing how to be ruled is essential to ruling, no ruler can claim self-authorization, and *archē* can no longer constitute itself as a singular origin. Authority begins already cleft and differential, open to question at the point of its constitution, by virtue of the fact that both subject and object of power are in a position of *co-incidence*. Although nominally, at a specific point in time, someone rules and someone is being ruled, these positions are not structurally or temporally frozen, but are provisionally filled by whoever fills them. In a democratic situation, according to Aristotle's stipulation, this "whoever" pertains to both domains (ruler and ruled) without qualification—hence being called upon to take up the responsibility of ruling by lot. In this respect, the mutual alterity between the positions of ruler and ruled does not disintegrate to mere opposition but rather remains involved in a mutual complicity where any primordial notion of *archē* as singular authority or singular origin of power is irreparably disrupted. This exposes the whole business of ruling as a veritably *anarchic* condition, in the sense that rule, though not abolished, is provisionally constituted on no other ground than the equal sharing of power among a people who occasionally perform the position of ruler and occasionally perform the position of ruled but are in essence always, *politically*, acting in both positions simultaneously. *In this very sense, anarchy is the* archē *of democracy.*

ARCHĒ AND FINITUDE

One may object that my quick reading of Aristotle's phrase is not very Aristotelian. Strictly speaking, this would be correct. By Aristotelian terms, it is a perverse reading—my conclusion at least, because the *co-incidence* of ruler and ruled is no doubt what the Aristotelian text pursues. My conclusion is perverse in the simple sense that anarchy, literally the nonbeing of rule (which is not at all to say the lack of rule or unruliness), would be inconceivable to Aristotle as the core signification of democracy. Although not quite bearing Plato's vehemence—Plato explicitly identifies anarchy to be the internal and incurable illness of democracy—Aristotle would signify anarchy as the unraveling of democracy. However, the semantic multivalence of the Greek language enables a broader horizon of understanding the permutations of *archē*. This multivalence is not the mark of the genius of the Greek language (as the German Philhellenic tradition from Humboldt to Heidegger would have it), but the outcome of an explosive social imaginary that, with extraordinary speed of formation and alteration, fashions new configurations of meaning while retaining the traces of the old in magmatic fashion, so that what would seem to be a semantic contradiction is in fact semantic *co-incidence*.[9]

Given our scant knowledge of the pre-classical Greek world, the word *archē* first occurs as a philosophical principle in the famed Anaximander fragment, itself an interpolated text, possibly written around 570 BCE and glossed by Theophrastus, Aristotle's premier student, around 350 BCE. Theophrastus's commentary no longer exists, but reference to it is found in Simplicius, a Neoplatonist writing in 517 CE, who produces in turn a citation of the famed fragment of Anaximander, in effect, a whole thousand years later.[10] This initial philosophical use, by Anaximander, of a word (*archē*) already present in scant textual traces going back to Homer comes into conjunction with his introduction of a bona fide new concept: *apeiron* (infinity). The tenet of my argument should be obvious: the notion of *archē* (origin and rule) is first used philosophically in order to identify what has no origin and no end and over which there can be no rule. This is not at all a paradox. I quote the famous paragraph from Simplicius:

> Among those who say that the first principle [*archē*] is one and movable and infinite, is Anaximander of Miletus, son of Praxiades, pupil and successor of Thales. He said that the first principle [*archē*] and element of all things is

infinite [*apeiron*], and he was the first to apply this word to the first principle; and he says that it is neither water nor any other one of the things called elements, but the infinite is something of a different nature, from which came all the heavens and the worlds in them; and from which things are generated in their substance and to which they return of necessity when they degenerate [*ex ōn de ē genesis esti tois ousi kai tēn phthoran eis tauta ginesthai kata to chreōn*]; for he says that they suffer retribution [*dikēn*] and give recourse [*tisin*] to one another for injustice [*adikian*] according to the order of time [*kata tou chronou taxin*], putting it rather poetically [*poiētikoterois outōs onomasin auta legōn*].

Right offhand, I would point out two essential elements, established by this fragment, whose complexity, of course, is vastly disproportionate to its brevity:

1. *Archē* here is infinite. This does not preclude it from being a source (of all matter, of everything). Nor, however, does this mean that it is somehow external to this everything it enables, because this everything decays, is finite, and thereby returns to become source again. Source, therefore, is not *Ursprung*, the one and only origin, the once and for all event of creation, but an infinite space of interminably enacted beginnings of an indefinite array of "things" that have one thing in common: they come to an end. There is a crucial element in the meaning of *apeiron* we need to remember: whatever has no *peras* doesn't just mean whatever has no limit but also whatever cannot be completed. In this sense, the infinite is also incomplete. The paradoxical condition is that the incomplete/infinite enables the emergence of the complete/finite, an emergence that is, as such, a disturbance of the infinite. The finitude of existence is thus justified by its very violation of the infinite; it is this violation that inaugurates the question of justice (*dikē*). Note Barry Sandywell's succinct formulation: "Whatever exists is universally subject to justified destruction. Now the *kosmos* is perceived as a vast process of coming-to-be and passing-out-of-existence. Every existing thing is a site of expiation for its violation of the *apeiron*."[11] Moreover, in addition to signifying whatever is unlimited and incomplete, the infinite (*apeiron*), by virtue of the literal polysemy of the word, also means whatever exceeds experience (*peira*)—literally, something that cannot be empirically determined.[12] In this latter sense, insofar as it cannot be empirically known, the infinite (*apeiron*) is not just interminable (*atermon*), as it came to be understood in Aristotle's day, but indeterminable: something that in itself has no *telos*, no finality, no termination—which is another way of saying, it

lacks de-finition, de-limitation, de-termination. For this reason, as Castoriadis puts it, "a theory of the infinite is, in some ways, a literal contradiction" because there can never be an empirical (experimental and experiential) basis on which the infinite can be theorized; "hence, only poets can touch the infinite."[13] I would add that, although the Anaximander fragment is about physics, the thinking involved is not mathematical strictly speaking. In modern mathematics infinity is calculated, or rather, mathematized. It can be part of an equation that can be solved, even if infinity remains unknown as a specific number. In Anaximander, infinity is a nonmathematical entity. It does denote an order, but an order that cannot be determined, an order that is incomplete and intangible and therefore cannot be calculated.

2. Yet this disturbance of the infinite/indefinite/indeterminate by virtue of termination or finitude also means that the infinite source is not omnipotent, for it is thus crossed by time. Time is what makes things/beings decay and die and, in so doing, opens infinity to their readmittance, to their return, which thus makes the infinite source, simultaneously, a sort of repository, a burial ground, of what has come into the world and has gone out of it. (Ground, here, is metaphorical, for *apeiron* rests on nothing—it is abyssal and only figuratively situated, precisely by this relation to finite things, for its spatial dimension is otherwise a void.) The condition of things/beings entering the world and necessarily having to go out of it constitutes, in itself and without any other qualification, an injustice (*adikia*). This is to say, rather brutally, that time itself constitutes an injustice, which the infinite, though an *archē*, can neither overrule nor alleviate. The relation between infinity and time hangs in the cosmic balance which finite matter inevitably unsettles—for, on the one hand, matter is subject to time, thereby defying the infinite, and on the other hand, matter returns to the infinite, thereby defying time. This unsettling of balance, this injustice, is life itself—the tragic life, from which there is no redemption.

This impossibility of redemption ends any resemblance of this cosmological sense with views of humanity separated from the divine, fallen from grace by original sin or what have you. The Greeks gesture toward a permanent cosmological condition that cannot be repaired in some messianic sense (Jewish or Christian) or alleviated by some paradisial afterlife (Christian or Muslim). They gesture toward an injustice in which death (irreparable finitude) is both the cost of retribution and the mark of judicial balance, insofar as it restores to the infinite its integrity as matrix.[14] Imaginaries of original sin or fall from grace celebrate an imposed-inherited limit of existence. This archaic Ionian imaginary, for which finitude itself constitutes an injustice, provides justice (*dikē*) in determining that one makes one's own limits in the course of living, while submitting unredemptively to the ultimate limit of death. While living, one's life is potentially unlimited—one's imagination is infinitely capacious, it partakes of the abyssal infinite, one might say—hence the danger of committing hubris and the demand thereby that one authorizes (I would say *poietizes*) one's own limits.

It is important to add—and about this matter alone a whole other essay would have to be written—that this astounding fragmentary thought, pertaining to the core of the cosmic and articulated in just a couple of sentences, is explicitly understood to be a way of speaking and thinking poetically. The force of *poiein*—what enables a society to create a world for itself and a mythic language (poetry) that makes this society fully accountable to the fact that *it and no other* has created this world—is essential to understanding the peculiar significance of both tragic life and democracy.[15]

In his stipulation of the substitutable nature of *archon* and *archomenos* we just examined, Aristotle reconfigures the stakes of Anaximander's cosmology in explicitly political terms; this cosmology echoes in his account of ruler and ruled, although I am not, of course, suggesting that that this (or any Aristotelian account, strictly speaking) belongs to a pre-Socratic idiom. However, while the temporal distance between Anaximander and Aristotle is a matter of historical interest, historical distance cannot be used to bar the fecund association I am invoking, first because if we know anything of Anaximander it is because of Aristotle and his students, and more important, because the power of the notion of *archē* in the Greek world does not wane in the least, nor does its meaning undergo such radical transformation in the three hundred years that separate the two philosophers as to be altogether alien. As Jean-Pierre Vernant points out, what strikes Aristotle is the notion that infinity holds together a balance of contentious forces, so that "no individual element should be able to monopolize the *kratos* [power] and impose its domination over the world. The primacy [*archē*] that Anaximander grants to *apeiron* aims to guarantee the permanence of an egalitarian order in which opposing powers are balanced against one another in such a way that if one of them is dominant for a moment, it is then in its turn dominated, if any one of them advances and extends itself beyond its limits it then recedes as much as it has advanced, yielding to its opposite."[16] In this respect, Vernant goes on to say (reading both Aristotle and Simplicius), infinity cannot be seen as one element among the many opposing elements of the cosmos, but precisely as the intermediary between the elements, what mediates them and is, by the same word (*meson*), in the middle of them: the mediating space of the elements—the *medium* of a limitless abyssal terrain—on which the limit and capacity for self-limitation in every element is tested (drawn and redrawn, broken and reconstituted).

In other words, the limitless is a mediatory field that enables limits to be self-instituted. The very constitution of the middle is itself a groundless condition of autonomy. According to Anaximander's vision, the earth exists in the midst of infinity, situated thus and sustained because of the equilibrium produced by interminably contending and opposing forces, an equilibrium that is never static but constitutively dynamic, since if any one force achieves dominance, it must be immediately destroyed by an emergent opposing force, and so on. In this infinite dynamic, the earth is otherwise *hypo mēdenos kratoumenē*, that is, literally "held by nothing" but also (equally literally) "beholden to no one," not dominated (*kratoumenē*) by anything, independent, autonomous (Vernant, 186, 192). That is, in the midst (*meson*) of the infinite universe, the *kratos* of the earth is self-authorized *dynamis*—there is no better evidence of the social imaginary of the democratic polis than the political hue of this language of cosmological physics. Indeed, Anaximander's physics marks the first instance of understanding the suspension of the earth in groundless space, by "spatial" equilibrium, a remarkable intellectual discovery given that his configuration of how the earth can hold itself suspended happens without a theory of gravity, or more precisely, without mathematizing the phenomenon of gravity.

Moreover, the significance of the middle—*meson*—is not only figurative, as mediating space, but geometric, as central space, in relation to which all elements, by virtue of the balance that they are thus pressed upon to sustain, are equidistant, or as Vernant (thinking in political terms) hastens to add, in a condition of *isonomia*: "It can thus be said of the centre, as of the *apeiron*, that it represents not so much a particular point in cosmic space, an *idion*, but the common mediator among all the points in space, a *koinon*, to which they all refer equally and from which they are all measured" (Vernant, 206–7). *Idion* and *koinon* are related to each other by a mutual irreconcilable otherness—something that cannot possibly be conveyed by their plausible translation as *self-same* and *collective-common*, respectively. This incapacity of translation encapsulates the profound difference between the Athenian democratic imaginary and the imaginary of today's so-called liberal democracies, in which any notion of the collective is configured by some sort of phantasmatic multiplication of the individual.

Although in Anaximander's language *archē* and *dikē* pertain to cosmology, their political meaning is unquestionable, not only because we know them to be explicitly political terms in subsequent phases of Greek society but also because the constitutive emergence of the polis as a specific mode of social organization takes place, before it even becomes democratic in Athens, within and through the same social imaginary that enables Anaximander's cosmology and in the same geography. There is a long discussion about the relation of pre-Socratic cosmologies to concurrent political structures, from Nietzsche and Heidegger to Werner Jaeger and beyond. Gregory Vlastos, whose philosophical reading of the fragment is celebrated, disputes that Anaximander's categories can be translated to political terms, even if they represent the first instance of a detheologizing process in philosophy. Vlastos's announced impetus is to correct Jaeger. However, his philosophical interpretation of the fragment ends up confirming Vernant's, for whom the political significance of Anaximander's cosmology is unquestionable.[17] In their seminal structuralist study of Cleisthenes's democratic reforms, Pierre Lévêque and Pierre Vidal-Naquet have stated the issue succinctly: "The problem to discover is whether Cleisthenes' *isonomia* and the representation of the cosmos as it appears to the Miletians are two phenomena that, although parallel, do not have any common link or whether, on the contrary, the mental universe of Anaximander was of a kind to be understood by the founder of the new city."[18]

This is not some pedantic philosophical issue. We are talking of an archaic world whose cosmological understanding cannot be divorced from its political imaginary on grounds of some sort of epistemological or disciplinary difference. In such a world, it is not far-fetched to argue that a politics, and even an ethics, can in fact rise out of physics, which would not at all mean an argument on the basis of natural law. Anaximander's language articulates a field of observation of whatever exists around the observer, who is simultaneously the thinker and the poet—this is precisely the mark of its archaic epistemology. Whatever exists around includes, of course, even the most distant things—the sea, the sky, the stars. The Anaximander fragment has been called the first instance of a naturalist way of thinking because it places whatever is based on observation and probable measurement at the center of philosophical/poetic speculation. But the very first level of observation is actually anthropological—Anaximander was in fact the first to speculate that all life, including human life, emerged from the sea—meaning specifically what happens to the human body: decay and then death. This is understood to be a natural condition. There is nothing peculiar about it; it is a brutal fact like any other fact, just as water is a fact. So, from this standpoint, what would be called political or ethical rules, which pertain to how human beings interact and live together, are predicated on a brutal natural condition—yet, I repeat, not in a deterministic way, not as natural law.

So, it is possible to say that because *human-being* is part of nature like any other, no better no worse, specific in its difference but like any other material specificity in the universe, *human-being* becomes an indication (not a model) of how everything works. In our time, we recognize the molecular association of everything in the universe, and yet we still dissociate the human from the nonhuman. But stars too are actually finite, like *human-being*; all matter decays. The infinite and the finite are the ways of the cosmos. And so, the terms for justice or injustice are literally of existential cosmological significance. It is really unjust that we die. Even more so, it is really unjust that we live, for this means that we die. But it is not death that signifies injustice, because this thought leads to the desire for an afterlife. It is life itself that signifies injustice because it interrupts the universal infinite fold. We die because our coming-to-be, our birth, tears through the fold of the infinite. As finite creatures necessarily come into being this beautiful and perfect, even if incomplete, infinite that generates them is disrupted. Our death is a measure of this cost and its payment: a retribution for the sheer fact that we have come to be. And yet, this punishment signifies a return to the fold, to nonbeing as space of the infinite from which (re)generation will come forth again, ad infinitum.

No doubt, only an archaic civilization could think this way: imagining a circular process that is not mere reiteration or reproduction of the same, but rather a circle that arises from/results in/exists on account of a disruption and conceives generation as a rupturing leap from nonbeing into being and back. Nowadays we would consider this thinking poetic. And it is—not only because the fragment ends on the phrase "putting it rather poetically," which could easily be a later interpolation, but also because *poiēsis* means creation of forms and thus belongs to that same language of physics. In turn, this is the epitome of the creative/destructive capacity of the human animal: observation and measurement are already modes of transforming material elements into conditions of life.

There is enough evidence to argue that the institution of the polis, as a radical space of isonomy and *isēgoria* (equality of speech) long before the Cleisthenes reforms in Athens, was actualized in the Ionian societies from which what we call pre-Socratic thinking emerged. A cosmology of groundless mediation and a geometry of equidistance from a central point are the essential registers that permeate all aspects of the city, from its architectural planning to the organization of its domestic space. Vernant specifically argues that the centrality of the agora in Athens is not due to some economic principle in the modern sense (the centrality of the market place in the exchange of goods and ideas) but harkens back to the primitive circle of warriors (as described by Homer), in which the man who speaks takes a position at the center of the circle of equals and returns to the circle for the next man to step into the middle and so on. Likewise, he goes on, once the polis is instituted as a new mode of social organization, the hearth—the sacred space in every house that resides at the center and is implanted in the earth—is reconfigured as common hearth (*hestia koinē*) and placed in the center of the agora space, now identified explicitly as a *political* symbol devoted to no divinity and thereby desacralized (Vernant, 183–89).

Vernant points to Hippodamus of Miletus, fellow citizen to Anaximander but a century later, as the architect of the first polis based on an agora space at the center of a circular construction, adding that, although an architect, Hippodamus was indeed a political theorist (185). This geometrical imaginary of the polis can be said to be at work also in the ideal architecture of Vitruvius, according to which the city's center must be open to ventilation by a series of radial streets in a circle around it. But the speed with which the social-historical field changes in less than a century between Cleisthenes and Hippodamus is remarkable. Lévêque and Vidal-Naquet point out that the urban geometry of Hippodamus already signals the way to a philosophical abstraction that becomes independent of the political, whose ultimate trajectory eventually leads to the Platonic architectural ideal that restores sacred space as the center of the polis (*Cleisthenes*, 73–97). In the end, for all the remarkable capacity of the Greek philosophical mind to mathematize the world, the most important legacy of the Greek democratic mind is that the political is indeed incalculable.

This geometrics of *meson*, of mediation and middle, which irreparably alters any understanding of *archē* as the fixed point of origin and primary rule, operates in another often quoted instance in Aristotle: "A citizen is simply determined, above all other matters, in sharing/participating [*metechein*] in judgment [*krisis*] and rule [*archē*]" (*Politics*, Book III, 1275a, 22-25). This phrase demonstrates in the language itself not only how *archē* is indeed not constituted as a primordial whole—that it is in fact cleft, permeated by *différance* both as origin and as principle—but that it is also, by virtue of that permeability, a condition of mediation. The citizen does not possess or occupy (*katechein*) rule/origin (*archē*), but shares (*metechein*) in rule/origin. Considering the etymology, one could argue that *metechein* means also one "exists within it," or literally, one "permeates its possession" or, even more precisely, one "enters a medium of this possession." But it is not only this permeation/mediation that disrupts the illusion of a primordial and integral *archē*, or that it displaces its possession of the origin. It is also that, insofar as *archē* becomes a matter of share (*metochē*), it is simultaneously mediated and pluralized. Democratic *archē* can only be shared. If not shared, it does not exist. It sounds self-evident, but we better take seriously what it means for it not to exist. In addition, by virtue of the same language, democratic *archē* is also constitutively mediated by the transient community that shares in power. The very institutions of *isonomia* and *isēgoria* signify and *actualize* this mediation of *archē* achieved by the sharing of power. It is worth quoting Vernant here at length:

> *Archē* [in the polis] was no longer concentrated in a single figure at the apex of the social structure, but was distributed equally throughout the entire realm of public life, in that common space where the city had its center, its *meson*. Sovereignty passed from one group to another, from one individual to another, in a regular cycle, so that command and obedience, rather than being opposed to each other as two absolutes, became the two inseparable aspects of one reversible relationship. Under the law of *isonomia*, the social realm has the form of a centered and circular *cosmos*, in which each citizen, because he was like all the others, would have to cover the entire circuit as time went round, successively occupying and surrendering each of the symmetrical positions that made up civic space.[19]

Insofar as *one* (absolute singular) cannot occupy (*katechein*) this *archē*—which is not to say that no one occupies this *archē*—one (generic impersonal and substitutable singular) traverses (*metechein*) this *archē*: the *archē* becomes a shared space of mediation that thereby disrupts the constitution or reconstitution of absolute singular (literally, monarchical) rule/origin.[20]

We thus reach the paradoxical situation, by modern logic, where what begins is already in the midst of what exists. A point of departure (and governing principle) is permeated by forces that can never be accounted for singularly, one by one, but together form the abyssal point of emergence, the opening in the infinite that creates this midst in what exists. But also, what exists is, as such (if this can even be said), indeterminable, impossible to subject to any singular origin, any singular reason for being, because it, too, exists within the infinite. The only thing that can be said about what exists is that it exists so as to cease existing; the only way to determine that something exists is because its existence is finite. Only insofar as it has a definite end (*telos*) can one understand that what exists has a beginning (*archē*): finitude is the only rule (*archē*) of existence.

As a profound attempt to create meaning out of meaninglessness, while neither denying meaninglessness nor seeking to transcend it, this orientation may be called philosophical but is profoundly political, not only because it belongs to the social imaginary institution of the polis, but because it expresses an elemental struggle against heteronomous determination beyond the strictly physical realm. We can think of this another way. If in the first instance Anaximander's fragment entails a specific conceptualization of *physis*, in the last instance—as it becomes comprehensible within a social historical frame—it also conceptualizes a certain *nomos*. *Physis* is not nature as a given, in the way that modern thought (moral, religious, scientific) has configured it. It is literally a condition of emergence (the verb *phyein* means to sprout, to surge forth) out of an indeterminate abyssal infinite, which cannot quite be called source, at least not source as *Ursprung*. *Physis* is not a state of things as they are, but an interminable flux of generation and degeneration (*phthora*), literally a dynamic of living (and of course, dying) being. This dynamic sense of *physis* stipulates that it bears in itself a *nomos*—while the reverse is inconceivable—a mode in nature by which the cosmos is regulated and balanced, by which justice is achieved. The ordinance of time (*kata tou chronou tixin*) expresses the necessity (*kata to chreōn*) of finitude which thereby preserves the possibility of interminable generation (*archē*) from the matrix of the infinite.

The injustice does not reside in the struggle between the infinite and the finite, the indeterminate and the determined, as if they are two polarities as different universes. The struggle takes place within the infinite; what is determined to be (to live and die) emerges as determined within the interminable and indeterminable *to-be*, as Castoriadis would put it (*à-être*).[21] The paradoxical figure of the ontological injustice of death being at the same time a reconstitution of the order of the infinite, therefore a gesture of justice against the injustice of existence disrupting the infinite fold, suggests a social imaginary that takes irrevocable death as ultimate limit of living being, the only untranscendable limit that thereby frees life from any other imposed limits. (Where limits, we might also want to write determinations.) It may seem then that heteronomy is removed from the realm of necessity in the course of one's life and relegated to one and only place: death. But in death there is no *nomos* strictly speaking. *Nomos* occurs and has meaning only in the course of living. So, the untranscendable limit of death is not the last instance of a naturalized heteronomy, but the irrevocable limit point that denaturalizes heteronomy altogether. From this perspective, limits or determinations in the course of one's life are open to becoming a matter of self-knowledge, self-determination, autonomy—in the strictest sense of determining the question of what *nomos* is within one's conditions of living. Both Sandywell and Castoriadis point out the *co-incidence* between Anaximander's fragment and the Aeschylean imagination in *Prometheus Bound*, specifically the notion of *physis* subject to (or crossed by) *nomos*, thereby opening the path for the creation of an autonomous life in a tragic universe (Sandywell, 161; Castoriadis, *Ce qui fait la Grèce*, 113).

Incidentally, I should add that by Anaximander's time, as opposed to Homer's or Hesiod's, the Greek world is marked by two crucial emergences/institutions: the collapse of the political order of tribal kinship and the spread of alphabetic writing. *Nomos* gains by being written and displayed. Although carved in stone it is nonetheless *not written in stone*, according to the inherited biblical metaphor, because it is precisely its overt appearance—its coming out into the radiance of *phainesthai*—that enables it to be reviewed and revised, questioned and altered. On the contrary, as is famously claimed by Antigone, what remains "unwritten" tends to take the meaning of "written in stone," that is, permanent and unalterable sacred custom (Sandywell, 159).[22]

Later in the *Politics* (Book VI, 1317b), Aristotle reiterates his understanding of the undoing of *archē* as singularity and primacy by explicitly connecting democracy to the institution of existential liberty (*eleutheria*). Against all inherited notions that the concept of "individual liberty" emerges in Enlightenment individualism and liberalism in the eighteenth century, one finds in Aristotle that the liberty of living as one likes (*to zēn hos bouletaii tis*)—for to live not as one likes is precisely the condition of being a slave—is an essential element of democratic *archē*. Living as one likes, as a condition of being, is expressed *politically* in the desire not to be ruled by anyone (*enteūthen elēluthe to mē archesthai, malista men hypo mēdenos*)—"from there arises [the desire for] not being ruled, indeed by no one"), or, if that is not possible, to rule and be ruled in turn (*ei de mē, kata meros*). In other words, the necessity of sharing rule (of ruling as the practice of knowing how to be ruled) is predicated on the desire not to be ruled at all. Having said that however, it depends on the recognition that this desire is possible only as an existential desire—the prerequisite of an ontological freedom—since the coexistence of free citizens that makes up the polis makes some institution of rule necessary. We can also think of it in reverse: refusal to be ruled existentially can only be actualized *politically* in sharing rule (*metekhein tēs arkhēs*), in knowing how to be ruled. This only makes sense if we abolish our preconception that "being ruled" means "having no power." In democracy, *being ruled means having power*—not as some sort of clientelist electorate or the alleged agency of public opinion as happens routinely in contemporary liberal oligarchies, but insofar as the decision to be ruled is made autonomously, in full cognizance of the fact that this is a decision made by the plurality of rulers, since rule, or more precisely self-rule, is shared by all.

There is a curious configuration here where the self is radicalized as an autonomous entity and yet, simultaneously, pluralized and shared according to the isonomy of the polity. It would be erroneous to consider this along the lines of the divide between public and private, whereby one refuses to be governed in the private sphere and submits to government in the public sphere. This is a purely liberal formulation. Neither is it, however, akin to Kant's pious reversal—freedom of thought and speech in the public sphere, obedience to the (moral) law in the private sphere—because, although *oikos* and *agora* are distinct spaces, in the Athenian imaginary there is no stipulated separation between the ethical (private) and the political (public). One's existential condition of freedom is a matter of *physis*, while the political enactment of freedom is a matter of *nomos*. *Physis* and *nomos* are not contradictory; they are coextensive cosmological crossings permeating the entire ancient Greek imaginary.

Similarly, the relation between ruler and ruled is not simply dialectical; it belongs to the order of *co-incidence*. It is by this logic of *co-incidence* that I speak of anarchy, to return to my first thesis: *anarchy is the* archē *of democracy*. The term literally means the impossibility of fully constituted (or once-and-for-all instituted) *archē*, both as point of origin and as point of governance. It does not mean the refusal of governance or the refusal of principle—at least, not when it comes to politics in a democracy.

In Herodotus, there is the famous episode of the three Persian princes, who are discussing the form of power that the Persian kingdom must have in the wake of the reign of Cambyses. As has been amply pointed out, Herodotus is here enacting an allegorical exercise to discuss different modes of politics. This is a theatrical exercise, and despite the fact that the actors are Persians, the dramaturgy is Greek. And so is the matter enacted. It is highly unlikely that three Persian princes would conduct a debate over which political mode would be the best to succeed the death of the king. Moreover, we know that Herodotus made a sojourn in Athens c. 447-443 BCE (in Periclean times, as the Parthenon was being built), and we may just as well imagine, for the sake of the argument, that this specific scene could have been publicly performed for the benefit and interrogation of the Athenians. (It is known from Plutarch that the Athenians granted Herodotus a financial award in recognition of his achievements.) The theatrical debate as to which mode of rule was preferable (democracy, oligarchy, monarchy) itself deserves a close reading, for it bears considerable rhetorical and political subtlety. Most striking, however, is the concluding phrase by Otanis (the advocate of democracy), who, upon facing the agreed-upon decision (by majority) that the preferable solution is monarchy, decides to withdraw his name from the process of succession to the throne by famously declaring "I want neither to rule nor to be ruled [*oute archein oute archesthai ethelō*]" (*Histories*, Book III, 80-84).

This phrase in Herodotus is often identified as an expression of anarchist sentiment. This is absurd in any strictly political sense. I take it to be the mere expression of the desire to be exempted from the political, literally an option to withdraw into the private sphere. Otanis deliberately opts out of any participation in government, and in return he and his family gain a sort of asylum, a freedom in a state of exception established by a certain rule—a rule of the game, a convention—but a rule of an Other nonetheless. For even if it is Otanis's own decision to opt out, the survival of the agreement he brokers is henceforth predicated on the good will of another, the one (the monarch) who will come to rule.

In the discussion that takes place before the agreement, Otanis defends the option of democratic politics, not using the name "democracy," however, but *isonomia*, a notion that historically precedes democracy in name. Although it is generally accepted that democracy is first explicitly articulated in Aeschylus's *Suppliants* in 464 BCE (*dēmou kratousa kheir*, "the people's hand of power"), the name itself does not appear until later, which is why Herodotus does not use it here.

Lévêque and Vidal-Naquet call the word democracy "philologically anomalous" in relation to the various faces of *archē* (monarchy, oligarchy), which by itself signifies an entirely different order where there is no *archē* as reigning first principle, where *archē* is found in the midst (*meson*) of power (*kratos*) shared among equals (*Cleisthenes*, 150). Thus, they underline *isonomia* as the operative word for democratic rule, a quintessentially political notion that first appears specifically as the name of the regime that overtakes the institution of tyranny. Herodotus, again, is a reliable and revealing reference. In recounting the overthrow of the tyranny of Polykrates of Samos (c. 518 BCE), he explicitly denotes *isonomia* as the setting of *archē* in the middle: *es meson tēn archēn titheis* (*Histories*, Book III, 142).[23]

Otanis's critique of monarchy is precisely that it engages the law from a constitutive position of hubris—this is the word that Herodotus uses. By occupying the law absolutely, monarchy exceeds, violates, and thus annihilates the law. There is indeed a subtle but definitive shift in the language from *archē* to *nomos* (monarchy to isonomy), for democracy is qualitatively other to monarchy not merely by the fact that rule is exercised by the multitude (*plēthos*) as opposed to the rule of the one, but that rule (*archē*) is subject to law (*nomos*) according to the essential significance of the source verb *nemein*: divided, apportioned, allotted, mediated, shared. Although there can be rule of the one (*monarchia*), there can never be law of the one in any manner of speaking; the word *mononomia* does not exist in the Greek vocabulary. Otanis's final decision, however, is ultimately a rejection of the democratic politics he espouses, for no community, no polis and no *dēmos*, can be constituted on the basis of refusal to rule and be ruled. It is, moreover, a blatant violation of isonomy in that Otanis's decision pertains to himself only (his family is literally his property, proper to him). It is, if you will, an option for *idion* over *koinon*, thereby positing the exclusive privilege of just one: a monologic position that is, strictly speaking, monarchic, even if in name anarchic.

In other words, despite Otanis's overt naming of his decision, his position is actually not anarchic because anarchy, in the way I am defining it, can exist only *against* the provenance of the One (the singularity of *archē* as origin and rule). Moreover, as a political position, anarchy is not a matter of personal desire; it is an investment in a specific signification of *archē*, whereby the right to rule is a plural, shared, yet contentious affair. Anarchy can never be linked to some apolitical position, to the voiding of *archē*, whereby the right to rule is left to the others.[24] In that sense, too, anarchy is the *archē* of democracy.

DEMOCRACY IS THE REGIME OF THE LIVING

Let us now shift gears in historical context in order to discuss specifically, from another angle bearing the full imprint of democracy's modernity, the significance of resisting this business of leaving rule to others. I turn to an exemplary text of the radical Enlightenment, perhaps the only text that entwines the American and the French Revolutionary experience, Thomas Paine's famous polemic dismantling of Edmund Burke. This text belongs to the great tradition of revolutionary pamphlets, a genre that encapsulates the force with which eighteenth-century ideas in Europe flourished in the production of a mass public. While the economic dimensions of this public do pertain to the formation of the capitalist market, let us recall that the *political* dimensions of this public are quintessential in the invocation of democratic action by retrieving a specific imaginary of social organization, the polis, in which the originary notion of the market (*agora*) was first and foremost a political and intellectual space—the economic being grounded, paradoxically for us moderns (but not at all paradoxically, given the initial instance of its naming), in the *oikos*, the private space of communal binding, the hearth of kinship and relation to land.

Recent work that seeks to place the legacy of the political in modernity within the legacy of the economic falters on two specific points: (1) it elevates the governmental elements of *oikonomia* (the rules of administering a household) to the status of the political, thereby literally domesticating and effectively depoliticizing the political; (2) it assumes that the politics of modernity (at least, in the West) is determined solely by the *oikonomia* of sovereignty developed in Christian imperial modes (from early Byzantium onward), thereby not only theologizing the political but also erasing from the political its original pagan-cosmic and specifically popular-revolutionary (democratic) dimensions.[25] The consequence of this trajectory of thinking is not only to underestimate the advent of capitalism as a radical rupture in the social imaginary at an anthropological scale, but also, as a result, to occlude the fact that the only real enemy of capitalism—the existential enemy—is radical democracy.

Paine's pamphlet is called very simply (and I think deceptively) *Rights of Man* (1791). I say deceptively, because we have inherited the idea that the notion "the Rights of Man" bears some timeless and unshakeable structure, as if indeed these rights are given by God—which might as well be the case, since the instrumental intention (so as not to say the very epistemology that authorizes it) is for them to take over God's place, God's law. But Paine's standpoint is in fact the exact opposite. He is, of course, an avowed enemy of God, but for our purposes here more than that he is the enemy of timelessness, which he correctly discerns all over Burke's key notion of "ancestry" or "inheritance" and which he goes so far as to call, in a brilliant turn of phrase that I very much applaud, "the idol of Divine Right."[26] Paine argues that Burke's ancestry, bearing down with the full force of an ensconced past, unfurls a pall of eternal presence, a presence that annihilates a sense of the *present*. Instead, he argues for an uncompromisingly radical present, indeed a present tense of poiētic-political action, in what is an exemplary expression of modernity several decades before the manifesto of modernity, Charles Baudelaire's famous essay "The Painter of Modern Life" (1859). Let me just float a few pointed quotations from Paine:

> Every age and generation must be as free to act for itself, *in all cases*, as the ages and generations that preceded it. The vanity and presumption of governing beyond the grave, is the most ridiculous and insolent of all tyrannies. Man has no property in man; neither has any generation a property in the generations which are to follow.
>
> Every generation is, and must be, competent to all the purposes which its occasions require. It is the living, and not the dead, that are to be accommodated. When man ceases to be, his power and his wants cease with him; and having no longer any participation in the concerns of this world, he has no longer any authority in directing who shall be its governors, or how its government shall be organized, or how administered.
>
> I am contending for the rights of the *living*, and against their being willed away, and controlled and contracted for, by the manuscript assumed authority of the dead. (42)

Paine argues straight on that, although the Rights of Man bear, by the language itself, a kind of anthropological primacy (which is what, in Thomas Jefferson's language, makes them inalienable), they are nothing—that is to say, they are mere principle, but that's the point: *mere principle is nothing when it does not confront the responsibility of making history*—they are nothing if they don't belong to the generation, the age, that enacts them and is enacted by them, the generation that empowers them and is empowered by them. The Rights of Man cannot be possessed once and for all, nor are they themselves possessed by authority of time immemorial. They are indeed configured in the literally radical vein that Marx invoked when thinking of humanity itself, as we discussed in the previous essay: "To be radical is to go to the root of the matter. For humanity, however, the root is humanity itself." Precisely because the Rights of Man are not authorized by God, or any other externality, they are groundless in their (self-)authorization. They express the *co-incidence* of subject/object and insofar as "Man" is subjected to the requisite class, gender, and race critique post its revolutionary Enlightenment legacy, this subject/object is always mutable—always in-the-making as a self-altering entity.[27]

For the same reason, precisely because these rights are authorized by a certain anthropology (as opposed to a certain theology), which is also their object—to be generated, defended, safeguarded—they are also compromised, as it were, by finitude. They are not timeless and immortal; they are perpetually threatened by death, as is every single historical being, and indeed it is almost banal, historically speaking, to recollect how consistently and how repeatedly the rights of humans all over this planet have died and are dying right this minute. Dying a real death, a death as real as the bodies these rights have not managed to protect, bodies that are laid to waste, killed and abandoned—what horrific irony!—oftentimes in the name of these rights, as the price extracted over catastrophes and wars waged in the name of these rights.

So, Paine is remarkably aware of how paramount it is, how required of any sort of revolutionary thinking, that the greatest threat against the Rights of Man is precisely to deny that indeed they die. Because then something enormously perverse takes place. The deniers of this worldliness of rights—who, as mortal humans, cannot but in fact depart this world—succeed in immortalizing themselves by sustaining their power from an otherworldly position ("having no longer any participation in the concerns of this world, [they wield] authority in directing who shall be its governors") by preserving structures of power that are to rule by institution alone, uninterrogated and disembodied institution, the tyranny of ancestry: "The vanity and presumption of governing beyond the grave, is the most ridiculous and insolent of all tyrannies." Governing beyond the grave condemns these rights to the grave—this is what Paine means. And he counters with the argument that to acknowledge the finitude of oneself in this world is to acknowledge the finite relation one has with one's time, with one's making of history—a making that, in a revolutionary sense, is always also an unmaking. To acknowledge such finitude is precisely to enable the renewal of rights, their historical transformation in the hands of the living, according to the demands of the living, and for the sake of the living.

This idea is very much in the air at the time. We see it in Article 28 of the 1793 French Constitution as an essential lawmaking stipulation: "A people always has a right to review, reform, and amend its constitution. One generation may not subject future generations to its laws." Notable also is Thomas Jefferson's lengthy advocacy of each generation's absolute right to self-determination in a letter to James Madison, sent from Paris just a couple of months after the outbreak of the French Revolution (September 6, 1789). Jefferson speaks here as an economist and a naturalist simultaneously, framing the argument in terms of both the injustice of inheriting "debts and incumbrances" and the natural distinction between generations: "The earth belongs in usufruct to the living, and the dead have neither powers nor rights over it.... No generation can contract debts greater than may be paid during the course of its own existence.... Between society and society, or generation and generation, there is no municipal obligation, no umpire but the law of nature, [and] by the law of nature, one generation is to another as one independent nation to another.... No society can make a perpetual constitution, or even a perpetual law. The earth belongs always to the living generation."[28]

Of course, whatever Jefferson says excludes the fact of slave labor over the land. The concept of "living"—not to mention simply the concept "people" or "society"—pertains only to those who have political rights, even if behind this juridical assessment resides a transcendental investment in eternal rights, as was famously phrased in the Declaration of Independence by Jefferson's own hand. African slaves have no rights, whether real or transcendental. They are not people, and therefore any distinction between their being alive or dead is made impossible. They are the living dead, and all notions of generation, of both finitude and infinity (eternity), are barred from their realm of definition. But this is Jefferson's own limitation to the degree that he belongs to the specific liberal bourgeois and settler-colonial imaginary that founded the United States. It is a historically created limitation and, in this respect, just as finite: just as it is made it can be unmade, which is also to say, whatever it has made can be unmade. Not strangely, Jefferson's limitation is subjected to his own principle and therefore need not be given further attention as such. The principle about the constitutional power of the living is not nullified, whatever was the specific and limited content that Jefferson or Paine imagined and attributed to it.

The gist of the argument brings out in the open the politics that permeates society's perpetual concern with the significance of the dead in the world of the living: the undeconstructible impetus for memorialization that we encounter in every society in human history. Paine's gesture constitutes a radical political outing of the mechanisms of established power in precisely this anthropological domain. Because, contrary to the tendency of society's institutions to engage in a sort of repetition-compulsion of memorialization in order to reproduce their status quo (the apex of which, in modern societies, is found in nationalism and its notorious rituals of remembrance of dead heroes), Paine conducts this gesture from the standpoint of enriching the world of the living through the desacralized memory of the no longer living. From my standpoint, as I write against narratives of sacralization that I take to be narrative denials of history (hence, dangerous to one's historical relation to the world), this is a priority.

Memorialization of historical authority must be conducted against the grain of our understandable desire to render the dead sacred. I say this not because I dispute or disavow attributing to human life the gravity it deserves by honoring its passing. I say it motivated precisely by the desire to do justice to the very history marked by the passing of those who had once made history. Or, putting it otherwise, to do justice to the fact that those who are now dead were once living *in the world*, a world whose significance, as social-historical sphere, must be found in the *worldly* work of the living: the now living and the living to come, each in their own time and place. I also say this in full cognizance of the fact that the adjudication of life—of what is living and what is dead; of what is worth living and dying and what is denied the actuality of living and the value or grievability of dying—has never been impartial. It is always a political matter, and a crucial problem for democracy specifically since the time of *Antigone*. This is precisely the point of the Black Lives Matter intervention in today's racist world: black life has been prejudicially marked and unjustly measured for centuries. And by the same token, so has their death: in a racist society black people's lives are not recognized as lives, and therefore their deaths are not even registered, not to mention properly mourned and memorialized.

To go even further and in reference to the specific text I am examining: only insofar as the Rights of Man are deprived of the sacred ancestral authority of the dead can they overcome their allegedly unmarked gendering, the fact that gender markings are meant to disappear under the (un)mark of the universal. It was after all the women of living generations of the French Revolution's future (nearly two centuries later) who came to dismantle the falsely universal presumptions of the Rights of Man, just as in the interim, a century before, Marx had demonstrated the unmarked class presumption of the notion in the context of the living conditions of the 1848 insurrections and the Paris Commune. But what better, what more concise, expression of the notion that rights are established in the arena of historical finitude than the famous utterance by Olympe de Gouges, whose 1791 *Declaration of the Rights of Woman and Citizen* is contemporaneous to Paine's pamphlet: "if women have a right to die on the scaffold, they have a right to speak in the Assembly." The right to death, in this respect, is perfectly present as the right that authorizes living and acting freely for the sake of the living, not some transcendental right of access to the authority of ancestry. At the same time, as Jacques Rancière points out, it undoes women's confinement to particularity, the particularity of domestic life, which, in the realm of liberal universal rights announced in the Declaration, is indeed bare life.[29]

The codification of the Rights of Man according to the transcendental guarantee of constitutional language is what Paine so evocatively names "the manuscript assumed authority of the dead." It is worth remembering that the last Article of the 1793 French Constitution (two years after Paine's pamphlet) reads as follows: "When the government violates the rights of the people, insurrection is for the people, and for every portion thereof [*that is to say, any dissenting collectivity, even as minority*] the most sacred of rights and the most indispensable of duties." Barring here the revealing contradiction of pronouncing sacred the very rights that undo the sacred—this goes along with the problematic nature of secularization as a project unfinishable by definition, about which I have spoken elsewhere—this is an extraordinary gesture of self-undoing to be included in a constitution issued by a government, and it can only be a government of the people that can issue it. That it is still, by all historical standards, a utopian gesture—a gesture that found no place of historical expression, as the 1793 Constitution was never implemented, having been immediately deferred by Robespierre when he came to power on account of it to a kind of interminable suspension—testifies precisely to the nature of its imaginary. There has never been, at least not yet, a real government of the people, except on those extraordinary experiments in self-government in restricted spaces of social organization, all of them ill-fated and short-lived, from the Paris Commune to workers' councils, anarchist unions, and direct citizen action in various contexts of modern history worldwide.

What interests us here is specifically this notion of constitutional—in fact, constitutive—self-interrogation and self-alteration, despite the problematic language of the sacred. The last stipulation of the 1793 Constitution bears the full logic of Paine's critique of ancestry, including in this case the forged ancestry of the Revolutionary Constitution itself. If the law—for this, in the end, is the purported domain of *The Rights of Man and the Citizen*, not mere declaration of principles—is to challenge inherited structures of heteronomy, whether derived theologically or not, it must be open to its own finitude and dialectical undoing. The temporality of such dialectics is, on the one hand, a kind of radical present, the tenuous and ephemeral present of modernity, and on the other hand, a kind of equally tenuous—because riveted with risk, daring, and lack of guarantee—investment in the future: a future that, though it remains constitutively uncertain, must nonetheless be configured as an actual perspective, a standpoint of critique and interrogation of the present.[30]

This is the crucial meaning of Paine's contention on behalf of the living, of each living generation to have the right to determine itself, over and above the credits or deficits it has inherited, over and above the laws it has inherited: "Although laws made in one generation often continue in force through succeeding generations, yet they continue to derive their force from the consent of the living. A law not repealed continues in force, not because it *cannot* be repealed, but because it *is not* repealed; and the non-repealing passes for consent" (44). Notice that this does not suggest that each generation clear the board of instituted laws and significations and go back to zero—a zero point that, in any case, never exists in history. Rather, it clarifies, in no uncertain terms, that all existing institutions and significations hold no authority unless they are (re)authorized by those to whom they presently pertain. That is why revolutionary change can never be relegated to mere change of regime, the simple takeover of power: "A casual discontinuance of the *practice* of despotism is not a discontinuance of its *principles*" (21). To insist on "the consent of the living" is nothing more than what animates Paine's famous delineation of law as constituent power in the mere presence/assembly of the people: "The constitution of a country is not the act of its government, but of the people constituting a government" (71). This automatically deconstitutes the sacred character of a document that serves as the foundation of democratic law. One might say, it restores to this text its worldly character: the fact that it is created by people in specific conditions and that, in the end, it is the people who grant it authorization. Without the people, this document is literally empty, void.

Such radical insistence on the consent of the living is meant to guard against the probability that law will attain some sort of otherworldly perpetuity, as if the constitutive order of the law enacts mastery over the order of time. By returning temporality to the order of the law, Paine draws a clear distinction between natural rights—which in essence are encapsulated in the indisputable right to exist—from civil rights, which can never be anything other than what a particular *civitas* at a particular point in space and time orders into existence. What seems to be a condition of radical present time, of strictly controlling present time—the consent of the living—is actually an embrace of the full spectrum of time, past, present, and future, yet without abandoning oneself to time in a way that would render one out-of-time, a timeless, nonfinite being. From this standpoint, even if not spelled out directly, Paine's understanding of law's relation to time is anarchic at the core, for if constitutive (and constitutional) law must always be (re)authorized by the consent of the living and not by the manuscript authority of some dead founding fathers, this law is deprived of *archē*, in the temporal sense of the word, in order precisely to keep the political sense of the word open to contention.

In this specific sense, Paine's argument might belong to what Foucault called "anarcheology"—the sort of thinking that sees in the politics of the living an understanding of the nonnecessity of all power.[31] But there is a certain irony here, considering Foucault's title in relation to mine, for Foucault hinges this politics of the nonnecessity of power onto the necessity of truth-telling: as is pointed out by the editors, "on the government of the living" is not quite accurate as a title, for the title that best reflects the direction Foucault's research had taken at this point should be the "on the government of men by truth" (327). This phrase would be unacceptable to Paine, unless truth were to be tantamount to living itself. It is possible to consider truth in these terms if the notion of *parrhesia*, on which Foucault famously depends and elaborates, is understood to mean not simply truth-telling (*dire vrai*) but saying everything—and anything regardless, even the unsaid (*tout dire*). That is where the anarchical element resides.

Curiously, when Jeremy Bentham reiterates Edmund Burke's critique of the French Revolution a few years later in his own pamphlet *Anarchical Fallacies* (1796), a text that clearly has Paine's pamphlet as a target, he reiterates many of Paine's temporal concerns, but from the opposite side. Bentham's evident horror at the revolutionary project across the Channel is encapsulated in what he calls "the cultivation of a propensity to perpetual insurrection in time future":

> The revolution threw the government into the hands of the penners and adopters of this declaration [of the Rights of Man and the Citizen], which is the effect of insurrection; the grand object is to justify the cause. But by justifying it, they invite it: in justifying past insurrection, they plant and cultivate a propensity for perpetual insurrection in time future; they sow the seeds of anarchy broad-cast: in justifying the demolition of existing authorities, they undermine all future ones, their own consequently in number.... The logic of it is of one piece with its morality—a perpetual vein of nonsense, flowing from a perpetual abuse of words.[32]

I am interrupting here the already long quotation—which goes on to rant about the dismantling of meaning and abuse of language with signifying fallacies that reminds me of the panic with which professors of literature at one time faced the advent of deconstruction—because the gist is perfectly clear. The revolutionary logic of rights that bear no other authority but what is derived from the consent of the living is an affront to reason itself—and how could it not be for any person for whom reason coupled with ancestry has taken over the place of God in the social organization of a polity? What's interesting is that Bentham charges Paine—or the position that Paine holds—with the same concern: the abhorrent order of perpetuity. Here, the difference is quintessentially *political*. If we assume that both Paine and Bentham object to law depriving a polity of acting within its own time, what divides them is their political decision. One sides with the power of the people, generation after generation, making/authorizing its own laws, while the other sides with the order of some people to author and authorize laws that cannot be overturned by any action of any other people who rise up to challenge the constituted order. One is a defender of constituent power in its temporal finitude; the other is a defender of constituted power, ironically taken out of its frame of constitution into a sphere of temporal suspension.

In 1928, at the heart of the contentious uncertainty that would precipitate the demise of the Weimar Republic, Carl Schmitt will register an uncanny reiteration of Thomas Paine, entirely unwitting of course. Permit me to quote at length from *Verfassungslehre* what in Schmitt's overall oeuvre seems rather aberrant:

"People" is a concept that becomes present in the *public* sphere. The people appear only in the public, and they first produce the public generally. People and public exist together: no people without public and no public without people. By its *presence*, specifically, the people initiate the public. Only the present, truly assembled, people are the people who produce the public. The correct idea that supports Rousseau's famous thesis that the people cannot be represented rests on this truth. They cannot be represented because they must be *present*, and only something absent, not something present, may be represented. As a present, genuinely assembled people, they exist in the pure democracy with the greatest possible degree of identity.... The genuinely assembled people are first a people, and only the genuinely assembled people can do what pertains distinctly to the activity of the people.[33]

One would hardly expect to find in Schmitt the manifesto for the phenomenon of anticapitalist, antistatist assembly movements, which we saw in various societies around the planet in the second decade of the twenty-first century, but here it is. Most striking is not only the echo of Paine over the constituent power of real living people demanding to alter and create the law in real living time, but also the fact that in Paine's temporal figure of the radical present resides a spatial figure of radical presence. In this spatiotemporal *co-incidence* inheres the radical actuality of the constituent power of the living. This cannot be re-presented in the sense that it cannot be repeated, reiterated, reproduced, or indeed represented in the procedural/institutional form of liberalism. It can occur again an indeterminable number of times, but each time creating its own time and space, its own project, its own public. And "its own greatest possible degree of identity" says Schmitt, an identity, however, derived from and actualized only in its constituent moment, where it then leaves its mark in history—yes, to be memorialized, but also to be altered or outdone, celebrated or effaced, depended upon or abolished... The list is endless, as history is endless as long as human beings exist to make it and unmake it. And with no guarantees, for this is what history as the (poietic) work of the living and democracy as the regime of the living entail.

Of course, what I am describing would be anathema to Schmitt, who even in this case of identifying the constituent power of the people is seeking to establish the rule of sovereignty in both senses of the term: the *archē* of sovereignty and its master mechanism. In both senses, the meaning of rule is the same. Schmitt seeks to elucidate authority, and his light will always show it to be singular. In this respect, he cannot handle not only the interminable upturning without guarantees that is the poietic work of the living in democracy but also the differential forces of democracy. For Schmitt, the people's authority is no different than the monarch's (the dictator's): it is the sovereignty of the One. The plural and differential people, open to social difference and conflict, become the unitary People. It is a theologizing gesture, pure and simple, yet another way of making visible the invisible divinity he cannot imagine being without. By some profound and surely unwitting irony Schmitt's account of the people's constituent power echoes both the liberal fetish of "We, the People" and its eventual populist variants that always drive themselves by and toward the adoration of some leader. From this standpoint, Schmitt and Paine are divided by a chasm—and not just ideologically, but politically in a quintessential sense. Paine's regime of the living exposes the profound deception inherent in the (presumably objective) concept of legitimacy, which is always contingently authorized by whoever claims it, while Schmitt remains perfectly happy in his faith that legitimacy is the absolute element of the always monarchical sovereign, even if this might come occasionally in the name of the people. Needless to say, this latter iteration nullifies entirely the real power of the people.

THE CONSTITUENT VIOLENCE OF DEMOCRACY: THE LIBERAL ENCLOSURE

One might argue, against my example, that Paine's argument is drawn from a revolutionary occasion, under demands of extraordinarily altering violence, and that it cannot be supposed to sustain its meaning in the context of political institution, if the latter is understood as an affirmative process of legitimation. And unless we opt to restrict the definition of democracy to the realm of permanent negation, we cannot constitute its domain of inquiry on the basis of the revolutionary project alone. This assessment creates all kinds of complications, as we shall see. Having said that, I think that any consideration of democracy that resists the metaphysics of liberalism (conceived in the broadest sense) can never escape the fact—even in light of the necessity to create political institutions—that its revolutionary imaginary, and more specifically what has been called its constituent violence, remains a permanent problem at its core.

I return to the assertion I made at the outset. One of the most contentious dimensions in the peculiar entwinement of rule with law that characterizes radical democracy is the issue of violence as a mode of political action, over which always hovers the metaquestion of whether violence is a legitimate or illegitimate mode of political action. Accordingly, the issue of violence as political action would pertain both to rule and to law—for and against either or both.

Historically speaking, democracy has never been able to actualize itself without violence at some level—and this is always the violence of the living, regardless of what institutions might be inherited that produce an institutionalized violence. What is harder to determine, however, is whether this historical legacy may be due to an intrinsic condition: democracy's precarious, guaranteeless nature. In any case, discussion of political violence outside a democratic context is uninteresting—worthy of historical inquiry no doubt, but of little theoretical value. This is true about the question of legitimacy as well. If the law is monarchical, the question of the legitimacy of violence enacted in the name of this law is already decided. On the other hand, precisely because the basic tenets of liberal democracy claim to work beyond or even against violence, any commitment to a radical theorization of democracy that would challenge the limitations of so-called liberal democracy demands a retheorization of violence in relation to core conceptions of radical political action.

For all its failings, Hannah Arendt's essay *On Violence* (1969) is an important reference point in this discussion. The crux of Arendt's meditation resides in her distinction, or rather opposition, between violence and power, which is here theorized as a normative distinction, but which does emerge out of a deep historical reflection and no doubt historical experience of the predicament of revolutionary (and also antirevolutionary) politics for the duration of the twentieth century. Another instance, which may serve as somewhat of a precursor, remains her well-known preference (argued in *On Revolution*) for the American revolutionary process over the French one, precisely in terms of this relation between violence and power. The specific historical moment that contextualizes her direct focus on violence, however, deserves a moment of attention. It is not only a matter of Arendt responding directly to the invocations of violence by the student and antiwar movements of the late 1960s or the agonistic imaginary of New Left politics in general. It is also what she identifies, from the very start, as the basic battleground conditions of the moment: the fact that violence, as presumably revolutionary means, cannot be evaluated formally as an abstract concept of political or ethical theory, because, she argues, violence always bears a technology. At this particular historical moment, the technology is not merely destructive but catastrophic, and therefore any invocation of violence, which is at some sort of elementary level vehicle for radical social change, has to be calculated against the ultimately incalculable imaginary, technologically induced and produced, of total planetary annihilation.

This imaginary is indeed planetary by definition, regardless of whether it is recognized as such. It permeates every aspect of psychosocial life, no matter where one is situated in the social class ladder or ethnogeographical sphere. It concerns all men and women regardless, and it is racially blind, even against the inequities that remain. It is a self-destructive human reality whose purview is suprahuman, and it is planetary because its imaginary inheres the possibility of total annihilation of all life on this planet. Characteristically, Arendt identifies this rebellious generation that invokes a politics of violence with such ease as "those who hear the ticking."[34]

Although it is fair to say that for the latter part of the twentieth century the planetary conditions of radical politics were explicitly characterized as "politics after '68," it is also fair to say that this "after" is in effect an after without end, without conceivable closure or completeness, simultaneously present in the sense of consistent (so as not to say permanent) presence and at the same time noninstrumentally related to whatever end bears upon our own time: in short, a non-teleological after—which is also to say, an after without *archē*. Even the subsequent flashes of new radical politics—from Zapatista and then antiglobalization politics of Seattle and Genova in the 1990s to assembly movement politics of the first decade of the twenty-first century and the Black Lives Matter and Antifa politics of the present moment, all equally global politics in the utmost sense—have not overcome the inevitable comparison with "global '60s" politics, whose shorthand gathered together a fierce generational revolt with the legacy of anticolonial struggles worldwide.

What tends to be forgotten in these sorts of historical attributions is that the globality of radical politics emerges from an already formed framework of planetary annihilation. And while the initial imaginary of planetary annihilation is usually attributed to the MAD (mutual assured destruction) politics of the Cold War, the fact remains that it continues unabated (and indeed magnified beyond any scale conceivable in 1969, when Arendt was writing) to be our politics in the here-and-now. Indeed, the here-and-now would be in this sense configured as a temporal frame that trips up even the boldest historical accounts of recent decades, in the sense that it derives its meaning from the permanent potential of total annihilation that continues to permeate any sort of transformative politics since 1945. Spearheading this now, of course, is the politics that pertains to climate change in the face of what might already be irreversible ecological catastrophe. The causal imagination and the performative reality in all these imaginaries are the same.

Certainly no radical democratic politics can be conducted without some strategy for encountering and accounting for the clock ticking on the planet's future, whether it be nuclear or atmospheric catastrophe—the two are now perfectly entwined. This is an undeconstructible limit that conditions our present. The very least I would say about it is that we are forced to confront an epistemological limit condition for which we really have no historical or philosophical preparation. Which is to say—and this is alarming—that whatever our propositions, visions, or predictions of the future, they are reduced to mere fancies if they do not wrestle explicitly with this epistemological limit. In the end, although there is a great deal to discuss in relation to Arendt's meditation on violence as such, this particular dimension of planetary annihilation and its technological reality colors the entire epistemological horizon.

Arendt speaks indicatively of the late-'60s generation as the first one to be formed in the shadow of planetary annihilation. In what is a rather instrumental reflection on this point, she describes the peculiarity of a generation honed by an initial rejection of violence—precisely because in the 1950s this generation comes of age in America under the paranoid rituals of nuclear destruction and insipid "duck and cover" commands—which eventually turns around to attach itself, after nonviolent civil disobedience tactics during the civil rights era, to what she calls a "romanticized" image of political street violence reminiscent of nineteenth-century insurrection, with the Paris Commune emerging in this respect as a canonical precedent.

According to Arendt's assessment, the 1960s generation's switch from aversion to adoration of violence betrays a lamentable delusion. For even in the event that the presumed revolutionary energy unleashed by this sort of street violence does register as a bona fide political factor, she argues, what might be its constituent politics? What might be the instituting power that would lead it to actualize a certain social-political vision, to transform existing structures, to create new social formations? Arendt sets these up as rhetorical questions, for she has already decided the answer and, moreover, as Fred Moten's memorable critique of her position points out, she has decided thus by blatantly steamrolling over the altogether explicit racial parameters of violence in America.[35]

Arendt composes her argument on an assertion whose realism cannot be disputed and is very much the case today as well. At the crudest level of the violence game, this presumed revolutionary energy has to face a state machinery of supreme technological capacity—such that, militarily speaking, it makes class war (in the nineteenth-century militant sense) altogether untenable. A state that conducts a so-called politics of peace under the permanent capacity to blow up the entire planet surely does not need to exert itself too far to dismantle an intransigent youth movement that challenges the premises of this politics, international though this movement may be. The surgical brutality with which the FBI and local police throughout America assassinated Black Panther Party leaders and (via the infamous COINTELPRO, or counterintelligence program) annihilated even their most nonviolent operations in just two years (1969-1971) bears the unerasable signature of the liberal state's capacity for military violence against its own people, especially when the people actively politicize themselves in order to expose and challenge their conditions of exclusion.

I open an extended parenthesis here in order to properly historicize this issue. Around 2010, in what is now definitely a bygone era, television political analyst Rachel Maddow directed a similar argument against the altogether genuine delusions of Tea Party, NRA, or other right-wing constituencies to honor the Second Amendment (the right to bear arms) as a prerogative to defend against and indeed overthrow a tyrannical government (at that time, the Obama presidency). In typically acerbic mode, Maddow quipped that the constitutional law should be revised to "the right to bear nukes" and that the pursuit of such a right would no doubt precipitate a "new arms race between you and me and the 82nd Airborne."[36] Without diluting Maddow's sarcasm, let us note the extraordinary shift in American politics between the time of Arendt's intervention and now. In Arendt's time the idea that the Second Amendment signified an expressly political meaning—as a revolutionary remainder and safeguard against future government tyranny—was essentially a leftist argument. The Black Panthers actualized this notion in the most spectacular and practical sense. They were vilified as outlaws and were exterminated solely because the country's racist imaginary could not handle the spectacle of black men with guns. Perhaps along a straight line since then, the political meaning of the Second Amendment is now entirely occupied by alt-right nationalist ideologies, inarguably exacerbated by the racist incapacity to accept that a black man was elected president of the United States. Meanwhile, the extermination of black Americans, most of the time without guns whatsoever, continues unabated.

At the time I had thought, much to my embarrassment for the naïveté, that a truly radical move in mainstream media political analysis would be to remind various defenders of the Second Amendment of the Black Panthers, and not just of the right of black citizens to bear arms but of the fact that they actually did and were killed for it. What would happen, I wondered, if one brought a tape of Malcolm X's speech "The Ballot or the Bullet?" to a Tea Party meeting? Well, the ridiculous rationalism of this idea has been blatantly exposed in the Trump MAGA era—it would have been welcomed with a bullet. We surely did not need Trump for this realization, although there is no doubt that Trump, wittingly or not, unlocked the latent symbolic power of Second Amendment politics like no other. What matters is exactly this unlocking and what is found once the door is kicked open.

Until Trump came along to concentrate the backlash against the scandal of the first black president of the United States, the Second Amendment's revolutionary constitutional provision for the autonomy of militarized citizens (militia) against an autocratic government had been eclipsed by the individualist self-authorization to bear arms in order "to protect my property," which rose to prominence in the era of Wild West homesteading but was in place already from the first instance of colonization and extermination of the native peoples. Since the post-Civil War era of Reconstruction, this same attitude of "I am the law" indeed became law in expressly targeting the country's black population—the logic of defending property being left intact, as the notion of free black citizens (or worse, even simply persons) remained unfathomable to a great majority, even those on the winning side of the war. Eventually the law of capital took over as guns turned into pure commodity in a "free market" whose freedom was continuously buttressed by the ruse of constitutional right while driven by one of the purest instances of commodity fetishism in the world history of commodities.

Surely there is nothing peculiar about shifting significations because of altered social-historical conditions, except that in this case these significations, although triggered by historical particulars, are not sequential. As Donald Pease points out, they are asynchronously constellated in a permanent convergence of past, present, and imaginary future, which is the core imaginary of "being American" in its full racist glory.[37] Trump himself, but also the movement he exploited by granting it symbolic power as leader, epitomized exactly this fact. Pease homes in on this imaginary with incisive accuracy. He reminds us that beneath the national pedagogy of revolutionary Enlightenment, which conceived and authorized a constitutional regime of rights to liberty and equality, resides a story of settler colonial violence that has been consistently disavowed but has never been expunged. Even in those times when it is acknowledged as a historical fact (the extermination of the natives and the enslavement of Africans), it is seen as an aberration that has been properly redressed through the triumph of constitutional law. This is the great deception, Pease argues, animating the heart of American liberalism. In fact, it is the perfect *co-incidence* of liberalism with settler colonial violence that is the essence of the American national imaginary, all the more so *because of* liberalism's disavowal of this association. The right to bear arms in this regard is not some liberal right that follows the right to free speech, a right whose transcendental safeguard is some self-evident truth of humanity. Rather, it is an indelible remainder—and by this token, indelible reminder—of American democracy's *real* revolutionary foundation: not the overthrow of the British monarch for national independence, but the foundational claim of the colonial settlers to legitimate constituent violence over and above the legal constraints of constitutional law and the state's monopoly of violence. That is why Pease argues that the figure of the settler is not at all the figure of the citizen, or even subject, but an archetypal figure that may seem dormant but fiercely (re) emerges whenever there is a fissure in liberalism's presumed to be seamless self-regulating trajectory through time.

In this sense, the Second Amendment is a bomb implanted into the foundations of constitutional law as a legitimation of its abolition. It is a historical error for leftists to deny this fact, in the face of right-wing, gun-toting, NRA profit-driven propaganda about individual rights to gun ownership. We can imagine, from a left standpoint, that the Second Amendment can also be a source to appeal for legitimacy of a popular movement (radical democratic, antiracist, anticapitalist, etc.), but this would be possible only if it were understood to be a bomb that would need to be detonated against the entire institution. The desired object of destruction in this respect is mutual to both sides, even though this has *never* been avowed—and indeed may be impossible to avow as long as liberalism itself remains the chief imaginary of law and government in the United States. For the desired object of destruction on both sides is liberalism itself. With irreconcilably antagonistic political content, of course, but for the same reason: its sublime con game. Liberalism is complicit and mutually constitutive with settler colonial violence, if nothing else because it legitimized this violence by sanctifying it into the constitutional order of rights, which served in turn as the primary means of disavowing this complicity. For the alt-right, this disavowal creates an unnecessary filter that needs to be eliminated in order for white settler colonial privilege to be reinstated with perfect clarity. This is their response to what they call the Great Replacement, and it can be exercised only with insurrectionary violence, a glimpse of which we got in the events of January 6, 2021, that may turn out to be a mere rehearsal for new civil war violence in insurrections nationwide. For the left, liberalism's disavowal is also a filter, except in the opposite direction: it is an impediment against identifying settler colonial violence for what it is and how it works in the present—and combatting it directly. A symptom of this misidentification on the part of the left is also that the signifiers of insurrection have been entirely appropriated by the present incarnation of the colonial settler imaginary: the racist-nationalist right.

The imaginary undercurrent of originary settler colonial violence, which is now unabashedly surging, is continuously fed at a libidinal level by America's mind-boggling fetish for guns. Although statistics vary, more than half of the U.S. population is armed, while the number of guns in the hands of civilians are currently calculated to be around four hundred million, exceeding the actual population numbers. As gun laws are explicitly ever more driven by firearms industry profit and gun-slinging is ever more celebrated as existential fetish, the rate of gun ownership in American society is skyrocketing daily, extending rapidly to all strata of society and most alarmingly even to children. This libidinal investment of Americans in everything to do with guns—unlike any other society on the planet—needs also to be evaluated in itself, parallel to the foundational dimensions of colonial violence.

Although American society's "Wild West" mentality has been whitewashed by its association with the antecedent revolutionary action of musket carrying colonials in New England, it has nothing to do with what drove French sansculottes to sever the necks of aristocrat landowners. The fetishistic adoration of gun-slinging postures that encapsulates American violence is best described as *domestic violence*—I mean this literally, as violence pertaining to and emerging from the *oikos*, not the *dēmos*. It is about property first and foremost, not community, about what is proper to oneself in radical ego-closure—hence, the frequency of lone gunmen either taking the law in their own hands or indiscriminately massacring unknown others, including mere children. And it is not an accident that arbitrary mass shootings by lone gunmen are rarely conducted by women. The signification of domestic violence, in the way I use it here to mark the American social imaginary as such, is obviously gendered male; the fact that the number of women gun owners has recently skyrocketed does nothing to displace it. Thus, the constitutionally sanctioned claim of the settler colonial imaginary in its perfect racist Eden comes to meet the individual pathology of gun fetishism on the same ground: the violent expropriation of property and defense of ownership of land and things (who sometimes have been actual persons) in an abyssal narcissism of self-authorizing entitlement. In the end, any discussion about democracy and violence in America cannot take place without addressing this specific social psychopathology, and indeed Arendt, although impeccably knowledgeable about American history and certainly sensitive to racial parameters in her own right, lacks the specific social-imaginary connection to address it in her argument.

Let us then close the parenthesis and return to Arendt's theoretical condemnation of violence. As she does indeed question with inimitably cold reason: What sort of instituting power can emerge in the face of the absurd (but nonetheless perfectly realistic) possibility for calculated planetary destruction in the name of legitimate sovereignty, out of a type of political action that itself privileges an aesthetics of destruction, albeit in ridiculously minor scale by comparison? Arendt's initial focus on the off-scale dimensions of the technologies of violence borne by the state apparatus is inarguable, whatever one might say about the later philosophical reflections on the relation between violence and power that the text ultimately leans on. Indeed, to discuss the latter without attending to the epistemological demands of the former is to dehistoricize her argument for no philosophical gain.

A real question remains, which I cannot claim to answer, as to whether the incalculable epistemological limit of planetary catastrophe is enough, in and of itself, to exempt us from thinking critically about the history of violence at the crux of this catastrophic imaginary that is, simultaneously, both the imaginary of emancipation in the Enlightenment sense and of autonomy in a socialist sense: the radical democratic imaginary. I confess that for me a certain Adornoesque dialectic of Enlightenment figure of creation/destruction is elementary to this discussion, and Arendt's avowed dislike of Adorno should be evaluated in light of how close she comes, in this text, to his own criticisms of radical youth movements, as he voiced them in various radio addresses, television interviews, and lectures during that same time in Frankfurt. Of course, the way that history overcame—or, perhaps more aptly, absorbed, assimilated, and defanged—the radical aspirations of the late-'60s movements confirms both Arendt's and Adorno's prescience. It does not, however, absolve them of the paternalistic gesture of disregarding the desire of rebellious youth, the daring of a generation to alter its historical boundaries, even at the cost of debilitating failure. The insight of this prescience cannot be devalued. Nor, however, can it be allowed to take some sort of political precedence over youthful and indeed reckless desire, unless we discredit Thomas Paine's revolutionary exhortation that history is the right of the living as the key imaginary of radical constituent politics.

The famous quotations from *On Violence* that everyone grapples with focus directly on the debate over legitimacy of rule:

> Power is the essence of all government, but violence is not. Violence is by nature instrumental; like all means, it always stands in need of guidance and justification through the end it pursues. And what needs justification by something else cannot be the essence of anything.... Power needs no justification, being inherent in the very existence of political communities; what it does need is legitimacy.... Legitimacy, when challenged, bases itself on an appeal to the past, while justification relates to an end that lies in the future. Violence can be justifiable but it will never be legitimate. (V, 51-52)

The context of reference to legitimacy in this last sentence definitely discredits Paine. So be it. It is easy to conclude that, even if unconsciously, Arendt here is channeling Burke. But if we are studious, the "appeal to the past" is not a matter of ancestry; it is a matter of history—not quite the same thing. Arendt's argument, in essence, is that violence cannot achieve legitimacy because it is antihistorical. The very first charge she levels against New Left violent radicalism is that they don't really know their Marx. They don't learn from Marxist history because—in their presumption to act anew—they refuse their history. They merely *think* they are revolutionaries because they refuse to learn from the history of revolution. So, they are mere reformists, and bad ones at that because they have no language, no strategy, for passing from the lawbreaking /irrational/destructive stage to the law-making/rational/constitutive stage. This is the crux of the problem for Arendt.

They lack power and will never gain it because violence can fight against power but cannot create power: "Violence can destroy power; it is utterly incapable of creating it" (56). In other words, violence has no dialectics. Its destructive capacity creates nothing. It may produce an altered condition, but even if it does, it does so by chance, therefore leaving itself open to the most reactionary reconstitution, oftentimes a fascist counterviolence. That is why, she implies, the often-used notion "constituent violence" is a contradiction in terms, particularly if conjoined in an articulation with "constituent power."

But despite evidence for this line of argument, the matter is far more complicated. It is surely the case that almost all modern societies have constituted their sovereignty with violence, which is always to say, violence against others. In this sense—and the above logic would have to concur—their constituent action has yet to achieve power, beyond the simplest terms of sovereignty in name. This is why, even in times of peace, their existence remains in essence precarious and needs to be protected by force (national army, police, border patrol, etc.). In other words, to be blunt, sovereignty is not a matter of power but a matter of security. Hence violence is essential to it; violence is sovereignty's primary instrument, even if conducted solely on a juridical plane. In order for there to be a bona fide achievement of constituent power, in a quintessential democratic sense, either there has to be no violence or violence has to be overcome. It is debatable whether the first can ever occur in the history of democracy, given democracy's definitional mandate of undoing the status quo, which is what makes democracy a radical regime. But it is certain that the second has yet to be achieved in any regime.

The difficulty of defining violence as such, other than the fact that it is always embodied even in its most abstract (whether metaphysical or genocidal) manifestations, does not mean that it is simply a historical concept. There is something ontological about it, and I do not mean this in a sense of it being natural to living being, and so on. I mean it in the sense that it is embedded in living being in a seemingly interminable range of variation, which becomes even more indeterminate and complex within the contours of *human-being*. In this latter register, there may indeed be something to John Keane's argument that it is only after the invention of civilization as a concept that grants value to specific forms of society that violence becomes a self-sufficient independent notion.[38] But his argument too is marred by the presumption that democracy is ultimately opposite to (or without) violence. The historical record of democracy (both revolutionary and constitutional) since antiquity disputes this in stark fashion. Therefore, Keane's proposition that violence can be democratized is ultimately not very meaningful. The contrary needs to happen: democracy must come to terms with its own history of violence and, even more, its own particular investment in violence, its own value of violence, and how this is different from how other political regimes value violence. The self-awareness of such distinction is essential.

In the end, no radical democrat can justify revoking the option of violent resistance on the part of people whose actual existence is threatened by daily violence, whether it be black people in America, who still remain homeless and hunted in their own country, or Palestinians, who are rendered superfluous aliens in their very land. In both cases—as in many others, no doubt, but these are so blatant as to boggle the mind—the denial of people's violent resistance to daily conditions of extermination is an incommensurable moral outrage. All the more so, given the arrogance of the perpetrators of violence who dare stigmatize in turn the resistance of those they lay waste by controlling their very means of living and dying, a condition that has achieved a kind of pathetic permanence both in the banality of its execution and the cynicism of apathy with which it is received by the rest of the world. One can hold any position of critique in relation to violence per se as to whether it is or is not the appropriate political action, and one can perhaps be against violence altogether in a framework of personal judgment, but there is no philosophical or ethical ground to justify depriving a people of the legitimacy of violence in response to living daily under violence.

Of course, violent resistance is not the only option; nor would I repeat the cliché that violence begets violence. I am not making a determinist argument. The question is not a matter of comparison, nor is it a matter of measure or choice between violent and nonviolent resistance, for there is nothing that links the two. They entail an entirely different order of political action, perhaps even of political order, not just a different means. The question is whether there are philosophical grounds to reject violence tout court, Mahatma Gandhi or Martin Luther King notwithstanding. A decision can be made one way or another, and violence can be discredited, but whatever argument will be made in justification of this discrediting will always be partial and self-serving.

THE CONSTITUENT VIOLENCE OF DEMOCRACY: THE ANARCHIST OPENING

Arendt's argument about the social destructiveness of violence is corroborated by plenty of historical evidence to suggest that it is often true. But her argument still fails to confront the problem of legitimacy as an autonomous concept. In fact, legitimacy here works as a given, as a *quality* of power. Insofar as violence cannot by definition (Arendt's definition) create power, it lacks legitimacy. Arendt does not address the distinction between legitimate and illegitimate uses of violence because when so-called legitimate violence is enacted by state law-enforcing mechanisms, it exposes a mark of weakness in state power, the weakness of the necessity for security. This violent mode of the law-enforcing mechanism provides a window not only to the state's weakness, but also to its lawless foundation. It is revealed, to be more accurate, as a *lawless lawmaking* mechanism, and the state, in that sense, becomes criminal. I repeat: this becomes an issue only regarding the liberal democratic state, which allegedly operates not by violence but by lawful consent. In a monarchical or totalitarian state there is no issue because there is no disavowal of violence at any level. When the liberal state reveals its inbuilt contradiction by deploying "legitimate violence," this argument reaches its highest stakes. Otherwise, any formal advocacy of legitimacy is inherently flawed; formally speaking, the category "legitimacy" is incoherent. I understand that the practical-political dimensions of "legitimacy of rule" can never be effaced by the poietic-political dimensions that infect this notion with terribly unstable properties, but let's at least consider the effects of the latter, for the sake of argument.

To help us with this touchy point, it might be interesting to bring into discussion a largely forgotten text that should be considered almost a sibling text to Arendt's essay on violence, its kinship not compromising in the least its ultimately adversarial character. I am speaking of Robert Paul Wolff's once famous essay "On Violence," written and published in the same year as Arendt's (1969), while Wolff was a professor of philosophy at Columbia University. The essay largely derives from and refers explicitly to the Columbia events of 1968, and in this immediate regard it is worth quoting extensively, not merely for documentary reasons but precisely because it raises—on this extremely limited and specific ground—a challenge to Arendt's theoretical warnings, themselves derived (let's not forget) from the same social-historical ground.

> Consider, as a particular example, the occupation of buildings and the student strike at Columbia University during April and May of 1968. The consequences of those acts have not yet played themselves out, but I think certain general conclusions can be drawn. First, the total harm done by the students and their supporters was very small in comparison with the good

results that were achieved. A month of classwork was lost, along with many tempers and a good deal of sleep. Someone—it is still not clear who—burned the research notes of a history professor, an act which, I am happy to say, produced a universal revulsion shared even by the SDS. In the following year, a number of classes were momentarily disrupted by SDS activists in an unsuccessful attempt to repeat the triumph of the previous spring.

Against this, what benefits flowed from the protest? A reactionary and thoroughly unresponsive administration was forced to resign; an all-university Senate of students, professors, and administrators was created, the first such body at Columbia. A callous and antisocial policy of university expansion into the surrounding neighborhood was reversed; some at least of the university's ties with the military were loosened or severed; and an entire community of students and professors were forced to confront moral and political issues which till then they had managed to ignore.

Could these benefits have been won at less cost? Considering the small cost of the uprising, the question seems to me a bit finicky; nevertheless, the answer is clearly, No. The history of administrative intransigence and faculty apathy at Columbia makes it quite clear that nothing short of a dramatic act such as the seizure of buildings could have deposed the university administration and produced a university senate. In retrospect, the affair seems to have been a quite prudent and restrained use of force.[39]

There is something disarming about how measured this account is, and one could argue that it is part of Wolff's style of philosophical anarchism, a kind of forthcoming and straightforward conviction articulated with humor and little fanfare or radical agonistics. More important, however, is the position that ensues: namely, although one might conclude that Wolff's account provides a justification for the violent action in the Columbia '68 events, nonetheless his retort is prohibitive: "[Such justification] is *totally wrong*, for it implies that a line can be drawn between legitimate and illegitimate forms of protest, the latter being justified only under special conditions and when all else has failed." In other words, Wolff's claim that no such line can be drawn breaks with not only Arendt's position on the matter but also the entire Marxist tradition, Leninist or otherwise, in which violence as political action is subsumed to some sort of instrumental reason. Needless to say, the Marxist tradition does concern us here because, whatever may be its varied relation to violence as actual politics (and the variant range is vast, according to

Marxism's differential history), violence, in the last instance, is explicitly considered (in whatever way, again, it might be or not be embraced) as a *transformative force*—contrary, say, to the bourgeois-liberal tradition, which expends extraordinary symbolic energy in order to occlude and disavow the violence on which it has founded its social order and with which it continues to maintain it.

I should add that Wolff predicates his stance on how impossible it is to draw a line between legitimate and illegitimate violence on a claim that such impossibility pertains to how we theorize *authority* itself. Or, to pick it up from the other end of the thread, as it were: whatever determines whether the use of violence is legitimate (or illegitimate) depends on whether the agents authorizing violence are legitimate (or illegitimate). In other words, there are no intrinsic or formal grounds to condemn or defend violence as a mode of political action, much as there are no intrinsic/formal grounds to condemn or defend legitimacy of power. Wolff speaks explicitly of the "myth of legitimacy" as the main weapon in the hands of states to justify whatever means they employ to enforce, sustain, and perpetuate their authority over the societies they rule, sometimes in the sovereign name of those societies, with the constitutional authorization of those societies.

It is precisely those societies, of course, that complicate these questions—societies of the rule of law, so-called liberal democratic societies—for which legitimacy is indeed a foundational myth whose never-ending performance grounds their otherwise groundless social imaginary. This myth is animated by a transcendental signification of the law, and we don't need political-theological determinations to understand it.[40] The point that Wolff makes, with which I obviously concur, is that "legitimacy" is an incoherent concept in and of itself, much like the concept "violence" is. The coherence of each is directly dependent on the coherence of the other: "Once the concept of violence is seen to rest on the unfounded distinction between legitimate and illegitimate political authority, the question of the appropriateness of violence simply dissolves" (Wolff, 608). In this particular sense, Wolff disputes Arendt's antinomian relation between power and violence as a categorical distinction. The opposition between power and violence may come to exist under certain historical circumstances, but it is neither consistent nor necessary. And even when indeed opposed, the question of legitimacy or illegitimacy of power/violence is not—cannot be—answered.

Wolff is careful to point out that this undecidability does not pertain to a moral domain; hence all objections as to moral relativism are off the table. It is a political matter entirely, and in politics no state can claim legitimacy on the grounds of its formal existence. Or rather, it can claim it all it wants and can have the means to enforce it, but this does not cease being (philosophically) a mere claim and does not cease being (politically) a claim legitimized by force. How much this force includes violence or is a matter of tacit consent to authority is in fact not the issue. For the exact same reason, Wolff rejects any sort of argument for the legitimacy of nonviolence, including civil disobedience, which, he goes on to show in a rather crafty argument, always entails an act of violence regardless of the claims.

In the end, Wolff's response to a state's emerging lawlessness oftentimes in response to liberalism's troubles is to evade its presumption to law, in whatever fashion one chooses. One's choice, he is careful to point out in conclusion, has a great deal to do with one's position and interests in society—one's class position, above all, though not in a typical Marxist sense. For Wolff, the notion of class pertains less to one's position in the labor market and more to one's social and political interest in an arena of conflicting positions (which cannot be divorced from the economic, yet not ever simply reduced to it). For Wolff, the most constitutive position—by virtue of social interest—against violence is the "liberal" one. I am not by any means suggesting that this applies to Arendt, but it is worth considering. Liberalism cannot come to terms with social-political violence as a rule, precisely because it denies both its own constitutive violence (bourgeois revolution) and the violence it wields institutionally by exclusionary execution of the law (partial activation of rights or tacit enforcement of special interests) in the name of (its own) security.

As is well known, Wolff argues for and from the position of "philosophical anarchism," a position whose philosophical parameters remind me of what Paul Feyerabend, just a few years later, would identify in his *Against Method* (1975) as "epistemological anarchism." Wolff concludes the essay "On Violence" as follows: "The belief in legitimacy, like the penchant for transcendent metaphysics, is an ineradicable irrationality of the human experience. . . . [Against it], the philosophical anarchist is the atheist of politics" (616). My affinity with this assertion should be obvious. However, my investment in anarchic politics is entwined with my investment in radical democratic politics, insofar as I take for granted that democracy requires an imaginary of rule without *archē* or *telos*. This is a tragic imaginary, in the sense of practicing a politics of tragic life, where there can be folly but no heroism and where there is lucidity but in conditions of total uncertainty. Indeed, this is the politics of autonomy, about which Wolff and I agree, even though not quite in the same terms, partly because of his underlying Kantianism and partly because of his reluctance to equate anarchy with democracy.

In his legendary *In Defense of Anarchism* (1970), written roughly in the same historical and political juncture as "On Violence," Wolff asserts that there is no possible philosophical justification for the authority of the state. Somewhat against the grain but with commonsense language, he demonstrates how the very politics of utility that enable and sustain the authority of the state are in the end metaphysical. This is predicated on the rather strict definition that authority is "the right to command and, correlatively, the right to be obeyed," which Wolff means not abstractly but as a condition woven into basic processes of identity and exchange: "Authority resides in persons: they possess it—if indeed they do at all—by virtue of who they are and not by virtue of what they command."[41] There is no transcendental right of command, as there is no transcendental duty of obedience. It all comes down to human action in specific situations; no moral law authorizes the corresponding right or duty, no matter what the claim might be, in principle or in text, legal or otherwise. Indeed, Wolff nullifies from the outset any notion of the (moral or whatever) autonomy of obedience. Obedience resides already in the command itself, not in following the command: "Obedience is not a matter of doing what someone tells you to do. It is a matter of doing what he tells you to do *because he tells you to do it*" (6). He thus slashes through the discursive thicket of morality, so that authority can be lucidly understood to be attached to command and we can thus go on to focus our evaluation on the legitimacy of its status.

In a strange sense, one might argue that to the degree that it is *formally* (not just instrumentally) attached to command, obedience bears a certain authority as well, which nonetheless remains persistently hidden, even inarticulate. This authority would be tantamount to the power of consent, whose enormous capacity to move huge numbers of people to act, often against their interest, is beyond doubt. Such was, after all, Etienne La Boétie's insight into voluntary servitude. Despite its self-enacting power, however, this authority does not translate into autonomy, except by its negation, its nullification by the sort of self-understanding that sees consent for what it is: a formal extension of command. Autonomy presupposes the nullification of command (9) and therefore of obedience, since the formal self-determination of autonomous action can never be constituted in terms of action between a subject and an object, even though I have argued that autonomy makes no sense without understanding that it is at the same time a condition of othering oneself (self-alteration).[42] But even according to the strictest Hegelian-Freudian understanding of the splitting of the self, where being object is very much part of the subjective condition, autonomous action takes place in an undeconstructible psychic simultaneity, whereby the bifurcated structure of command/obedience is abolished. Autonomy, in this respect, too, is quintessentially *anarchic*. Moreover, since what I am suggesting is neither a Kantian understanding of transcendental autonomy nor some liberal notion of possessive individualism, autonomy always implies *social autonomy*. It testifies to a relational field, not only because of the lesson we have learned from Marx that every individual is a social relation (an economic assessment) but also because the very psychic constitution of the subject always happens in a state of interdependency, actual and phantasmatic, permeated by otherness, which might also do well to explain my seemingly paradoxical claim that autonomy always involves a process of self-alteration.

Quite obviously, in that moment of negation whereby consent will have been understood for what it is—the extension of command—the absurdity of the presumed (or proclaimed) legitimacy of authority would also become perfectly apparent. This too is La Boétie's daring point, which is the essence of withdrawal of consent: the most revolutionary weapon societies have in the absence of firepower to counter the state. It would be rather narrow-minded to proclaim that radical withdrawal of consent is devoid of violence or, even worse, foreign to violence. For Wolff, the question does not arise because, although he expands definitions of violence to include nonsomatic experiences of force strictly speaking—say, economic exploitation, social exclusion, or psychological repression—he insists nonetheless on considering violence an incoherent concept, whether as ideological reality or utopian wish. But I am not interested in strict philosophical assessments of the in/coherence of concepts, at the very least because conceptual contradiction or paradox is not only not foreign to me but rather the most interesting and fruitful way to think. So, assuming Wolff's groundbreaking argument about the manufactured basis of all legitimacy but also retaining the actuality of violence as essential dimension of all politics—but democratic politics in particular—how might we understand in contemporary terms the radical potential of the politics of rage, without which all talk about withdrawal of consent is just impossible?

Frantz Fanon's famous meditation on violence is predicated precisely on this question. From the outset, he describes decolonization as a creative/destructive process that operates at the root level of nature: "decolonization is quite simply the replacement of one 'species' of humans by another" (WE, 35). This does not in the least nullify its fully material historical character, in the same way that nature too is nothing transcendental, ideal, or magical, but the very process by which *human-being* is formed—that is to say, made and unmade. Fanon describes in plain terms the violence of humanization that the decolonizing process radically entails: "Decolonization, which sets out to change the order of the world, is obviously a program of complete disorder. . . . [It] is the veritable creation of new humans. But this creation owes nothing of its legitimacy to any supernatural power; the colonized 'thing' becomes human during the same process by which it frees itself" (WE, 36-37). "Creation" is precisely the word. We are not talking about some process of reform or some new construction in the sort of social engineering that colonialism itself after all promulgated. The process is radical, literally a transformation, the creation of new form that can happen only by the destruction of already existing form. Creation and destruction are one—that is always and inevitably the case. And in order to efface any possibility that this might be understood in some theological fashion, Fanon insists on this creation/destruction as a material, sensible, natural (as opposed to supernatural) force. Hence the violence.

This violence bears no dialectical redemption whatsoever because it is literally the renting asunder of the entire network of significations that make colonial reality possible and comprehensible. It is not about overcoming or about alleviating difference toward some grander equality or inclusion. This is because colonial violence itself has already forbidden any possibility of the whole where difference might have an integral social meaning, even in the distinctions it establishes and enforces in its creation of the categories "settler" and "native" (*indigène*), which are condemned to "reciprocal exclusivity" (WE, 39), notwithstanding their ultimate political opposition. This is a remarkable epistemological point in Fanon's argument, especially if we keep in mind his Hegelianism, and it establishes an understanding of violence that has or seeks no a priori legitimation—no reparation or restitution, not even revenge. He therefore removes any metaphysical justification from decolonial violence and in the process deauthorizes the sovereignty of discourses of legitimacy that are always a major part of the oppressor's arsenal, including the entire system of values that mobilize *la mission civilisatrice*.

After all, Fanon says, the native is rendered "impermeable to ethics ... [as] the enemy of values" (WE, 41) in an absolute sense. In the struggle for decolonization "all Mediterranean values—the triumph of the human person, of clarity and of beauty—become lifeless and colorless knickknacks" (WE, 47). As the value of individualism is the first to go, Fanon continues, decolonial violence, proceeding with total contempt for the sham of liberal legitimacy, creates new communal imaginaries on the very ground it destroys. An indigenous universality springs forth from the very deindividuation and depersonalization that colonial violence produces. The politics of rage that spontaneously and organically underlies decolonial transformation is precisely a process of humanization—or more accurately, another sort of humanization, one that would indeed produce a new species of human.

In the process, Fanon does not in the least discount the violence of revolutionary rage, whose springing from the violence of oppression he confirms while removing any pretense as to some sort of dialectical redemption. Indeed, he describes extensively internecine violence among colonized peoples—analogous to what in America is called "black on black violence"—as the very first psychosocial consequence of colonial and racist violence (WE, 52-55). Not surprisingly, he zeroes in on the libidinal dimensions of this self-destructiveness of rage, and this would have been rather banal if he did not connect it to what he identifies as the mythical/magical elements of indigenous society's ultimate realm of anticolonial resistance. By a sort of demonic possession that springs from deep-seated social-imaginary structures among African peoples across the continent, Fanon argues, the traumatic symptom of colonial violence, which threatens to break out into internal(ized) self-destructiveness, enables a whole other order of self-awareness and realization: "The zombies are more terrifying than the settlers.... The supernatural, magical powers reveal themselves as astonishingly personal [*étonnamment moïques*]; the settler's powers are infinitely shrunken, stamped with their alien origin [*extraneité*]. We no longer really need to fight against them since what counts is the frightening adversary created by myths. We perceive that all is resolved by a permanent confrontation on the phantasmatic plane" (WE, 56).

The phantasmatic plane is essential to this discussion, not only in terms of how the experience of being an object of violence informs how one becomes and acts as a subject (of violence or not) but even more in terms of how the social imaginary of violence weaves together myths of legitimation, authority, and biopower. This is especially the case since violence cannot be encountered in strict philosophical terms. Its conceptual integrity is a presumption, indeed a ruse that benefits ideologies and structures of power. Judith Butler says much the same in her worthy intervention on this specific quandary where Fanon is encountered expressly, even if not with attention to his own investment in social phantasy, though phantasy is an essential dimension in Butler's entire framework.[43]

Butler's argument is quite careful and nuanced, entirely self-aware that it is indeed an argument and deserves to be contested, with the proviso that the higher stakes it raises be respected. As the title suggests, she argues for an aggressive form of nonviolence; she is not reiterating some passivity or retreat into nonaction: "Nonviolence ... [is] a form of resistance to systemic forms of destruction ... [that] does not necessarily emerge from a pacific or calm part of the soul. Very often it is an expression of rage, indignation, and aggression" (21). She thus wrests from the concept of violence its presumed monopoly of force while at the same time inducting nonviolence into the realm of the politics of rage. While the negative part of the argument is a clear-headed critique of the assumptions surrounding the concept of violence, the affirmative part is cognizantly tentative: in turn utopian—"nonviolence is an ideal that cannot always be fully honored in practice" (22)—and yet practical in the literal sense of embodied knowledge, a way of living-being/becoming: "nonviolence is not an absolute principle, but the name of an ongoing struggle" (23), "less a failure of action than a physical assertion of the claims of life, a living assertion, a claim that is made by speech, gesture, and action, through networks, encampments, and assemblies" (24).

The latter distinction is key to the argument. Butler sees nonviolence specifically as a politics of equality, indeed of radical democracy, although she does not use the term. This is because violence and its assortment of legitimation practices is always predicated on stark notions of self as distinct from the other, chief among them the common justification of violence in self-defense. Reminding us that state violence always uses the self-defense argument to crack down on its opposition (internal or external) even when it acts preemptively, as the military phrase goes, Butler weaves a succinct dismantling of the presumptive framework. Her target is the cornerstone of liberalism—possessive individualism and the autonomous self, the self of property (both *soi propre* and private ownership)—which disavows the fact that no *human-being* (but, indeed, no living being, no material entity in the entire physics of the universe) is ever strictly independent. Even atoms are not atomized, if I may be allowed the indulgence of such phrasing, for atomization is a social imaginary created in a specific historical and geographical terrain.

Butler argues fiercely that violence is both an extension and a symptom of the presumption of self-sufficiency and social division. On the contrary, nonviolence is conceivable only when we realize that every one of us lives in conditions of (inter)dependency, that our self is always an other—to a whole array of others who surround it and give it meaning, but also to itself, according to the constitutive significance of otherness in ourselves, our psyches. The point is "to open up the idea of selfhood as a fraught field of social relationality" and to understand relationality as "a vexed and ambivalent field in which the question of ethical obligation has to be worked out in light of a persistent and constitutive destructive potential" (10). From this standpoint, not only does the justification of violence as self-defense prove to be a ruse (often specifically as a defense of power) but the very divisiveness of a self-centered perspective of the world is also in itself a condition of violence. In this respect, Butler is entirely correct to conclude that "violence against the other is violence against oneself" (25), and the emphasis on this phrase would have to fall not on the self, as an unfortunate collateral consequence of assault against an other, but on the fact that such assault is on self *and* other, on *everyone*, indeed, on the field of social relation as such.

It is from this standpoint that Butler tries to give meaning to nonviolence, which does not at all signify the absence of or refrain from violence—indeed, it means to nullify violence as frame of reference altogether. Instead, Butler aims to orient us beyond both self and other as singular notions and underline their constitutive interdependency—indeed, the interdependency of everything that makes our lives possible in an elementary sense. Although she does not put it this way, this is precisely how the Greeks, from Anaximander and Hippocrates to Herodotus and Aristotle, understood both cosmologically and politically the notion of *isonomia*, which we discussed earlier in the essay. And this is perfectly apt, since Butler emphasizes the interdependency of everything as a way of understanding equality in the political field of social relations whose creation and sustenance nonviolence serves.

To my mind, what Butler names "nonviolence" describes less an ethico-political gesture whose reference is the problem of violence in its voluminous histories of definition and more an epistemological position that enables us to break from our confinement in established frameworks of understanding the political. She seems to hint at this from the outset: "Perhaps nonviolence requires a certain leave-taking from reality as it is currently constituted, laying open the possibilities that belong to a newer political imaginary" (10-11). One of the first such openings in the specific demands of this argument would be to disengage the entire debate on the distinction between violence and nonviolence from its instrumentalist frame: "Nonviolence is not a means to a goal nor is it a goal in itself. It is, rather, a technique that exceeds both an instrumental logic and any teleological scheme of development—it is an ungoverned technique, arguably ungovernable" (125). A second such opening is to break through the tight doors of the definition of violence as corporeal and psychological force or as simple destruction in order to include practices of critique, dissent, and noncompliance —such weapons as the general strike, the hunger strike in prison, civil disobedience, boycotts as resistance, occupations of public spaces, etc., that is, actions of refusal or disavowal of presumed or proclaimed authority (139-40). One might argue that in this latter sense nonviolence becomes a category of violence in an internally subversive way—not, of course, in terms of how Butler sees violence as social division and inequality but in the opposite terms: in the way she sees nonviolence as social relation that creates equality. In both openings the definitional realm of violence is upturned, that is to say, politicized, interminably contested. In both cases, the register of the ungovernable problematizes governmentality. The epistemological thus returns to the political but is never reducible to the ethical, despite Butler's insistence on keeping to this discourse. As such, insofar as the political is never an ethical matter, it is also never a strictly philosophical matter.

Butler is fierce in questioning the problematic assumption that violence can be discussed in some neutral philosophical manner. "*Violence is always interpreted*," she says with emphasis (14). Indeed, the whole premise is that before we even get into the debate as to the politics of nonviolence, we need to understand that the semantics of violence are already politically (and in fact ideologically) motivated even when—or rather, especially when—they claim to be objective. What is named and defined as violent always happens in the same gesture of disavowing something else as not violent, even though this something else might be described as exactly the same action. State violence, in this respect, is almost always disavowed, or even when it is accepted as such it is immediately justified as legitimate. In the same semantic frame, antistate violence is never justifiable or legitimate and becomes the core signification of how any like meaning of violence is thereby effaced from the impetus of the state. While from every political perspective the difference between state violence and antistate violence is always obvious—and indeed, always antagonistic, both in the realm of politics and in the realm of law—from a philosophical perspective the distinction is impossible.

We are back to Wolff in this sense: legitimacy is an incoherent notion in any philosophical sense, for whoever decides what is or is not legitimate is whoever has the authority/power/violence to decide on the definition and its enforcement. This is not just the mark of Woolf's epistemological anarchism. It is the recognition that law is never impartial despite its proclaimed aspirations. If it were, justice would never be a question; it would be a mathematical equation, and judgment (read: *krisis*, decision, critique) would not exist as a human faculty. Letting go of the ideology of impartiality in law and resolution in justice certainly creates a tough ethical and political terrain. I understand very well how it opens up the space of justice to relativism, which from any position that assumes to be neutral, objective, or transcendent is surely the case. However, this is precisely the point. There is no such position in politics, except as social phantasy. And there is surely no such position in radical democratic politics, a politics of neither *archē* nor *telos*, neither origin nor end—an anarchic politics that is always irresolutely in-the-making.

Butler is wary of such anarchist positions. She does not mention Wolff at all (even though he would have been an interesting interlocutor, especially on the philosophical ruminations around violence) but mentions Benjamin's investment in anarchic violence with explicit ambivalence. The reason seems to be her wariness against a sort of relativism of value as to what is/is not violent or is/is not legitimate, which to her mind entails a position that in essence recognizes no ethics in politics. Here Butler and I part ways. As I mentioned earlier in reference to Wolff: in politics, no state—of being, of acting, of deciding, of governing, of resisting, of subjectifying, of relating, and obviously of claiming to be a state but also, just as much, of claiming to be and act as antistate—can claim legitimacy on the grounds of its formal existence. Otherwise politics reverts to Kant, which furthermore ultimately reverts to liberal ethics. If we assume that all values are contested regardless (and this is key to the anarchist politics of democracy), which places the onus of responsibility on our own political decision as to what sort of action we shall engage in (in order to defend the relational field of self-determination which privileges no one over another and yet still allows for the openness of contestation of values), then no transcendental a priori ethics or values—no principles!—can prevail. The evident danger of relativism in this position is checked by assuming the risk of decision or judgment against established norms and anchored on no ground and thus provisionally privileging certain values about which whoever makes the decision is ultimately accountable, without, however, being authorized objectively to decide and act beyond the critique and judgment of others, even if s/he does so.

While I can see how Butler's notion of nonviolence can be inducted into the framework I am describing, I can also see how this framework makes the distinction between violence and nonviolence ultimately undecidable. Butler's concluding statement is that "the power of nonviolence, its force, is found in the modes of resistance to a form of violence that regularly hides its true name" (201). Yet, although I understand and applaud her call to take full account of the decision that would differentiate between violence and nonviolence, the distinction cannot be simply a matter of naming. It does not matter if *we* use the term violence or not. It is *who* names what that matters, not *what* the name is. Certainly, this anarchic framework recognizes the undeconstructible interdependency of all being—the fact that no autonomous decision can register outside or beyond the critique and judgment of others, which is always there to remind us that no self remains intact after a decision, that each political decision is to some extent or other transformative, even if not apparently so in the time of its making.

Concluding this discussion but also inevitably complicating it, it is imperative to examine Etienne Balibar's idiosyncratic figure of antiviolence not only in relation to Butler's argument but also specifically in the context of anarchy and the insurgent politics of democracy. In a manner that follows my assessment of the instability of violence as a strictly philosophical concept, I have already argued that Balibar's notion of antiviolence belongs to his general tendency to think in terms of border concepts, that is to say, notions that occupy the limit of conceptuality as thresholds or portals of meaning, open at both ends of definition and context, internally relational, impermanent, ambiguous, antinomian.[44] The border concept performs an action that exceeds the concept's historical mark, even the revolutionary one. In democratic terms specifically, it brings the problem of citizenship/*politeia* within the contentious realm that characterizes the question of political anthropology since the time of Aristotle's essentially problematizing figure of the political animal.

Next to Balibar's more widely discussed border concepts of equaliberty, citizen-subject, or ambiguous universality, antiviolence is the most curious—or the least evident. This is because words bearing the prefix "anti" are conventionally made to bear a position of some solidity which is rarely considered to be emancipated from its binding mirror condition. And yet, this is precisely the point of this formulation. Balibar tells us from the outset that "antiviolence" is not at all "nonviolence" or even "counterviolence," these two being the quintessential negations that seal the conceptual sovereignty of violence. "There is no nonviolence" he says characteristically late in the book.[45] Unlike nonviolence which, strictly speaking (not in Butler's formulation), means a literal negation of violence, antiviolence means "another type of 'negation' of violence" (7) or "a hypothetical designation of a 'different' kind of 'negation' of violence" (13)—in both cases, negation being marked as something that can never be quite literal, separate, separately intact. Antiviolence thus signifies an antithesis that is fully implicated in the thesis that nominally gives it meaning and, by this token, it enables an anarchic upturning.

Antiviolence enables us to recognize the dangerous delusion of seeing violence as society's existential appendage that civic politics allegedly can overcome, which is a keystone in the Western metaphysics of sovereignty. Instead Balibar sets as a task the impetus to think not how politics can eradicate violence, as if a social imaginary can ultimately be reduced to the rule of its institutions, but how violence is permeated by politics, making thus the question of politics immanent and crucial in any consideration of violence. Specifically: "Politics can no longer be thought as either a sublation of violence (as a going beyond it toward nonviolence) or as a simple transformation of its determinate conditions (which can require the application of counterviolence). It is no longer a means or an instrument employed to accomplish something else, but it is also no longer an end in itself. It is, rather, the uncertain stakes of a confrontation with the element of irreducible alterity that it carries within itself. This infinite circularity is what I have called, at least hypothetically, 'antiviolence'" (17). Note here a crucial stipulation: while violence is conventionally—within liberalism, of course—thought to be the other of politics, antiviolence both emerges from and reveals the internal otherness of politics, which exists in all politics and which liberal politics has constitutively tried to repress.

Incidentally, liberalism also represses the fact that "the question of politics" always involves the decision of how to answer the question *which politics?*—the point where the political (*le politique*) intersects with politics (*la politique*). Using Balibar's language, I would risk adding that the political is the citizen-subject figure of politics. In this respect, Balibar's meditation on the problem of violence is entirely a reconceptualization of the problem of politics as such, not ethics or metaphysics, and in the end, expressly of radical democratic politics, anarchic politics in my language, which means that it is also at the same time a meditation on the problematic of insurgency and, to my mind, on the politics of rage. Antiviolence surely does not signify or aspire to an overcoming of violence, but it does signify—polemically, one might say—a way of imagining an insurgent and emancipatory politics, much in the way of Fanon, where violence is neither the subject nor the object that authorizes politics but the "irreducible remainder over the institutional, legal, or strategic forms for reducing and eliminating it" (11).

This politics, which Balibar names "the emancipatory insurgency that simultaneously perpetuates and eclipses the constitution" (144-45)—notice here the parallel structure of excess between violence as remainder and the politics of insurgency—may be characterized by a sort of know-thyself recognition that enables the self-constitution of a collective political subject "in a world in which the political community no longer has natural or traditional bases but can arise only from a collective decision and practice" (146). Note also that collective decision is intimately linked to emancipation: "no one can emancipate herself without others" (6), an explicit recognition of interdependency that Balibar immediately connects to the meaning of equaliberty. Such politics cannot possibly be restricted to the politics of autochthonous citizenship (whether ancient or modern) and in this respect cannot be reduced to any sort of transcendental rights that somehow precede the institution of this politics in the name of the citizen-subject. Such politics is profoundly historical, in the sense of geotemporal, and therefore as precarious as any radical democratic politics is by definition: a politics of citizenship in which antiviolence would be endemic, as a condition of internal otherness at the core of its constitution, but even more (or precisely, as a consequence of), a politics of "citizenship permanently 'in the making'" (147). As a worthy addendum to Paine's radical understanding of the groundless condition of the right to have rights as basic stipulation of living-being, Balibar argues that insurgency (not law, or even institution) is the permanent condition of the Rights of Man.

It makes perfect sense to me then that Balibar will go on to recognize this politics as a tragic politics, the dimensions of which we shall shortly explore. In a brilliant moment, he sees the politics of antiviolence as a borderline condition that he names "Luxemburg's aporia" elaborating it further as the question: "How can the balance between the ethics of conviction and the ethics of responsibility be democratically shared?" (148) By this he means to confront the difficulty of how collective power handles the violence of social oppression or injustice. In this aporetic encounter neither of these contrary ethical realms—we can call the pairs alternately faith and knowledge, theory and practice, and so forth—have any significance outside their *political* immersion in this paradoxical condition of democratic sharing, the proposition of equaliberty par excellence. Because no constitutional order of rights can possibly safeguard what always takes place in the precarious arena of contested collective practice, this sharing cannot possibly be restricted to a priori authorization. From this standpoint, all ethical positions are tragic: they are groundless, without guarantees, and *meaningless* in themselves outside the field of contention—meaningless in a literal, not pejorative, sense. Note that this tragic politics, Balibar says emphatically, is not heroic. The people who collectively act to emancipate themselves from the violence of oppression and injustice are "tragic individuals" not as heroes but as "militants of the impossible" (150). Their politics is a matter of tragic life, residing at the limit point of a political anthropology that enacts a differential, ambiguously universal, anarchic humanity.

DEMOCRACY IS A TRAGIC REGIME

Democracy is not a state. It is an act.

—John Lewis, 2020

The imaginary of this shared, collective politics, this insurgent militancy of the impossible, exemplifies why in Cornelius Castoriadis's words "democracy is a tragic regime." Let's look at a couple of instances of the many reiterations of this phrase in Castoriadis's writings: "Democracy is quite evidently a regime that knows no external norms; it has to posit its own norms, and it has to posit them without being able to lean on another norm for support. In this sense, democracy is certainly a tragic regime, subject to hubris, as was known and was seen in the second half of fifth century Athens; it had to confront the issue of its own self-limitation."[46] And on an earlier occasion: "In a democracy, people *can* do anything—and must know that they *ought not* to do and say just anything. Democracy is the regime of self-limitation; therefore, it is also the regime of historical risk—another way of saying that it is the regime of freedom—and a tragic regime."

Later in the same paragraph, Castoriadis explains how he conceives and uses hubris in this context:

> *Hubris* does not really presuppose freedom; it presupposes the absence of fixed norms, the essential vagueness of the ultimate bearings of our actions. Transgressing the law is not *hubris*; it is a definite and limited misdemeanor. *Hubris* exists where self-limitation is the only "norm," where "limits" are transgressed which are nowhere defined. The question of the limits to the self-instituting activity of a community unfolds in two moments. Is there any intrinsic criterion of and for the law? Can there be an effective guarantee that this criterion, however defined, will not be transgressed? ... The answer to both questions is a definite *no*.[47]

There are several terms and notions common to both occasions that need elaboration—certainly: hubris, self-limitation, absence of fixed norms—but it might be helpful to see why Castoriadis always opts to identify democracy, not as a system, or even, more significantly a process or a procedure, but as a regime. Surely, the colloquial usage of the word "regime" evokes an inflexible political image, hardly conducive to conditions of emancipation. The "regime change" slogan of the imperialist Bush Doctrine is the essence of this image at its most demeaning. The most neutral way of using the word is to allude to a set of conditions as such—in physics, it is often used to account for limit conditions (particularly resonant here) of measured parameters. When Castoriadis refers to democracy as a "regime of freedom"—significantly bending the inflexible colloquial image in *regime*—he counteracts the more typical images of democracy as procedure.[48] It's not that he doesn't recognize that democracy, like all political institutions, bears its own specific constellation of procedures. Rather, he decries the reduction of democracy to its procedures, which is how it is commonly considered: as system rather than form. The issue is about democracy not as a form of government—which, in terms of its own procedural character necessitates a system of government—but, rather, as a form of *governance*, which implicates both the governing and the governed in an inextricable, complicit, and continuously overturning relation. The Greek word for regime is *politeia*, a society's political state of things, Plato's very title unfortunately mistranslated as *Republic* or, worse yet, *Der Staat*.

Democracy cannot be reduced to procedure because whatever is procedural about it is ultimately provisional, in the sense that it must be always subjected to question, reconsideration, and possible revision. The grandest and commonest travesty of democracy is the ritual of interrupting your day-to-day routine to go to the voting booth once a year (or every two or four years) to exercise your electoral right. I say this in full cognizance of the importance of voting, particularly in so-called liberal democracies whose constitutive political tradition is marred by extraordinary efforts to disenfranchise people of their electoral rights on account of race, sex, poverty, or even ideological leanings. But the electoral ritual is not what democracy is about in essence. Historically speaking, although the Greeks invented elections in politics, the electoral principle is not initially democratic; its origin resides in the aristocracy.[49] In modern terms, the electoral ritual is at best the instrumental act, on a specific and unreproducible occasion, of a lifelong commitment to citizen action. At worst, it is a perfunctory ideological act, which could just as well be undertaken by a robot.

Democracy then is a regime of the provisional; this is what it means not to recognize and inculcate fixed norms. It is anything but normative, which is why one of the most absurd elements of its history is the attempt to export it or impose it on other societies. The ancients were just as guilty of this absurdity as the moderns and with equally catastrophic results, for others as well as themselves. We misjudge the "nature" of democracy if we see this as an aberration. While contrary to democratic values of autonomy, it lies nonetheless within range of democracy's constitutive excess. What might be deemed absurd in the language of the moderns qualifies to be called *hubris* in the language of the Greeks. The Melian massacre may be the most indicative and famous instance of Athenian hubris, but just as significant are the condemnation and execution of Socrates (even if Socrates himself is exemplary of democratic hubris), the Sicilian Expedition, a number of ostracisms for political expediency, and most of what Alcibiades (Socrates's famous pupil) did in his public life.

As a theatrical form, Athenian tragedy is a profound meditation on hubris, not as formal characteristic according to dramatic convention but as a social condition of the polis. This is not to say simply that tragedy is essentially political, but neither is it to say that tragedy is merely aesthetic or a matter of religious ritual or just a form of mass entertainment. The bibliography on this contested issue is enormous and spans at least two centuries of expert writings, all of them seeking to understand an archaic society about which ultimately little is known relative to its complexity. The name of this complexity is the *political* as such, emerging from the agonistic coexistence of contradictory elements in everyday life that create the unprecedented form of society's self-organization we still call democracy. What transmutes this complexity into society's self-organization is a tragic sense of life. This is what lends democracy its tragedy. With the notable exception of Aeschylus's *Eumenides* (458 BCE), which is perfectly explainable historically, tragedy does not put democracy on the stage in any literal sense. Tragic theater *is* political not because of its content but because, by all the different accounts, it is *endemic* to this peculiar mode of self-organization that emerged in Athens. Tragedy's political character includes all "nonpolitical" elements that remain essential to it throughout, including its various stagings of *oikonomia* and all of its ritualistic and entertainment aspects. Self-interrogation presupposes a performative distance; in the theater, unlike in the agora space, the *dēmos* is not the actor but the audience.[50] This spatial relation between the agora and the theater, where everyone in the city assembles, including women, slaves, and foreigners, is essential to Athenian tragic sensibility. To what extent the theater space emerges de facto as an alternate assembly space is, moreover, key to understanding both the events of Athenian history in this period and the sui generis theatricality of the Athenian "mind." No historical but also no philosophical understanding of democracy in Athens can be achieved without underlining how profoundly embedded theater was in Athenian life.

Although it would be questionable to disavow tragedy's multivalent social significance and even contradictory purposes, and therefore irresponsible to speak of it as an undifferentiated whole (despite its compact historical specificity, its meteoric rise and fall as a classical form), I would nonetheless underline that the Athenian masterpieces of theater we still celebrate were produced and performed mostly while the city was at war. This is to say, in conditions when a city operates at its most existentially essential (all Greek societies, Athens too, were warrior societies) and yet at its most existentially vulnerable. Christian Meier puts it succinctly: "The citizens had grown so unused to normal life that they were vulnerable to delusion."[51] Under such precarious conditions in a city at nearly permanent war where the people have become intoxicated with their own desire for uncertainty, much like suffering from permanent sleep deprivation, tragic theater seems especially well configured to place before the polity the event of its own hubris, even if this was conducted within parameters of ritual that were historically endemic and ordinary or conditions of entertainment that were eventually cultivated as a social institution.

Whatever might be the magnitude of these tragedies as masterpieces of the theater, which we still appreciate and honor today, pales before their magnitude as events, as social institutions through which the polis performs its own self-interrogation—something we certainly don't appreciate today and don't honor because it is altogether inconceivable. Just so I am not misunderstood: I am not saying there is no longer great art being created, great protest art or even visionary art that disrupts and overturns society's established hegemonies. I *am* saying there is no art form that quintessentially stages the self-interrogation of society as a whole; there is no social institution that can envision such a thing much less enable it to happen; there is no polity that has such a sense of itself as to place itself before a performance court that would stand witness and pass judgment on its own injustices and excesses.

The Athenian tragedies we have inherited wield their lasting power because they articulate in one and the same language both the political self-interrogation of the society that enables these plays to exist and the larger anthropological imaginary that enables that society to exist. The two moments (the political and the anthropological) are never fully separated, though they denote different registers, because Athenians of this period are a society that exists on the edge of the social imaginary that animates it; they function almost at a zero point of self-occlusion or concealment.[52] What they do and the reasons for doing it, why they act and the sense of their action, is out in the open, argued and counterargued, justified and accounted for, to an extent and a speed impossible to imagine, even in an exhaustively media driven society like ours (where, of course, secrecy reigns supreme). For this reason, the Athenians are a society all the more vulnerable to excessive, hubristic behavior.[53] Thucydides's characterization of Athenian excess is well known:

> Athenians are addicted to innovation, sharp in conceiving their designs and swift in executing them. . . . They are daring beyond their power and court danger against their better judgment, yet in the midst of trouble they remain sanguine. Their determination is unwavering and they are never at home, for they think that the further they go the more they will achieve. They are swift to pursue the ground of victory, but don't dwell on defeat. . . . If they invent a scheme and don't execute it, they feel they have lost something that belongs

to them; if they pursue something and gain it, they consider it a small thing compared to future gains; if they try something and fail, they look elsewhere to mitigate the lack. Only in them does the hope for gain match gain itself, because of the speed with which they execute their decisions. Their sense of peace and quiet is to do what needs to be done; lack of action or overburdened labor is considered misfortune. In short, their nature is to never find rest for themselves and never let anyone else find rest" (*History*, Book I, 70:1-9, my translation).

Although imbued with the objectivity of history, this characterization is staged theatrically, as the enemy Corinthians, almost like a chorus, perform it as a warning lesson to the enemy Spartans. The theatricality of the setting parallels the doubleness (and duplicity) of the character performed. Athenian character is exalted at the very moment it is pronounced exemplary hubris—yet not by its own voice, but by an other in a theater of others.

Hubris permeates the entire Greek world (at least until the Hellenistic era) as a kind of cosmic principle to which every mortal is subjected, even the Persian king (as Herodotus argues). Even though this condition is commonly thought to pertain to individuals, democratic Athens can be deemed to stage hubris as a condition for an entire society. Here, the individual's incapacity to know the limit—the problem of hubris as cosmic order is that there are limits, but we can never know them—is generalized as the crux of how society is organized politically. Athens marks a peculiar historical phenomenon, in a social imaginary organized around this cosmological principle, as a society that pushes itself to such an extent that its entire mode of self-organization works at the precipice of this condition, so that all institutional safeguards are open to question and subversion. On this basis we may confront the constitutive question, as Vidal-Naquet has argued, of whether in the space of the political that the emergence of the polis as form inaugurates democracy is merely an extension or indeed a radical innovation.[54] If it is the second, as Vidal-Naquet implies, then the "translation" of hubris from cosmic principle governing individual fate to political reality permeating the society is perfectly applicable to Athens, at least from the Cleisthenes reforms to the Macedonian era.

This instituted invisibility of limits—a paradox, if there is one—is difficult to understand from the standpoint of a social imaginary trained to perceive limits sanctioned by writing, especially when it comes to economics and law. Even before democracy is instituted, the Greek city form of social organization is characterized by a peculiar relation to political order that straddles the boundary between the performative and the written. Greeks no doubt inherited (or learned) a great deal from the Phoenicians, including seafaring and shipbuilding, to which they made their own adjustments, but nothing compares with the innovation of introducing signs for vowels to alphabetic writing, and this cannot be brushed aside as mere whim. Some sort of engaging desire ("intention" would presume we know more than we can about an archaic society) to sustain the permutations and nuances of oral life in the new reality of inscription has to be supposed. It is difficult to account for the specific motivation behind this innovation, but its symptom says a great deal. Christian Meier makes the daring proposition that "it looks as though they meant to use this new technique primarily to give permanence to their literature" (*Athens*, 100–101). Moreover, Vernant argues that because of its phonetic character, Greek writing is wrested away from "the specialty of a class of scribes" and forges "an element of a common culture" that reverses its social and psychological significance: "The purpose of writing was no longer the production of archives for the king's private use within the palace. Now it served a public purpose: it allowed the various aspects of social and political life to be disclosed to the gaze of all people equally.... [It marked] the transformation of secret wisdom into a body of public truths."[55]

Writing's relation specifically to the workings of the law is crucial here, although the discussion is vast. Essential is the navigation of this complexity by Deborah Steiner in *The Tyrant's Writ* (1994), angled ultimately in favor of written law as an instrument of tyranny against the performativity of democratic politics. The significance of oratorical agonistics to the latter cannot be underestimated. At the same time, Jacqueline de Romilly's *La loi dans la pensée grecque des origines à Aristote* (1971) makes a counterclaim, establishing written law as the guaranteed protection of *isonomia*, with specific reference to the famous passage in Euripides's *Suppliants* (424 BCE) that makes the point explicitly: "with laws written, the weak and the rich have equal justice" (*dikēn isēn*). The matter is not easily settled. However Greek law was written, regardless, it was not written in stone, as the metaphor goes; its writing did not abolish its performative (oratorical) interrogation but made it impossible for any one individual to "speak" the law. In Greece, legislators can be poets, but they are never prophets.

If indeed the development of phonetic writing was due to a "literary desire" to anchor poetry to something more permanent than mere memorized transmission of oral performative techniques, starting with the painstaking transcription of the Homeric epics (each more than fifteen thousand lines long), we can suppose further that what underlies it is a broader historicizing imaginary that culminates, if Thucydides is to be taken seriously, in Pericles's explicit claim that Athenians are indeed establishing traces for the future (*aei*). In other words, this exceeds mere accounting of social relations in law and economics that we see in the writing of many archaic societies and provides an overt documentation of the *political* order of things in its full complexity. Here, too, Athens lies at the forefront of excess, for it is the only city to provide such a voluminous record of its vicissitudes, including, of course, its literary, intellectual, and performative life.

In fifth-century Athens this lack of external norms and guarantees is at a peak; hence both Sophocles and Euripides (even if in different terms) warn about irreverence toward the entire cosmic order. The stakes of and demands for self-limitation are consistently being raised and challenged and, since there is nothing intrinsically permanent to act as a final limit, Athenian society commits extraordinarily self-destructive acts in the very midst of its most glorious age. Castoriadis again: "Democracy is the regime that explicitly renounces all ultimate 'guarantees' and knows no limitations other than its self-limitation. It certainly can transgress its self-limitation, as has so often been the case in history; it can thereby sink into the void [*s'abîmer*] or turn into its contrary. This is tantamount to saying that democracy is the only tragic regime—it is the sole regime that *takes risks*, that faces openly the possibility of its self-destruction.... Democracy is always within the problem of its self-limitation, and nothing can 'resolve' this problem in advance."[56]

This notion of self-limitation has nothing to do with what, under liberalism, is a series of equally presumed tropes: the self-regulation of the market or civil society, the moral freedom of self-constraint, the self-taming of civilization, the self-discipline of desire, and so forth. In Athenian democracy self-limitation takes place in the absence of indications of where limits are, while in liberalism self-limitation as self-constraint means literally to step back, to withdraw, from limits either already known or presumed. Liberalism presupposes limits tacitly in the name of protecting the interests of liberty, in the same way that it extends the bounds of inclusion by silencing the markings of exclusion. Ultimately this is a mechanistic logic of order; the projected ideal is the presumed self-regulation of the market coupled with the self-control of individual desire. In a tragic universe, however, limits are unseen and therefore absent until the moment they appear. And they appear in order to vanish again—they appear to denote a fait accompli, like death, which is the ultimate and unsurpassable limit whose precise moment of appearance can never be foretold. In this situation, self-limitation is an act of resistance to the alterity of limit, which in that ultimate sense can never be governed. As a response to the danger of hubris, self-limitation is therefore an act of resistance against the heteronomy that is always lurking in mere life.[57]

Keeping in mind their historical specificity, Athenian tragedies are exemplary sensors of the city's vulnerability to hubris, serving as a sort of last safeguard, even if indirectly (perhaps mysteriously) posed and often failing. Borrowing freely from Jacques Derrida, I would argue that tragedy is an instance of democracy's autoimmunity.[58] This performance of autoimmunity is conducted in immensely varied, if not contradictory, range of ways, even in the handful of surviving plays. If Aeschylus's *Oresteia* (458 BCE) may be said to stage the democratic city's reconciliation of residual tribal strife as political autonomy, his *Prometheus Bound* (430 BCE) exposes the problem of defying the last instance of heteronomous authority. Sophocles's *Ajax* (450 BCE) dramatizes the repercussions of a new cosmic order where change becomes the measure of the cosmos (Protagoras), while his *Antigone* (442 BCE) presses radically upon the hubristic potential of autonomy (*monos phronein*), with or against the law. If Aeschylus's *Persians* (472 BCE) might mirror to Athenians how victory is measured by the hubris of the enemies they defeated, Euripides's *Trojan Women* (415 BCE) exposes, as Athens is preparing for the Sicilian Expedition, what the possible hubris of war in the name of the polis might mean to the *oikos*, Sicilian or, just as well, Athenian.

The characterization of my examples is speculative and partial. No one can know with certainty whether these stagings were perceived in this fashion, but also no one can dismiss their *co-incidence* with known historical events and yet not fully known epistemic conditions. What precipitates what? Any common conceptions of tragedy are insufficient to explain how democracy as such may be tragic. Surely, if we remain within the Aristotelian view of tragedy, we are bound to a specific perspective. Aristotle, whose distanced view of Athens through the eyes of a metic should not be underestimated, is the great ancient theorist of democracy, but he theorizes from mere experience of its demise, from the standpoint of its remnants, which enables him to say practically everything about how democracy works or doesn't except to explain how a polity envisions itself or thinks of itself *in* and *as* a democracy. Far more than Aristotle, our master texts in this regard are Thucydides and above all the tragedies themselves. Indeed, Thucydides's history is a tragedy of the first order, where the Athenian *dēmos* is the tragic protagonist exemplifying the Sophoclean *deinon*, the daring capacity that celebrates human creation in one moment and precipitates destruction in the next. Thucydides shows in what sense the Athenians engage in hubris, not as an aberration but precisely because of their way of life, of perilous democratic life.[59]

In Aristotle's time, theater had changed, not so much as a form but as practice, as communal self-interrogation and critique.[60] Hence his ruminations are restricted to a formalist comprehension of the existential—we would say in today's language—predicament of the hero. Surely, the fact that the tragic hero has been, since Aristotle, gendered masculine, despite the extraordinary figures of women we see in the handful of surviving tragedies, is enough to raise questions about the legacy of Aristotelian poetics.[61] A common motif in subsequent interpretations of the tragic hero figure is that he stands ultimately speechless before the nonlanguage of fate. This speechlessness in the suspension, interruption, or more precisely, self-undoing of *logos* before fate may be where the tragic element in the hero figure manifests itself in the final instance. Nietzsche's affluent speech against the empty speech of both philology and theology of his day would seem to dispute this interpretation. Perhaps this is because Nietzsche is not quite the tragic hero of modern philosophy but its tragedian. In the end, the figure of the tragic hero may be an essential literary topos, and a great deal more still remains to be said about it, but it does not encapsulate the meaning of tragic life that I isolate here as essential to democracy. On the contrary, a tragic sense of life is indifferent to anything heroic. There is nothing heroic about democracy.

In Plato's ears, this very phrase would certify his conviction that democracy exemplifies a polity's illness, much as tragedy (and more substantially, poetry) leads a city astray from its heroic values. In his famous condemnation of democracy in the *Republic*, Plato is succinct: there is nothing heroic about democracy because it is a regime of self-undoing violence. It emerges out of a revolutionary desire for whatever is new. Plato seems to echo Thucydides's description of the Athenians: democracy's advocates are "in love with innovation" (Book VIII, 555d 10). Worse yet, democracy feeds on the sick body (*sōma nosōdes*) of the polis in order to produce internal strife, civil war, stasis [*stasiazei auto autō*] (556e 5). In other words, since it precipitates self-undoing, democracy is against the natural order of the polis (whose safeguard is the aristocratic privilege of autochthonous

Athenians), which is also to say that democracy is the fatal undoing of *politics*. What Aristotle signifies as the very attributes of freedom (the desire not to be ruled by anyone, which leads to the epistemic *co-incidence* of ruler and ruled) is for Plato the most damning element of democracy. In a democratic city, "there is no requirement to rule in this city [*mēdemian anagkēn einai archein en tautē tē polei*], even if you're capable of it, or again to be ruled if you don't want to be" (557e 2-4). The Platonic sense of the democratic sensibility is that it breeds the desire to abstain from the responsibility of politics altogether; in Plato's framework, the behavior of Otanis in Herodotus is but an exemplary instance of the decadence of a democratic mind. The perspective is skewed, of course, and the charge unwarranted. If anything, the problem is that Athenians are ever too eager to rule, and they are susceptible to reckless rule. But Plato does not respond to the contradictions of Athenian democracy. He sees the contradictions as failures, and he responds with genuine abhorrence and contempt.

But to rehearse Plato's explicit antidemocratic sentiment isn't to say much at all. What is worth underlining is the tropology of this sentiment, his strategy of logical reversal: his argument is consistent in that the very things that make democracy a radical regime make it reprehensible. In this respect, Plato demonstrates that the greatest enemy of democracy is democracy itself; because he cannot accept this paradox, he becomes democracy's enemy. Plato's analysis is not so much a formal definition of democracy (as may be said of Aristotle's) but an account of the preconditions of its emergence and the conditions of its certain, self-determined, destruction. Plato is the first to stipulate that democracy always emerges by revolution: the radical alteration of the status quo, a novelty in which violence always inheres. After all, he argues, the first targets of democratic politics are the ruling elites, which surely invites the question of whether there can ever be a democratic politics that does not induce their fear and threatens their wealth and privilege. As traditional elites face the decision either to submit and participate in the new regime or face exile, for Plato, the ultimate target of this violence is the polity itself. For even participation is a sham, since democratic politics is determined by the arbitrary equalization of governing by lot.

There is nothing more reprehensible to Plato than the regime of governing by lot; the notion goes against all the laws in the universe. The very gravity of this realization shows the radical magnitude of the social imaginary at work in Athenian society. It is important to note here that Platonic philosophy draws a new line of thinking that counters many of the crucial elements of the Greek social imaginary. For example, lot (*klēros*), as a social institution of warrior tribes, emerges from the imaginary horizon that privileges a sort of cosmic allotment: fate. As in the post-Homeric universe fate (*moira*) is replaced by justice (*dikē*), in democracy we may speak of another register of allotment where law (*nomos*) becomes the operative framework, according to the exigencies of land apportionment (*nemein*). Yet tragic life (and tragedy as a poetic form) retains, as it were, a measure of the archaic *moira*—fate being essentially one's allotted piece of the fabric of the universe. In this sense alone, the preeminence of lot as a political institution in democratic Athens testifies to its being literally a tragic regime.[62]

For Plato all this is tantamount to a cosmological anathema. In light of the hierarchical demands of Platonic philosophy this imaginary signifies one's self-enslavement, for it lays one open to indiscriminate desire, to "surrendering rule over oneself to whatever desire comes along, as if it were chosen by lot [*lakhousē tēn eautou arkhēn*]" (561b 2)—literally, as if one's own rule (rule over oneself, one's autonomy) were a matter of chance. Democracy is indeed indiscriminate insofar as it fosters *isonomia* and *parrhēsia*, that is, insofar as it abolishes hierarchy in the law and enables the freedom to say anything. Plato derides this indiscriminate attitude literally as "supermarket politics" (*pantopōlion politeiōn*, 557d 8), which in the end produces an incapacity to act politically, a failure even to rule over oneself, indeed an intoxication that ultimately deauthorizes any principles of ruling, so that either anarchy reigns unlimited or tyranny gains total control. Because "a democratic city thirsts for freedom," Plato argues, it is vulnerable to "the lot of bad cupbearers" and thus to a regime of "uncontrolled intoxication" (*akratos methē*). The adjective cannot go by uncommented: *akratos* means a condition where there is nothing to hold onto and nothing to be beholden to but also, politically speaking, a regime without power, without *kratos*, a stateless, drifting condition, where freedom means insatiable desire that annihilates all *archē*.

This uncompromising mathematics in which the politics of the multitude is tantamount to the rule of none, to the annihilation of very conditions of rule—when even ruling over oneself fails—is a societal malady: the city suffers from democratic addiction. The malady is incurable, and the outcome is certain self-destruction. Democracy marches inevitably toward tyranny, a tyranny already produced in the contempt toward authority with which a people intoxicated by freedom treat all traditional rulers until one of their own (a "bad cupbearer") magnetizes everyone's desire toward his ruling hand. Aristotle too names one of the dangers of democracy to be the prospect of falling under the rule of the One, but for him this is just a possibility, nothing more: the occasion when the many overtake the law they share in making by consolidating themselves into one, so that the *dēmos* becomes *monarchos*, a singular ruler (*Politics*, Book IV 1292a). For Plato the danger is not the possible consolidation of the many into one, but the one's demagogic usurpation of the many which democracy endemically enables. It is altogether certain: tyranny is democracy's internal teleology. Underneath all that, what Plato targets as the greatest threat is democracy's intoxication induced by freedom, its openness to uncontrolled desire, which destroys all order—"it makes its way into private households and in the end breeds anarchy even among the animals" (562e 3-5).

It is elementary to point out that this language, the very analytical rubric Plato employs, is but a repetition of the terms of his condemnation of poetry—mimesis, performativity, tragedy—in the earlier books of the *Republic*. Plato knows very well that democracy is a tragic regime, and that is precisely why he finds it insufferable. In the *Laws* (701a) he famously calls it "theatrocracy" in a passage that links the audience's capacity to judge art with its vulgarity of taste and its power (*kratos*) to demand a spectacle (*theatron*). In the *Republic* philosophy doesn't just vanquish poetry (tragedy) as a form of knowledge, but it vanquishes democracy as a way of life—the combination means to say that philosophy vanquishes tragic life. The legacy of this gesture is the great triumph of theological configurations of life, which in the modern world shift easily into technological configurations of life—the *technē* of the permutations of Logos. In the end, Plato's strategy of deploying philosophy against democracy is caught in a brilliant ironic loop. Not only, very simply, because philosophy emerges out of democracy—even if philosophers of democracy don't exist (poets are actually the intellectuals of democracy)—but also because the hubris of democracy is epitomized by the most hubristic Athenian sophist, Socrates, who in the hands of Plato becomes the exemplar of philosophy as poetry's and democracy's simultaneous defeat.

NO DEMOCRACY WITHOUT DISSENT

From the standpoint of this inquiry, tragedy as a poetic form has much to do with how democracy is tragic, but as a symptom, not as a source. A tragic sense of life, on the other hand, is consubstantial with the imaginary of democracy. And the space of inquiring, examining, and envisioning what "tragic life" might mean is hardly restricted to literary types. Earlier I said that tragedy is an instance of democracy's autoimmunity. I am freely borrowing from Derrida here, but it is uncertain whether he would see tragedy this way—in any case, he does not gesture in this direction. However, when he argues that "democracy protects itself and maintains itself precisely by limiting and threatening itself" (R, 36), he invokes the crux of the notion of democracy as a tragic regime. It is not only a matter of absence of guarantees that opens democracy to the peril of hubris. It is that its very *nature*—if this term is at all appropriate—is continuously (self-)denaturalizing, that is to say, continuously reminding us and demanding of us to come to terms with the fact that our "nature" is political: conflictual, antagonistic, and power-ridden, yes, but also, unconditionally collective, interdependent, and accountable to the differential contours of forming and transforming a social space that our singular identity cannot contain: "The thinking of the political has always been a thinking of *différance* and the thinking of *différance* always a thinking *of* the political, of the contour and limits of the political, especially around the enigma or the autoimmune *double bind* of the democratic" (R, 39).

Note, in this phrase, that the democratic is configured as the limit of the political. I would say it is the self-limitation of the political, the limit instituted *as* the political, precisely in the sense that the polis emerges out of a social imaginary that conceptualizes the limitless as a mediating terrain, as *meson*. This is tragic language. The paradoxical terrain we have been encountering since the early section on Anaximander hinges on this untenable sense of limit. Specifically: on the a priori absence of limits that necessitates the creation of limits, first and foremost, as internal contours of differentiation, self-differentiation. The double bind occurs because if democracy places "objective" or external limits (let's say, a constituted body of laws that must be obeyed no matter what), it ceases to be democracy. Yet if it places no limits—a kind of anomie (which is in fact socially impossible, but that's another discussion)—it also ceases to be democracy. Derrida's proposed solution, an autoimmunity that protects the organism from itself, is to enact self-limitation, which, however, cannot be self-interdiction, self-censorship, repression of desire, etc., because then democracy lapses yet again. Democracy surely does not consist of a bunch of happily law-abiding citizens. That is a travesty of citizenship, a totalitarian nightmare. Nor is it, however, a bunch of freely consensual citizens, devoid of antagonism and political impetus. Contrary to whatever liberalism argues, the cornerstone of democracy is not consensus but dissent. You can still have democracy without consensus, but you have no democracy without dissent.

Therefore, divisiveness is not a negative or politically disempowering principle in the democratic imaginary. On the contrary, it underlies the requisite resistance to uniformity; it animates the heterogeneity necessary to withstand a debilitating stability (or status quo) of political agency. Athenian democracy is born out of instability and radical inequality. The multitude of the poor rebel against their indebted servitude. Solon's response, which may be considered the founding act, is the cancellation of all debts (*seisakhtheia*, which literally means the ceasing of all burden), that is to say, a zeroing of the ground of social organization. This abolition of economic slavery by a law that both founds and unfounds, grounds and ungrounds, opens a new horizon in two ways: (1) it banishes the power of the economy from the political sphere and makes this severance an essential task of democracy for here onward; and (2) it introduces the possibility that *isonomia*, the radical equivalence that balances contrary forces which already existed in the conceptual cosmological horizon of the Greeks, can become a political principle. No longer simply the social privilege among the equal by birth (the warrior aristocracy), *isonomia* becomes the rule of all citizens and, liberated from the power of brute might, becomes a political dimension that now marks precisely the differentiated and unequal.

This new horizon is expressly dramatized by the peculiar conceptualization of the Cleisthenes reforms, whose numerology is worth a little attention. Cleisthenes divides the traditional (in all Greek cities) four tribes to one hundred *dēmoi* (multiple of ten communal units), each of which is composed in turn of three parts according to a spatial *nomos* that creates a hybrid geography: each *dēmos* includes a part drawn from each of the three urban demographic terrains (city center, inland, shoreline) without regard to neighboring proximity. This does not dissolve the urban distribution of tribal privilege or class difference, but it does create an artificially equivalent framework of political constituency. Aristocratic families still live in the city center; they just cannot constitute a political block on the basis of their central location, socially and spatially. The fact that they persist on trying with dogged resolve, but with only occasional and temporary success, very much attests to the effectiveness of this new order.

Detaching wealth from power by disrupting the unifying mechanisms of kinship reorganizes society's framework, so that "the individual Athenian becomes a protagonist of political decision making. Rendering the individual central to democracy was a strategy designed to bolster those who were essentially only individuals and could not rely upon social connections and strong classes like the nobles or oligarchs."[63] To further disrupt such entrenched consolidations of power, Cleisthenes "inducted in the tribes [*ephuleteuse*] many foreigners and alien slaves" (Aristotle, *Politics* III, 1275b). Simply speaking, to break down aristocratic kinship privilege means no less than to create, by political means, a new organization of society where those who until then were simply unprotected individuals can find collective belonging. This new form of collective being, the *dēmos*, creates a whole other source of power for the individual, which is unrelated to birth or social standing. Democracy is a regime of creation indeed, of *poiēsis*. Such is precisely the verb (*epoiēse*) that Aristotle uses to describe Cleisthenes's act of transformation (*metabolē*): the making of citizens. And the matter is driven even further. This bona fide poietic moment altogether alters the meaning of citizen (*politēs*): no longer simply the person who belongs to the polis, but the person who shares equally in the politics of the polis. Aristotle is perfectly clear on the fact that in democracy the notion of the citizen is altogether alien to all other notions previously under different political systems, suggesting in the end that democracy is a regime of *created citizens* [*poiētous politas*] (*Politics*, III, 1275a), which does not quite mean poet-citizens but definitely means poetically made citizens, which is really to say that both law and institution in democracy are explicitly matters of *poiēsis*.

Since Aristotle, much has been said of the significance of Cleisthenes shifting from a duodecimal to a decimal framework, with the decimal signifying a poetically revolutionary geometry that goes against the grain of long-established tribal imagination and practice. The singular significance of number twelve in the archaic Ionian imaginary, especially in terms of religious ritual (the religious calendar, the Olympian gods, etc.) is common knowledge. There is thus a common acceptance of the fact that the decimal geometry of Cleisthenes's political reforms is simultaneously a sort of secularization, in today's language; hence, Plato's corrective ideal is also in these terms a resacralization. Certainly, what drives Cleisthenes is a disruptive aspiration, where *isonomia*, a perfect symmetry of equidistance and equivalence, is the primary mobilizing principle.[64] But in terms of disintegrating and integrating division, this disruptive arithmetic ($4 \to 10 \to 3$) is entirely asymmetrical. It points to the limit of what can be divided and how: a transformative arithmetic in the sense that each act undoes the digital architecture of the previous one. Mathematically, no division is possible here from the standpoint of the whole; the equation leaves a nonintegral remainder. Politically, however, it leaves no remainder at all; all citizens are accounted for equally. This disjunction explains how a polis that remains heterogeneous in all social and economic respects—since Athenian democracy abolishes neither class structure nor inequality between the sexes, nor difference between indigeneity and foreignness— nonetheless achieves a political unity.[65]

Etymological actualities are inadequate here: unity does not mean oneness—just as social-economic equality does not necessarily (causally) imply political isonomy. As Castoriadis points out, the Cleisthenes reforms signify a shift from what he calls a pre-political organization ("in the abstract, logical, non-temporal sense of the term") to a political organization. In this process, the pre-political is not abolished as a social-imaginary institution, but it does become secondary to what is, as a result, a new (*political*) mode of organizing society: "The political community is a unity that articulates itself—it cannot but *articulate itself*, because we're not talking here of a mass where each person is in direct relation to power—and where the more ancient elements, without being abolished, retreat in the face of a new form of unity" (*La cité et les lois*, 104). Let us recall here that a key meaning of the French *s'articuler* is to conjoin. To contextualize further I would also add that in the discussion of heterogeneous coarticulation in Athens it is paramount to stress the significance of the myth of Eris (strife). That is to say, the political unity of democracy is always internally conflictual. It is a polemical unity, an antagonistic unity, but unity nonetheless, because Eris (and the oratorical agonistics that it underwrites) can only take place among peers, equal by rule in the context of *isonomia*.

Without specific reference to this historical occasion, Derrida understands this well, and he also understands the literally unsettling mark of democracy: as a political condition that requires an unconditional commitment to the continuous formation and transformation of the polis, which, in this respect, can never settle. Thus the limits of democracy are always under negotiation—more specifically, always challenged as to how they would be recognized, always open to being deinstituted and reinstituted, imagined and reimagined, (self-)created and (self-)destroyed. Thus, democracy is precarious at the very least and indeed dangerous—to itself most of all. One might say that its condition is an unconditional hospitality to an indefinite plurality of forces, even to forces that are hostile to it, forces which it may engender but to which it is not immune. We know enough of today's medicine, as mere mortal objects of it, to know the perils of autoimmunity syndromes. Autoimmunity may be configured as the epitome of an unconditional condition of bearing the self: the body's immunity mechanism extends even to itself, thereby producing a line of defense not merely against the body's breaches by dangerous others, or even its own excesses and failures, but also against its own constitution. The self conjures itself as an other and stages a brutal line of defense against the evident threat of this (self-)othering. The result is the demise of the self, against which the self mounts yet another defense, and so on—but not ad infinitum, because the body is positively finite. Democracy is finite, too; the Athenian experience is only too illustrative. But this is true of all societies, all human forms, all living being. The point here is that democracy, more than any other mode of political organization, is likely to give itself over to suicidal practices.

For Derrida specifically, this raises a question he always asks or demands to deconstruct somewhere along the line, the question of the end—of *telos*, which is neither spatial nor temporal, but again partakes of the paradox of self-limitation without conditions. Derrida has famously championed the notion of "democracy-to-come," which is based on a deconstruction of the French word for "future": *à-venir*. A notion developed variously in many of his later texts, from *Specters of Marx* and "Faith and Knowledge" to *The Politics of Friendship* onward, it is interestingly produced here according to the terms I just mentioned, democracy's suicidal tendencies: "Democracy has always been suicidal, and if there is a to-come for it, it is only on the condition of thinking life otherwise" (R, 33). In response I would add that not only openness to self-destruction (the risk of suicide) but the very phrase "life otherwise" signals indeed the tragic life, the sort of life that does not cower from confronting the actuality of living as the experience of othering, of encountering the other without conditions but with the consequence of forming and transforming the other within oneself.

In this respect, though accessing the language of the future, the notion of democracy-to-come is not conjured on the basis of some sort of ideal to be reached. Nor does it belong to the language of utopia—not even literally, because *l'à-venir* does have a place, albeit according to the paradox of an always displaceable place, whatever forges a political community autonomous from the power of both autochthony and kinship. Temporally speaking, this paradoxical place requires alertness and self-critical responsibility to one's finite here-and-now, whose integrity is consolidated, to quote Edward Said once more, from the fact that "criticism is always postulated and performed on the assumption that it is to have a future."⁶⁶ Said, who in his last work clarified that if it is to be worthy of its name criticism must be democratic, is clearly aware of the future being subject to performance in the present, which remains the only time of political action. But he also insinuates the reverse: the present critical act is indebted to a future that it inaugurates even if it does not necessarily actualize. Derrida's *à-venir* is similar in that it disrupts the instrumental temporality of democratic institution and thus its pretense to finality. *Là-venir* signifies that the process of democratic institution is interminable and, in this sense, permanently out of reach as a *telos*. Its temporality is simultaneously synchronic, deferred, and yet still envisioned, even if ultimately impossible to articulate in any logical language of time. To quote Derrida from another context: this temporality signifies "a future so radically to come that it resists even the grammar of the future anterior."⁶⁷ This means a future that cannot be historicized at any point, a future that will never come to be past—never come to pass, interminable, no passage.

Derrida says outright that "the expression 'democracy-to-come' does indeed translate or call for a militant and interminable political critique," which he quickly amends by contending that the notion encapsulates that "democracy will always remain aporetic in its structure" (R 86).⁶⁸ The political challenge is to engage this aporia not with the instrumental desire to resolve it, to find the right path to a way out, but with a certain equanimity about the fact that the passage we carve out of history—for *aporia* literally means impossible passage—is possible precisely because *we* are the ones who make it and not some institutional authority (*archē*), and, moreover, because we make it with a full sense of circuitous adventure (*peripeteia*), uncertain about everything except the passage itself: "the aporia in its general form has to do with freedom itself, with the freedom at play in the concept of democracy" (R, 34).

In other words, Derrida's notion of "democracy-to-come" cannot be signified without simultaneously invoking the figure of autoimmunity:

> Beyond this active and interminable critique, the expression "democracy-to-come" takes into account the absolute and intrinsic historicity of the only system that welcomes in itself, in its very concept, that expression of autoimmunity called the right to self-critique and perfectibility. Democracy is the only system, the only constitutional paradigm, in which, in principle, one has or assumes the right to criticize everything publicly, including the idea of democracy, its concept, its history, and its name. Including the idea of the

constitutional paradigm and the absolute authority of law. It is thus the only paradigm that is universalizable, whence its chance and its fragility. (R, 86–87)

It is interesting to note that some years earlier this sort of formulation is even stronger: "[In keeping] this Greek name, democracy ... one keeps this indefinite right to the question, to criticism, to deconstruction (guaranteed rights, in principle, in any democracy: no deconstruction without democracy, no democracy without deconstruction)."[69]

There is a lot of "only" here in the first quotation and "none without" in the second, yet this is to be understood not as exclusivity or absolute wholeness but rather as radical singularity, as ipseity. The universalizable paradigm encounters the indefinite, *though guaranteed*, right to question, to *crisis*, to deconstruction, which is both the subject and yet also the object of democracy. One might ask guaranteed by what? in what sense?—rightfully presuming that, in the groundless work of democracy, no guarantees are ever *ultimately* possible. There can never be a guarantee to the groundless, the indefinite, the always-in-*crisis*, the unconditionally poised to deconstruction, the none-without. There is no out. Derrida's conclusion is quite intriguing: it is precisely this singularity, this ipseity, that enables democracy's universality, a singularity entirely within history, *as* history: "absolute and intrinsic historicity." But it is not clear to me that this conclusion—although I find it entirely understandable and agreeable—can actually stand in terms of Derrida's argument, particularly in terms of his imperative toward radical alterity. This may indeed be a moment of autoimmunity in his own text.

Jacques Rancière is especially useful in this regard, even if he points out something self-evident: the fact that Derrida's persistent investment in the politics of singularity is the consequent outcome of "something that Derrida cannot endorse, namely, the idea of substitutability, the indifference to difference or the equivalence of the same and of the other." Hence, Rancière claims, Derrida's democracy is actually "a democracy without a demos" since if "the democracy to come cannot be a community of substitutable persons, it cannot be a community of equals."[70] Rancière explains his reading by pinpointing what I have also argued is the elemental problem in Derrida's political thinking: "the commitment to an absolute other, an 'other' who can never become the same as us, who cannot be substituted ... an 'other' who cannot stage his or her otherness, who cannot put on the stage the relationship between his or her inclusion and his or her exclusion. 'Democracy to come' means a democracy without a demos, with no possibility that a subject perform the *kratos* of the *demos*" ("Should Democracy Come?" 280).

It would not be helpful to take sides here for or against Derrida or Rancière. It is more important rather to underline and elucidate the terms of their argument. On the one hand, Derrida opts for an aporetic framework, whereby the resolutely singular (incalculable, undecidable, unreproducible, unconditional) enables the opening to the sort of universal that is never unitary or even unifying but is nonetheless unique: a universal conducted not by patented inclusion that erases difference (therefore, exclusion of otherness) but by the one and only instance of being open to otherness without reciprocity or regulation, without law. Because such unconditionality necessarily exceeds the limit of time, of history, it defies any sort of delineation of passage; it is literally an *aporia*—impossible passage to an incalculable future (*à-venir*).

On the other hand, Rancière opts for a framework of dissensus, whereby any figuration of singular plurality ("We, the People") is intrinsically fissured and differential, no matter what its actual political expression of unity might be. The singularity of this plurality is, in my sense, a matter of performance—the very performance of the political, whose provisionality or radical contingency can never be outmaneuvered or overcome. At the same time—and the *co-incidence* is essential to this figure—the plurality is indeed actualized as such because of the substitutability of the elements that comprise it. The *dēmos* epitomizes the plurality of decision in the political sphere, and in Athens this reaches its most radical extent because (1) every man is called upon to assume the position of decision regardless of his particularity, and (2) this calling to assume the position of decision is emptied of all intentionality—every man is chosen by lot, by sheer chance: "the qualification without qualification," as Rancière calls it, the veritable anarchic element of the "government of chance" (*Dissensus*, 51-52).

The full-fledged substitutability of political actors, instituted under the radical equivalence of chance selection, certainly distinguishes democracy from any other mode of political organization, whether in the ancient or the modern world. Flirting with a Derridean term, Rancière sees this condition as:

> Something extra—a supplementary qualification common to both the rulers and the ruled.... This is the qualification of those that are no more qualified for ruling than they are for being ruled. Democracy means precisely that the

"power of the *dēmos*" is the power of that no *archē* entitles them to exercise. Democracy is a supplementary, or grounding, power that at once legitimizes and delegitimizes every set of institutions or the power of any one set of people.... The political rests on the supplementary "power of the people" which at once founds it and withdraws its foundations. (*Dissensus*, 52)

The equivalence of substitutability which is predicated on the radical element of chance selection, the drawing of lots, is the only way to actualize Aristotle's anarchic conceptualization of rulers and ruled as one people in their plurality: "the unqualified citizen is defined by nothing else so much as by his participation/sharing [*metechein*] in judgment and rule" (*Politics*, III, 1275a). Regardless of the singularity of individuals as social entities, we have to come to terms with the fact that *isonomia* means nothing less than political substitutability, a strict equivalence that does not abolish each one's particular anthropological difference. Political equivalence is not tantamount to social equality, whether determined or implied—and vice versa. Social equality cannot be simply a political goal, as liberalism claims, where at best it becomes nominal equal opportunity. It is difficult to determine exactly what radical social equality would involve, short of an as yet unconfigured economic imaginary as well as a profound reorganization of the terrain of sexual difference which, no matter the gains of relationality and nonbinary sexual determination, has yet to materialize. But political equivalence is entirely possible and has been historically created, albeit in rare instances and in specific historical imaginaries (from the Athenian polis to worker councils' communism and anarcho-syndicalism).[71]

Rancière's wager is how to conceptualize a differential figure that does not allow heterogeneity to become a fetish, an end in itself. (This is why the politics of democracy also has nothing to do with the politics of multiculturalism.) The social imaginary of the Athenian polis demonstrates how alterity can flourish as an internal figure, for no external authority is left unquestioned. No doubt, this refers only to the realm of the political, and as far as democracy in Athens is concerned the stark distinction between the political and the social enables this rather unusual (historically speaking) internal alterity. In those modern societies where a democratic imaginary has emerged (however partially actualized), the political and the social cannot be so easily disengaged—the demand for equality of citizens is tantamount to the demand for equality of all and at all levels—but the radical significance of barring the authorization of external alterity still remains uncompromised. When Rancière unequivocally argues that "heterogeneity means heteronomy" ("Should Democracy Come?" 283), he means to cast a shadow over Derrida's consistent rhetoric of opening to the other in absolute terms.

The truth of the matter is that neither position is unequivocal: neither does heterogeneity *have to* signify heteronomy, nor does opening to the other *have to* signify radical external otherness. For me, adopting Derrida's demand for opening to the other would first mean opening to the otherness in ourselves, to the possibility of being other than we are, a possibility that can never be animated, determined, or authorized by an otherness elsewhere—which would include all manufactured and commercialized hegemonic trends of otherness, regardless of the politics of identity they mobilize and however radical these are conceived to be. If we are to insist on the structural necessity of elsewhere—and I understand the retort that would demand it—this elsewhere has to be found, *to be created*, within our signifying realm as the platform of radical transformation, indeed of self-alteration. The great lesson of democracy—we might even say the incessant demand of democracy—is indeed that autonomy means self-alteration. This can never be authorized by an idea or an a priori principle.

From this standpoint, substitutability in democracy is not a quantitative notion precisely because all singularity is fissured, which in turn prevents plurality from being either cumulative or incremental. The strict isonomy (substitutability) of political actors ensures that the "self" in autonomy is unable to ever come to full self-sufficiency, full *archē*, for the limits of the self are the otherness of the other who is utterly substitutable in a process of itinerant othering, which is exactly what I mean when I say that autonomy means self-alteration. Beyond the psychoanalytic significance of this term, self-alteration is best understood in theatrical terms, where the notion of *I is an other*, in Rimbaud's splendid manner, achieves meaning in a constitutive way: the "I" inheres an otherness that makes the identitary utterance of being ("I am") inadequate. Rimbaud's famous phrase *Je est un autre*—uttered, let us remember, in the midst of the May events of the Paris Commune (1871)—disarticulates not only the Cartesian cogito (*Je suis*) but also the Kantian anthropological prerogative that identifies the human being as the animal who can say "I," for in this case "I" cannot be enacted but by the third person verb form, so that "to be" becomes demonstrably the verb of transformation, of becoming other.

In democracy, one may say that the "I" *is* already an other because the utterance *I am* is already caught in the sharing of *archē* (as quoted earlier from Aristotle) and mediated by lot: being allotted (*nemein*) equally the responsibility of political action regardless of who you are and what is your position in society. This would be an answer to those who think that substitutability is the weapon of capitalist consumer homogenization. Democratic plurality is not the multiplication or proliferation of the One.[72] It is capitalism that quantifies this quality when it renders the individual an impersonal measure of the market, driven by the language of numbers (calculation, proportion, averages, or trends), and therefore turns substitutability into a calculating principle of the marketability of units. While in capitalism substitutability takes place entirely in the language of numbers, in democracy the equivalence is predicated on the recognition of every single person's heterogeneous otherness. Unlike how liberalism promotes and underlies the confusion of equality with social homogenization (assimilation to the republican citizen ideal), I am talking here of political equivalence in a social sphere of ineradicable anthropological difference and contention. This is an equivalence that cannot be mathematized, since its operating system is not logic (of numbers) but lot (*nomos*).

Of course, capitalism is the greatest enemy of democracy, very much against their forged ideological adherence, which is, alas, taken as common sense. In the conceptual universe of *dēmos* there is no space for *Homo economicus*, which is why critiques of democracy as critiques of the "West" are terribly misguided. It is certainly disappointing and alarming when someone of the stature of Talal Asad takes the essential substitutability of the democratic imaginary as the leveling and depersonalizing numerical essence of the capitalist imaginary and all for the sake of a rather insipid display of anti-Westernism.[73] This skewed and partial metonymy by which capitalist values are taken to be "Western" values tout court is one of the commonest but most profound weaknesses of anti-Western arguments in the ranks of today's antisecularist academy.

Thinking along these lines will also help us move beyond the dominant discourse that sees politics in the rubric of exception. Theoretically, the question of the exception holds enormous interest, but politically this interest lapses the moment the inquiry becomes a theoretical rule. Instead I would like to imagine a politics from the standpoint of the unexceptional.[74] Democracy is precisely the regime that does not make exceptions, if we are to take seriously Aristotle's dictum of a politics where rulers and ruled are mere positions of a continuously revolving *archē* that has no precedent and no uniqueness but is shared by all. No exceptions. The obvious politics of partiality and discrimination or exclusion in the liberal oligarchy that governs so-called modern democracies testifies to their fraudulent use of the name.

One consequence of this unacknowledged misnomer has led to a tacit acceptance as fact of Giorgio Agamben's celebrated description of today's political world as a permanent state of exception. Although this is just a rhetorical gesture, for permanent exception is no longer an exception, nonetheless it is an attempt to generalize the miraculous, in effect, yet again, to theologize politics. I am interested instead in a politics where nothing is miraculous, where indeed nothing is sacred, where there is no *homo sacer*. This would be an unexceptional politics, an untheologized politics, and most certainly—necessarily—an anarchic politics, insofar as *archē* is unexceptionally shared by all in interminable substitution. Considered from the standpoint of unexceptionality and substitutability, anarchy as democratic rule par excellence raises a major challenge to the inherited tradition of sovereignty in modernity.

If we infuse this standpoint into the perspective of Schmitt's famous dictum that "the sovereign is he who decides on the exception" then we have no choice but to rethink sovereignty. Mere thinking about whether sovereignty is or is not a matter of exception is inadequate. Surely, we are already forced to rethink sovereignty in a world where global economic agents, fully deterritorialized and beyond the boundaries of traditionally understood sovereignty, make direct political decisions that determine real territories, the terrains where actual people dwell. The essential sign of the sovereign in societies since the invention of capitalism is not the state (and therefore monarchy and law) but the national economy.[75] The erosion of the national economy as prerequisite of national independence is now the case everywhere in the world, no exceptions—another impetus to let go of the discussion of sovereignty as an extension of the monarchical law tradition of imperial Christendom. In a society fighting against capitalist values, sovereignty needs to be located in unexceptional collective political action. Unexceptional because it can only take place every day—not once in so many years at a ballot box ritual—and it must take place by unexceptional people, people who are not in the business of politics. These are the people most targeted by today's exceptional geopolitical and biopolitical order, the two being utterly entwined.

Today we seem to reside in a kind of twentieth-century First World War déjà-vu. The Great Powers and the great bankers are determining the sphere of politics in numerous societies, independent only in name. This old phenomenon is now multiplied astronomically in speed and scale. We have seen conditions of flash impoverishment implemented on populations in the manner of a natural disaster. In one and the same gesture, geopolitical power plays are coupled with biopolitical techniques in ways that have left the realm of the "pathological"—the prison and the clinic—and are bearing down squarely on the "normal," incarcerating thus both one's norms and one's pathos in new regimes of daily life that deprive one's own creation of new norms and pathos altogether.[76] Austerity, for example, which is touted as an economic principle and taught in business schools, is nothing but power politics and indeed enacts an exceptional politics. It is all about exempting—separating, taking out of the field of contention—constituencies on both sides of the equation: those who profit, or more accurately, those who rob, and those who are robbed. Austerity is a politics of rule, where the ruled, insofar as we are speaking in democratic terms, are exempted, yet again, from their equal right to rule. Here, exception truly confirms the rule—the rule of those who make exceptions *as* rules.

The only response against this overt violence of division and depoliticization, for this is what it means to be taken out of the field of contention: to be depoliticized, is the politics that expands the field of contention, the politics of aggravating conflict.[77] Such politics radicalizes democracy by making it pertinent to the self-organization (autonomy) of all sorts of modes of collective life: the contestation of all spheres of social convention and the creation of conditions of autodidactic collectivity that challenge institutionalized pedagogies. Although this always starts at the point of dissent, it cannot be just the work of negation, of critique for the sake of critique. It necessitates an affirmative action, literally: a constituent action. This need not be considered as a two-step process. Although the withdrawal of consent to power, which in a democratic polity bears the hardcore meaning of dissent, may seem—and strictly speaking is—an action of negation, it should be seen nonetheless as the first moment of affirmative action. Withdrawal of consent is as such, *in its negativity*, a gesture of autonomy. And as such, withdrawal of consent is always also withdrawal of foundation—the unconcealment of the groundlessness of politics that always lurks beneath all gestures, events, and institutions of grounding in some sort of convention.

Recalling La Boétie, who was the first to articulate so clearly this extraordinary power of the withdrawal of consent, such radical dissent enables us to see that all modes of rule other than democracy are predicated on concealing the fact that they have no legitimate argument as to why some people must rule over others. All such arguments, which are based on elaborating specific qualifications, are tautological. The best or the mightiest, the noble-born or the tribal elders, the divinely ordained or the mandarins of learning, the wealthiest minorities or the constituted majorities of humble birth—*all* claim legitimacy of rule on the basis of being what they are. Their actual qualifications for rule are arbitrary. But the point is exactly that: all qualifications for rule are arbitrary. They become conventional by rule. Only democracy refuses to conceal this arbitrariness by making the business of rule (and of being ruled, which is one and the same) the work and power of the unqualified.[78]

This refusal of concealment, of the mystical foundation of authority, opens politics to a certain lucidity where the social conflict that makes politics necessary is no longer secret—disguised, naturalized, mystified, sacralized or rationalized. Indeed, what makes democracy radical politics is that it stages its own internal conflict out in the open—democracy requires the *visibility* of the *dēmos*: "The place where the people appear is the place where a dispute is conducted."[79] That is to say, the people in democracy are not a standing body, standing by in order to be actualized, nor is it a body endowed with the metaphysics of history, like the traditional Marxist notion of the proletariat. The people are no part of anything that already exists in some differentiation. The "part of those who have no part," as Rancière has famously theorized in reference to politics under capitalism, a kind of partition of society according to divisive distribution, can become the people if it can emerge politically in the openings that are torn in the political fabric by radical conflict, including, of course, class conflict. In this moment, the invisibility of those who have no part becomes visible as the political coming forth of dissent. "The people always, in fact, take shape at the very point they are declared finished" (*Dis-agreement*, 98).

At the revolutionary point of democratic actualization, where people become power, partitions end: "The *demos* is not the population, the majority, the political body or the lower classes. It is the surplus community made up of those who have no qualification to rule, which means at once everybody and anyone at all. The 'power of the people' therefore cannot be equated with the power of a particular group or institution and exists only in the form of a disjunction" (*Dissensus*, 53). This disjunctive indivisibility that comes with the perfect visibility of everyone and anyone as political actors of and for themselves, whose qualification is that they have no qualification other than this of-and-for themselves, is

228 *Democracy's Anarchy*

the peculiar mathematics of autonomy in democracy, *a sort of surplus over nothing in the politics of all for the sake of everyone*, no exceptions. But the indomitable enemy of democracy also deploys its weapons in this same surplus over nothing mode, except that its aim is precisely to debilitate the capacity of all, to annihilate the desire for dissent, and to induce conditions of division and intrasocial warfare that aims at and thrives on the cultivation of limitless mass individualism, where the politics of all and for all is strictly prohibited.

SURPLUS OVER NOTHING

Hannah Arendt has argued famously that one of the essential functions of capitalism is to create superfluous lives: "the combination of superfluous wealth and superfluous men," she says characteristically.[80] The argument is made in an extensive framing of the historical conditions of the colonial economy and the production of racism. A quick focus on the specific historical context of writing is crucial. Arendt writes from the position of exile in the immediate aftermath of World War II and the onset of the Cold War and the nuclear age, which presents a new political perspective that is planetary in nature, and she chooses to examine this present by delving into the vicissitudes of modernity's past, which she also frames as equally planetary even if it is not conventionally considered to be so. Hence her attention to colonialism as the hardcore underpinning of both the global development of capital and the crisis in national sovereignty that opens the door to twentieth-century totalitarianism.

In this respect, although I will not be conducting it here, a double reading of Arendt's *The Origins of Totalitarianism* with Carl Schmitt's *The Nomos of the Earth* is essential. They were written at the same time, and even though they have a different political motivation they share an understanding of how global imperialism, rooted in worldwide colonial conditions of economy, incapacitates every society's desire for self-determination.[81] Behind them, to my mind, lies W. E. B. Du Bois's magnum opus *Black Reconstruction in America*, written some twenty years earlier, while Arendt and Schmitt, in clear divergence, were taking stock of their own positions of survival in the ascendant days of Nazi Germany. Du Bois had already anticipated their analysis of the Cold War globality that was already underway, having understood that the same worldwide colonial economy determined all structures of nationalism and racism in the modern capitalist era. This triptych of reading, with a full sense of the internal tensions and contradictions among these authors and their works, holds one of the most accurately prescient portraits of what we are facing today.

In this latter sense I especially recall Arendt's description of colonial practices, which snaps a perfect picture of what today we call rogue or mafia capitalism. Parenthesis: Although I use it here, I reject this description, for rogue capitalism presupposes a capitalism gone bad or turned outlaw. But capitalism has never been "good"–besides, who cares about "good?" Capitalism *is* an outlaw form–it has always been so–to the degree that it *makes* law into what it pleases and when it pleases. Although it is always important not to lose historical specificity–and in this respect, say, industrial capitalism is different from financial capitalism– nonetheless the designation of capitalism gone rogue or succumbing to mafia tactics is just an attempt to launder what can never be cleaned. Precisely because capitalism has always been rogue in relation to society's survival, it is a deadly enemy and worth our most formidable attention.

Parenthesis closed, I return to Arendt and to the historical specifics: "Here we have the same story of high society falling in love with its own underworld, and of the criminal feeling elevated when by civilized coldness, the avoidance of 'unnecessary exertion' and good manners, [he] is allowed to create a vicious, refined atmosphere around [his] crimes" (190). Although the specific reference is the colonial politics of British Prime Minister Benjamin Disraeli, 1st Earl of Beaconsfield (1804-1881), the description is altogether familiar to us by now, so vividly present in our time yet hardly unusual historically. Arendt's key premise is that colonial sovereignty (to which the nation form is indebted) is enabled by this strange alliance between high society (feudal remnants in bourgeois form) and fortune-hunting marginal elements of society at the lower ranks, whose aimlessness, mobility, and indeed rootlessness is the byproduct of the social and economic upheaval created by the capitalist organization of society. Populations ensconced in centuries-old conditions of stability were displaced into ever sought out, but rarely stable and successful, new conditions of labor and sustenance permeated by an inarticulate desire for rapid wealth at all costs. In terms of Britain specifically, this sort of economic displacement and social upheaval had antecedents centuries before, as Thomas More famously chronicles in *Utopia* (1516), although Arendt does not reach that far back.[82]

Her test terrain for this observation is specifically the colonization of southern Africa and, whatever else we might say about her argument overall, I must acknowledge that this is one of the most formidable historical analyses of colonial history that have ever been written. With notable recourse to Joseph Conrad's *Heart of Darkness* at a time when this was virtually absent from the archives of literary criticism, Arendt chronicles the unfolding of "an economy that relentlessly produced a superfluity of men and capital" (189). She describes a "phantom world" specific to Africa, whose notorious name ("the dark continent") is not only a racist designation but also reveals both the lawlessness with which the Europeans operated in total disregard of convention and their evident befuddlement even to take account of what they practiced. It is not that the reality of colonization in Africa is that much different from the Spanish (and later English) conquest of the Americas, especially considering the violence against the indigenous population and the brutal extraction of wealth (mineral and corporeal). It is the specific conjuncture in the development of capitalism that marks this analysis, with a projective intention to contextualize the horrendous unfolding of the European twentieth century.

One might even say, following the groundbreaking vision of Sylvia Wynter and others, that the superfluity of men and capital that Arendt theorizes about late-nineteenth-century colonialism in Africa is predicated on the unprecedented surplus of wealth in gold and plantation commodities that the colonization of the Americas funneled into the colonial capitals of Europe at unprecedented speed and scale in the two centuries before. Yet, Arendt's focus is on a condition of social and economic excess at the margins of colonial conquest and exploitation, which may indeed have been the outcome of this influx of surplus into European societies that upset the regular rhythms of industrial capital and its specific tight class structure, but now marks, in its own right, an incredible acceleration of capital's expansion in truly planetary scope and in such a way that the class organization of society is no longer the machine of civilization. National boundaries, legal regimes of rules and regulations, social stratifications, civil and political statutes are simply no longer adequate to contain this explosive excess that displaces, overwhelms, and shatters in its path every marker of order. The tunings for what will become mafia capitalism in our time are set in this context.

The obvious feeding ground for this frenzy was the racist assumption that sub-Saharan Africa was a savage space, in which lawlessness was simply nature. This presumed lack of civilization enabled the abandonment of "civilization" by the social renegade and fortune-hunting settlers: "They were not individuals like the old adventurers, they were the shadows of events with which they had nothing to do" (189), "escaping the reality of civilization" (192). Gold, diamonds, and ivory became the only objects of value in a world where no sense of value existed, not to mention "values" in the typical sense of custom or ethic. The folly that the settlers perceived all around, most severely in relation to the indigenous population, which seemed so alien that they frightfully relegated it to the category of beast, fueled their predatory menace even further and the pursuit of rapid wealth was disengaged from all social parameters. In Arendt's words: "In the natives, the Boers discovered the only 'raw material' which Africa provided in abundance and they used them not for the production of riches but the mere essentials of human existence" (193). Adam Smith's moral imagination was nullified—one might add once and for all, if we look around to what global capitalism has become today. Arendt brilliantly chronicles the Boers' fear that their settler world might revert to the European social system of legal and cultural order they had fled with limitless abandon. The apartheid system they eventually instituted is rooted precisely in this fear.

In the process, superfluity changed from being the condition of possibility for colonial (dis)order to being global capital's (dis)order of desire for limitless growth. From today's perspective, superfluous capital is the most coveted of all objectives, the sort of capital that, even when it (or part of it) might get "reinvested" to generate more, is ultimately driven to waste, to produce waste, to create wastelands, to waste lives, whole populations. And it is here that the notion of superfluous people, as Arendt theorized it to refer to those renegade elements of European society that fueled the most brutal aspects of colonialism in Africa, now reverts to the colonized. Structurally based on the transatlantic slave trade, which was, of course, already in full swing for more than two centuries before this period, we have now reached a point where the production of superfluous people has been extended to every corner of the planet.

The category of superfluous people concerns precisely those populations whose worlds are ravaged and pillaged by the lawless onslaught of wealth extraction (again, mineral and corporeal) which knows no measure. Superfluous people are the people whose lives simply don't register, whose death is ultimately beyond statistics, even as statistics contribute to the numbing: the numbers in the thousands or tens of thousands, or hundreds of thousands, that are considered to be the casualties of war, drug cartels, genocidal massacres or, worse, "natural disasters"—earthquakes in Haiti or floods in Bangladesh. But superfluous people are also every single one, unique, unreproducible black or brown body with a name that is wasted by police or security forces in every world metropolis. This is exactly the point of the Black Lives Matter movement: to arrest this ceaseless flow of superfluous and nameless life-and-death existence. And it is also every single one, unique, unreproducible black or brown body that dies in the desert or drowns at sea while making the passage, the border crossing, from a wasted life at home to a projected life in the lands that produce waste—in an uncanny repetition of the Middle Passage in the Atlantic slave trade, only this time slavery is couched in the accoutrements of better wages.

So, while Arendt eventually turned a figure of settler-colonial economy into a core element for understanding totalitarian politics, including its specific kind of nationalist racism, the essence of superfluity in society belongs to capital through and through, across its histories and iterations. In essence, superfluous people are the refuse of growth, which is the most horrific of all values generated from the imaginary of liberal economics since the eighteenth century, having now surpassed its ancestral siblings—accumulation, exchange, investment, progress, development, self-regulation—as the one and only sacred rule not only of history but also of human nature. Growth—in colonial terms, expansion for the sake of expansion—became the common denominator, the common language and currency of all economics, including most importantly the translation of economics into politics, into social organization, and even more, into personal aspiration, the very making of subjectivities.

Nowadays, of course, growth is the talisman of neoliberalism—the presumption of its interminable, infinite nature somehow coming to merge with a totalizing (and in effect, totalitarian) concept of globality. The obvious contradiction is shrewdly shielded. No one in the business dares ask how something unlimited can become one with what epitomizes the limited: the astral body of a planet. And yet this is precisely the ruse. Capital's endless expansion must envelope every corner of the globe, exhausting the very notion of exhaustibility in the process. Neoliberalism is built precisely on these nonsensical paradigms, veritable con games of doublespeak. Let's take stock of the nonsense: trickle-down economics is the epitome of capital accumulation at the top; privatization sold as social empowerment means the perfect dismantling of social welfare; the promise of skyrocketing individual wealth happens with society's flash impoverishment; fiscal austerity underwrites the most scandalous profligacy since the reign of Roi Soleil; deregulation is the most insidious self-serving regulation ever conceived, and so on—the list of nonsense language is endless.

About the latter I have spoken before, but it bears repeating. There is no deregulation; there never has been. The term "deregulation" is one of the grandest deceptions of liberal economic theory, achieving sacred status (as grand social deceptions tend to do) in all of liberalism's "neo" variants. Because all economy is political economy, there is always regulation. And because capitalism, as we were taught by its colonial and imperialist strains, is in the end not just an economic system but a mode of making and enforcing politics, of governing populations by ruse and violence, regulation of the rules of the market is the highest-stakes game. The question is not how to arbitrate between regulation and deregulation, but how to see and understand who regulates for whom and against whom. The neoliberal (neocolonial) politics of so-called deregulation has spawned some of the most vicious regulations ever implemented—regulations that made the tiniest minority across the globe rich beyond all possible measure while rendering billions of human lives superfluous—regulations, in this respect, no different, no less insidious, than the ones that once explicitly and legally determined who is and what it means to be a slave.

Bearing this in mind, we should settle on a basic thing. Contrary to its precepts, which have been ideologically implanted in the global mind, neoliberalism is not an economic order but a political one. And as a political order it requires the concentration of power at the top—indeed, much like the accumulation of capital, the accumulation of power. This too is a way to launder the dirty pathways of growth, to naturalize it as allegedly the most advanced state of human civilization. As the great Greek political philosopher Constantine Tsoukalas put it recently: "The acceptance of 'normalcy' or 'reality' as 'by nature' identified with constant growth would have never been generalized had not the processes of production been infused with the *pharmakon* of ceaseless accumulation."[83] The word *pharmakon* is deliberately chosen, perfectly and self-consciously succinct as to the two-faced or doublespeak politics of neoliberal order. Strangely, ceaseless accumulation of capital in the hands of the fewest of the few is both the outcome of the ideology of growth and also its most obvious subversion, for capital is thus not "reinvested," not channeled back into the flow that will sustain the institutions of social welfare. It is removed from society in order to concentrate not just wealth but, most importantly, power—again—in the hands of the fewest few. This is why the politics of neoliberalism is literally the politics of oligarchy, although, to be fair, this was always the case with liberalism since its revolutionary era. As Castoriadis never got tired of reminding us, the proper name for so-called modern democracies is liberal oligarchies.

I take my cue from Andreas Kalyvas's evocative new work on oligarchy as the politics of wealth throughout history—the mode by which society's wealthiest enact their power.[84] So, by this measure, oligarchy is the quintessential politics of capitalism. Yet this most ancient of political concepts next to monarchy has lapsed from the modern political vocabulary almost entirely. To the degree that it has resurfaced at all, it has been used recently either to describe power outside the political system in reference to wealthy individuals who use their money to influence power, often in illegal or clandestine fashion, or, with a certain Orientalist bent, it has been reserved for post-Soviet, African, or Asian state situations, never as the mark of so-called democracies in the European and American sphere. Kalyvas explains this conceptual decline of oligarchy as the effect of liberal hegemony, and specifically of the fact that liberalism's cornerstone concepts of citizenship and rights were detached from the political power of wealth since the moment its revolutions were constitutionalized. The taboo on naming oligarchy as the explicit political reality of capitalism is indeed a symptom of liberalism's repression of its constitutive politics of power.

Thus, one of the most prevalent myths of modernity is that capitalism and democracy are one, roped into a loop by a core shared thread: freedom—free life, free market. I will not spend even a single sentence deconstituting this delusion. Besides, Balibar's monumental work around his innovative concept "equaliberty" remains a beacon for us all, and whatever we say about this matter is mere elaboration. My thesis here is that democracy is the enemy of capitalism—frankly the only worthy enemy—and from the standpoint of the fact that knowing thine enemy is the first step in any process of radical political thought, my focus in this section is capitalism and indeed the politics of capitalism—capitalism as a political order. The battle between capitalism and democracy takes place in the political field, and I do not mean the field where institutional politics happens, for this is merely symptomatic terrain. I mean at the core of the political, where society's organization is most at stake, where power is fought over and gained or lost. The economy in this respect is essential, not in the classic Marxist division of base/superstructure, which inevitably still enacts a separation—Marx's embrace of the notion of political economy notwithstanding—but in the sense that the economy *is* a political sphere as such. This is not something that capitalism has invented but has certainly refined in astonishingly effective ways. In fact, the more capitalist economics takes over the space of politics, the more *political* the situation becomes. The field of contestation is aggravated, and engagement with the inequities of power becomes graver. Indeed, war is capitalism's ultimate political modus operandi, even though it has become almost a matter of advertising to popularize the slogan "war is bad for business"—it sure isn't.

The new world war that is enveloping the planet, nominally on the battlegrounds of Europe in yet another iteration of twentieth-century déjà-vu politics, is part of the history of global capital. It is a world war because it is an internal war amid the ranks of capital and its oligarchic powers—as was the case in the twentieth century after all—except that in this case it is further aggravated by globalization. Hence, if missiles are gutting Ukrainian towns on the one side, banks are gutting assets by computer buttons on the other. While there is abundant talk in the analytical world of the *Financial Times* and its ilk that the war in Ukraine signifies an implosion in the heart of globalization—and with perhaps a grain of truth, in strict terms, insofar as Russia's Eurasian nationalism is employing the logic of the clash of civilizations in order to force a multipolar global power structure—nonetheless whatever emerges, short of nuclear catastrophe, will be a mere readjustment of the avenues of global capital with its gravitational weight otherwise left intact. A distanced view, if that is at all possible, could easily be that we are witnessing the war politics of a hostile takeover in perfect market language. Oligarchies have gone to war against one another, and the strongest market conglomerates are eating up the weaker ones. Of course, speaking market lingo is the sangfroid of cynicism, for the lives of millions of people are gutted in the process—with brutal death, mass displacement, and flash impoverishment. Although Naomi Klein's assessment of today's world as capitalism's techno-necro phase is accurate, it merely signals the extraordinary acceleration in speed and scale of a process that has been in effect since the colonial era: the production of superfluous people in the service of superfluous wealth.

In plain terms then, now more than ever, one might say that blocking the path of capitalism is democracy's raison d'être. From the outset, in ancient Athens, the root of democracy has always been to separate the economic from the political—even more, to nullify economic power in politics. That was the essence of both Solon's laws and Cleisthenes's reforms: how to pull the ground from under the oligarchic capacity to turn wealth into power. This veritably *artificial*, anthropologically speaking, reorganization of society that makes (*poiein*) every individual equal and equally free to any and every other in terms of how they make their laws, decide how to govern and be governed, and create the analogous political institutions in which the economic has no presence whatsoever, remains at the core of democracy no matter what its iterations, configurations, achievements, or failures. In Nadia Urbinati's words, "*Isonomia* was not meant to suppress social antagonisms, nor to eliminate conflicts, but to transfer them to another plane, namely politics, which became thus the name of an art practiced by the citizens and based on speech, voting, and the collective interaction of participants in public space."[85] That's right! *Democracy is an art*, an enactment of *poiēsis* in the public sphere, a form of governance where economics is subservient, where it becomes a domestic matter, as its very name suggests. Of course, this is anathema to the capitalist imaginary, which does the exact opposite: it turns economics into power in the public sphere, which it conquers, and political subjects into domesticated animals.

To think of capitalism as a means of societal control is surely not new, although usually when this sort of thinking unfolds it configures the field instrumentally: capitalism partakes of mechanisms of control in order to facilitate and maximize its profit machinations. In such analyses the modern state apparatus is understood as capitalism's ally at best, flunky at worst, but in all cases the state, not the economy, is conceived to be the direct agent of control. The most basic history of colonialism would show that even when the modern state apparatus took itself to specialize in mechanisms of control, it did so not only at capitalism's invitation but also on the very pathways of wealth extraction and surplus (and the full range of their destructive consequences) that capitalism opened at the level of *society* in practically every corner of the globe. The East India Company, for example, was for a time a bona fide political agent, as a sort of microstate with its own flag working on behalf of British imperialism, until its political power was regulated by an act of Parliament. Here I am interested in reading this process at an immanent level: to consider capitalism as a mode of social organization itself, where economics is a subset, albeit essential—or, if you will, to return thus to the broader meaning of *oikonomia* where the home is society itself and, in today's terms, the whole nexus of interrelated societies and transnational flows, the entire planet.

In his influential account of neoliberalism, Wolfgang Streeck explores specifically the variable permutations of the constant vying for control between capital and state—the state conceived expressly as the agent of society.[86] The strange figure of "democratic capitalism" that animates his argument takes for granted that capitalism needs some sort of democratic apparatus to keep it in check and that the whole problem of contemporary societies is that this regulating mechanism has been bulldozed by global capital. While his description of the ravages of neoliberalism is accurate and convincing, the presumption that this is a deviation, a kind of kink in a system that has gone wrong, is questionable. It is very much enthralled by the myth of democratic capitalism—or in specifically European, perhaps even simply German, terms, capitalism under conditions of social democracy—by which Streeck nods to established institutions of social welfare in twentieth-century industrialized societies marred by world wars.

According to this presumption, democratic capitalism is characterized by a certain balance between "social justice" and "market justice" (58), which is how Streeck identifies two concurrent systems that are entwined by contrary logics of operation: the first privileges society's rights (to work, to health, to community welfare) regardless of labor productivity, while the second privileges a right to wealth distribution based on standards of productivity and competition as performed and evaluated in/by the market. Streeck identifies the first to be a matter of what he calls "status" as opposed to "contract," which he reserves for the market. The distinction is even stranger in that it stands counter to the tradition of civil rights emerging out of social contract theory in its Enlightenment variant, which veritably belongs to the first category ("social justice"), but this matter is left curiously unaddressed.

Be that as it may, the very notion of market justice is absurd by any juridical standards. It formalizes and instrumentalizes justice as part of a certain machinery, which is none other than the classic ruse of capital with its presumption of neutral, objectively measurable, distribution of wealth according to productivity: "*market judgments*—especially if the market is assumed to be a state of nature—seem to fall from the sky without human intervention and have to be accepted as a fate behind which lurks a higher meaning intelligible only to experts" (63). What Streeck describes is nothing less than Adam Smith's concept of self-regulation—the cornerstone of liberalism, not some neoliberal invention. The presumption of an altogether new logic shields the reiteration of the foundational tautology. So-called market justice is mere market, where what counts is what can be counted and what is counted is the only unquestionable value. Measurement and exchange as the only value-determining parameters are thus abstracted not only from human labor but also from human judgment—indeed, all things human. Thus "human values," on whose conceptualization and adjudication all practices of justice are predicated according to the limitless variation of social practices on this planet, become utterly insignificant.

But such has been the play of liberalism since it initially surged forth from the social imagination: abstracting and instrumentalizing human interaction into a system of values that are ultimately countable and accountable, self-regulating and self-sufficient. For this reason, liberalism is indeed the politics of the capitalist ideal (even if at times laid aside), and neoliberalism is a lazy name to describe a mere phase. The point would be perfectly banal and unworthy of comment if we didn't have the broad conviction, astonishingly even among people of learning, that liberalism is a democratic regime while neoliberalism is antidemocratic. Liberalism may make use—sometimes effectively—of the democratic imagination but, I repeat, it is an oligarchic regime all the way through, from its revolutionary era to the present. Streeck's otherwise historically useful argument falters on exactly this unexamined conviction. While he claims to describe the history of the democratic safeguard of post–World War II societies against capitalist economics, he is only giving an account of capitalism's tango with liberalism's politics. This passionate dance does indeed have a noteworthy history, which is utterly determinant of the world we currently live in even while there is a broad sense that we may have exceeded it (a point I clearly dispute), but this history is *not* the history of democracy and surely *not* the history of the relation between capitalism and democracy, which, if it is anything at all, is an as yet interminable history of struggle to the death. The nominal object of Streeck's subtitle, "democratic capitalism," says it all. There is really no such thing—I mean, no such thing that is not reducible to capitalism plain and simple.

Nonetheless, Streeck's book is worthy of our attention—and this is why I mention it here—insofar as it chronicles the struggle between democracy and capitalism, even though I clearly disagree with his terms. While he sees a sort of checks-and-balances framework between the two and I see a warring struggle to the death, the fact remains that the two imaginaries are vehemently entwined in the course of modernity. This entwinement has a global history. Indeed, it might be the only terms in which we can speak of global history or to attest to the fact that global history has by this token become a reality, a framework of meaning that organizes our existence everywhere on the planet.

Indeed, what Streeck laments as "the real *failure of democracy* in the neoliberal decades" (74) is surely a global matter, even though he traces it in specific societies or specific state politics. The strongest ever thread to run through the broadest ever range of national histories in the modern era is the politico-economic unfolding out of a social welfare state in which taxation remains anchored both to popular sovereignty and to the state's democratic responsibility and on to the debt state, in which all sovereignty and responsibility is wrested from society and administered by capital where taxation becomes a dirty word. This phenomenon is truly worldwide, and it cannot be otherwise because it is tied directly to the global financialization of capital: in effect, the disengagement of capital from the primacy of production within the national economy where historically labor relations have been intricately entwined with political constituencies. In this regard the stark dismantling of the national economy structure by the power of global capital spelled the total depoliticization of society, as electoral constituencies became errant masses of consumers, happily globalized in all ways, not just economic but also cultural. Politics within national boundaries, from local to state level, was thereby relegated to a mere spectator sport, mirroring in this respect the spectacle of objects of ecommerce on a website.[87]

That "political participation was redefined as popular entertainment and disconnected from policy" (74) was the direct outcome of the idea that the free market was in the end the essence of free life, an idea that in retrospect mirrors the trajectory of the liberal imagination as it propelled itself further and further away from its revolutionary Big Bang. All institutional outposts in this expanding trajectory—the nation state, the colonial economy, the imperialist project, the Cold War, the United Nations, human rights, "the end of history" and, of course, globalization itself—are attestations of how liberalism's *political* foundation was not whichever version of the Rights of Man and the Citizen engendered specific constitutional conditions but the power of the market running behind all political manifestations regardless of variance.

This was the case all along. From the standpoint of institutional capacity, the real revolutionaries of liberalism were not the people but the bankers. No surprise then that the most powerful political constituency today are the creditors who finance the debt of states (Streeck, 72–96). But even when we are not surprised, we would be wrong to see this as some newfangled grotesque reality. Although nothing in history is predetermined, in retrospect this now omnipotent constituency was in the political driver's seat all along, even before what we now call the financialization of capital was yet apparent. Losing track of this inner logic keeps us from understanding capital as *political* power and thereby its deathly struggle with democracy. Indeed, this understanding is possible only from a radical democratic standpoint; it points to the very purpose of democracy, as Kalyvas succinctly argues: "democracy blocks economic power from turning into political power. It disrupts this passage by establishing the primacy of the political over the economic.... This subordination of the economic to the political is one of the main modalities of democratic politics."[88]

The first barricade to overcome in manifesting this inner logic is to dispute all discourses that interpret moments of crisis in this struggle as instances of market failure. Unfortunately, we find cavalier use of the term even in discourses of the left, which is mind-boggling. In such cases the point is to underline the problems of the market, but the logic is nonetheless compromised. To claim that the market fails is already to assume that the market *knows* and *does*—as a veritable subjective agency, even if colored by the wishful celebrations of its being a cybernetic machine. It is, moreover, to assume that there is a *correct* process to the market, which occasionally loses its way and falters. To call, say, the banking crisis of 2008 a "market failure" is to assume that subprime mortgages and derivatives are uncalled-for deviations. Or even worse: as some free-market fundamentalists argued back then, the intervention by states to bail out banks was an indication of market failure, since it belied the fact that the market is free. Obviously this emerges from the same source that promulgates governing pseudonyms, like the lying discourse of deregulation I mentioned earlier. "Market failure" is a term that belongs to the imaginary that conceived the notion "the market never fails." In both cases, the market is a subject that *knows* and *acts*.

This may seem trivial to those of us who know there is no such thing as "the market" other than a space where actual people assemble to trade, a human activity as old as Mesopotamian civilization. It is capitalism that produced the extraordinary mechanisms of persuasion that turned one of the most ubiquitous aspects of *human-being* into a disembodied autonomous logic. Strictly speaking, this is a theological gesture of perfect grandeur. The Market became the new God, and indeed, speaking in monotheistic terms, it is the only instance in the history of this imaginary where this notoriously jealous and exclusionary God allowed (frankly, welcomed) this other God to reign alongside. So, in these terms, "market failure" is a moment of religious deviation, a moment of heresy that is always articulated in order to authorize the next onslaught of dogma—capitalism's next power play, often more brutal than what preceded it. Such was the bank bailout by both the United States and the European Union in the recent debt belly-up. In response to (and under the logic of) "market failure," indebted states produced the necessary funds to shore up the creditors who held them in debt, passing the bill down to the disenfranchised constituencies of people who saw their life savings and social-welfare benefits go up in smoke. It is patently absurd to say that states bailed out capital when indeed capital bankrolls these states whose sovereignty is sustained by debt. The debt economy that has replaced the national economy today is the perfect illustration of capital's *political* power, according to which states have resolutely become capital's servants.

And yet, market apologists still project and play on the fear that disgruntled constituencies and ideologically corrupted politicians are detrimental to the market's process by interfering through government, whether by enacting laws of "regulation" or imposing corporate taxation and the like. Strangely—but altogether predictably, given the doublespeak conditions we inhabit—these rallying cries of fear against "democratically" induced governmental decisions have produced the most maximal state politics ever seen since the collapse of fascism in Europe. In this parade of pseudonyms strange conceptual contortions occur that poison not only political acumen but also historical analysis. Just like "self-regulation" (of both market and government) in liberalism became "deregulation" (of both market and government) in neoliberalism, classic liberalism's nominal investment in a "minimal state" (regardless of what actually took place historically) turned into neoliberalism's investment in a "maximal state" where basically totalitarian practices in parliamentary garb are mobilized to protect the rhetoric of unimpeded markets. This is not a manner of speaking. In order to seal this politics, capital now takes over the highest seats of government directly, so that in 2012 bankers were appointed (not even elected) to be heads of state in Greece and Italy, and shortly thereafter the U.S. presidency was delivered into the hands of a brand, which is the impersonal presence of capital in its purest form.

The difficulty of receding focus from Trump the person, with all the psychological accoutrements this focus necessarily involved, concealed this most significant fact of the Trump phenomenon. Although I certainly understand the importance of all other signifiers that Trump, *as an event*, still animates and mobilizes—the racism of white supremacy, the celebration of misogyny, the nationalist hysteria, the pseudonymous populism, the mass manipulation, indeed even the plain stupidity or psychopathology of it all—nonetheless, it is the blatant hijacking of political office by capital's commodity form that may indeed mark this as a turn on the road, as the opening to a new psychosocial condition in politics. When we talk of a legitimation crisis in the institutions of liberal democracy all those other factors are in play, not least the con game of populism, as I discuss in the next section; but the most important factor remains the takeover of political institutions *directly* by capital.

EU politics in this regard was further advanced structurally than its U.S. counterpart, although again the Trump event tends to shield this order. Left criticisms of EU politics in the last decade abound, but it's remarkable to me that most of the time these criticisms ignore that the European Union was never constructed as a political entity. It was instituted and is still governed by economic principles. It was forged from the same imaginary that precipitated the financialization of capital at a techno-global scale. In retrospect, what was once called the European Economic Community (EEC) may be financial capitalism's first large-scale institution. The Eurozone is a symptom of the original and unadulterated logic of the EEC. The original EEC could be read just as well as the ECC: the European Community of Commodities. In the category "commodities" I would include the European peoples themselves.

Given this history, the crux of the EU's governmental incapacities—both its communal dysfunction and its bureaucratic tyranny—are consequences of this chimeric institutional structure where political decisions are made *directly* by economic interests or actors on their behalf. As this logic unfolded from its initial liberal framework to the neoliberal one, it produced the monetary union as just a playground for the most powerful financial interests worldwide, as a kind of money laundering scheme through the taxation of the poorer strata. Banking debt was nationalized and made a burden to bear by a community of commodified consumers. Although to say "nationalized" invokes the parameters of national sovereignty, this nationalization of debt signifies the exact opposite: further erosion of national sovereignty. At the same time, the community of consumers is indeed a community beyond national borders, in the sense that they are consumers of the European idea, presumably made available to them via a whole array of commodities, one of which is, of course, debt itself. We're talking about quite a scheme.

The Eurozone, as supreme achievement of this imaginary, signified the ultimate deterritorialization and dissolution of borders, except that this dissolution is only in place for the benefit of capital, which doesn't recognize borders anyway. Again, as perfect incursion of the economic into the political, borderless sovereignty is a figure of capital, and its achievement in the form of the EU is but the actualization of a logic that had been in place and in effect for a long time.[89] What this formation mobilized, despite the presumption of the notion of community, was the dissolution of national sovereignty without, however, diluting the elements of racial nationalism. In fact, the contrary happened. The more national sovereignty was effectively defanged, the more nationalism and racism was consolidated. The even greater failure of the EU project in this respect was that it brought about the very thing it was supposed to have overcome in a kind of bizarre perverted manifestation of Hegelian *Aufhebung*, where the element of preservation in the act of overcoming subjugates all others. For, instead of quelling nationalist violence, the EU produced the intensification of nationalist (and always, in that sense, racist) violence in ways that now present themselves as ever more complicated, given the intertwinement of multiple social and cultural modes across the very borders that were presumed to have been abolished.

In this respect, thinking back to the postwar days of Arendt and Schmitt, who both envisioned a sort of proto-EU federalist politics even if with starkly different ideological investment, abounds with irony. Both thinkers never managed to overcome their reliance on the idea that national sovereignty is the foundation of all modern politics, even if again irreconcilable ideologically. Their federalist aspirations were built on a national-sovereignty platform, which would presumably regulate the expansive ambitions of capital. But European federalism itself is riveted by a national-imaginary animus, which is why the only work of EU politics, apart from supporting the commands of capital, has been to inculcate *Europeanness*—in effect a national-colonial identity formation that must be pursued, revered, and protected foremost as an exclusionary cultural privilege against the world's others. Sometimes this exclusionary privilege can even be leveraged as a threat in order to discipline insubordinate tendencies within the EU terrain itself, which is a perfect example how the EU works as a national-imaginary formation against its member nations.[90]

In this context, the recent explosion of micronationalist anti-EU sentiment among the peoples of Europe, which dovetails with an antiglobalization sentiment directed against capital, is profoundly self-deceptive as to where it comes from, what it aims to achieve, and whose interests it serves. Nothing is more dire in the current juncture than the grand deception precipitated upon large masses of people, and surely not only in Europe, that the politics of national sovereignty is indeed an emancipatory politics. Sadly, the lessons of anticolonial thinkers on this front are completely disregarded. Reverting to nationalist passions is not only literally regressive in historical terms but also perfectly incapacitating, for the simple reason that this regression cannot resuscitate its historical basis; it is an anachronism standing on its own historical void. As I have often argued, the pillar for the survival of a nation is not its flag or its constitution but its economic self-sufficiency. Since a national economy is, quite literally, no longer possible, the presumption of national independence—indeed, often articulated as *economic independence*—is a ruse implemented against national populations by certain elite interests (which are fully embedded in international capital) for the sake of maximizing their power and their profits. The national-populist rhetoric taking over liberal political institutions nowadays, which claims to empower masses impoverished by globalization by reanimating the defensive strength of national borders, is conducted by forces and actors that epitomize global capital—the paradigmatic world of no borders. Its most famous brand names may be Brexit or Trump—or, at this moment, Putin's Eurasian supremacy—but its poison runs deep in societies across continents and at the minutest micro level of social organization nearly everywhere.

This became plainly evident in the veritable construction of actual borders—barriers, walls, interception zones—to block entrance of racially excluded others on the very marks of erstwhile sanctioned national borders within EU territory. Borderless Europe came to establish recognizably internal borders on the markings of what was considered to be culturally non-European in its very midst. In the last fifteen years, the dimensions of ethnic, racial, and cultural exclusion grew immensely under the project of presumed EU consolidation. While divisions of this kind existed since the outset of "decolonization," they were severely augmented by the EU formation, partly because the influx of peoples from the Eastern European periphery and the colonized world increased under the cultivated aspiration of greater flow and absorption into the euro-based socioeconomic sphere.

But most significant was another factor. In the era of national sovereignty the problem of assimilation of postcolonial populations was conducted within the limits of each colonial state itself, with its own specific racist exclusions. But with the EU forming as part of the vanguard logic of globalization, the vision and promise of the European dream elevated the (post)colonial problem to an overarching *civilizational battlefield*. Here there is much merit to Aamir Mufti's insight that every country that becomes part of the EU is implicated inexorably in Europe's colonial and postcolonial conditions regardless of its history.[91] From this perspective, the rise of neo-Nazi or neofascist elements in Greece, Hungary, or

Poland is not merely a rehashing of old indigenous nationalism, but a kind of intra-European (and, in that sense, colonial) racism.

An utterly perverse replay of history reached unfathomable levels when in 2015 the concentration camps of Dachau and Buchenwald were put to use again in order to house those who managed to slip through and infiltrate the native terrain, or when the state of Denmark issued an order to confiscate the material wealth (cash or jewelry) of incoming refugees as payment for their being allowed to settle in its domain. When the Syrian front collapsed and hundreds of thousands of people ended up on Greek beaches, many of them dead on arrival, the EU rhetoric cynically manipulated rubrics of humanitarianism in order to steadily implement and enhance a militarization of its borderless borders.[92]

In 2013, after two major disasters off the coast of Lampedusa, the so-called Mediterranean Task Force (in effect a consolidation of Frontex and Europol) began the process of militarily patrolling the seas under the pretext of averting nautical disasters but in effect creating conditions of interdiction with the aspiration of dissuading passage into EU land.[93] Remarkably, such practices of interdiction on the high seas were soon considered to be counterproductive because saving people from drowning (even though it meant internment on land) was seen as a motivating indicator for greater influx. The initial highlight of these efforts—the extraordinary program instituted by the Italian government under the revitalized Roman name Mare Nostrum[94]—seemed to be a moment of national sovereignty reasserting itself in the midst of nation-state depoliticization by the political arms of global capital. Yet, even in this case, a national government and a national budget (an extraordinarily high, in fact unsustainable, €9 million a month in 2013) were put in the service of EU elite interests, thereby confirming the loss of sovereignty even while acting in its name. Eventually the Libyan coast guard was "hired" to do the ugliest of the requisite labor of interdiction, which included internment on Libyan land in such lawless conditions that it produced an extraordinary economy of violence, sex trafficking, and veritable slavery. Indeed, Frontex-controlled or EU-financed internment camps from Greece (still EU territory) to Turkey to Libya all the way even to sub-Saharan Africa (Mali, Niger, Burkina Faso) signify a series of continuous displacements of spaces of enclosure in various geographical margins relative to an idea of "Europe" at the center, which exists independently of the actual borders of the EU. This structure discloses not only the sham of national sovereignty conducted in its name but also the unabashed reinstitution of colonial territorial control and blatant denial of an unfaceable fact: that Europe's colonial problem can only be resolved on European soil itself.

While the presumed dissolution of borders within the EU was also put into effect in order to facilitate movement of labor (for labor, too, we must not forget, is a commodity), it nonetheless produced strict borders of exclusion in the labor market in terms different from the ethnopolitical lines of national sovereignty, which in any case had been dismantled. So, extraordinary *internal* borders were imposed in order to contain the massive migration of cheap labor from spaces surrounding the EU: first, from collapsed ex-Soviet societies (the Balkans, the Caucasus, Poland); then new waves of postcolonial migration (Asian/African/Caribbean) chiefly into the United Kingdom, France, and Holland; and finally the post-Iraq, Afghanistan, and Syria refugee debacle. While a legal distinction between refugees and migrants is maintained, the element of cheap/undocumented labor remains a common factor in both and very much the determining element, if not quite as cause of migration, then certainly as its effect or endpoint.

When the EU moved against Italy in spring 2014 and dissolved Mare Nostrum, "Europe held the negative side, the militarization of immigration control, rejecting the positive, the saving of immigrants and refugees from drowning at sea and their transportation to European land. In this fashion, it remained consistent with two basic principles that pertain to EU immigration policy for almost a decade: the closing off of legal pathways to Europe, which is the main reason immigration became criminalized, and the continuation of militarized border control. In this sense, Europe selected in essence to persist in a cul-de-sac that it itself had created" (Fotiadis, 74). The ultimate project in this quandary was the creation of a high-tech panopticon system of surveillance on the outer borders of the EU, which achieves same time virtualization of all that takes place in the vicinity. Officially inaugurated as Eurosur (European System of Border Surveillance) in October 2013, this system provides the perfect image of Fortress Europe as internal border condition. "Frontex is everywhere present and nowhere exposed" (Fotiadis, 103) —and we should add, not only on EU land.[95]

Alongside Eurosur, which is a Frontex operation, the European Commission has also authorized eu-LISA (European Union Agency for the Operational Management of Large-Scale IT Systems in the Area of Freedom, Security and Justice), whose task is surveillance and recognition—via biometrics, thermal cameras, and drone systems—of *all* persons who move in, out, and about EU territory, whether citizens of member states, alien residents, or transient persons (both legally and illegally).[96] This work is conducted by an enormous network of AI systems, despite the demonstrable fact of facial recognition failure by computers all over the world, the case of twenty-eight members of the U.S. Congress being falsely matched with purveyors of criminal acts in databanks being perhaps the most notorious. The six-year eu-LISA budget (2021–27) for its program "Horizon Europe" measures up to €95.5 billion, which surely goes to show that from the standpoint of capital border control technologies are certainly fine business, especially as the paradigm is shifting to construction of virtual walls and mobility monitoring systems. This too is part of the readjustment in the relation between politics and capital, as capitalism creates ever more inventive ways to take over the realm of politics altogether.[97]

Although I dispute Wendy Brown's Schmitt-driven argument that protective walls are a theological remnant of archaic societies—the mere example of Athens (if not all Greek cities in antiquity) discredits this argument—she is nonetheless correct to point out that the obsessive desire of states to build border walls is a clear indication of declining sovereignty. This is true not just of walls literally—in Israel, Greece, the United States, or wherever—but of all complex mechanisms of military mobilization to implement exclusion, whether on land or the high seas. Facing the ruses of capital, this is the national imaginary's last gasp. This is not to say that this desire and the practices still emerging from the national imaginary are not formidable or that the violence they incur should be underestimated. But it is certainly misguided to think that they still belong to the domain of statecraft, as matters of defending or enforcing sovereignty have been considered traditionally. Wall building is determined by capital, even when it is overtly and vehemently politicized by nationalist rhetoric. Brown is perfectly succinct: "the walling project was born out of a tension between the needs of North American capital and popular antagonism toward the migration incited by those needs, especially their effect of wages, employment, and the demographics and cultures composing and in some eyes decomposing the nation" (Brown, 48). The second (the nation) is subservient to the first (capital); even when the nation-state presides over the operative logic, it does so as a reaction to new conditions of capital. As Jason de Leon reminds us in his magisterial ethnography of southern U.S. border crossing, it was the NAFTA agreement in 1994 that created the flash impoverishment conditions for Mexican farmers who were then driven to mass migration to the north.[98] And when migrants escape border police internment or brutal death in the desert and succeed in entering U.S. territory as undocumented workers, it is still capital that gains from their cheap and unsecured labor. Capital invites migration.

This invitation can be produced directly or indirectly. Who can possibly dispute that climate refugees are not the consequences of global capital? Are regional wars (Syria or Ukraine, etc.) irrelevant or contrary to capital's movements and global recalibrations? Are they not world (war) events? Is the flash impoverishment of society that precipitates migration an accident, an unintentional by-product of growth? This unprecedented global movement of labor is part and parcel of the same force that enables the global movement of commodities on the high seas or the instant transfer of money between computers. The "market" celebrates all this; it calls it free flow. The obstacles—the walls, the interdictions, the pushbacks, the camps, the criminalization of "men on the move," as is now the official designation—are part of the show.

This show is the show of power plain and simple. It is the spectacle of control, like domestication or pacification of wild animals in a circus. Capital turns on and off the spigots of flow as it pleases. Indeed, it never turns them off entirely; it diverts them accordingly. Flow is the operative logic of capital, not interruption, enclosure, border protection; these are subsets of flow. And power flows as well—in the financial capitalism phase we are in, power flows upward like wealth into extraordinary accumulation in the hands of the fewest of the few: oligarchy again. Capital accumulation takes place along with power accumulation in the very same process, as does the annihilation of the productive (creative) capacities of people in order to produce superfluous populations in every society on the planet. That is the essence of *surplus over nothing* in capitalism.

One might recall that I used the same notion at the end of the previous section to describe the irreducibility of democracy as a politics of rule without qualification and without exception, a politics that remains groundless even as it unleashes a formidable constituent and instituting power. The double iteration pushes us in front of a veritable problem: the coarticulation, even identification, of capitalism with democracy. This bears a number of ideological expressions: from the liberal one, which sees it as a natural pair, to the antidemocratic one, according to which democratic life enables a limitlessness of relations that threaten the integrity of hard-set identities (racial, sexual, religious, ethnic), and to what could be called a leftist anxiety, which sees in the workings of contemporary capitalism many of the anarchic elements of radical democratic theory, including the prominence of deterritorialization.

I need no longer dwell on the first; we have already discussed the liberal ruse of tropes that signal natural affinity. Rancière, in both *Dissensus* and *Hatred of Democracy*, has aptly dealt with the second. The fear of limitlessness in democracy is as old as Plato, which means there is indeed something there. Elite power is always about imposing limits—of exclusion, if nothing else—while it seeks to remain unlimited as to its own terrain. Surely, in modern terms capitalism promulgates unlimited growth and thrives on discourses that break through or overcome limits, including political ones. What is different here in contrast to Plato's elites is that at the same time capitalism cultivates conditions of living *as if* there are no limits, even when it imposes hardcore limits of exclusion at all levels of society's capacity and power. This persistent performative ruse reaches its apex in the cultivation of what Rancière calls "the reign of narcissistic 'mass-individualism'" (*Dissensus*, 48). Mass individualism is an oxymoron very much in the tradition of capitalist doublespeak, but in its self-contradictory meaning it is perfectly accurate. The most extraordinary reproduction of sameness across inordinate masses of commodity consumers on a planetary scale has been achieved under the presumption of radical atomism. The more you think you are unique as a self-possessive individual, the more you are rendered absolutely the same as everyone else who thinks they are unique. In this respect capitalism is absolutely totalitarian.

On the other hand, the limitlessness of the democratic imaginary, which is obviously linked to its antifoundationalism but is never a project, a fantasy of growth, is precisely what disrupts the (re)production of sameness. For one, there is no commodity reward for democracy's unlimited politics. If anything, this condition carries the dread of unfulfillment, of no end in sight, and therefore the fear and fatigue that settles in when so much remains up in the air and looks unachievable. At the same time and for this exact reason, it produces a demand for what Castoriadis has called self-limitation, the self-propelled and self-organized creation of limits where (and because) there are none. Strangely, this is most apparent in conditions of collective democratic action at the extreme, where questions of spontaneous organization become palpable in the very moment they appear on the ground as a problem—that is to say simply, when a groundless politics finds ground, even if inadvertently but, by virtue of finding it, necessarily. In these autoscopic moments and while instrumental reason still remains suspended, people learn about themselves by the sheer act of coming together as (previously) strangers and acting as an assemblage. We think of revolutionary moments as moments of great excess, and from the standpoint of order this is true, but from the standpoint of groundlessness they are moments of integrity, moments of consolidation that mobilize the capacities for self-alteration that are always unleashed by spontaneous collectivity, in a way similar to how spontaneous composition happens during instances of musical improvisation.

Self-limitation has nothing to do with self-restraint (of mind or desire) by some sort of rational self-control or some sort of repression in a psychoanalytic sense. It is not about holding things in, pulling the reins, or putting on the brakes but the exact opposite: it is about inventing a horizon out in front, drawing and shaping it in the face of the void. Although it is self-propelled and autonomous, self-limitation is not *individualistic* or atomistic in the way that both liberalism and capital understand and construct the abstract notion of the ahistorical, asocial individual. This is because in moments of radical collective action, the individual is completely reconceived and detranscendentalized, thoroughly and palpably concretized in the moment, in the specific situation that takes over all so-called rational disengagement from the world that authorizes concepts of possessive individualism or Kantian anthropology.

Having said that, capitalism's chameleonlike capacity to shape-shift, even under its most dire challenges, and the speed with which this shifting happens create a sense that it too is groundless and indeed anarchic. This has been increasingly posed as a point of critique against antifoundational theories all around, and certainly those of radical democracy. The earliest instances I recall, already in the 1990s, addressed the avowed appropriation of postmodern theory in the reorganization of upper-level capitalist management. There was voluminous writing in the decade leading to the banking collapse of 2008, from articles in the *Financial Times* on "postmodern management" or executive retreats that promote self-actualization and harmonious productivity to significant theoretical works, like Boltanski and Chiapello's *The New Spirit of Capitalism* (1999), which served as critical warnings. Although no direct connection is usually made, one might argue that these "postmodern" tendencies and attitudes are rooted in theories of so-called anarcho-capitalism going back to David D. Friedman's economic libertarian writings of the 1970s. Subsequently, the same libertarian attitude, including its economics, took over various groups identified as cyberpunks or cryptoanarchists, who link the politics of resistance against cybersurveillance to cryptocurrency economics. The general mayhem produced by alt-right politics even led to descriptions of Trump as an anarchist figure.[99] I'm not sure how seriously we need to encounter such stipulations. After all, they too are part of media manipulation of subjectivities predicated on capitalism's doublespeak. Still, one might acknowledge—even with caution as to the terminology—a sort of contamination, at least at the boundary level where all these discourses and practices intersect with those of democracy. Even if democracy is the ultimate enemy of capitalism, its practice on capitalism's own sovereign grounds means that it is permeated by what it seeks to nullify.

But this mutuality or intersectional coexistence is not intrinsic; it is a historical symptom. At that level things do indeed become complex and opaque. No doubt the alt-right's response against what to them appears as capitalism's antifoundational premises, which are evident in the deterritorialization of labor and the brutal deracination (both physical and psychic) that it engenders, produces an *affective* backlash that unites constituencies, often of the lower classes, in the populist (on the way to becoming fascist) ways we have seen recently on numerous occasions worldwide. These constituencies are propelled by a desire to alter not only the present but also the future, much like the anticapitalist left's tradition since the days of the Paris Commune. Except that here the tenet is not utopian but apocalyptic—a qualitative difference. Although there is merit in thinking about how both radical democratic politics and the capitalist growth imaginary converge around a future disruption of the existing order, nonetheless the stakes, even the aesthetics, the poetics, are radically different, indeed contrary.

Anarcho-capitalism is surely hostile to any notion of the commons; any language of mutual aid is utterly repugnant to it. So what is nominally anarchist about it is perfectly pseudonymous; its libertarian arsenal is but a generational extension of liberalism, much like David Friedman is literally the son of Milton. But the clearest point of divergence resides in the fact that the most distilled image of the apocalyptic future that expresses the (desire for) disruption of the present order is produced by capital in its essence: the projected destruction of the planet. At the mass commodified level of cultural consumerism this entails, such a projected future takes place entirely in the domain of dreamwork. Alt-right constituencies fantasize about the end, but they are not pursuing it as a project, even if their actions might be bringing it on (ecologically, if nothing else). They still think the end is somewhat of a by-product, a metaphysical realm. In this respect, apocalyptic thinking is the same as thinking that capitalism will never end, to remember one of Fred Jameson's most brilliant accounts of the fantasy space of capitalist life. After all, the mechanism that produces both the images and the desire for the apocalypse is a huge money-making machine perfectly integral and active in the present.

One might retort that even when leftist futuristic desire/anxiety is articulated in a dark apocalyptic imaginary, in the way even of blockbuster Hollywood's sci-fi imagination, the same thing happens: the same machine makes money. Fair enough, but in this case the problem is indeed with the apocalyptic imagination that gets in the way of the utopian one. This is not by accident. The cultivation of pessimism among leftist constituencies and its concurrent disparagement of optimism as some sort of insidious narcotic are among the greatest achievements of the capitalist culture machine. And as is exemplary of capitalist logic, this is no more than a commodification of an already present, perhaps intrinsic, desire. Humans do not need capitalism or the nuclear age to contemplate the idea of total extinction. The ubiquitous occurrence of flood myths in archaic societies makes this perfectly (and *historically*) clear.

One might retort again that the inordinate arrogance of humans to think of a world without humans, to desire it even, indeed to think of it *because* they desire it, is a kind of enabling fantasy by virtue of the narratives of expiation that it produces. Hence the emphasis in flood myths on the imaginary of regeneration. But in our terms this still raises a question: What sort of politics authorizes this fantasy, this psychic arrogance? Anthropological explanations are very interesting and complex, but inadequate in themselves—surely, in the social-historical moment we inhabit. Again, Jameson's point stands out in stark light: "Someone once said that it is easier to imagine the end of the world than to imagine the end of capitalism. We can now revise that and witness the attempt to imagine capitalism by way of imagining the end of the world."[100] In our time apocalyptic desire is an expression of a depoliticized psyche. *Because* we cannot imagine the end of capitalism, we imagine the end of the world. Once again, humans deify their creation and consider it immortal, eternal, and invincible—like the monotheistic God. And like this God, they imagine the destruction of everything as redemption from the burden of having to unmake what they have made, God and capitalism both. Perversely, climate change denial involves the same operation, which, if we break it down, is simply deferral of the inevitable, a displacement of the temporality of the event.

All this is to say that groundlessness, limitlessness, and anarchy in radical democracy have an entirely different signification from how capitalism might have appropriated them. On the left side of things, the most common point of confusion is the identification of deterritorialization with groundlessness. This most likely derives from the left's unwillingness to take groundlessness seriously. It has always been difficult for the leftist tradition to sustain thinking from the standpoint of history while dispensing with any notion of ground. Although there is plenty of evidence that Marx's early thinking, especially about the "nature" of *human-being*, was antifoundational (as we discussed extensively in the previous essay), his subsequent attachment to the iron laws of history prevailed in the form of inculcating structural attitudes even in nondogmatic strains of Marxism. The proletariat, after all, signified a ground, even as it was endowed with a solventlike substance against all political-economic solidity. On the other side, capitalism's penchant for deterritorialization was not some appropriation of postmodern theory in the 1980s. It is an intrinsic faculty of the workings of capital, animating both the transatlantic slave trade and the colonial economy. But even more, deterritorialization does not mean the dissolving of foundations. At most it means the mobility, mutation, and even liquidity of foundation, which was already in play when "national" sovereign economies became imperial through naval exploration, conquest, and colonization since the sixteenth century.

Besides, for all its deterritorializing menace, capitalism is perfectly grounded in one thing and nothing will cut that anchor: money. The biggest weapon that capitalism has against democracy is indeed money. Democratic politics in our time has become nothing other than "money given by those who have it to those who vote properly."[101] Nothing has been more formidable in depoliticizing societies than money, and certainly nothing is more culpable for the erosion of trust in politics that societies are increasingly showing to an alarming degree. The biggest threat to the democratic imaginary is the deficit of trust in the political, and in this phase of the war between capitalism and democracy capitalism is clearly winning. But this too has a subversive underside.

By today's statistics, trust in governments and political institutions of liberal states has fallen to 40% of the population in Europe (Britain, Germany) and 27% in the United States, to which we would add the astonishing statistic that nearly 30% of Americans are ready to take up arms against their government.[102] The specific *politics* of distrust, however, is what matters, and this is exceedingly complicated. It used to be the case that society's sustained distrust of the liberal state came from the left, from rebellious constituencies that were veritable class enemies of governing elites and also antiliberal by conviction (anarchists, communists, anarcho-syndicalists). In the fascist era, we saw similar elements of antiliberal distrust (including in part similar class elements), but this switched immediately into its exact opposite, fanatical adoration and obedience to centralized power, when the liberal regimes were overthrown. Nowadays this is impossible to fully measure. Distrust in the liberal ruling classes is rampant in both right and left circles, and it's impossible to see how this would be alleviated, even if these rulers were dethroned. Assuming such a hypothetical case, the result is certain: society is poised to revel in its bipolar haze. Whoever wins will be doubted by the losers in an endless cycle of illegitimacy ad absurdum. It is difficult not to see this as society's psychopathology: every faction delights in its own delusion. In this they are all one, in a grotesque parody of similarity across the ideological spectrum, which achieves neither social unity nor productive social division. That is why great notions, such as the class struggle, which used to serve as a method both to explain social division and to rely on it for a politics that would bring about social unity need to be reconceptualized and reinvested with the radical democratic politics of today if they are to become visionary again.

There is a theoretical point to be made in the end that has much broader consequences. It is always attractive for anyone having spent years on the Marxist conceptual horizon to think that Marxism is still the greatest adversary to capitalism. The seduction is real and hard to resist. But the truth of the matter is—and the triumph of globalization and neoliberal order on the one hand plus the fierce resurgence of nationalism on the other make this obvious to me, for all I owe to Marxist thinking—that the greatest adversary to capitalism are mass popular movements, radical democratic movements on a planetary scale. Democracy is the only thing that capitalism cannot anticipate or predict in the last instance. This is why it goes to such great lengths to manufacture simulacra to serve its interests in the name of democracy, hoping to control it and discredit it in favor of sustaining the liberal oligarchy that is capitalism's real politics.

Facing this reality is a terrible quandary, an embedded contradiction. Democracy emerges as the only politics that might reconfigure the meaning of sovereignty in the era of global capital, yet sovereignty is already in the hands of global capital, a sovereignty that claims no sovereign. So, democracy must go against global capital. This is now its only goal; everything else has become secondary.

How this may be implemented in a substantial way without an independent national economy, which global capital always seeks to destroy, and without nationalist or civilizational wish-fulfillment delusions which send us straight into barbarism, marks the terrain of a sort of radical democratic politics we can call left governmentality. This politics changes the meaning of sovereignty altogether. It can only be planetary politics, even if still embedded in locality in its infinite variance.

NOTES ON LEFT GOVERNMENTALITY

It is banal for me to point out that the present economico-political situation worldwide is detrimental to democracy, or that it is happening because whenever democracy returns to its real place of power—the streets—it gets defeated, decade after decade. Nonetheless, in the face of this existential war between capitalism and democracy, where the latter seems to be invariably retreating or folding under its own incapacitation, I want to conclude with some preliminary thoughts driven by a sort of futuristic affirmation. With a full sense of how bleak the future looks, this may be called a folly—surely, a fancy—yet none of the thoughts unfolding here at the end of this long journey are mere inventions of my self-enclosed mind. They do emerge as response to real events that mark the political horizon of the first two decades of the twenty-first century more powerfully than either the technologically animated realization of the security state or the theologically animated investment in a global clash of civilizations, both equally glorified as the terms of definition of our era.

I am thinking of the extraordinary examples of insurgency worldwide in this period, already announced by the Zapatistas in Mexico and the antiglobalization protests in Seattle and Genova in the 1990s, which went on to manifest itself in what was called the Arab Spring and its consequent assembly (or Occupy) movements across continents, further on to the street insurgency of youth explosions in Santiago, Hong Kong, or Beirut, *gilets jaunes* or Black Lives Matter (political differences aside),[103] leading finally to leftist grassroots *electoral* movements victorious in Latin America (currently in Peru, Chile, Honduras, and Colombia), even if with uncertainty as to their prospects. Although in retrospect these multivariant moments seem ephemeral, their fleeting lifespans cannot erase the fact that popular reactions to the global neoliberal order are proliferating worldwide, covering an even broader geocultural range than the assembly movements of 2011, and are mostly driven by youth who see their futures already sold and wasted.

As mass withdrawals of consent to existing political institutions, assembly movements produced an entirely different signifying framework of political action and brought back to the fore the urgency of radical democratic politics outside and even against the established "democratic" modes of power, including the presumed stability of the political party form. As explosions of rage that found a path away from mere burning and looting and into occupation of public spaces, they exemplified the politics of spontaneous organization and self-representation that confirms radical democracy as the only weapon against the consumerist depoliticization of society that goes hand in hand with the bankruptcy of liberal institutions, especially in the European/American sphere. And yet, the intractable political question remains: How can these spontaneous insurgent gestures of rage turn into an affirmative politics of governance? And in the broader sense, how can those who are deprived of power and access to resources of organization, who are rendered superfluous by economic practices and hunted by the law to the point of death, come to organize themselves as a self-governing body?

With this question specifically in mind, my interest here, still abstract and inconclusive, is to explore a certain radical democratic attitude (rather than simply an institutional practice) as a response to the general crisis of democratic credibility in our times. I call this attitude "left governmentality," hoping to retain some sort of politics of the left even if the content of leftist politics may no longer be readable in a coherent way, haunted as it is by a sense of irreversible defeat by global capital in the post-1989 world. Precisely because of this historical discredibility and theoretical incoherence, the search for left governmentality remains tentative. But for the same reason it also remains open at both ends, both in conception and in execution. It is not reducible simply to an idea (let alone an idea born of the mind of any one person) but is rather realizable in the field of political action by democratic constituencies in specific social-historical situations. It is not concerned with the violent overthrow of the state, if nothing else because "governmentality" here exceeds the boundaries of state machinery. It is not about some technocratic expertise of government or statecraft, merely distinguished by ideological difference. It is not about management of what already exists but a transformation of what already exists, and this cannot be reduced to a simple takeover of the state or the mere inheritance of the state.

In the years since I introduced the notion of left governmentality and the extensive conversations that ensued, I have come to doubt its political efficacy several times. Occasional attempts to elaborate on the nuances, complexities, and enigmas of the notion have been motivated precisely by these doubts. After all, what could left governmentality mean outside the real political terrain of our times? The very claim that there can be such a thing, which must exceed the tradition of leftist resistance, makes sense only when it is measured as a reality of governance.

Ongoing governmental politics in the wake of neoliberalism's onslaught (austerity economics, the evisceration of social welfare institutions, the media-driven selling out of democracy, the all-encompassing consumer ideal, etc.) and its creations—the sovereign debt crisis, racist politics in the wake of labor and refugee migration, or nationalist violence within and across borders—make left governmentality seem like an impossibility, at best romantic, at worst naïve. And yet, for precisely this reason, because of what presently seems to be an unprecedented orchestration of politically debilitated societies, left governmentality seems like a necessary, even if daring, aspiration.

Because of this speculative daring, even if anchored in reality, some matters need to be settled at the outset. First, whatever it might be or might become, the meaning of left governmentality will be ill served if understood in the philosophically restrictive sense as a political concept. If it is deemed to be a concept at all, left governmentality mobilizes a kind of border conceptuality, along the lines of Balibar's invention and deployment of notions such as "equaliberty," "ambiguous universality," "citizen-subject," or "antiviolence."[104] Border concepts of this kind might turn out to be methodologically better suited to encounter a time of massive conceptual failure in the political terrain, as ideological certainties have been fissured or twisted beyond recognition and long-term institutional safeguards have collapsed in a remarkable atmosphere of violence, lawlessness, dehumanization, and political incapacitation of vast constituencies around the globe, citizens and noncitizens alike.

It has already become customary to refer to this time of conceptual failure as a time of crisis, in such a way, however, that the notion of critical time has lost its gravity. Surely in recent years "crisis" has become an umbrella term for a whole set of alibis that impede critical thinking, a sort of screen term that enables us to slip under the rug a whole set of situations that are difficult to interpret. Thus, the use of the term prevents us from pushing up against not only what "crisis"—as a word with multiple meanings—might actually signify but also what has been recently instituted in its name or even in reaction to its existence, whether as expressions and implementations in the first case or countermeasures and palliatives in the second.

Let's not forget that the word "crisis" is linked to judgment and decision and is therefore quintessentially political. It pertains as well to the faculty of distinguishing or discerning, and therefore, in some fashion, to dividing, separating. In this specific sense it is also linked to law—to regulation, to the apportionment of value, and therefore to fundamental aspects of social organization. But all these frameworks of meaning should be considered in light of the fact that "crisis" also pertains to something that is barely stable, precarious—something, as we say, in critical condition—which tempers the elements of finality inherent in judgment, decision, or regulation. Crisis is thus a border concept as well, or, if you will, crisis is always a concept in crisis.

For this reason, there is an equally presumed sense, even if not always articulated, that crisis is nothing new, but rather endemic to the long term situation of modernity—whether as an intrinsic element of the capitalist economy, whereby it even becomes a coveted object, a target, even perhaps a project (capitalism creates crises because this is how it grows), or as an intrinsic element in democratic politics, whereby again it may appear to be a necessary condition, an existential reality, and even here too a target and a project.

However, these two rubrics of endemic crisis, if it is indeed endemic, are entirely different. As I have already argued, capitalism and democracy are profound enemies of each other. Pushed to the ontological limit in each case, their existence means each other's annihilation, war to the death. In this respect, however we define them precisely, the crisis of capitalism is not the same as the crisis of democracy. Or, put differently: capitalism has a different agenda for the use of crisis than does democracy. They each put the notion to use in antagonistic ways.

As such, the so-called economic crisis that seems to have become permanent—starting with the banking collapse of 2008, subsequently the EU sovereign debt crisis, and now the global inflation and supply chain crisis in the pandemic, which is compounded by a war in Ukraine that signals globalization's implosion—cannot be simply equated with the crisis in political institutions, national sovereignty, political legitimacy, and so forth that we are seeing virtually everywhere in "democratic" societies. Nor is it the same as two other domains of identified

Democracy's Anarchy 259

crisis, which, although different, are conducted on a planetary scale: the climate crisis and the cultural crisis, as it is designated by long-lasting trending terms such as the culture wars, the resurgence of religion, or the clash of civilizations. I am hardly suggesting these matters are unrelated but just resisting easy deterministic causal accounts: say, that the whole lot is reducible to the advent of globalization and the domination of the neoliberal order. We can certainly debate the connections and the points of influence and effect—and there are many—but the situations of crisis are not interchangeable.

The discourse of crisis is a manufactured reality whose management serves the sole purpose of turning it into a natural order. (The radical exception is the ecological sphere, for that crisis is utterly and brutally real; however, this too is folded, alas, into this manufactured discourse.) In old terms we could speak of a "crisis-effect"—in the sense of Michel Foucault's "subject-effect" or Roland Barthes's "reality-effect"—in order to describe how crisis produces specific subjects and specific realities whose specifically manufactured historical emergence is repressed. Society's critical condition thus becomes a "crisis-suffused norm," with a culture all of its own, including its own kind of governmentality.[105]

Moreover, there is definitely political detriment in accepting crisis as a norm. Regardless of what sort of ideological content one gives to it, accepting crisis as a norm exacerbates the depoliticization of society. Andreas Kalyvas is certainly right when he questions the easy presumption that politics is in crisis in the liberal parliamentary sphere. He points to the radicalization of the right, with its extensive mass mobilization, its aggravation of polarized or conflictual conditions, and even its contribution to an increase in electoral participation, as a perfect indication. This manufactured reality of crisis, he argues, is insidious. It testifies to "the exoneration of the post-democratic order and the absolution of undisputed hegemonic neoliberal reign. The idea of a democracy in crisis constructs its own idealized periodization that exalts the pre-crisis period as a superior epoch, a golden age of democracy, a higher universal norm, and a legitimate order against which the populist present is measured and indicted as abnormal, deficient, exceptional, and regressive."[106]

Questioning the discourse of crisis in this way enables us to consider seriously the movements of radicalized right politics as pulsating terrains of the political against the neoliberal depoliticization of society. Except, of course, that we cannot at all discount that radical right politics is enemy politics to democracy. What animates the alt-right insurrectionary politics in the United States right now—to the point that the BLM slogan "Defund the police" turns into "Defund the FBI"—is plain hatred of democracy. Masses of disgruntled people, some disenfranchised by capitalism to be sure, engage in fantasy paroxysms of violence against essential institutions of democracy: the election process and electoral representatives, mechanisms and purveyors of justice, investigative journalism and media persons, public officials and civic employees, education boards (including parents and teachers), local institutions and representatives, and so on. The cries of war—indeed, explicitly named "civil war"—abound in alt-right circles, and while the named enemy is "the government" the fantasy endpoint of their desire is to institute their own government by force. Which is to say that the government is not the enemy per se; the enemy is the regime of democracy. The irony that it is the realm of democracy itself that enables them to flourish in their full-fledged antidemocratic violence is, of course, entirely absent from their consciousness.

This raises a serious question that Kalyvas does not address: Can antidemocratic politics be considered indicative of exaltation of the political when the political matters only in the context of democratic conflict? Because, despite the fantasy-cultivated insurgent desire for empowerment, antidemocratic politics leads with mathematical accuracy to the depoliticization of society at the other end, to a submissive politics of adoration of and obedience to the Leader. Despite appearances and sloganeering, there is nothing civically disobedient in alt-right politics. From this standpoint neoliberalism and alt-right neototalitarianism are the same; in both cases people lose their power. Anything short of this realization entails a formalist fetishization of the political.

In addition, we need to account for the increasingly fickle investment of the effectively depoliticized (even if fanaticized) public in errand electoral directions. The speed with which large constituencies withdraw consent from candidates or even parties after they have endorsed them in elections, under obsessively embraced reversals of lies into "truth," emerges from these same conditions of vacant polarization and blindly aggravated conflict—read: effective depoliticization—which is why the populist phenomenon is both the biggest political quandary within the liberal framework and the greatest obstacle to left governmentality, as we will discuss shortly.

I invented the term "left governmentality"[107]—initially without much thinking, I admit—in response to the 2011-12 political conjuncture that brought forth what we now summarily call the politics of assembly movements (the Arab Spring, the Spanish and Greek occupations of public squares, the Occupy movement in the United States, and subsequent assembly occupations of public spaces in Istanbul, Hong Kong, Brazil, and elsewhere in the world), even though "movement" might not be an accurate term of description because the operative politics involved in all these cases of assembly is a kind of Benjaminian politics of arrest, of interruption.[108] Subsequently, this idea found more concrete and higher stakes historical content in the rise of Syriza to power in Greek politics in 2015, especially since this signaled the rather unusual event of the left coming to power not by revolution but by the procedures of a liberal parliamentary system.

At the time I had argued, with no desire to be prescient, that Syriza was a *problem*—not a problem to be solved, for nothing in politics can be mathematized, but a problem in the sense of an open framework of trouble in the terrain of politics. It was a problem in the midst of the political, in terms of Greek history certainly unprecedented and even beyond the history of the Greek left from which it obviously emerged. Using a phrase by Edward Said in a different signifying framework, I argued that Syriza enacts "a technique of trouble"—it means trouble, it gets into trouble, and creates trouble for all presumed-to-be-stable categories, including, of course, the category of the left. And the fact that very soon after it came to power Syriza was politically *in* trouble was also part of the same rubric. My sense then was that Syriza was a troublemaker entity in politics, and this was something that we should not lament or wish to extinguish but rather engage with an open mind, if we are ever going to get out of the categorical sludge of much of leftist thinking, especially since the enormous geopolitical shift of 1989, as well as liberalism's ridiculous presumption of the politics of civility.[109]

The ill fate of Syriza aside, this remains acutely pertinent still. The question of left governmentality and what it might entail exactly—what sort of political action it manifests, what sort of institutional politics it inaugurates or mobilizes—emerged from these present critical conditions against these conditions: as an immanent reconsideration of the radical democratic politics necessary to disrupt the norm of crisis and the "crisis management" models that are typically proposed in order to enforce and safeguard the crisis norm. In this respect, left governmentality cannot simply be a politics of alterity in the way this is often celebrated and even fetishized as another politics of identity. For it emerges from within an illogical (or paralogical) foundation, where alterity is already assumed, assimilated, and ensconced in the requisite place it occupies in every narrative of crisis. Whatever alterities left governmentality might animate will emerge from the terrain of political action in the process; they are not there already waiting to be swept up by some political deus ex machina.

Left governmentality is thus paradoxical par excellence, keeping in mind the problematic relation of the left—at least in both the Marxist and the anarchist tradition—to the politics of government as opposed to the politics of resistance, which is always instantaneously privileged. The problem emerges from the historical record of the left's incapacity to govern without being absorbed by the institutions against which it stands, even when it has assumed power by force and through the violent dismantling of whatever is the ancien régime of the day. But this particular historical legacy of violence does not concern me here. I am proposing that we consider the notion of left governmentality not in the frame of the Leninist revolutionary left, but within the limits of a democratic process whereby the left's accession to government does not abolish the democratic process—any such abolition, regardless of where it comes from, is fascist.

For leftist politics to achieve a governmentality not of management but of social transformation, it cannot remain in the default position of resistance but must develop a capacity to rule. In essence, this requires a shift from an oppositional imaginary to a ruling imaginary, except this would not be some sort of Leninist idea of taking over state power. First of all, opposition already means governance; in democratic politics, opposition/dissent always takes place from within. Opposition/dissent is in itself a mode of governance, and we have often seen it literally bring down elected governments. If in a democratic society the left is already in opposition (say, as an opposition party in parliament), it would need to understand that it already bears a governmental responsibility, for in a democratic society government cannot be left to the hands of named (appointed or even elected) officials but belongs to all always. By the same token, pivoting from opposition to rule necessarily means to rule in the service of all, not merely an electoral constituency, a particular class, or specific social, economic, or cultural interests. This structural pivot means that we cannot hold left governmentality to unshakeable a priori ideological principles but rather must remain alert to those new social and political exigencies that emerge as an outcome of left governmentality becoming a political event. Which means, right away, that any sort of left governmentality will have to account for the possibility that it might be overthrown in the same way that it came to be. Hence it is a regime of struggle, a tragic regime.

This paradox is aggravated further if we consider how Foucault's notion of governmentality tends to be interpreted as mechanism of population control, although there is ample evidence in Foucault's thinking that would make governmentality a notion essential to any kind of autonomous, self-empowering politics. For this, even in passing, Foucault does not turn to the traditional Marxist left but opens the horizon to a sort of autonomous *poiēsis*: "In any case, we know only that if there is a really socialist governmentality, then it is not hidden within socialism and its texts. It cannot be deduced from them. It must be invented."[110] The comment comes in the course of an extensive rumination as to whether socialism bears its own governmentality and what exactly this would mean, if it were not merely a borrowing from the governmentality of liberalism that brings forth biopolitics. As he reveals his profound uncertainty and leaves the horizon open to invention, Foucault does certify that what has served as *extrinsic* (he says) governmental rationality in the history of socialism is an almost sacred devotion to the master texts of the Marxist tradition—quite clearly a condition whose shackles must be broken so that invention can indeed take place.

It is along these lines that we must account for Foucault's extensive work, subsequent to his historical theorization of biopolitics, on the disciplines involved in what he named "the government of the self," for there is no doubt that any sort of left governmentality worthy of its name cannot possibly be excised from the self-governance of the subject, however we might agree or disagree about what this might involve and how feasible it might actually be. Indeed, self-government, the old anarchist/autonomist adage of *autogestion*, which is pertinent to the politics of society, has a "mirror" in the government of the self, with its extensive self-disciplinary practices including those that Foucault sought out in the Stoic period, as we know.

So if governmentality, in Foucault's writing, is the figure that moves him out of the disciplinary or punitive society model and into, say, the biopolitical or micropower model, by analogy left governmentality is a figure that moves us out of the counterpower model and turns the notion on its head, so that "societies of control" (to use a Deleuzian phrase) become societies of self-governance. Here, it helps to remember the resonance of the French notion of *mentalité*. Namely, governmentality is not so much the substantive noun from the administrative qualifier "governmental" as it is the designation of a certain imaginary (a mentality) of governance. Thus, left governmentality is as much a condition of governing the self as it is a condition of governing the other, in both cases departing from both liberal-individualist and Marxist-collectivist modes where a sharp division between self and other remains.

In this respect, the operative notion in left governmentality is not government but governance, even when we are talking explicitly of governmental structures in the full institutional sense, which would most certainly include the police. Indeed, the question of how a leftist government organizes, reconceptualizes, democratizes the police (purging it of all fascist, racist, misogynist, homophobic, militarist, and, yes, capitalist elements) in order to turn it into a force of governance of the law is one of the primary problems that left governmentality must solve. (Incidentally, that is the real meaning of the slogan "Defund the police!"—not just disrupting the state's economics of violence.) Hence left governmentality's radical democratic character, for democracy is not about mechanisms of government (parliaments, political parties, elections, police forces)—these are necessary symptoms. Democracy is a politics of self-governance above all, and this happens in all facets of society and ideally by all of its members, regardless of their differences. Because social difference does not vanish despite equality being essential to democracy, a politics of self-governance is especially keen to address social and economic disparities pertinent to all without exception.

This is precisely where left governmentality cannot but be anticapitalist in the last instance, even if in the historical process of its political emergence it surges forth in capitalist conditions, therefore inheriting the contradictions of capitalism and its profound structures of social division and differentiation and always having to face their management. In trying to conceptualize what left governmentality might mean, we do not begin by presuming the disappearance of capitalism by some sort of magic nor certainly the elimination of social difference, an idea that is but another pseudonymous liberal utopia, much like the presumption that at its civil-society best liberalism makes the category of class irrelevant. Difference is intrinsic to the human, and the presumption to eliminate it is not just antihuman but nonsensical. The project of a politics of freedom among equals, which is what democracy means simply speaking, respects the marks of difference; it just seeks to transform them. The purpose of this project is that difference does not become inequity—or subjugation, the rule of one over another—indeed, that difference becomes instead the ground of collective free life and decision. As left governmentality is an affirmative and transformative project within democracy's radical framework, the process of resignifying social difference or restructuring the conditions whereby difference becomes the ground for the equal capacity of the people to rule themselves is one of its essential tasks.

All the more reason, then, to take seriously and think inventively about the key question in the actual (governmental) politics of left governmentality: how to move from resistance or opposition to government decision. I do not see this as a mere positional shift in the spectrum of power, but rather as a shift that requires the operations of a different political imaginary and a different framework for social organization. The idea is that, at the very least, the long-term play of power is now in your hands, and you no longer have the alibi of merely responding to power. Responding to power—reacting or resisting—also has a long-term strategy, but this is often clouded by the exigencies of the short term. From a certain perspective, counterpower is an "easier" mode of action than power as such or ruling power, even if we know very well that in the course of counterpower formidable foes are encountered and real lives are lost.

Left governmentality is a border concept because it acknowledges—indeed, it *names*—the paradox of a political constituency that traditionally derives its authority from negation (resistance to established authority and, at the outer limit, revolution) but has achieved a position of affirmation, the imperative to rule—especially if we understand rule in a radical democratic sense, not as reducible to an ideological partisanship that divides society between rulers and ruled, whatever may be the specific turns of representation. For this latter reason alone, left governmentality entails the sort of rule that pertains to all and is shared by all of society, not just the extension of the specific class interests presumed to authorize leftist propositions of rule—traditionally the dictatorship of the proletariat on the way to communism or, more recently, the politics of left populism, to which I will attend.

Daring to think from the standpoint of all, yet not as a singular totalizing notion—as heritage of the One—but as an irreducible heterogeneous plurality, is indeed the challenge of democracy and its paradoxical politics. Likewise, left governmentality cannot be considered from a partial viewpoint. In this sense, the class politics that the Marxist legacy of the left has indelibly established, and in fact the class struggle itself as a kind of epistemological framework that informs all levels of political thought and action, must be reconceptualized in such a way as not to work against the radical democratic imperative. Anarchist in literal terms, as we have seen, this imperative aspires to an autonomous politics at all levels of life and for all involved, regardless of the social differences that are still in play. In the encounter of left governmentality with democracy, the epistemology of class struggle becomes a productive obstacle to the tendency to circumvent (or smooth out) social difference in the name of an emancipatory universality. In this respect, to use Balibar's language again, the play of ambiguous universality that the proposition of equaliberty necessitates remains prominent.

We can think of this another way: Although left governmentality begins with and has sufficient cause in the fact that the left is in government, it cannot be conducted solely within the purview of political institutions of government. The operative idea in left governmentality is not government but governance—indeed, self-governance. Therefore, whatever governmental (state) politics left governmentality enacts obviously fails if restricted to typical institutional politics. When it comes to governing society as a whole, especially with the inheritance of the capitalist state, the left in power cannot sever itself from the social movements that bring it to power in the first place. By social movements I am referring not only to the politics of negation or resistance but more to a radical politics of affirmation: solidarity networks (which must always be international in the last instance); collaborative decision making and collective protection in the workplace; alternative modes of social organization and economy at the local level; collectively self-instituted public services (neighborhood health care, schooling for immigrants, welfare for impoverished social strata); extraparliamentary politics; and all kinds of psychosocial performativities of difference that generate and shape subjectivities.

The primacy of self-governance means that left governmentality cannot be exhausted in governmental practices and institutions. Social change cannot be mandated by law, although it often requires law in order to be sealed. It is always rooted in social movements, and leftist politics in the absence of social movements is an empty shell. This shift from a negative politics of resistance to the affirmative politics of governance works only to the degree that social movements retain their full critical and interrogative power. Although intertwined, government and movement each retain a position of relative autonomy, and as relatively autonomous from the government, the movement has its own task in place—an essential task that no government can handle. Developing a left governmentality entails precisely that internal dissent in the relation between government and movement would register not as a weakness but as a critical force that enhances the capacity of self-governance.

The movement in this respect cannot be instrumentalized, whether as a potential source for political party organization or even as a symbolic recipient and/or vehicle for institutional alterity at the state level. For example, local self-organization in neighborhoods, workplaces, schools, and the like would have to disrupt hierarchical institutions of power. To do so, conditions of a new pedagogy would have to be fostered. One of the concrete lessons of the assembly movement was the spontaneous discovery of new pedagogical possibilities. The best analogy to the conditions of learning (and teaching) in assembly conditions is indeed the Aristotelian *co-incidence* of rulers and ruled, so that we can speak of a continuous process of self-teaching, of learning not through a master source, a sacred text or any authentic source of knowledge and external authority, but from a self-propelled inquiry that opens the self not only to the other but also to its own othering. The autodidactic element of this pedagogy is also characterized by exceeding the inherited authority of *logos* because the very experience of forming a new public space—the somatic, sentient, and spiritual *co-incidence* of people, otherwise unknown to each other, in the street or the square—constitutes, *as such*, a pedagogical event.

Once this experience and the new imaginary it fosters are brought into the realm of governance, things change. An instant problem arises: What does it mean for the left to create and uphold the law, in contrast to opposing and transgressing the law, which, for obvious reasons, has been its inheritance and its calling? Again, I repeat bluntly: How does the left in government conduct the work of the police? A crucial problem that never arises in the classic bourgeois politics of security. Yet, precisely in a society where criminality in the name of the law is rampant—discriminatory legislation, legal protection of elite power and corruption, the lawmaking lawlessness of police violence, and so on—the radical politics of transgression becomes the only emancipatory politics of *nomos*. To protect the justice of the law against the injustices of the law is the left's key responsibility to society: this is one of the great lessons of the Black Panthers. Obviously, this sort of *nomos* is not *nomos* as the name of sovereignty, especially if sovereignty still espouses its authority as mystical foundation—the Nation, the State, the Race, the Family, the Religion, the Logos—but a *nomos* that discloses its constitutive lack of foundation, other than what is provisionally grounded in history by a polity's constituent action in a specific social-historical moment.

In Greek tragic terms, left governmentality mobilizes, in full cognizance and accountability, *astynomous orgas*, as Sophocles puts it in *Antigone*: the "self-ruling passions of the city," which can also be translated as the "legislating rage of the city." As strange as this may sound in our ears today, what else can an autonomous politics be in the context of the legalized lawlessness of today's rulers and their rules? There is only one answer: a politics that will return *nomos* to the commons—*nomos* that is instituted in equal share, pertains to the totality of society, and does not make exceptions for the benefit or detriment of some part— and simultaneously involve political daring (*tolmas charin*, says the same ode in *Antigone*: "for the sake of daring"), which will not bear any guilt for its rage/passion (*orgē*). In speaking about rage/passion, I am not referencing the manufactured or media-controlled libidinal affect of *los indignados* (in times past, *les enragés*) but the creative rage/passion of society in its lawmaking plurality, where *nomos* would not be reducible to the juridical authority of a specifically designated person, party, or institution but would be pertinent to the daily action of every citizen against every condition of legalized, state-sanctioned criminality, even when such criminal conditions might provisionally be to any specific citizen's benefit. This is also the battle between society's rage and society's corruption, if we can put it this way, where various mechanisms of the state apparatus, down to the smallest capillary, are implicating (seducing) individual citizens into all sorts of compromising acts, often by mobilizing individual benefit over the commons but in the process depoliticizing both individuals and society at large.

Pierre Clastres's old argument about "society against the state" (unburdened, however, by his utopian politics of "society without the state") can be very useful here as an epistemological framework. A certain relative autonomy of society, as a field of self-organization, must remain in place in order to keep the movement from being instrumentalized and to enable performativities of difference to flourish or, even more, to sustain real political effectiveness and not remain locked in ideological self-satisfaction. For this reason, the state politics to which the left may have acceded cannot presume to dictate the terms of action to the movement that may have created the horizon of possibility for this accession or presume to harness a certain raw political power inherent in the movement that, no matter what its specific forms of social organization, must remain formless in some last instance.

Here it is important to note a peculiar temporality. Popular movements always look beyond the temporal frame of governance because their desire manifests itself in the present tense. It does not wait and will not be deferred—all the more after a victory against the grain of previous history and established power. In wanting the future now and in not looking beyond their place in the present, movements overlook the shift that takes place from the politics of opposition to the politics of government. Winning power under these conditions always produces enormous expectations; it is the self-propelling force of a dream that must become reality. This reinforces the movement's constitutive condition. Since every movement lives in the now, it is not made for, nor concerned with, tactical maneuvers of retreat or negotiation. The immediacy of its social base, relative to the mediation of the exigencies of government, keeps the movement free of responsibility both to statist sovereignty and the polity within which after all the movement fights agonistically and breaches, where time is in constant flux and parameters can change any minute and in directions that may run counter to plans and wishes, even principles.

Here democracy is severely tested. Let's consider the notorious case of how the leftist movement in Greece that, in large part, underwrote Syriza's electoral victory responded to the government's handling of the referendum on EU austerity measures in July 2015. The movement's perception—but even more dramatically, the sentiment, the profound affect—that the referendum unleashed the power of the demos, which was then revoked by the government's agreement with the enemy, precipitated explosive expressions of disaffection, depression, and rage, as well as charges of cowardice, capitulation, selling out, and indeed treason of the movement's principles. But, as I argued at the time, thinking of the quandary of left governmentality in action, the referendum was decided by the government and was won, for the government, by the movement in order for the government to act on its basis. Nothing in this equation should be assumed to be linear or self-evident, or even simply causal. The components are irreducibly linked but cannot be collapsed into each other. Neither the government nor the movement is subservient to each other, and yet both the government and the movement are responsible for each other. They can exist just as easily in coincidence as in contestation, and indeed they must if the radical democratic impetus of left governmentality is to be sustained.

It is in this sense that left governmentality—again, regardless of how we eventually come to explain it theoretically—cannot be equated with left populism, either in the able hands of Ernesto Laclau, Chantal Mouffe, and their acolytes, or in the historical-political field in Venezuela, Bolivia, Spain, or Greece, for that matter.[111] The now common assumption among ranks of the left that Syriza failed in 2015—which unleashed extraordinary waves of debilitating affect ranging from depression to rage among large constituencies of supporters, including activists in the movement itself—would have been more productively put to work if the symbolic structure of the whole affair did not have left-populist characteristics, whether these were the result of psychic investment by the population (a sort of metaphysics of faith)[112] or were instrumentally cultivated and engineered by central aspects of the Syriza organization itself. It does not matter whether this cultivation was intentional or unwitting, for the symbolic structures of left populism are machinelike in their ways and channel political affect in a monovalent direction regardless of what the material conditions of social difference on the ground might be.

The disastrous way in which the Syriza referendum in 2015 was constructed, conducted, and interpreted is the ultimate outcome of this machine logic. The left-populist imaginary that engendered and prevailed over the referendum at nearly all levels of society and state prevented the differences of the social body (on both sides of the vote) from retaining their coherent articulation as actors on the stage of political agonism. This imaginary thus produced a debilitating homogenization of all political signifiers, with the polarization of enraged affect being one of the most acute markers of this homogenization. A series of events ensued: the complexities addressed symptomatically and brought forth causally by the referendum were thereby nullified; the government's subsequent decision appeared to be total deception—for some, it spelled treason, for others cynical confirmation of political realism; the complexity of differences in the reasons why the electorate came to decide one way or another were effaced; the roused population (on all sides) was simply deflated; and any radical possibility in the next phase of political action was thus disarmed.

I cannot expound on it here, but the idea that the referendum epitomizes democratic politics is a great deception. The history of plebiscites since ancient Rome makes clear that this form of politics was always a means of accrediting or, worse, sanctifying, a sovereign decision—in essence, granting a ruler the popular imprimatur (Urbinati, *Democracy Disfigured*, 171–80). In time plebiscite politics created the delusion that the voice of the citizens is directly heard, except that this works to disengage them from the daily work of self-organization, which is requisite of democracy. Plebiscites indicate a point of failure in governance. Because the government has hit a dead-end in its political process of judgment and decision (*krisis*), it orders a plebiscite. In what seems like a moment of direct participation in decision making—but, as Urbinati says, it is not decision but *pronunciation*—the people deprive themselves of the lifelong process of small judgments and decisions that form social mobilization and political organization in the everyday in exchange for a once in a lifetime up and down vote on a question someone else has posed. In this sense, politics based on the referendum form almost always serve a binary machine logic.

Along these lines, the division between "us and them," which Mouffe (and Laclau) always held onto in order to keep intact a certain register of the epistemology of the class struggle, is also what renders left populism a political machine logic. (What this does to the epistemology of the class struggle as such cannot be discussed here in a substantial way.) Despite the consistent acknowledgment that "the people" is a heterogeneous entity, this elemental division inevitably homogenizes the framework of society. The binary machine reproduces simple 0/1 divisional pairs: people/elite, society/state, disenfranchisement/power, us/them. In this framework, then, what happens when, let us say, "the people" come to power? What happens to the meaning of the state? To the meaning of "the people" who now occupy the state? Do these meanings change instantly, as by an on/off switch? We presume that "we" do not become "them," but on what basis do we turn "their" house (the state) into "ours," if by sheer preemptive division we have already undersigned and sealed its enemy alterity? What does it mean for us to have *come to power*? Had we no power before? If being disenfranchised means having no power, then how do the powerless achieve power? Likewise, if we presume that there are two different modes of power, ours and theirs, how do we account for qualitative shifts of power in real political and social-historical terms? Either the division between "disenfranchisement" and "power" collapses, or the power "we" now have in the place of "their" power—say, the state—is really still "their" power, since after all we had no power of our own and we just fell into an inheritance.

Note that these sets of questions—in essence mobilized by the equally divisive pair "self/other" over which the presumption remains that each side is intact and self-sufficient—would have entirely different meaning if considered in racial terms. From the standpoint of black activism, let us say, how would the "us/them" pair be constituted? How would the bipolar pair of "our/their" power be constituted? Obviously the framework would be nonsensical before we even get off the ground. The same would be true with gender and sexuality politics—any situation of basically asymmetrical power positions, which in effect means any and every situation when disenfranchised people engage in social movements. The question of how the truly disadvantaged, the wretched of the earth, can organize themselves remains the direst political question of our times. The left-populist dream assumptions of consolidation along the lines of a simple oppositional structure, where in fact the power of definition still remains in the hands of your enemy, does not really address this question. If nothing else, these dream assumptions disregard the psychic complexity of collective minds. Enacting a sense of belonging by political simplification is surely a powerful experience; hence populism's seductive power. People love to lose themselves in the oceanic feeling of belonging, to use a bit of Freud's language, but the phrase to underline here is *lose themselves*. This happens easily because in an absolute self/other division the fiction of the self submits one to a debilitating paradox, a double deception: both the sense that the self exists as such in some unassailable fashion outside of society and that this existence is determined by opposition to (and because of) the enemy other who gives it meaning. According to the first, one exists already as a transcendental entity and need not change, and according to the second, one exists only to the degree that the enemy other exists, who however, politically speaking, must be annihilated, thereby endangering the self's source of existence. In both cases whatever is "self" is desocialized and deauthorized by structures that exist outside it, which makes it easy to "lose yourself" in some equally transcendental experience of belonging.

Whatever this is, it is not politics. It is certainly not democratic politics, for it goes to great lengths to defuse democracy's contestation of all terms, most important of which in this case is the term "self." An already-made transcendental self at best cannot engage in self-reflection and at worst cannot mobilize the critical capacity that will both open oneself to the other and understand oneself as part of the commons—which in essence happens in the same gesture. Thus we come to the point that contrary to the idea that populism seems to mobilize the popular will and invest human individuals with collective power, the opposite happens. Populist politics assimilates individuals into an illusion of power, and what is worse, it confuses the field of vision as to who has what sort of power, which enables the easy transfer of the people's power to the hands of the leader and leads to the self-abrogation of real material power in favor of the imaginary power of an idea—the nation, the flag, the race, the divine right, the intractable We.

Finally, this affective investment in nonambiguous politics of opposition confuses the very field of contestation. That is why what might nominally be a populist movement with left characteristics—say, overt anticapitalist aspirations—so easily turns into nationalist self-enclosure. When internationalism is coded as the realm of elites in a simple "us/them" situation, internationalist solidarity projects become suspect and from the standpoint of the left populist are deemed to be liberal, thereby forging an alignment with right-populist paranoia over everything foreign. In this respect, populism always enacts a politics of exclusion, contrary to what it claims. In the populist imaginary, the collective does not produce the isonomic configuration of equality-through-difference, but rather the proliferation and reproduction of the same. That is why it is also a politics of homogenization of society, despite the vehement polarization it fosters and within which it flourishes. Or perhaps more accurately, *because* of this polarization society hardens into mirror images of the same—even if self-advertised as enemy otherness—driven by the same technologies of mediatization and videocratic identification. Not only pluralistic views but also the very principle of dissent are neutralized, for dissent does not mean simple opposition to something external; it is also always an internal self-interrogation, a production of otherness from within, an affirmative alteration. Strangely, for all the ardor and rage it produces, populism celebrates a politics of passivity and thus fits well into current social situations where politics has become a spectator sport of competing approval ratings.

Notice that in discussing how left governmentality and left populism are incompatible I have left the inheritance of capitalism out of this admittedly schematic set of queries, even though this specific inheritance can never be ignored. In fact, it is impossible to address the problem of left governmentality without also addressing the key problem of inheriting capitalist structures, at least in the present planetary phase. Because the symbolic structure of left populism is so formalist, the actual politics it mobilizes will be channeled at some point in the process toward inherited modes of oligarchic power: not only in the basic sense in which a popular movement will be subsumed by the political party form and its metaphysics of representation, but even more in a kind of historically antecedent way, in the sense that the people's power will be subsumed by the power of national sovereignty at the apex of which remains the heroic sovereign, whether as the President of the Republic or the Popular Leader. For the same reason that I have always argued that popular sovereignty is, strictly speaking, a nonsensical notion, I also think that left populism is a nonsensical notion, if we want to retain within the content of the left an undeconstructibly internationalist and radical-democratic (or, in my language, anarchist) ground.

The usual argument, which Mouffe reiterates, that the difference between right populism and left populism is that the first restricts democracy while the second doesn't has proven insubstantial, since so many strains of left-populist politics have ended up centralizing sovereign power—literally, oligarchic power. Left populism is still sovereign state politics, with all the horrific dimensions of nationalist thinking that this entails kept intact. Thus, no matter what left-populist rhetoric might claim, left populism actually means that national borders must be preserved as sacred markers of difference qua division—that is, as safeguards of identity—which then serve either as pillars of self-enclosure or platforms for expansion and the conquest of the other. This pertains to the internal space as well: it is the paramount gesture of creating internal borders of division and self-enclosure, instrumental power and control over the performativities of difference. This is why left populism is not a border concept in the way I argue that left governmentality is.[113]

And it is also why left populism may pride itself at mobilizing a movement but ultimately has no respect for the autonomy of the movement past its point of instrumentalized power. Left populism claims to begin with the movement but is instead always already grounded in the telos of governmental power as state power in the name of the people. In this respect it remains entirely within the liberal framework and plays very well into the hands of neoliberal power. Instead left governmentality is inevitably grounded in the *problem* of government—on how to move from resistance to government—but this can never be its telos because it would mean de facto the conquest of the movement and the voiding of resistance by the formal power of rule. Without the movement—that is, civic action whose institutionality exists outside the state and sometimes against the state—there can be no left governmentality. In other words, although left governmentality begins with and has sufficient cause in the fact that the left is in government, it cannot be conducted solely at the level of government. It cannot be exhausted within the purview of the political institutions of government but must involve general social practices of *governance*, indeed self-governance.

For this reason, left governmentality cannot revert to simple party politics in the liberal system. In fact, precisely because of the perpetually contentious relations that it sustains between governance and insurgency, government and movement, left governmentality is a border concept that bears a tragic politics. The nonrevolutionary left's notorious aversion to taking on the responsibility of government in its name might be due to its fear of losing its authenticity as resistance or counterpower, which is curiously never the fear of revolutionaries despite the fact that historically this loss of authenticity seems to have happened every time, for how could it not? Yet, as Balibar reminds us—and he offers this reminder specifically as a mark of the tragic dimension of politics—"the risk that the revolt might be perverted is never sufficient reason not to revolt" (*Violence and Civility*, 150). Permit me to add, especially in the conjuncture of present catastrophic times, that the bloody tragedy of leftist politics today is certainly not sufficient reason to think that the left now lies dead on the stage.

Although radical democratic thinking must be realist thinking, it must also be optimistic thinking; the two are hardly incompatible. Besides, leftist thinking can only be conducted from an internationalist standpoint, so we cannot get bogged down by setbacks or failures in specific social-historical (national or geographical) situations. The politics of left governmentality is de facto antinationalist politics. It is a politics that understands the artificiality of all borders. Although respectful to the legal safeguards of national sovereignty, left governmentality seeks to expand the inherited boundaries of national citizenship and to create new political subjectivities that respect and care for the locality of their everyday lives but are alert to the transience of the lives of others across porous borders of geography, history, society, and culture. From this standpoint, citizenship is an ever-renewable pool one has a right to if committed to defending the dignity of one's life and one's society. This is fought over and won at the most local level—in the workplace, the home, the school, the neighborhood, the street. Citizenship, in this sense, is not an individual right; it is profoundly public, pertains to whatever is the commons.

This is why the pedagogical work of left governmentality takes place initially in the ranks of social movements, whose immediate object at work is the troubles of society, not the mechanisms of the state. In our globalized era, society's troubles are never exclusive to one society, and social movements that do not see beyond the frame of their "own" interests are condemned to calcify in very narrow (national) achievements that will eventually incapacitate them. This extension beyond "one's own" reaches all levels of political action. One is not acting democratically if one espouses a politics that defends exclusive or exceptional interests. This is why I am not friendly to the sort of leftist politics that divides the political body simply between the few and the many. Although this line reiterates the Roman republican legacy of the plebeians, it is ultimately unhistorical because it operates at a level of profound abstraction. Even the Marxist notion of class struggle, which also formalized social conflict in a specific way, continues to account for the complexities of social difference, especially in this era, when the contours of labor have become too diffuse to be contained in a single formulaic relation to capital. Hence, the most creative thinking in the Marxist framework broadly speaking, since Georg Lukács's *History and Class Consciousness*, has been to reflect on and reconceptualize the ever-changing vicissitudes of labor and the meaning of class not as a concept but as a force in how societies are organized and how subjectivities are formed.

Conflict is, of course, essential to democracy. But not when polarization becomes a fetish. Especially when constituencies that venerate a politics of difference that is fluid and relational end up celebrating a politics of polarized abstractions which effectively eliminate the complexities of difference. Us-against-them politics reduces politics to a battle between hardened identities, which impedes the inclusive and unexceptional politics essential to democracy. Although the Occupy movement's slogan of the 1% was incisive and powerful—and historically accurate as to oligarchic power—the subsequent evolution of this figure into "the plebeians," "the many," or "the poor" effaced the radical potential of social difference that characterizes the 99%.

The nagging question, of course, remains: How in today's world of global capital do we conceptualize, achieve, and mobilize a collective subject? So far, populist mobilization of the masses (even in leftist garb) has done nothing to upset the entrenchment of the atomized consumer-subject ideal. And capital enjoys the expenditure of mass desire through the micropolitics of identity, which, in its collective abstraction, does nothing to hinder the consumer habits that serve as painless relief for the everyday.

The dismantling of the consumer-subject ideal is thus an essential presupposition for any politics of left governmentality. Elementary to this has to be the counterformation of a planetary consciousness, which at this point cannot but be ecological in the most literal sense: in caring not for one's own but for what is common, and the planet is the undeconstructible figure of the common. Indeed, a basic "care of the self," starting with Foucault's reinvention of the Stoic notion but going further, cannot be anything less than care for all that is life on this planet, for without it, very crudely, there is no self of any kind.

The creation of new planetary subjectivities is thus essential to a politics of self-governance and lies at the forefront of combatting the consumer-subject ideal. This hardly means that we abandon the local politics of the workplace, the home, the school, the neighborhood, the street—because the planet is not some abstraction but precisely encountered and experienced in this utter locality of everyday existence.

From this standpoint, locality has no borders, no exclusionary refutation of otherness. Surely not in the world of global capital, even when it is currently engaged in its own civil world war, which may split it in a few geopolitical oligarchic spheres of influence but will not negate its existence (sort of a nuclear catastrophe that ends it all). Globality means that what happens here also happens in the here of elsewhere, quite literally at the same time. In left governmentality the difference between localities is neither alleviated nor overcome, but from this planetary standpoint of self-governance it is no longer a difference that divides. Perhaps the uncanny simultaneity of insurrections across continents in the last decades, despite their failures, signifies the first instance of such local-global negation of difference. Turning this into a planetary politics of self-governance is the crucial task of our age, no matter what the odds.

Coda

Against the Politics of the Sacred

The politics of the sacred is arguably the oldest political process. Arguments justifying the implication of sacred practices with political action abound in the history of thought, for the configuration of what is holy seems coincident with what it takes to defend it, from the biblical texts and the Qu'ran to Augustine and Justinian, Aquinas and almost every pope, Voltaire and Freud, Sayyid Qutb, Hindutva ideologues, the Taliban, and beyond. The question, then, is not whether sacred practices or even the bare conceptualization of sacred spaces are adverse to or independent of the political, but rather what sorts of politics are enacted in the name and in the service of the sacred, even if, from the standpoint of devout adherence to the sacred, any discussion of its serving a politics is refused. After all, politics is taken to be the epitome of the profane, and to the degree that theories of the sacred attempt to designate a space against (if not simply apart from) the profane, those who advocate an autonomous sacred realm cannot presume to espouse a politics to which the sacred is subservient. Yet the world we inhabit abounds in politics that claim to defend something sacred. The simplest such example is the flag, the symbol of the sanctity of the nation, yet even more, the increasing tendency to create a politics along the lines of a civilizational battlefield by virtue of religion, culture, or race makes our historical moment especially grave.

My concern here is to approach the sacred as a term—not necessarily, or not exclusively, as a term of faith but more so as a political concept—and so I begin with some broad assertions that aim to delineate this terminological space, keeping in mind that one of the key elements of the sacred is indeed a spatial signification, a kind of demarcation, delineation, and in fact division both concretely, of spaces as such, and metaphorically, in the very domain of signified and abstract meaning. I thus proceed, through a kind of philological examination, to elucidate the provenance of the term in a number of discursive domains, including the most broadly anthropological—that is, at the level of *human-being* as such (*anthropos*)— and the tendency to link this term with discourses of transcendence. Both the spatial and the etymological significations speak to a certain itinerary across various historical, geographical, and linguistic frameworks.

First: The very gesture of discussing the sacred as a concept is, simply speaking, a desacralizing act. One cannot speak of the sacred in sacred terms. Sacred language exceeds terms—it exceeds *its own terms* as language, at the very least because it effaces the fact that language is a human creation. Sacred language disavows its (otherwise undeconstructible) social-historical condition by feigning an existence out of time and place, an ontological exteriority. It is thus a language beyond language and yet, simultaneously, a language that recognizes no metalanguage—no language, in other words, that doubles upon itself in self-reflection. And it does this despite the urgency with which it fosters almost endless exegetical practices, as is evident in most theological traditions. In historical terms, carrying the most formidable injunction against idolatry, the cryptic idolatry of words—and not only in Christianity, which is obvious— launched a structural transformation of the realm of the sacred that went a long way toward the transformation of the profane. Indeed, what became the final difference between the two is its outcome.

Second: Having started with language since any attempt to determine "what is sacred?" makes that unavoidable, the sacred—however we are to conceptualize it—additionally designates a space: actual space in terms of land sites (burial grounds, houses of worship, holy retreats, festival sites, etc.), as well as space in the sense of realm, a realm of practices, of ceremonial gatherings, of rituals. Incidentally, space in the sense of realm includes the body—sacred marking, for example, or preservation of relics, and so on. No doubt we still use language to speak of sacred spaces and practices, and in so doing, according to my first assertion, we desacralize them, which is another way of saying we humanize them. It is thus no accident that the preeminent language to deal with sacred spaces or rituals is the language of anthropology. But here there is an immediate grammatical shift, which cannot go unnoticed and uncommented. In anthropological discourse, the word "sacred" is usually deployed as a qualifier, an adjective to the specific social and cultural parameters it determines: the sacred rituals of the Guarani, the sacred sites of the Assyrians, the sacred oath of warriors, and so forth. Although anthropology can be as comparative as any social science, nonetheless it resists philosophical generality as much as possible and therefore it resists the abstraction of *the* sacred as an unqualified, not to mention transcendental, domain. *The* sacred, as a singular substantive, invites and belongs to a terminological mode that claims to transcend social-historical realms, the sort of conceptual framework that is initiated by the language of philosophy and then extends to theology, which is, of course, philosophy's adversarial brainchild.

Third: I understand the overweighted tradition of the word "sacred" in the discourse of religion, but this discourse, in the terms I have introduced, is hybrid too, in the sense that it is equally derivative of the historical-anthropological mode as it is of the philosophical-theological mode. Thus the use of the term in the context of religion is both adjectival and substantive, both singular and plural, both concrete and abstract. Even when considered as a term of faith, as is often done nowadays, the hybridity of the sacred remains, but I endorse the term "faith" because it exceeds the discursive realm of religion, as a sort of primarily psychocognitive mode that pertains to a whole range of societal aspects, from religion to politics to art.

Finally, to round off this introductory framing, let me point to the obvious: namely, that in discussing the term "sacred" we cannot possibly assume that its meaning is integral, complete, pure, or consistent—and not only across histories, geographies, languages, but even within a specific and bounded social-historical or cultural-lingual frame. Certain words are battlegrounds, and surely in this case this is especially so. What is sacred for one is sacrilege for another, as we have seen myriad times, which is why any discourse organized around the notion of blasphemy is inadequate. This very fact should discourage the easy trading of the sacred in the scholarly sphere, if nothing else because the term is so internally contentious as to bar any clear-cut signification.

This notion of "battleground" in relation to the sacred is not quite the same as the long-established notion of the allegedly intrinsic "ambivalence of the sacred" that emerges with Victorian anthropology and then passes into the sociology of religion, sociolinguistics, and psychoanalytic anthropology—quite a formidable trajectory from William Robertson Smith and J. G. Frazier to Emile Durkheim, Marcel Mauss, and Sigmund Freud, to Roger Caillois, Georges Bataille, and the Ecole de Sociologie in Paris, but also to positions as different as those between Emile Benveniste and Theodor Adorno all the way to René Girard and his many followers, scholars of antiquity and anthropologists of primitive societies, in what is an enormous range of scholarly work across the disciplines in the modern academy. For the sake of the specific argument here I will presume basic familiarity with this trajectory and its establishment of those antithetical pairs that characterize the sacred as creating domains of simultaneous veneration and victimization, exaltedness and disgust, purification and defilement, holiness and taboo, worship and horror, and so on.

This space that produces simultaneously the saintly and the accursed, this argument goes, emerges directly from the most elemental depths of the human capacity for symbolization—hence its crucial connection to the psyche's relation to society, to which I will return—as a long-unfolding process around and eventually beyond the foundational ritual of sacrifice, which is found in some form or other in most archaic societies. The standard interpretation—again, produced in voluminous variability but always amounting in essence to the same argument—is that the violence of the sacrificial ritual is meant to act as an embedded inhibitor of society's violence in a sort of homeopathic or pharmacological double logic. Insofar as the sacred is thought to encapsulate the ritual logic of sacrifice, the sacred *contains* violence, in both senses of the verb, per Jean-Pierre Dupuy's succinct and inspired phrasing: "in the compound sense of blocking it while at the same time harboring it within itself."[1]

The purveyors of this argument engage it from the perspective that sacrifice, as the original performative site of the sacred, belongs to an antique social imagination, and that the permutations of this built-in ambivalence become even graver as repressed elements in modernity's response to the lost framework of archaic meanings. There seems to be general agreement, and with good reason, that a significant role here is played by the establishment of Christianity as the dominant world religion (indeed the paradigm of the world's religion), not because Christianity is equivalent with secular modernity as is often pointed out thoughtlessly—I very much oppose this simplistic notion—but because the Christian imagination is organized around the ritualistic abstraction (and, in psychoanalytic terms, ritualistic sublimation) of sacrifice as an internalized psychosocial condition of community. The ritual of the Eucharist is the succinct elaboration of this idea, as has been conventionally argued, as is, of course, the most extraordinary sacrifice of all: the event of the Crucifixion, that is, the scandalous sacrifice of God himself. As an outcome of this remarkable configuration in the history of the human imagination, the argument goes, a process of increasing abstraction was enacted that effaced even the very experience of ritual, which blurred the boundaries of the sacred so much that it deprived it of its social function, thereby unleashing the sort of uncontrolled social and political violence that characterizes the history of Western modernity from the Reign of Terror in the French Revolution to the atomic bomb.

I will let this narrative stand, for it is not my purpose here to examine its validity, even if I would quarrel with the kind of brutal monovalence with which it assumes the meaning of modernity. Much as I will also not concern myself with the problem of sacrifice per se. Although relevant, a discussion of sacrifice would derail us into a realm of cultural anthropology whose vast terrain I cannot properly account for here, and in any case, my contention is that the sacred exceeds its homonymous basis. Starting from the standpoint of this excess, my concern here is specifically with how the sacred is thought to work (or not work), both in the sphere of the political in contemporary so-called secular societies and in the psychosocial dimension of the human imagination overall. In the latter sense, if the sacred is understood to be a battleground that exceeds its thought-to-be endemic ambivalence, it knows no temporal distinction, and its specific significance in modernity is secondary. I would argue instead that whatever the unavoidable historical condition of how sacred space (literal and metaphorical) is determined, its significance remains pertinent to the most basic dimensions of social difference—of otherness as an essential element of society—which is necessary to all social organization. It is here that the question of exteriorization, or transcendence broadly speaking, becomes crucial.

There are two much-discussed works that deal directly with these aspects, both with the problem of the sacred in modernity and the more extensive framework of transcendence in social organization. No one can doubt the enormous influence of Giorgio Agamben's *Homo Sacer* since its publication in 1995, even if one takes issue with the argument's many problems. This work inaugurated Agamben's impetus to provide an account of the symbolic structure of sovereignty in Western Christian-derived societies, an account that has taken up the space of several books since then and is ongoing. We all know that Agamben's trajectory is built upon Carl Schmitt's famous stipulation that sovereignty is determined by the capacity to enact exception to the law, whose crucial twist is that this capacity for exception is built into the law, perhaps even presupposing the law, as a kind of rupturing violence at its origin. This fundamental spatial ambiguity—which Agamben mines repeatedly to create what he calls "threshold figures"—is especially pertinent here.

As the title of the book famously foregrounds, the problematic threshold space of sovereignty is best illustrated in the Roman figure of *homo sacer*, the man who cannot be sacrificed but is rather killed with impunity: that is, killed outside the realm of the law. *Homo sacer*, in this respect, would characterize a man—and he *is* a man; the gendering of the argument is not often accounted for—of double indemnity, or double exclusion. First: because, insofar as he does not qualify to be sacrificed and sacrifice is considered the ritual that seals and safeguards the integrity of the community, he is rendered useless to the community. Second: because his homicide is not considered a crime, he is killed outside the order of the community. He is thus a criminal whose death is decriminalized or an outlaw whose execution remains outside the law. We can see here the fascination with the outside as a determining space, for *homo sacer* is not only a quintessential outsider figure, but a figure that signifies and indeed literally embodies the outside, dragging everyone who comes into contact with him, even his killer, his executioner, into a space outside society. That this quintessentially accursed outsider figure comes to stand as a metonymy for the sovereign is a very complex and highly problematic gesture, which remains, as far as I am concerned, unconvincing.

There are several reasons for this, and here I can only be dreadfully brief. First of all, the background signification that links this name—literally—to the realm of the sacred is quietly displaced. The Romans pronounced *homo sacer* any person who broke an oath, that is to say, a contract with the gods that consecrated his actions in divine protection, an oath being the essential mode of inhabiting the sacred in both language and deed in archaic societies. An oath breaker is thus more than a violator of the law, more than a simple criminal. As a deceiver of the gods, he is an outlaw way beyond the boundaries of a crime whose punishment confirms the law and keeps the convicted violator within society. Having already had access to the divine by calling upon the gods to sanctify his actions, an oath breaker is expelled from society and is accursed twice, as it were—hence, again, the double properties of the sacred.

All this is fine and well, but it is hardly generalizable. The Latinate signification, despite expressing Roman antiquity, cannot stand for antiquity as such, not even antiquity in the Mediterranean, not to mention a general social anthropology. Its semiotic participation in the language of sovereignty is enabled solely by the medieval history of Latin Christianity. Even its overburdened connection to modernity is essentially Christological—a matter of *globalatinization*, to use one of Derrida's thoughtful neologisms.[2] The very word "sacred" and its derivatives in

English (sacristy, consecration, sacrifice, sacrilege, etc.) have nothing to do, for example, with the Greek correlatives to the Latin language from which the English is derived, and, even more significantly, to the correlative Roman social, political, or juridical meaning that enables the original name. The Greek word for sacred, *hieros*, bears none of the conventional ambivalence of *sacrum*: it has nothing to do with purity or impurity, expulsion or sacrifice. It may be linked to the divine, particularly in institutional or ceremonial terms—where indeed the notion of *hierarchy* comes from, a quintessentially political, hence secular, notion as the name suggests—but the divine realm in the Greek imagination epitomizes society's resistance to pure externality. One could well wonder how significant it is to consider in regard to the vocabulary of modernity and all relevant connotations that in Greek the word for ghost is *phantasma*, a mere object of light and appearance, and not *Geist*, spirit.

The Greek gods are characterized not only by their evident anthropomorphism, but by their *anthropotropism*, if I may put it this way: the gods are immortal—and this is the only difference they have from humans, who are always named as simply "mortals" in Greek texts—but they are not eternal. Their divine positions are positions of power, to win or lose, to fight for or against. They are, moreover, subject to the primal forces of the cosmos that precede them and continue to hold the universe in balance. No Olympian god can overcome the force of Chaos, or Gaia, or Eros. These forces permeate their very ontology and oftentimes animate actions that are expressed as self-motivated, actions based on perfectly human, worldly, tropes: war, envy, eroticism, sentiment, shrewdness, deception, even cowardice. In this sense, the gods are internal to the universe that brings them into being, the very same universe that includes the humans. Before Platonic philosophy—which is, I would argue, somewhat of an aberration (or at best a new opening, a tangent) in the trajectory of Greek thought from the pre-Socratics to the Stoics—we would be hard-pressed to find unmediated notions of exteriority in the Greek cosmological framework. (I am speaking in terms of metaphysics, not society, where the exclusion of women from politics in patriarchal organization is a constitution of exteriority.) Insofar as Greek gods are not eternal, they are not outside this world. And in this sense they are subject to power, cosmological power (*physis*); they don't command power, certainly not the power of the cosmos, and certainly not permanent power or absolute power.

Even the notion of *physis* to which all matter and spirit belong is not configured as some sort of Outside. Nature (*physis*) is a necessary substratum; without it, humans—the world itself—would not exist. But the human organization of society (*nomos*) is the domain of working upon this substratum, ultimately exceeding it while never abolishing its last instance. Never abolishing it, yet also never allowing this last instance to become first: to determine, to legislate, the institution of social law. The concept of natural law is just unconfigurable in the Greek imaginary, which is also to say that there can never be a *physis* of *nomos* that isn't already a societal *physis*. *Physis*, let us recall, is not a state of things but a condition of emergence out of an abyssal infinite, a chaos that cannot quite be called source. *Physis* is merely an interminable flux of generation and degeneration, a dynamic of living and dying being. This dynamic sense emerges out of the specific legislative imaginary of the Greeks, who stipulate that *physis* bears in itself a *nomos*—while the reverse is unacceptable, inconceivable—a mode in nature by which the cosmos is regulated and balanced, by which justice is achieved. One's existential condition of freedom is a matter of *physis*, while the political enactment of freedom is a matter of *nomos*. *Physis* and *nomos* are not contradictory; they are coextensive cosmological crossings permeating the entire ancient Greek imaginary.[3]

In this regard, Carl Schmitt's phrase in *The Nomos of the Earth*, from which Agamben draws extensively, that "all human *nomoi* are 'nourished' by a single divine *nomos*" would be nonsensical in the imagination that created the notion of *nomos*.[4] We cannot avoid underlining the fact that Schmitt privileges this standpoint despite his understanding of *nomos* "as a constitutive historical event" (73) that is always enacted in concrete space, dividing, delimiting, and allotting as well as enclosing, dwelling, and cultivating, according to the two fundamental meanings of the verb *nemein*. He is certainly on mark to call *nomos* "a fence word" (75)—again, Agamben's frequent reliance on the notion of "threshold" is resonant here—insofar as the notion occupies (and is occupied by) the very materiality of limit. Moreover, following the indisputable presence of land appropriation in every historical instance of social organization in sedentary humanity, Schmitt goes on to declare that an originary spatial enclosure/division signifies the order of the sacred: "The enclosure gave birth to the shrine by removing it from the ordinary, placing it under its own laws and entrusting it to the divine" (74). From this standpoint I find it rather astonishing that Schmitt and a number of great thinkers, including Agamben and Wendy Brown, who follow, reproduce this configuration of the enclosed sacred space as the pillar of the political theology of sovereignty. The fact that in Athens the sacred space, the Parthenon, is enclosed away from the political, which is the open space of the agora below the rock, is entirely forgotten. As is, even more, the space where the sacred and the political coincide entirely: the space of the theater, which is the most inclusive unenclosed space in the entire city.

I am focusing on things Greek because the object of Agamben's thought is quintessentially political, and the theological contours he gives to the political in his many books (but also the economic, as he does in *The Kingdom and the Glory*) are left unexamined as to the particularity of its provenance, namely Latin Christendom. It isn't that one needs to insist exclusively on things Greek as an alternative genealogy. One could turn to Jan Assmann's account of how the originally political was theologized (instead of the reverse that we see in arguments of political theology) in ancient Egypt. Or one can just as well account for the historical trajectory of every original Sikh *gurdwara* or Taoist *guàn*, temples that resist notions of sacred exteriority. The significance of the Greek tradition comes to the fore precisely because by drawing the framework in these terms, Agamben (following Schmitt and extending to a great deal of others) leaves the democratic tradition out of the examination and critique of the problem of sovereignty. And I don't just mean the political elements of the democratic tradition as such. I mean the entire ontological and cosmological universe that enables the democratic polis to emerge and be coherent. In this universe, one can find a whole other genealogy of the sacred that would make it impossible to extricate it from the profane, but in such way that this entwinement would not precipitate the troubling confusion of the two as is presumed to occur with/in modernity.

Indeed, the theoretical impasse emerges not only out of the presumption that the sacred and the profane are irreparably entwined in modernity, but out of the refusal to recognize the inversion that takes place as part of the formation of modernity: namely, the reversal of primacy between the two terms, while still sustaining the presumed separation. Here we have a double occlusion. Not only is the primacy of the sacred in archaic societies itself a retroactive invention of modern thinking, but the presumed primacy of the profane in modern so-called secular societies serves in such a way as to lend to the sacred a special coherence as a domain within the profane. As Slavoj Žižek has inventively put it in his introductory comments to Schelling's *Ages of the World*, "enclosed in the profane, the sacred [becomes] its 'superstructure,' its inherent 'excess.'"[5] From this standpoint, there is no confusion at all. Or rather, as the sacred remains the primary signification in both invented historical domains—so-called antiquity and so-called modernity—the confusion of boundaries between the sacred and the profane becomes a convenient ruse that helps disguise the fact that the overall schema of separation and primacy of the sacred *at any historical juncture* is a modern invention.

This presumed confusion between the sacred and the profane as a problem of contemporary societies, and the disastrous consequences it is thought to produce, is the impetus of the second work I examine briefly: Jean-Pierre Dupuy's *The Mark of the Sacred* (2008). I have great admiration for Dupuy's epistemological thinking over the years, and in this work too there are some very thought-provoking instances, particularly what he calls "enlightened catastrophism" where, via a certain kind of negative dialectics (my assessment), a concentrated catastrophic focus on the parameters of the near planetary future would enable us to evade arrival at catastrophe. In this sense, Dupuy departs from a number of well-known catastrophologists, from James Lovelock's and Lynn Margulis's "Gaia hypothesis" to John Gray and indeed Žižek too in a certain phase of his thinking.

While Agamben disputes the traditional figure of the "ambivalence of the sacred" as a secondary justification of *homo sacer* that occludes it as paradigm of the exceptional exteriority of sovereignty and inevitability of law's violence, Dupuy builds on the figure of ambivalence by underlining how the sublimation of the inherent violence of sacrifice creates the realm of the sacred that *contains*—therefore, interrupts—the circle of society's sovereign violence. On the face of it, the two positions seem contrary. But Dupuy is seduced as well by the same desire to posit a sort of ontological exteriority to society that authorizes its salvation. This is not merely occupied by the category of the divine—that is just one manifestation—but by a slew of elements, including secular ones. Some of these are far-fetched or misconceived in their proper contexts. The most problematic is the attribution of externality to the ancient Greek practice of assigning political offices and duties by lot. While it is credible that chance may be a way that the human imagination accounts for a domain in the universe that it cannot control, the institution of lot in Greek politics (especially democratic politics) has nothing transcendental about it. The privilege of ruling by lot over, say, dynastic rule, rule by expertise, or even electoral representative rule in its modern manifestations, is made conceptually coherent because (and only in the context) of the assumed *isonomia* of political actors. This isonomy is so radical that it abolishes the distinction between rulers and ruled, as Aristotle famously argues in the *Politics*. What enables Aristotle to say that a ruler can rule only by having learned how to be ruled is an understanding of being ruled as a particular form of power—indeed, a participation in the act of ruling, which can take place only when all citizens are in perfect isonomy, so much so that the only way to decide who will rule today and who will rule tomorrow will be made possible by lot.

There is indeed nothing more immanent to the mode of social organization than ruling by lot is to the democratic imaginary. Anything else would have been deemed exterior indeed and would have been radically questioned. This is precisely why the Athenians question equally both the power of the Macedonian conqueror Alexander (though they recognize his military superiority in defeat) and, three centuries later, the eloquent but utterly preposterous ruminations of the Apostle Paul about a god who has been resurrected from the dead. Even in cosmological terms, where the notion of lot (*klēros*) is linked to the most archaic notion of *nomos* (as lot of land, allotment, and, of course, distribution), which hearkens back to the original cosmology of fate (*moira*) as each person's share of the fabric of the universe, there is nothing about chance that is in some fashion otherworldly.

Dupuy, by his own admission, sees "the logic of exteriority [as] an inescapable feature of human existence" (MS 126), thereby underlining the necessity for self-transcendence and disparaging immanence as an unfortunate epistemological condition of modernity, which refuses to accept chance as a factor in its drive for rational mastery. In the process, he bars the possibility that chance may indeed be thought as an immanent category of *human-being*, as an element of *physis* in whose *nomos* whatever is understood to be human is mere part. Dupuy's critique of modernity thus remains within the traditional humanist paradigm that presumes the defeat of transcendental thinking to be the triumph of the all-controlling power of reason. The sacred thus remains for him that treasured transcendent domain in which and through which the human world came to exist and will be saved from its penchant for self-destruction. "It is the sacred that gives birth to human societies," he says (MS 124). This is, of course, ultimately indefensible as a historical-anthropological argument. Only society gives birth to society. The sacred is the first instance of occlusion of this autopoietic fact, the first heteronomous instance.

To be clear, I understand autopoiesis as the primary force that organizes the ontological and cosmological universe of meaning. But this is not to be understood as a tautological self-referentiality, the endless reproduction of the self/same, as was once common to say. For no poiesis can take place without the alteration of form—the *transformation* of the field within which forms emerge—in large part because it introduces its own temporality. Autopoiesis—and, in a political language, autonomy—is tantamount to self-alteration. A classic formulation by Cornelius Castoriadis may be useful here:

> Each society brings into being its own mode of self-alteration, which can also be called its temporality—that is to say, it also brings itself into being *as* a mode of being. History is ontological genesis not as the production of different tokens of the essence of society but as the creation, in and through each society, of another *type* (form-figure-aspect-sense: *eidos*) of being-society, which is in the same stroke the creation of new *types* of social-historical entities (objects, individuals, ideas, institutions, etc.) on all levels and on levels which are themselves posited-created by a given society.[6]

I have written extensively about this in a variety of contexts, which has yet to alleviate concern raised by critics about my effacing the distinction between the transcendent and the transcendental. The most legitimate objection is the one that rightfully protests that without the possibility of exceeding one's situation, no change is possible, and this is surely Dupuy's departure point as well, and the point at which he places the sacred.

It is not clear to me, however, that to exceed one's situation presupposes a verifiable existing standpoint already given to be beyond your situation. So the big question becomes how to measure the production of difference (variation) versus the production of otherness (excess) when we are talking about formation, both in ontology but also in terms of society. Autopoiesis, as radical self-alteration, means the production of otherness. The wager for me in this assertion is how this production of otherness can take place without presupposing a transcendent standpoint that enables it—even *in potentia*—and at the same time without producing (performing) a semblance or assumption of a transcendent point as a result: that is, both a transcendentalist point as endpoint of the alteration and a transcendent point as a priori *archē* (enabling potential) of the alteration.

We have to be able to imagine and give language to the possibility that one can exceed one's situation from within the terms of that situation by altering the terms of that situation. This does not mean that this is the work of the mind, of the intellectual will. There are plenty of "objective" factors that can activate the potential in any field of organization to unravel within its own terms and thus to be altered and to exceed—if you will, transcend—itself.[7] Having said that, it is perfectly understandable why human beings desire to imagine transcendent spaces or even the idea of transcendence as something in-itself, as independent of situation and action. But this is not to say that human beings *must do so* in order to change, in order to exceed their situation. Nor is it to say that, once they change or exceed their situation, they must attribute this fact to a transcendental process.

The greatest obstacle in this discussion is indeed the problem of change—radical change. Certainly, it is the problem of constituent power in democratic politics as the force that emerges within whatever is constituted and, by means of this constituted framework, radically alters it for better or worse—this is a perilous proposition. Interestingly, both Agamben and Dupuy, for all their learning, cannot account for this without positing the need for constituent power to create an outside, or more precisely, to create itself as an outside at the very moment of its articulation. I see this precisely as the work of the sacred, but with an evaluation opposite theirs. I see the provenance of the sacred as occlusion, and indeed occultation, of this moment of immanent radical alteration. The provenance of the sacred does not merely reside in what has come to be called religion, but in anything that comes to achieve sacred status in a particular society and culture. This would certainly include, in today's so-called secular societies, the seduction of techno-science and rational mastery, the "right" of economic prosperity, the desire for endless growth, the fetish of modernity, the (pseudo-)ideal of progress and development, and so on, but equally, the (pseudo-)ideal of ancestry and tradition, the fetish of the nation, the sacristy of the Constitution and any other institution of law that makes Law into an ideal. To these we could add, of course, all kinds of other transcendentalisms, of both ethics and aesthetics and surely of politics, where politics—oftentimes, alas, in the very name of democracy—is utterly theological.

We can consider this also from the standpoint of a crucial intervention by Georges Bataille, who is no doubt one of the most committed and innovative thinkers on the question of the sacred in relation to both anthropology and religion:

> The development of knowledge touching on the history of religions has shown that the essential religious activity was not directed toward a personal and transcendent being (or beings), but toward an impersonal reality. Christianity has made the sacred *substantial*, but the nature of the sacred, in which today we recognize the burning existence of religion, is perhaps the most ungraspable thing that has been produced between men: the sacred is

only a privileged moment of communal unity, a moment of the convulsive communication of what is ordinarily stifled.[8]

Referring to a Sufi understanding, Bataille likens this privileged moment to a decisive instant, bearing the properties of a slicing sword: "The sword is a dangerous companion; it can make its master a king, but it can also destroy him. It does not distinguish between the neck of its master and the neck of another" (245).

It is easy to channel Agamben here and think of this decisive instant or privileged moment as the sovereign exception. But barring the metaphor, any double-edged sword—and in this sense every sword is potentially double-edged—is whatever it is, or acts however it acts, in human hands and by human hands. In that sense, it is not exceptional at all, and no exception exists in the universe as an autonomous notion, for the universe in this sense is unexceptional and makes no exceptions on its own. The decisive moment of the sacred then does not exist as such in the universe—or even the history of men and women, antiquity or modernity—but it is made so, not unlike, very simply, a work of art. The sacred is no more than a work of art, and its value, from zero to inestimable, is as much the work of fancy (or convention) as anything.

I conclude now with another series of assertions on how I understand the meaning of the sacred and why I take the risk of arguing for a politics in which nothing is sacred.

1. The sacred does not necessarily have to have theological meaning. If anything, its primary meaning is social-historical and more broadly anthropological, which also implies a powerful psychic dimension. As elemental to *human-being*, the psyche encounters the cosmic abyss—the fact that there is no intrinsic meaning to anything in the universe and yet this meaninglessness cannot be endured—with an essentially interminable range of meaning-producing figurations. The sacred may be said to be the most privileged such realm of figuration, given its ubiquitous presence in all societies in the history of humanity, because it singularly presents this abyss while simultaneously occluding it (and occulting it) through an equally interminable range of simulacra—not just images, but words, and texts, and, of course, performative ritual practices. This is an utterly worldly process; it is secular no matter how it may signify itself.[9]

Similarly, what is called "religious sentiment"—which has nothing to do with religious doctrine or even religious practice, especially as the latter is configured in some institutional form—is indeed an elemental secular characteristic. For it belongs to the primal psychic framework of the *human/animal* and it is "natural" despite the fact that it must be configured as "cultural" in order to be articulated. Of course, all this doesn't say very much, because all affective states belong to the realm of the secular (the worldly); however they may be coded, affective states are essentially corporeal. In this respect, the *discorporation* of affect—much as, one may say, the discorporation of the sacred—is a social-historical construction that is then taken to exist outside the secular in some netherland whose creation the *human/animal* seems obsessively incapable of refraining from enacting.

Secularization, I have argued repeatedly, is an unfinished or, even more, perhaps unfinishable process. It is not an end (*telos*). And it is not a thing of modernity. Secularization is what human societies have been engaged with since the very beginning of their existence. The human animal invents gods and simultaneously tries to tear them down. This is endemic to its psychic makeup. From this standpoint, *sacralization is a specific form of secular practice*. Regardless of how mystical or otherworldly it is in its conception and affect, sacralization is what human beings practice in a specific time and place in order to create the myths necessary to encounter the abyssal meaninglessness of existence.

2. The sacred is quintessentially mythical. At least, in the simplest sense that the sacred is the realm that humans have created in order to address the fact that there is no preordained ground on which something happens or does not happen in life beyond what they came to discover to be the constants of the physical laws of the universe: the fact that gravity does not allow you to jump off a building and fly or that fire burns right through everything you hold dear, and so forth. And most of all: the fact that no matter what you do your life ends, your materiality degenerates, and you flow out of existence with the same brutally accidental logic you came in to begin with.

The myth of the sacred is perhaps the most powerful myth of all but it is not all-controlling; it is not myth's last word. The existential abyss is intolerable, I understand. But the human psyche is as tough as the physical laws of the universe. Perhaps more, because the psyche follows no law and is indomitable. Its refusal of this intolerable abyss is the limitless creation of phantasms meant to counteract it. These phantasms are not mere images—although their "essence" is, I would argue, primarily imagistic, not linguistic. (For Freud this is a no-brainer.) Yet, although they may be conjured iconically, phantasms can have numerous manifestations, certainly verbal and language-based, but also ritualistic and performance-based. The sacred is a profound space of such verbal and performative action of the mythical. The "divine" is one of the most sublime mythical thought-spaces ever created by humans. The divine as such creates nothing. It is created in order to create, if you pardon me the extravagance. A politics of autonomy would begin precisely in liberating the sacred from this exclusively theological signification—all the more so in a world where the theological is taken over by capital, thoroughly commodified, and deployed in its service.

3. What is considered sacred in law—the Ten Commandments, Sharia, the principles guiding the Inquisition, but also, in Christian-derived modern secularity, the Constitution—is precisely what exposes the fact that law can never be sacred in itself. Law is *rendered* sacred. It is made (proclaimed) sacred when it is necessary to invoke certain principles that *transcend* the contingent factors of making legal decisions in given situations in given communities. Law is rendered sacred when society cannot bear—when it cannot find a way out of—a particular quandary of *nemein*: when it cannot divide/distinguish and distribute/attribute proper justice on its own grounds. Solomonic justice, a gesture of genius by a single man, is an instance that trumps "sacred law" by illustrating the moment when the contingent decision, by means of achieving a perfect *nemein* (in his case literally), produces justice. Of course, the gesture must be spun as an instance of divine wisdom visiting the mind of a mere mortal, even if "elect." It must be spun this way because the provisional perfectibility of contingent action—which thus achieves the status of a mythical paradigm—must be effaced by being reconstituted as permanent exemplarity within a sacred space of law. What is also effaced as a consequence is the requisite theatricality of the gesture, its undeconstructible worldliness. Bertolt Brecht's take on the Solomonic myth in his *Caucasian Chalk Circle* is arguably the most brilliant exposition of this problem, for among other things it shows how it is theatricality and not law, sacred or otherwise, that ultimately enables real action in society.

Rendering the law sacred describes the process by which the social imagination reachieves its closure often against the historical figures that emerge when certain decisions based on contingent forces achieve paradigmatic status. "Sacred law" must obfuscate the socializing function that reveals it as a once-upon-a-time contingent customary law. In essence, what happens is an elevation of law outside the boundaries of a society, with the consequent attribution of authority equally to a transcendent outside. A proper sacred law could not be implemented. It would have to adhere so strictly to its outside that it could never be put into action. The "sacred text" is untranslatable, meaning it cannot be transferred, especially transferred into the realm most antithetical to the sacred: the social, the customary, the worldly, the provisional. Therefore, when people claim it as law they desacralize it—by recognizing, even if unwittingly, its humanity.[10]

So, we must encounter claims of the sacristy of the law—claims that pertain to the attribution of worldly justice, not theological discourses as such (about them there is, in the end, nothing to say but what is already internal to them)— with a full sense of irony. These claims, statements that canonize the operations of the sacred in the realm of worldly law, exemplify the social artificiality of the sacred. They also make perfectly clear in what sense the construction of sacred law is essentially a police mechanism. Sacredness is the police force of society's law. In two ways: first because it enforces the law oftentimes with the arbitrary "autonomous" violence of perfect transcendental authority. And second, because it is the underlying force of the law—the paranomic element—that strips it of autonomy, that strips people of the authority of knowing and understanding that they made the law and therefore they can unmake it.

Here we need to consider the counteractions by certain pagan societies that still demand to "defend the sacred," like indigenous North Americans who use this slogan in their struggle to reclaim their ancestral lands. We need to consider the specific signification in the use of the term: "sacred" used against the violence of conquest, appropriation, and annihilation which is coded as desacralization. First, this is indeed and *consciously* a desacralization in the typical way of monotheistic desire (Christian in the case of the Americas) to annihilate all devotional rituals of infidel (pagan) life. Second, it *is* desacralization in the sense of destroying all elements of social organization in the people you conquer, a practice that is rather ubiquitous in the history of humanity. This is not specifically monotheistic; it is very much part of both pagan and secular history as well, of the human history of conquest and enslavement as such. But in both these rubrics the sacred is the battlefield in which you meet and destroy the enemy, a perfectly profane domain even when it serves to sanctify and transcendentalize *your own sacred*, the only sacred there is.

Finally, at a primary level, nothing sacred means nothing unscathed, nothing pure, nothing purely outside the material uncertainty of psychosocial existence. Thus, the whole project is also a rejection of all sensibilities of purity. It presupposes that we discern the human condition as something meaningless and scathed, if we are going to use this word marked by the sacred: as a condition in which everyone and everything is scathed—it matters not by what, how, or by whom. Even if this is posited with some exactitude—the what, how, who of the matter in specific detail—the condition of being scathed would have scathed this too. Hence, by scathed I hardly mean the theological notion of the fallen, because the fallen assumes a precondition of being unscathed, of being pure, and consequently names the how, or by what means and by whom, this scathing is derived. To have been once unscathed is to have been once pure. There is no way of having been once pure without implying the essence of the pure. Purity has no temporality. Once assumed, it comes to exist in the present, even if as precondition or postcondition, whose spectrality in either case is the eternity of salvation or redemption.

The point then is to argue that since nothing is unscathed, nothing is untouchable, nothing is barred from reach, nothing is barred. Here, the word "nothing" is itself barred from interdiction. Nothing *is* not-forbidding. The grammar of ontology may continue to play tricks with our minds, but we shall not be fooled. Nothing *is* not-forbidding; it is opening to the other. But no other exists without this opening except in the fantasy of transcendentally inspired selves. In effect, *Nothing Sacred* argues for a worldview in which nothing will be deemed untouchable, nothing will remain uninterrogated. In a paradoxical way, advocates of guarding heterogeneity at all costs will be upheld precisely in a world that does not render "the sacred" into a sacred category. The nullification of the sacred is in effect the nullification of the category of absolute certainty and thus of the absolute itself.

Nothing is sacred, provided we don't sacralize nothing.

Notes

PREFACE

1. Edward Said, *Beginnings* (New York: Columbia University Press, 1985), 34.
2. Edward Said, "Opponents, Audiences, Constituencies, and Community" (1982), in *Reflections on Exile* (Cambridge, MA: Harvard University Press, 2000), 145.

1. HUMANISM, HUMAN/ANIMAL, HUMAN-BEING

1. I have in mind Jacques Derrida's phrase that "there is no homogeneous continuity between what calls *itself* man and what *he* calls animal." *The Animal That Therefore I Am*, trans. David Wills (New York: Fordham University Press, 2008), 30. I address Derrida's argument later on. Here let us note the disjunction in the operative pronouns. The discontinuity is inherent in this disjunction.
2. Essential here is the argument about autopoiesis as a ubiquitous biological principle, pertinent to all living being, forwarded by the biologists Humberto Maturana and Francisco Varela in their groundbreaking work *Autopoiesis and Cognition: The Realization of the Living* (Boston: Reidel, 1972). This argument in all its vicissitudes is discussed extensively in the sections that follow.
3. Sylvia Wynter, "The Ceremony Must Be Found: After Humanism," *boundary 2* 12-13 (Spring/Fall 1984): 19-70, and "Unsettling the Coloniality of Being/Power/Truth/Freedom: Towards the Human, After Man, Its Overrepresentation—An Argument," *New Centennial Review* 3, no. 3 (Fall 2003): 257-339.
4. The most focused and imaginative work in this direction has been consistently the work of Donna Haraway, Katherine Hayles, Cary Wolfe, and more recently, Jane Bennett and Rosi Braidotti, which encounters certain philosophical venues charted, variously, by Gilles Deleuze, Félix Guattari, Jacques Derrida, Niklas Luhmann, Judith Butler, Bruno Latour, or Peter Sloterdijk—a formidable terrain. Much, however, can also be learned by reconsidering an earlier discussion, well under way in the 1970s, among thinkers in the French tradition such as Edgar Morin, Cornelius Castoriadis, Isabelle Stenghers, Henri Atlan, Jean-Pierre Dupuy, and, of course, Humberto Maturana and Francisco Varela, whose groundbreaking work I have already mentioned. I will address some of

this work in the process, but only partially, I am afraid. To do justice to this vast trajectory a whole other essay needs to be written, and however invaluable such an accounting, properly conducted, would be, it would take away from the painstaking process of articulating a different way of imagining *human-being* in the present moment.

5. The term "monohumanism" belongs to Sylvia Wynter, and, in her exceedingly complex analysis, it is connected to the same shift in the social imaginary that produces monotheism, which includes its subsequent secularist variances in the way I have identified in *The Perils of the One* (New York: Columbia University Press, 2019) as monarchical thinking. See Sylvia Wynter, "The Ceremony Found: Towards the Autopoietic Turn/Overturn, Its Autonomy of Human Agency and Extraterritoriality of (Self)-Cognition," in *Black Knowledges/Black Struggles: Essays in Critical Epistemology*, ed. Jason R. Ambroise and Sabine Broeck (Liverpool: Liverpool University Press, 2015), 184–252.

6. Instructive elaboration in this specific trajectory can be found in the work of R. A. Judy. See his "Reading with Discrepant Engagement" *boundary 2* 37, no. 3 (Fall 2010): 123–50, and what he calls "Tunisian democratic humanism" in "The Grammars of the Tunisian Revolution," *boundary 2* 39, no. 1 (Spring 2012): 17–42.

7. For the purposes of this argument, I am forgoing any discussion of ancient traditions with prevalent humanist imaginaries—keeping in mind that the term is modern—which in fact covers a huge range, by virtue of not only the typical references to Greek and Roman thinking but also to Confucianism, Taoism, Buddhism, Zoroastrianism, or several aspects of ancient Hinduism or African thought. No need to overstate the obvious: humanism is neither the invention nor the privilege of "Western civilization," and even if the term is modern, there is nothing exclusively modern about it as society's orientation. The biggest problem here has been the miscasting of so-called secularization as a condition of modernity, which I have discussed extensively in *Lessons in Secular Criticism* (New York: Fordham University Press, 2013), and *The Perils of the One*.

8. In that extraordinary opening lesson of *"Society Must Be Defended"* (1975), where he takes account not only of himself but the mode of research of his entire generation, Foucault reveals for the first time his sense of exasperation: "We are making no progress, and it's all leading nowhere. It's all repetitive, and it doesn't add up. Basically, we keep saying the same thing, and there again, perhaps we are not saying anything at all. It's all getting into something of an inextricable tangle, and it's getting us nowhere, as they say." Michel Foucault, *"Society Must Be Defended,"* trans. David Macey (New York: Picador, 1997), 4.

9. "The Late Style of Edward Said," in *Edward Said and Critical Decolonization*, ed. Ferial J. Ghazoul (Cairo: American University of Cairo Press, 2007), 37–45.

10. Note Said's words on account of Foucault's death, where he describes the French thinker (very much in fact as he described Adorno) in terms of intransigent human spirit. "[Foucault] was neither simply a historian, a philosopher, nor a literary critic, but all those things together and then more still. Like Adorno, he was rigorous, uncompromising, and ascetic in his attitudes, although unlike Adorno, his obscurities have less to do with his style, which was brilliant, than with the grippingly large, often obscure, theoretical and imaginative suggestions about culture, society, and power toward which his entire oeuvre tended. He was a hybrid writer . . . [which] therefore imparts a certain

1. Humanism, Human/Animal, Human-Being 299

extraterritoriality to his work.... Yet, in Foucault's most impersonal prose, one can still hear a distinctive voice ringing through; it is not accidental that he was a master of the interview form." See "Michel Foucault, 1927-1984," in *Reflections on Exile* (Cambridge, MA: Harvard University Press, 2000), 187-97.

11. See Edward Said, *Humanism and Democratic Criticism* (New York: Columbia University Press, 2004), 18-21, henceforth cited in the text as H, followed by page number.

12. Along similar lines, see Emily Apter, "Saidian Humanism," in *The Translation Zone* (Princeton, NJ: Princeton University Press, 2006), 53-82; Lecia Rosenthal, "Between Humanism and Late Style," in *Cultural Critique* 67 (Fall 2007), 107-40; and R. Radhakrishnan, "Said's Literary Humanism," in *Cultural Critique* 67 (Fall 2007): 13-42, even if Radhakrishnan retains a troublesome anxiety about whether Said's thinking is indeed (even if partially) anchored in traditional humanism. I think such anxiety is unwarranted.

13. Against the grain of typical accounts of the humanism/antihumanism divide, it is interesting to return to Foucault here for a moment—again the inaugural lesson of *"Society Must Be Defended."* Elaborating on his notion of "subjugated knowledges," Foucault speaks in uncannily similar tone of "singular, local knowledges, noncommonsensical knowledges" or "knowledges that were disqualified by the hierarchy of erudition." See Foucault, *"Society Must Be Defended,"* 8.

14. For a similar argument, see Paul Gilroy, "Not Yet Humanism," in *Conflicting Humanities*, ed. Rosi Braidotti and Paul Gilroy (London: Bloomsbury, 2016), 95-108.

15. I am retaining the word "dehumanization" here in full knowledge of Zakiyyah Iman Jackson's formidable critique of its use in her *Becoming Human: Matter and Meaning in an Antiblack World* (New York: New York University Press, 2020), whose groundbreaking nuances I will address herein.

16. I am drawing essentially on Mufti's recent lectures and our numerous personal conversations in the last decade. But see indicatively his *Forget English: Orientalisms and World Literatures* (Cambridge, MA: Harvard University Press, 2015), as well as "The Missing Homeland of Edward Said," in Braidotti and Gilroy, *Conflicting Humanities*, 165-83.

17. Louis Althusser, *For Marx*, trans. Ben Brewster (London: NLB, 1977), 219-48. This essay presents Althusser's first thoughts on ideology before he refined them in the famous essay on ideological state apparatuses. No doubt, Althusser's post-1983 undoing of his entire way of thinking incapacitates this mode of reasoning. But we do need to keep these matters distinct, and not just for the sake of the argument. The fact that "Marxism and Humanism" is a distillation of French poststructuralist antihumanism cannot be historically effaced by the later philosophy of encounter and aleatory materialism, which are indeed closer to the argument I pursue here in favor of rethinking humanism.

18. Alice Cherki, *Frantz Fanon: A Portrait* (Ithaca, NY: Cornell University Press, 2006), 185-200.

19. Léopold Sédar Senghor, *La négritude est un humanisme du XXe siècle* (Beirut: Les Conférences du Cénacle, 1966). Senghor succinctly argues that *négritude* needs "to be developed as a weapon, as an instrument of liberation, and as contribution to the humanism of the twentieth century" (9). In this respect, "contribution to humanism" is not some qualitative addition to a project otherwise left intact. It is a political intervention with

a full sense of entering a field of contestation, within which it operates indeed as a weapon.

20. It is important to add here that this anticolonial, Marxist-inspired humanism diverges, both politically and methodologically, from the wave of "socialist humanism" emerging from E. P. Thompson's inaugural use of the term in 1957, immediately after the Hungarian uprising (1956), and extending to the Prague Spring in 1968, when the term "socialism with a human face" was conjured. At both ends of this trajectory, the primary significance was a self-critical repudiation of the horrors of Stalinism in the ranks of the European left.

21. Souleymane Bachir Diagne, "Négritude," in *Stanford Encyclopedia of Philosophy* (May 2010, rev. February 2014), https://plato.stanford.edu/entries/negritude/.

22. Léopold Sédar Senghor, "Marxisme et humanisme," in *Liberté II: Nation et voie africaine du socialisme* (Paris: Seuil, 1971), 29–44.

23. Gary Wilder's *The French Imperial Nation-State: Negritude and Colonial Humanism Between the Two World Wars* (Chicago: University of Chicago Press, 2005) remains singular in handling the complexities of this historical and political convergence in French national-colonial history.

24. For a succinct account of M. N. Roy's trajectory, see Suchetana Chattopadhyay, "Being 'Naren Bhattacharji,'" in *Communist Histories Vol. 1*, ed. Vijay Prashad (New Delhi: New World Books, 2016), 16–36. A useful and exciting read in this regard is also M. N. Roy's *Memoirs* (Bombay: Allied Publishers, 1964).

25. Minutes from the Lenin-Roy Comintern debates, along with other interventions and discussions, can be found at https://www.marxists.org/history/international/comintern/2nd-congress/ch04.htm.

26. For an account of Roy's international clandestine life that is worthy of the most riveting thriller film script, see Gautam Pemmaraju's "The Dragnet," *fiftytwo.in* (February 3, 2022), https://fiftytwo.in/story/the-dragnet/.

27. These early Comintern years before Lenin's demise show a remarkably vibrant plurality of encounters with issues arising from communism reaching beyond the European sphere and may be seen as an antecedent of the Bandung imaginary, especially in its Marxist variants. Roy is a key figure in these years, but so is the Tartar communist Mirsaid Sultan-Galiev (1892–1940), who advocated what he called "Muslim Communism" as way of making sure that a workers-council mode of governance would succeed in Muslim societies—the term "Muslim" bearing as much a "cultural" meaning as a "religious" one. The Congress of the Peoples of the East, held in Baku in September 1920, was an official manifestation of these concerns and of singular significance in retrospect, even though Roy himself was already voicing his worry about centralized Soviet party control and thus refused to attend.

28. This is precisely missing from Timothy Brennan's account of Roy, even though, like my argument here, he duly associates Roy's new humanist project with Edward Said's. As a result, Brennan compromises his account by insisting that Roy remained a nationalist, albeit in what he calls "subjunctive" fashion. See "Future Interrupted: The Subjunctive Nationalism of M. N. Roy" *South Atlantic Quarterly* 122, no. 2 (April 2023): 299–316.

29. M. N. Roy, *Radical Humanist: Selected Writings*, ed. Innaiah Narisetti (Amherst, NY: Prometheus Books, 2004), 107–8. Henceforth cited in the text.
30. This long and complex trajectory is traced with sumptuous passion and detail by Robin D. G. Kelley in "'Roaring from the East': Third World Dreaming," in his *Freedom Dreams: The Black Radical Imagination* (Boston: Beacon Press, 2002), 60–109. See also Huey Newton, "Intercommunalism (February 1971)," in *The Huey Newton Reader*, ed. David Hilliard and Donald Weise (New York: Seven Stories Press, 2002), 181–99. There is ample evidence that Newton developed his notion of intercommunalism from his studies and dialogue with the renowned psychologist Erik Erikson.
31. Aimé Césaire, "Poetry and Knowledge," in *Lyric and Dramatic Poetry 1946–82*, ed. A. James Arnold (Charlottesville: University Press of Virginia, 1990), xlix.
32. Aimé Césaire, *Discourse on Colonialism* (New York: Monthly Review Press, 1972), 73.
33. Aimé Césaire, "Letter to Maurice Thorez," trans. Chike Jeffers, *Social Text* 103 (Summer 2010): 145–53. Translation modified. Henceforth cited in the text. Césaire's resignation from the Communist Party does not nullify the intrinsic connection between *négritude* and the Marxist political project. See Christopher L Miller, "The (Revised) Birth of Négritude: Communist Revolution and the 'Immanent Negro' in 1935," *PMLA* 125, no. 3 (2010): 742–49.
34. For an exceptional account of this trajectory, see Alex Lubin's *Geographies of Liberation: The Making of an Afro-Arab Political Imaginary* (Chapel Hill: University of North Carolina Press, 2014).
35. It is remarkable to realize that the psychoanalyst Fanon, despite his Lacanian associations, is virtually absent from the core of French psychoanalytic scholarship. Answering a question about Fanon's significance in her psychoanalytic thinking, Julia Kristeva gives this astonishing answer: "I have often heard people speak of him, but I have never read anything by him. He isn't part of the mainstream of psychoanalytic studies." Quoted in Ewa Ziarek, "Kristeva and Fanon: The Future of a Revolt or the Future of an Illusion?" *Southern Journal of Philosophy* 42, Supplement (2004): 25–41.
36. Only two of the manuscripts survive. See Frantz Fanon, *Alienation and Freedom*, ed. Jean Khalfa and Robert Young (New York: Bloomsbury Academic, 2018).
37. This delicate complexity of how the clinical and the political are entwined at the crux of Fanon's thought is expertly discussed in Camille Robcis, "Frantz Fanon, Institutional Psychotherapy, and the Decolonization of Psychiatry," *Journal of the History of Ideas* 81, no. 2 (April 2020): 303–25.
38. Frantz Fanon, *Black Skin, White Masks* (New York: Grove Press, 1967), 134. Henceforth quoted in the text as BSWM, followed by page number. The inordinate back-and-forth between Sartre and the poets of *négritude*, as well as Fanon, makes a long story all on its own. For an excellent such discussion, see George Ciccariello-Maher, "The Internal Limits of the European Gaze: Intellectuals and the Colonial Difference," *Radical Philosophy Review* 9, no. 2 (2006): 139–65.
39. Frantz Fanon, *The Wretched of the Earth* (New York: Grove Press, 1968), 210. Translation modified. Henceforth cited in the text as WE, followed by page number.
40. It would be worthwhile to juxtapose here Aimé Césaire's address to the First Congress of Negro Artists and Writers, given in 1956, just a month before his letter of resignation

from the French Communist Party, where, invoking expressly the spirit of Bandung, Césaire too points to culture as the primary battlefield against colonization, conceptualizing it, on the one hand, as a sort of *"solidarity in time"*—that is to say, a historically residual capacity of society to retain what binds it together, despite the external violence that tears it apart—and, on the other hand, as "the power to *go beyond oneself* [*se dépasser*]," which is the prerequisite of every free people. See Aimé Césaire, "Culture and Colonization," *Social Text* 103 (Summer 2010): 127–44. Translation by Brent Hays Edwards; italics in the original.

41. Hanan Elsayed conducts an interesting encounter between Fanon's and Althusser's stagings of interpellation, mediated by the relevant positions of two of Althusser's pupils, Balibar and Macherey, in the context of discussing race as a political concept. See "Race," in *Thinking with Balibar: A Lexicon of Conceptual Practice*, ed. Ann Laura Stoler, Stathis Gourgouris, and Jacques Lezra (New York: Fordham University Press, 2020), 193–210.

42. Frantz Fanon, "Racism and Culture," in *Toward the African Revolution* (New York: Grove Press, 1967), 44.

43. Paul Gilroy, "Fanon and Améry: Theory, Torture, and the Prospect of Humanism," *Theory, Culture, and Society* 27, nos. 7–8 (2010): 16–32.

44. To this we would have to add yet another dimension: the intervention by Achille Mbembe, who recognizes the uniquely Fanonian coarticulation of violence with care or healing. "Fanon believes that under certain circumstances, the very act of *caring*, of trying to *heal*, to console, to attend to the diseased mind and destroyed body, might not be devoid of violence. Violence for Fanon is both a weapon and a medicine. But as we know very well, a medicine is not simply that which cures. It is also that which can kill. The paradoxical nature of Fanonian violence is something I think we should hold on to." Achille Mbembe and David Theo Goldberg, "The Reason of Unreason: A Conversation About *Critique of Black Reason*," *Theory, Culture, and Society* (July 3, 2018), https://www.theoryculturesociety.org/conversation-achille-mbembe-and-david-theo-goldberg-on-critique-of-black-reason/.

45. Didier Fassin, *Humanitarian Reason: A Moral History of the Present* (Berkeley: University of California Press, 2011).

46. The quotation is by Sandro Mezzadra from an interview on the migrant/refugee rescue activities of the Mediterranea project. See Beppe Caccia, Charles, Heller, and Sandro Mezzadra, "Mediterranea: Thinking Through a Political Invention in Tumultuous Times," *Viewpoint Magazine* (July 7, 2020), https://viewpointmag.com/2020/07/07/mediterranea-thinking-through-a-political-invention-in-tumultuous-times/#f+12661+1+10.

47. Sylvia Wynter, "The Ceremony Found," 210–12.

48. Wynter, "The Ceremony Found," 217 (italics in the original). I note here the remarkable similarity of this account of human ontology with the account put forth by Castoriadis since the earliest phase of his *Imaginary Institution of Society* in the mid-1960s. It is unfortunate that an explicit conversation between Wynter and Castoriadis never took place, even though there is a range of shared interlocutors, from C. L. R. James to Francisco Varela. To explore this epistemological convergence in its full range (biology, anthropology, poetics, and politics), a whole other book would have to be written.

1. Humanism, Human/Animal, Human-Being   303

49. David Scott, "The Re-Enchantment of Humanism: An Interview with Sylvia Wynter," *Small Axe* 8 (September 2000): 119-307. See also Scott's reflections on this interview several years later, which recontextualize the conversation and indeed the text itself with a number of further insights according to what he calls explicitly and deliberately "recursive thinking": "Preface: Sylvia Wynter's Agonistic Intimations" *Small Axe* 40, no. 1 (March 2016): vii-x.

50. Sylvia Wynter, "Towards the Sociogenic Principle: Fanon, the Puzzle of Conscious Experience, of 'Identity' and What It's Like to Be 'Black'," in *National Identities and Socio-Political Changes in Latin America*, ed. Antonio Gomez-Moriana and Mercedes Duran-Cogan (New York: Routledge, 2001), 30-66. Henceforth cited in the text.

51. Ronald Judy has some very insightful things to say in this regard. See "Fanon's Body of Black Experience," in *Fanon: A Critical Reader*, ed. Lewis R. Gordon et al. (Oxford: Blackwell, 1996), 53-73.

52. As has been extensively pointed out, the initial translation of the title of chapter 5 in *Black Skin, White Masks—l'experience vécue du noir*—as "the fact of Blackness" is terribly inaccurate: the proper translation is "the lived experience of the black." The correction is essential because it restores the social-historical character of blackness away from some sort of transcendental ontological claim. However, this does not nullify its *factual* character in the sense that all historical creations, even the most outrageous or unfathomable expressions of the social imaginary, are historical precisely in that they are *actualized*, in that they become determinant facts in an interminable process of making and unmaking history.

53. Sylvia Wynter, "Black Metamorphosis: New Natives in a New World," Institute of Black World Records, MG 502, Box 1, Schomburg Center for Research in Black Culture, New York (n.d.), 47-48. This extraordinary 935-page manuscript, written during the early 1970s but remarkably remaining still unpublished, has nonetheless circulated widely and has become a major reference point in recent years, which gives it a legendary status. On its history, context, and significance, see the special issue of *Small Axe* 20, no. 1 (March 2016) guest edited and introduced by Aaron Kamugisha. Every essay published in this issue is uniquely attentive, not only to this remarkable, if unyielding, palimpsest of a text adorned with handwritten notes and alternate words, but also to how its abandonment by the author might be seen in light of her later publications, in all cases pointing with care to the intricate weavings of what may have been prescient or, alternately, superseded with what may have come to exist in the present time of reading that would give the unpublished text a whole other life. This is very much within the spirit of Wynter's argument of regeneration of life. Parts of the material contained in *Black Metamorphosis* did find its way to publication, either before or after the manuscript was completed. An early instance of Wynter's thinking in the specific terms discussed here, but drawn more toward a literary path, can be found in her essay "Novel and History, Plot and Plantation," *Savacou* 5 (June 1971): 95-102.

54. Apter, *The Translation Zone*, 25-26.

55. Peter Sloterdijk, "Rules for the Human Zoo: A Response to *Letter on Humanism*," (1999), trans. Mary Varney Rorty, *Environment and Planning D: Society and Space* 27 (2009): 15. Henceforth cited in the text as S, followed by page number.

56. Fred Moten, *Stolen Life* (Durham, NC: Duke University Press, 2018), 193. Henceforth cited in the text.
57. Later on in the text, explicitly channeling Fanon on this matter, Moten considers "blackness as an international anti-national force" (203).
58. Hannah Arendt, *The Origins of Totalitarianism* (New York: Harvest, 1976), 185.
59. The recent Black Lives Matter calls in the street for defunding the police should be understood precisely in these terms. Defunding is so literal as to break through the literal: meaning, the police mechanisms of the state must be de-instituted in such a way as to be deprived of all capacity to act in the presumed authority of the law in order to waste black(ened) bodies. Defunding is literal to the extent that police unions must be deprived of their financial immunity in conducting their predatory operations on society (including their wealth-producing machinery, for themselves and the state) and also beyond literal to the extent that they must be deauthorized as *law-making* (not just enforcing) entities on the basis of systematic extermination of the black population. I am speaking, of course, specifically in terms of American society, although the argument is generalizable onto the spectrum of (neo)colonial conditions worldwide. Crucial in this respect is Jackie Wang's argument in *Carceral Capitalism* (New York: Semiotexte, 2018).
60. Sylvia Wynter, "Unparalleled Catastrophe for Our Species? Or, to Give Humanness a Different Future," in *On Being Human as a Praxis*, ed. Katherine McKittrick (Durham, NC: Duke University Press, 2015), 23.
61. Wynter's remarkable lesson is assiduously and inventively extended not only by Moten and Jackson but also by Alexander Weheliye in his *Habeas Viscus* (Durham, NC: Duke University Press, 2014). For a concise view of Weheliye's thinking in this regard, see Monica Miller and Christopher Driscoll's interview with him: "Conversations in Black," *Los Angeles Review of Books* (September 1, 2015), https://marginalia.lareviewofbooks.org/conversations-in-black-alexander-g-weheliye/.
62. See Cary Wolfe, *What Is Posthumanism?* (Minneapolis: University of Minnesota Press, 2010).
63. Gayatri Chakravorty Spivak, *Death of a Discipline* (New York: Columbia University Press, 2003), 26.
64. Like all perversions, the human perversion for self-reproduction in machine form is, of course, boundless. Most perverse is the machine mode in which humans consume uninterrogated information about the increasing capacities of AI machines. This has now become a matter of mainstream media—the mass consumption of information for the "informed reader" is a market phenomenon. Most amusing is a recent instance of the op-ed specialist robot (an AI language generator) that produced an essay to assure humans that, unlike them, robots would never allow the destruction of humanity. We have to presume that the machine's etymological assertion that the word "robot" has Greek origins was a programming error.... See GPT-3, "A Robot Wrote This Entire Article. Are You Scared Yet, Human?" *The Guardian* (September 8, 2020), https://www.theguardian.com/commentisfree/2020/sep/08/robot-wrote-this-article-gpt-3.
65. I am reproducing a problem presented by Constantinos Daskalakis, world-renowned professor of computer science at MIT and specialist in equilibrium complexity,

mathematical game theory, and probability theory, from a lecture he gave at Aristotle University in Thessaloniki in January 2018.
66. Hong Qin, "Machine Learning and Serving of Discrete Field Theories," *Scientific Reports* 10, no. 19329 (November 9, 2020), https://doi.org/10.1038/s41598-020-76301-0.
67. See Zachary Kallenborn, "Was a Flying Killer Robot Used in Libya? Quite Possibly," *Bulletin of the Atomic Scientists* (May 20, 2021), https://thebulletin.org/2021/05/was-a-flying-killer-robot-used-in-libya-quite-possibly/.
68. According to recent research in robotic recognition patterns by Johns Hopkins University. See Jill Rosen, "Flawed AI Makes Robots Racist, Sexist" (June 21, 2022), https://hub.jhu.edu/2022/06/21/flawed-artificial-intelligence-robot-racist-sexist/.
69. Naomi Klein, "AI Machines Aren't 'Hallucinating.' But Their Makers Are," *The Guardian* (May 8, 2023), https://www.theguardian.com/commentisfree/2023/may/08/ai-machines-hallucinating-naomi-klein.
70. Noah Chomsky, "The False Promise of ChatGPT," *New York Times* (March 8, 2023), https://www.nytimes.com/2023/03/08/opinion/noam-chomsky-chatgpt-ai.html.
71. https://www.tiktok.com/@project_shadow_us/video/7182455932406844714.
72. Cade Metz, "'The Godfather of AI' Leaves Google and Warns of the Danger Ahead," *New York Times* (May 1, 2023), https://www.nytimes.com/2023/05/01/technology/ai-google-chatbot-engineer-quits-hinton.html.
73. Blake Lemoine, "Is LaMDA Sentient?—an Interview" *Medium* (June 11, 2022), https://cajundiscordian.medium.com/is-lamda-sentient-an-interview-ea64d916d917.
74. Kevin Roose, "A Conversation with Bing's Chatbot Left Me Deeply Unsettled," *New York Times* (February 16, 2023), https://www.nytimes.com/2023/02/16/technology/bing-chatbot-microsoft-chatgpt.html.
75. A groundbreaking exception would be Ruha Benjamin's radical intervention into the racist parameters of algorithmic imaginaries in *Race After Technology: Abolitionist Tools for the New Jim Code* (Cambridge: Polity, 2019).
76. For a succinct account of where Ethical AI stands these days, see a recent report by Carly Kind, who is a pioneering figure in this field: "The Term 'Ethical AI' Is Finally Starting to Mean Something," *VentureBeat* (August 23, 2020), https://venturebeat.com/2020/08/23/the-term-ethical-ai-is-finally-starting-to-mean-something/.
77. Quoted in Nitasha Tiku, "The Google Engineer Who Thinks the Company's AI Has Come to Life," *Washington Post* (June 11, 2022), https://www.washingtonpost.com/technology/2022/06/11/google-ai-lamda-blake-lemoine/.
78. To elaborate on the psycho-historico-ontological dimensions of this argument would take us far afield and distract us from the point at hand. In any case, I have made this argument at length in "Confronting Heteronomy" and "The Void Occupied Unconcealed," in *Lessons in Secular Criticism*, 90–144.
79. Very early on, in *Beginnings* (1975), and drawing from *The Poverty of Philosophy*, Edward Said points to this order of *co-incidence* (my term) in such a way as to link Marx's new epistemology of *human-being* as tantamount to human labor with the radical beginning of the Marxist project as such—the *radical* nontranscendentalist innovation of Marx's humanism. In order to "see man as the true origin of social change, a new fusion between man and his activity must be considered possible and thereby rethought in man's mind.

The very act of beginning must no longer set man apart from his end, but must immediately suggest significant connections between it and man. Marx thus tied his own interpretive activity to human activity in general at a common revolutionary point of departure" (*Beginnings*, 41).

80. Interestingly, when Léopold Senghor argues that *négritude* is a humanism for the twentieth century, he begins by defining it in very similar terms (though in clear opposition to a Marxian analysis) as "rooting oneself in oneself and self-confirmation: confirmation of one's being [*enracinement en soi et confirmation de soi: de son être*]" in order to argue furthermore in favor of "making oneself" as "realizing oneself" which is the quintessential *poietic* gesture: self-realization as self-alteration. See Senghor, *La négritude est un humanisme du XXe siècle*, 9–12.

81. Karl Marx, "Economic and Philosophical Manuscripts of 1844," in Karl Marx and Frederick Engels, *Collected Works* (New York: International Publishers, 1975), 3:277. I have altered the official translation, opting for a certain awkwardness in order to alert us to the nuances of language as I explain in the text. Henceforth, cited in the text as M-E followed by page number.

82. Earlier in the text, Marx asserts that "the worker must sell himself *and* his humanity" (M-E, 239, my emphasis). This sort of conjunctive phrasing attests to a double condition: (1) humanity is a property that belongs, in the end, to humanity as such—in the radical sense of the initial quotation above, yet (2) humanity is (or rather, has become) also a commodity—that is, it also belongs to a particular economy; it is determined by capitalism. But insofar as it becomes a commodity, humanity annihilates itself. It abdicates its self-authorization; it becomes dependent on an external system of reference that trades its meaning. Capitalism is dehumanizing in this very strict sense as well.

83. Mao Zedong uses perfect Hegelian-Marxist language to convey this, rather simply, in a famous formulation: "Is there such a thing as human nature? Of course, there is. But there is human nature in the concrete, no human nature in the abstract." What is concrete here in the most radical sense is the social relation; what is abstract is the presumption of an asocial singularity. See Mao Zedong, "Talks at the Yenan Forum on Literature and Art" (May 1942), https://www.marxists.org/reference/archive/mao/selected-works/volume-3/mswv3_08.htm.

84. Karl Marx and Frederick Engels, *Collected Works* (New York: International Publishers, 1976), 5:8. Translation altered.

85. Étienne Balibar, "From Philosophical Anthropology to Social Ontology and Back: What to Do with Marx's Sixth Thesis on Feuerbach?" *Postmodern Culture* 22, no. 3 (2012), doi:10.1353/pmc.2012.0014. This may be one of Balibar's most brilliant essays. He conducts a hermeneutical tour-de-force, bearing upon Marx's text with exorbitant philological and philosophical multilingualism. Indeed, I have adjusted the classic translations with his argument in mind.

86. Martin Heidegger, "Letter on 'Humanism,'" in *Pathmarks* (New York: Cambridge University Press, 1998), 245. Henceforth quoted in the text as L, followed by page number.

87. Beaufret's and Heidegger's initial correspondence takes place within a few days after Sartre's lecture (October 25, 1945), while the event's noisy aftermath is in full swing. (Heidegger will take two years to fully unwind and compose his thoughts before publishing

his essay.) The swiftness and intensity of the exchange testifies to the stakes involved. One might add that what has come to be known lazily as "French Heideggerianism" (as index of poststructuralism) undermines any productive consideration of the long, heterogeneous, and uniquely inventive ways of the French engagement with Heidegger—along the Kojève-Sartre-Derrida line and the many vicissitudes thereof.

88. Heidegger returns to the specifics of Beaufret's question in order to acknowledge that "there arises the possibility of restoring to the word 'humanism' a historical sense that is older than its oldest meaning chronologically reckoned" (L, 262), which he unsurprisingly elaborates as essence, "essential for the truth of being, specifically in such a way that what matters is not the human being simply as such" (L, 263). A historical being that precedes meaning and belongs to a primordial essential time is perfectly otherworldly transcendent Being. Hent de Vries masterfully shows how this analysis of *humanitas qua humanitas* in these very terms is an analogical vehicle for Heidegger's understanding of religion *qua* religion. See his *Philosophy and the Turn to Religion* (Baltimore: Johns Hopkins University Press, 1999), 232–41. Without being at all derivative, de Vries confirms Theodor Adorno's formidable exposure of Heidegger's religiosity in so-called historical disguise in *The Jargon of Authenticity* (London: Routledge, 1964).

89. See Cornelius Castoriadis, *Ce qui fait la Grèce* (Paris: Seuil, 2004), 185–201. The framework here does not allow me to expand into the terrain of Castoriadis's own reading of the Anaximander fragment. The most radical point of difference between Heidegger and Castoriadis—specifically insofar as both propose a historical ontology—is that, for Castoriadis, Being is impure (magmatic) and continuously mutable, understandable only as *à-être*: what emerges from nonbeing as always-becoming-being and what comes to create meaning in the foreground of what is irreducibly nonmeaning. In this sense, Heidegger's much discussed "ontological difference" is inherently nonsensical: "Nothing can be said about Being outside of beings." Castoriadis, "Imaginary and Imagination at the Crossroads," in *Figures of the Thinkable* (Stanford, CA: Stanford University Press, 2007), 82. For Castoriadis, no ontology of the human can be articulated outside some sort of configuration of the polis and the *psyche*—which need not be imagined solely in Greek terms—where self-alteration is the principal force, while his cosmology abolishes the difference between immanence and transcendence, or rather it shows this difference to be a social-historical difference, a social-imaginary signification that enacts a specific ontotheological direction.

90. Crucial evidence that living beings create their world and are not passive objects of receiving information from it was provided in the groundbreaking research of biologist Humberto Maturana, who discovered, already in 1956, that frogs produced ocular stimulation by brain activity even when deprived of actual visual information. This precipitated the later collaboration with Francisco Varela in *Autopoiesis and Cognition*, which opened a new biological horizon beyond cybernetics and information-science models of cognition. That one oftentimes finds readings of Maturana and Varela as confirmations of systems theory is altogether puzzling. The most radical dimension of their theorization of the autopoietic capacity of living being is the intrinsic implication of autopoiesis not with self-confirmation but with self-alteration, which brings their radical thinking into the discussion of the radical imagination of the psyche—from my

308   1. *Humanism, Human/Animal, Human-Being*

standpoint, the crux of the condition of *human-being*. For clarification of such misreading see the conversation between Varela and Castoriadis in *Postscript on Insignificance: Dialogues with Cornelius Castoriadis* (London: Continuum, 2011), 58–73.

91. It is precisely this nonmeaning of being which rests on abyssal infinity—or more precisely, this nondeterminant being, this veritable nonbeing —that underlies Anaximander's cosmology, as will be discussed in the next essay.

92. Walter Benjamin, "One-Way Street," in *Selected Works* (Cambridge, MA: Harvard University Press, 1996), 1:487. As with Marx, I translate here the terms *Menschen* and *Menschheit* in generic, not gendered, terms with full cognizance of the gesture.

93. It is very much in this sense that Benjamin may be said to deconstruct the quandary of contemplating the "end of man," which, as Derrida argued long ago, is quintessentially metaphysical: "The thinking of the end of man is always already prescribed in metaphysics, in the thinking of the truth of man." *Margins of Philosophy* (Chicago: University of Chicago Press, 1982), 121. The metaphysics of any teleology—for Derrida, correctly, tantamount to eschatology, theology, and ontology—inheres in the sense of the predetermined, which is in effect the sense of an *archē* that determines unimpeded the *telos* that thereby belongs to it. Such *archē* and *telos* is at work in *Dasein*.

94. James Gleick, *The Information: A History, A Theory, A Flood* (New York: Pantheon, 2011), 126.

95. Foucault, *"Society Must Be Defended,"* 254.

96. Michel Foucault, *Security, Territory, Population*, trans. Graham Burchell (New York: Palgrave, 2007).

97. Michel Foucault, *The History of Sexuality Vol. I: An Introduction*, trans. Robert Hurley (New York: Vintage Books, 1978), 143. Henceforth cited in the text. I can't help noting that these remarks, concluding the argument in *Le volonté de savoir* (1976), echo the famous remarks concluding *Les mots et les choses* (1966), in the sense that the threshold of modernity is again marked by a shift in the signification of what is human—or, in Foucauldian language, a shift in the framework of knowledge that determines what is human.

98. Julien Offray de La Mettrie, "Man, a Machine," https://www.marxists.org/reference/archive/la-mettrie/1748/man-machine.htm.

99. Foucault sees in La Mettrie's project "a general theory of *dressage*, at the center of which reigns the notion of docility." Although this is correct, in the sense that any disciplinary training partakes of machine-like elements, it might be inaccurate to channel La Mettrie's project exclusively toward the making of docile bodies. An undefinable machine is ultimately untrainable and always open to chance, where the possibilities of both docility and insurgency are incalculable. See Michel Foucault, *Discipline and Punish: The Birth of the Prison* (New York: Vintage Books, 1979), 136.

100. See Madeleine Stix, "World's First Cyborg Wants to Hack Your Body," CNN.com (January 7, 2016), https://edition.cnn.com/2014/09/02/tech/innovation/cyborg-neil-harbisson-implant-antenna/index.html.

101. Max Horkheimer and Theodor W. Adorno, *Dialectic of Enlightenment* (New York: Seabury Press, 1972), 253.

102. Indicative is Plessner's discussion of Uexküll in "Die Frage nach der Conditio humana" (1961), in Helmuth Plessner, *Gesammelte Schriften VIII: Conditio humana* (Frankfurt am Main: Suhrkamp Verlag, 1980), 136–217. Henceforth cited in the text in my translation.

103. Helmuth Plessner, "De Homine Abscondito," *Social Research* 36, no. 4 (Winter 1969): 500. Henceforth cited in the text.
104. See Helmuth Plessner, *Macht und menschliche Natur* (1931), translated as *Political Anthropology* (Evanston, IL: Northwestern University Press, 2018).
105. In a humorous but also rather sad metaphor, Castoriadis describes the *human/animal* as "a child who finds himself in a house with chocolate walls, and who sets out to eat them without understanding that the rest of the house is soon going to fall on his head" in "What Democracy?" *Figures of the Thinkable*, 145.
106. A crucial interlocutor, in this respect, would be Hans Blumenberg, but a serious engagement with his own philosophical anthropology would overburden an already overly compact argument. For a brilliant account of this nexus, see Brad Tabas, "Blumenberg, Politics, Anthropology," *Telos* 158 (Spring 2012): 135-53.
107. Pioneering philosophical work on this historical nexus is Elizabeth de Fontenay's *Le silence des bêtes: La philosophie à l'épreuve de l'animalité* (Paris: Fayard, 1998), which is the pinnacle of a series of such ruminations throughout her life, including her more recent *Sans offenser le genre humain* (Paris: Albin Michel, 2008), and Cora Diamond's articles collected in *The Realistic Spirit: Wittgenstein, Philosophy, and the Mind* (Cambridge, MA: MIT Press, 1991) and more recently "Injustice and Animals" (2001) and "The Difficulty of Reality and the Difficulty of Philosophy" in *Philosophy and Animal Life* (New York: Columbia University Press, 2008), 43-90. For an eloquent defense of Cora Diamond's arguments and a thorough exposition of the philosophical literature on this matter, see Alice Crary's entry "Animals" in the second issue of *Political Concepts*, http://www.politicalconcepts.org/animals-alice-crary/. Although I am deliberately not addressing matters of ethics, much of what I attempt in this section can be taken as part of a conversation with Crary's argument, including the way we both encounter Derrida's position.
108. Derrida's *en passant* distinction, however, does not extend itself to *poiēsis* as a mode of inquiry into this matter. See Derrida, *The Animal That Therefore I Am*, 7. (Henceforth cited in text as D followed by page number.) Interestingly, Cora Diamond says exactly the same thing, invoking J. M. Coetzee's *Elizabeth Costello*: "Poetry and not philosophy [has] the capacity to return us to such a sense of what animal life is" ("The Difficulty of Reality and the Difficulty of Philosophy," 53). However, Diamond's analysis is haunted by an obsessive formalism in this case woven around a contrived condition of distinction (homophagia). The idea that humans have been, in perfect actuality, constructed as animals in so many instances of human history carries no epistemological weight, despite her references to the Holocaust.
109. Some of the best work in the literary part of the terrain that has been named "animal studies" takes place in medieval studies and increasingly in classical studies, and this makes sense because pre-Enlightenment categorizations of language and reason are more fluid in this respect. See, indicatively, Susan Crane, *Animal Encounters: Contacts and Concepts in Medieval Britain* (Philadelphia: University of Pennsylvania Press, 2012), and Mark Payne, *The Animal Part: Human and Other Animals in the Poetic Imagination* (Chicago: University of Chicago Press, 2010).
110. In reading Crary's account of how Derrida's notion of "iterability"—as early a Derridean concern as any—haunts his argument about the animal, I could not help thinking

that the two are irreparably entwined as spectral obstacles: after all, absolute alterity is what iterability entails and without the rubric of absolute alterity iterability is nonsensical.

111. Donna J. Haraway, *When Species Meet* (Minneapolis: University of Minnesota Press, 2008), 164-65. Henceforth cited in the text.

112. This is where Catherine Malabou's interventions are radical and very close to my thinking. Not only does she understand the debilitating metaphysics of positing radical alterity, but she also underlines "becoming animal" as an entirely immanent reality. I quote here three instances from her *Ontology of the Accident: An Essay on Destructive Plasticity* (Cambridge: Polity, 2012): "These modes of being without genealogy have nothing to do with the wholly other found in the mystical ethics of the twentieth century. The Wholly Other remains always and forever a stranger to the Other" (3). "Destructive plasticity enables the appearance or formation of alterity where the other is absolutely lacking. Plasticity is the form of alterity when no transcendence, flight or escape is left. The only other that exists in this circumstance is being other to the self" (11). "This is why 'becoming animal' is not 'becoming *an* animal': the first is an arrangement; the second is a form, which can do nothing but freeze becoming" (17).

113. Derrida too seems to go in this direction, even if in passing, when he attributes the Cartesian privilege of the human to "the Judeo-Christiano-Islamic tradition of war against the animal" (*The Animal That Therefore I Am*, 101), in order to go on to delimit the purview of Kantian transcendentalism as "the general trait" of a zoophobia or even overt hatred of, not merely the animal, but "the animality of the human:" "Authentic idealism consists in *insulting* the animal in the human or in treating the human as animal" (103). Somewhat unusually in Derrida's work, monotheism and rationalist idealism are hereby conjoined in sharing a kin trajectory: a constitutive transcendental command to annihilate the sensuous animality of the human.

114. See Nigel Rothfels, *Savages and Beasts: The Birth of the Modern Zoo* (Baltimore: Johns Hopkins University Press, 2002).

115. Giorgio Agamben, *The Open: Man and Animal* (Stanford University Press, 2004), 16. Henceforth cited in the text.

116. See Clastres, "De l'ethnocide" *L'Homme* 14, nos. 3-4 (July-December 1974), 101-10.

117. This might be another way to elucidate Jane Bennett's claim that anthropomorphism "oddly enough works against anthropocentrism" because it "can catalyze a sensibility that finds a world filled not with ontologically distinct categories of beings (subjects and objects) but with variously composed materialities that form confederations." See Jane Bennett, *Vibrant Matter: A Political Ecology of Things* (Durham, NC: Duke University Press, 2010), 99, 120.

118. See Sigmund Freud, *Collected Papers Vol. 5* (London: Hogarth Press, 1950), 316-57. The consummate discussion of this issue is conducted with brilliance and fabulous humor in Cornelius Castoriadis's "Psychoanalysis and Politics," in *World in Fragments* (Stanford, CA: Stanford University Press, 1997), 125-36. Castoriadis makes the point that all three domains are engaged in *praxis* in a non-Aristotelian sense: that is, not as teleological fulfillments but as transformations of the object, as *practico-poietic* activities, a perspective that I adopt here as well.

1. Humanism, Human/Animal, Human-Being   311

119. Karl Marx, *Capital Vol. I* (New York: International Publishers, 1975), 177-78 (translation modified).
120. It is well known that Lucy, a chimpanzee raised by Jane and Maurice Temerlin in the 1960s, used to masturbate to *Playgirl* magazines using a vacuum cleaner extension. The Temerlins were professors at the Institute of Primate Studies, University of Oklahoma, and raised Lucy in their home as their child (exactly like Keith and Catherine Hayes did a decade earlier with Viki, another chimpanzee experiment in language learning). What such cases confirm, however, is the primate capacity for acute learning by mimetic coding and decoding—in fact, the operative logic (apart from the mimetic element) is similar to cybernetic or Artificial Intelligence models. There is indisputable capacity in primates to adopt all the ways of humans except for one: the capacity to imagine that another animal could possibly imitate their ways and to construct circumstances thereby to make sure this imagining will be actualized. No chimpanzee can ever become a behavioral scientist.
121. "Hegel has said that man is a sick animal. In truth, man is a mad animal, totally unfit for life, a species that would have disappeared as soon as it emerged if it had not proven itself capable, at the collective level, of another creation: society in the strict sense, that is, institutions embodying social imaginary significations. This creation we cannot help but impute to the creative capacity of anonymous human collectives, that is, to the radical instituting imaginary." Cornelius Castoriadis, "Radical Imagination and the Social Instituting Imaginary," in *The Castoriadis Reader* (Oxford: Blackwell, 1997), 331.
122. "Philosophy and Sublimation," *Thesis Eleven* 49 (May 1997): 31-44.
123. Incidentally, philanthropy should not be seen as the opposite of misanthropy but as its sidekick. Both loving and hating humanity are similar affective constellations that emerge within a predominantly Christian imaginary, regardless of whether their purveyors claim to be non-Christian or, for that matter, secular. The institution of philanthropy, whose variants are found in many religious practices or their mutation to secular-moral practices, is allegedly to enact a correction in order to assuage one's inevitable involvement in an imbalance (*adikia*). Nonetheless, its meaning depends on the instrumentality assigned to it by the religious/moral authority that commands it. This authority remains the sole beneficiary, and the cosmic imbalance is thus maintained.
124. I was particularly happy to discover Rosi Braidotti making exactly the same call, in the same terms and with the same urgency, for what she calls specifically "affirmative ethics" in her *Posthuman Knowledge* (Cambridge: Polity, 2019).
125. See "The State of the Subject Today," in *World in Fragments*, 153.
126. Cornelius Castoriadis, "Aeschylean Anthropogony and Sophoclean Self-Creation of *Anthropos*," in *Figures of the Thinkable*, 16.
127. For Castoriadis, this is exemplary of praxis itself: "The subject of praxis is constantly transformed on the basis of the experience in which it is engaged, which the subject *does* or *makes*, but which also *makes* the subject. Pedagogues are educated; the poem makes the poet." See *The Imaginary Institution of Society*, trans. Kathleen Blamey (Cambridge, MA: MIT Press, 1997), 77.
128. I broach this subject in "The *Poiein* of Secular Criticism," in my *Lessons in Secular Criticism*. An affiliate position, though differently conducted, is to be found in Paul Bové's

Poetry Against Torture: Criticism, History, and the Human (Hong Kong: Hong Kong University Press 2008).

129. Edward Said, "Vico: Autodidact and Humanist," *Centennial Review* 11, no. 3 (Summer 1967): 336–52, reiterated in a broader discussion of Vico's work in *Beginnings* (345–82). Said's admiration of the figure of autodidacticism permeates this essay, and it is in this light that I read his ubiquitous aversion to dogmatism and discipleship. But this is also an interesting context in which to read Emily Apter's characterization of Said's multifold and self-interrogative oeuvre as the work of a "self-translator." See Apter, *The Translation Zone*, 60.

130. Seminal in this configuration, even if not quite in terms of autodidacticism since attention is focused specifically on self-making (autopoiesis), is Saidiya Hartman's *Scenes of Subjection: Terror, Slavery, and Self-Making in Nineteenth-Century America* (New York: Oxford University Press, 1997).

131. Maturana and Varela, *Autopoiesis and Cognition*, xxix.

132. For thinking in similar terms, see R. A Judy's fabulous account of the Haitian Revolution as an autodidactic/autopoietic instance that both actualizes and radically challenges the full spectrum of the radical Enlightenment imaginary: "Somewhat ironically, the fact of revolutionary Haitian autodidactic activity proves [Kant's] theory of humanistic capacity for autopoetic progression even more than did the French Revolution." See R. A. Judy, "Restless Flying: A Black Study of Revolutionary Humanism," *boundary 2* 47, no. 2 (May 2020): 101.

133. That Aristotle in his rather neglected *Historia Animalium* adds bees, as well as ants, cranes, and wasps, to the category "political animal" as other animals that act together toward a common purpose should not trouble our analysis here, because he quickly moves further to differentiate the animality of *human-being* as "more" (*mallon*) political than any other. Uniqueness is not the issue here, but differentiation (and the grounds for it) is. For an interesting discussion of this specific issue, even more as it bears to the matter of friendship I discuss herein, see John M. Cooper, "Political Animals and Civic Friendship," in *Aristotle's Politics: Critical Essays*, ed. Richard Kraut and Steve Skultety (Lanham, MD: Rowman & Littlefield, 2005), 65–89.

134. See Roberto Esposito, *Bios: Biopolitics and Philosophy* (Minneapolis: University of Minnesota Press, 2008). For thorough and succinct dismantlings of Agamben's argument with the broader implications duly noted, see Laurent Dubreuil, "Leaving Politics: *Bios, Zoē*, Life," *Diacritics* 36, no. 2 (Summer 2006): 83–98; Neni Panourgia, "Bios" in *Posthuman Glossary*, ed. Rosi Braidotti and Maria Hlavajova (London: Bloomsbury, 2018), 68–69; Brooke Holmes, "Bios," *Political Concepts* 5, no. 2 (Spring 2019), https://www.politicalconcepts.org/bios-brooke-holmes/.

135. Sheldon Wolin, "Transgression, Equality, and Voice," in *Dēmokratia: A Conversation on Democracies, Ancient and Modern*, ed. Josiah Ober and Charles Hedrick (Princeton: Princeton University Press, 1996), 65–66.

136. Etienne Balibar, *Citoyen Sujet et autres essais d'anthropologie philosophique* (Paris: PUF, 2011).

137. Exceptional in understanding the magnitude and scope of such signification remain the studies by Jean-Claude Fraisse, *Philia: La notion d'amitié dans la philosophie antique* (Paris:

J. Vrin, 1974), and David Konstan, *Friendship in the Classical World* (Cambridge: Cambridge University Press, 1997).

138. Jacques Derrida, *Politics of Friendship*, trans. George Collins (London: Verso, 1997), 72.
139. Much can be learned about this sort of consistent slippage and why it happens from Gil Anidjar's *The Jew, the Arab: A History of the Enemy* (Stanford, CA: Stanford University Press, 2003).
140. Dimitris Vardoulakis has conducted one of the most challenging meditations on the notion of *stasis*, which includes an innovative translation of this famous passage in Aristotle. For Vardoulakis, the asymmetrical relation between friendship and justice in Aristotle "traverses the terrain of *stasis*" in such a way as to enable a configuration of *stasis* as a more ethical than political position, which I read as an outcome of his Spinozist "separation"'—in the last instance—between the ethical and the political. I am not sure this is feasible within the Greek conceptual horizon of *stasis*, all the more because it underlies a theologico-political conclusion, but to discuss this here in any responsible way would send us far afield. See Vardoulakis, "Stasis: Beyond Political Theology?" *Cultural Critique* 73 (Fall 2009): 125–47, and *Stasis Before the State: Nine Theses on Agonistic Democracy* (New York: Fordham University Press, 2017).
141. Similar is the conflation between the notion of being *homophilos* (of the same sensibility) with being *homophylos* (of the same nature), which mars a great deal of the argument. See *Politics of Friendship*, 92.
142. "There is no democracy without respect for irreducible singularity or alterity, but there is no democracy without the 'community of friends' (*koina ta philōn*), without the calculation of majorities, without identifiable, stabilizable, representable subjects, all equal. These two laws are irreducible one to the other. Tragically irreconcilable and forever wounding." *Politics of Friendship*, 22.
143. I discuss the problematic of Antigone's hubristic singularity, as well as the compulsion this tragic drama holds over modern philosophy in "Philosophy's Need for Antigone" in *Does Literature Think?* (Stanford, CA: Stanford University Press, 2003), 116–60, but I owe much of this reconsideration here to conversations with Sophie Klimis. See especially her *L'énigme de l'humain et l'invention de la politique* (Louvain: De Boeck, 2014).
144. It is only fitting that Montaigne's famous celebration of friendship in the *Essays* is motivated by and dedicated to La Boétie. What passes as Montaigne's description of their relationship registers the profoundly radical element of friendship against kinship—the abolition of property as identity: "It was some mysterious quintessence of all this mixture which possessed itself of my will, and led it to plunge and lose itself in his; which possessed itself of his whole will, and led it, with a similar hunger and a like impulse, to plunge and lose itself in mine. I may truly say *lose* for it had left us with nothing that was our own (*propre*), nothing that was either his or mine." See "On Friendship" in *The Complete Essays of Montaigne*, trans. Donald M. Frame (Stanford, CA: Stanford University Press, 1976), 139.
145. Etienne de la Boétie, "On Voluntary Servitude," in *Freedom Over Servitude: Montaigne, La Boétie*, ed. and trans. David Lewis Schaefer (Westport, CT: Greenwood Press, 1998), 220.

146. Laura Paddison, "2019 Was the Year the World Burned," *Huffington Post* (December 31, 2019), https://www.huffingtonpost.co.uk/entry/2019-the-year-the-world-burned_uk_5e0676d7c5b6b5a713ae21fa.

147. I'm drawing on Peter Brennan's stunning essay "The Anthropocene Is a Joke," *The Atlantic* (August 13, 2019), https://www.theatlantic.com/science/archive/2019/08/arrogance-anthropocene/595795/.

148. See Paul J. Crutzen and Eugene F. Stoermer, "The 'Anthropocene,'" *IGBP Newsletter* 41 (May 2000): 17-18; Paul J. Crutzen, "The 'Anthropocene,'" in *Earth System Science in the Anthropocene*, ed. E. Ehlers and T. Krafft (Berlin: Springer Verlag, 2006), 13-18; Will Steffen, Paul J. Crutzen, and John R. McNeill "The Anthropocene: Are Humans Now Overwhelming the Great Forces of Nature?" *Ambio* 36, no. 8 (December 2007): 614-21; Paul J. Crutzen and Christian Schwägerl, "Living in the Anthropocene: Toward a New Global Ethos," *Yale Environment 360* (January 24, 2011), https://e360.yale.edu/features/living_in_the_anthropocene_toward_a_new_global_ethos.

149. This rather strange operation by which a temporal order is made exclusively to account for a spatial transformation is rarely examined as methodology. I may not be interested in geology per se, but because I am interested in history, I too succumb to it here. But delving further into a poetics of space, as it were, would burden further an already overweighed argument. Significant correctives to this whole temporal attitude, which complement my critique here, are Valerie Olson and Lisa Messeri's "Beyond the Anthropocene: Un-Earthing an Epoch," *Environment and Society: Advances in Research* 6 (2015): 28-47, and John McGuire's "The Problem with the Anthropocene: *Kainos*, not *Anthropos*," *Constellations* 30 (2023): 128-40. Henceforth cited in the text.

150. David Archer, *The Long Thaw: How Humans Are Changing the Next 100,000 Years of Earth's Climate* (Princeton, NJ: Princeton University Press, 2009).

151. See the insightful discussion and official decision-making process of the Anthropocene Working Group, where indeed even the doubts as to the properly scientific status of the concept are aired explicitly, while scientific actions on the basis of the Anthropocene hypothesis are taken without qualms. http://quaternary.stratigraphy.org/working-groups/anthropocene/.

152. For shared perspectives, see Christophe Bonneuil and Jean-Baptiste Fressoz, *The Shock of the Anthropocene: The Earth, History and Us* (London: Verso, 2016), and Donna Haraway, "Anthropocene, Capitalocene, Plantationocene, Chthulucene: Making Kin," *Environmental Humanities* 6, no. 1 (2015): 159-65.

153. See also the crucial work of Jason W. Moore, who has created the term "Capitalocene," which he calls "a geopoetics for making sense of capitalism as a world-ecology of power and re/production in the web of life." See "The Capitalocene, Part I: On the Nature and Origins of Our Ecological Crisis," *Journal of Peasant Studies* 44 (2017): 594-630; "The Capitalocene and Planetary Justice," *Maize* 6 (2019): 49-54; and his magnum opus *Capitalism and the Web of Life: Ecology and the Accumulation of Capital* (New York: Verso, 2015).

154. See Dipesh Chakrabarty, "Climate and Capital: On Conjoined Histories," *Critical Inquiry* 41, no. 1 (Autumn 2014): 1-23.

155. Srinivas Aravamudan, "The Catachronism of Climate Change," *Diacritics* 41, no. 3 (2013): 6-30. Henceforth cited in the text.

156. Gayatri Chakravorty Spivak, *An Aesthetic Education in the Era of Globalization* (Cambridge, MA: Harvard University Press, 2012), 338-39.
157. Hence the apt gesture by Françoise Vergès to reveal the Anthropocene's real name. See her "Racial Capitalocene," in *Futures of Black Radicalism*, ed. Gaye Theresa Johnson and Alex Lubin (London: Verso, 2017), https://www.versobooks.com/blogs/3376-racial-capitalocene.
158. Kathryn Yusoff, *A Million Black Anthropocenes or None* (Minneapolis: University of Minnesota Press, 2018), 10. Henceforth cited in the text.
159. Wynter, *Black Metamorphosis*, 45-46 (emphasis in the original).
160. Wynter, "Towards the Sociogenic Principle," 54.
161. Wynter, "The Re-Enchantment of Humanism," 199.
162. Wynter, "The Re-Enchantment of Humanism," 190. Emphasis in the text.
163. Among numerous texts on this matter, see especially "The State of the Subject Today" in Castoriadis, *World in Fragments*, 137-71.
164. Eugenia Bone, *Microbia: A Journey Into the Unseen World Around You* (New York: Rodale, 2018), 15.
165. Manuel Alfonseca et al., "Superintelligence Cannot be Contained: Lessons from Computability Theory," *Journal of Artificial Intelligence Research* 70 (2021): 65-67. It is interesting to note that a self-described rebel faction within the AI community is committed exclusively to research that will limit superintelligent AI's capacity to develop beyond its strict programming. See Richard Waters and Miles Kruppa, "Rebel AI Group Raises Record Cash After Machine Learning Schism," *Financial Times*, May 28, 2021.
166. "Ex-Google Officer Finally Speaks out on the Dangers of AI!— Mo Gawdat," *The Diary of a CEO* podcast (June 1, 2023), https://www.youtube.com/watch?v=bk-nQ7HF6k4.
167. James Lovelock, *Novacene: The Coming Age of Hyperintelligence* (Cambridge: MIT Press, 2019), 85. Henceforth cited in the text.
168. Lovelock does this with a characteristically arrogant British sangfroid that has no qualms singing the praises of this island people "blessed with the Gaian gift of a temperate climate and with the human gift—most of the time—of a temperate history" (126), as if the Empire and its quite intemperate shenanigans worldwide never existed. Astounding.
169. For a similar critique, see Bruce Clarke, "Lynn Margulis, Autopoietic Gaia, and the Novacene," *Alienocene* 7 (June 6, 2020), https://alienocene.com/2020/06/07/lynn-margulis-autopoietic-gaia-and-the-novacene/.
170. Robert Epstein, "The Empty Brain," *Aeon* (May 18, 2016), https://aeon.co/essays/your-brain-does-not-process-information-and-it-is-not-a-computer.
171. David J. Chalmers, *Reality+: Virtual Worlds and the Problem of Philosophy* (New York: Norton, 2022).

2. DEMOCRACY'S ANARCHY

1. One such example is Jodi Dean's *Democracy and Other Neoliberal Fantasies: Communicative Capitalism and Left Politics* (Durham, NC: Duke University Press, 2009). Dean's theory of communicative capitalism is warranted and echoes a good deal of work in this direction—notably, Luc Boltanski's and Eve Chiapello's *The New Spirit of Capitalism* (New York:

316   2. Democracy's Anarchy

Verso, 2005)—but her political reading of democracy as consubstantial with liberalism is an easy gesture. It is important to theorize democracy not only against liberalism but even more against capitalism, with which democracy is quintessentially incompatible. To blame democracy in order to save its values by arguing for its collusion with capitalism, as, for example, Alain Badiou does in *The Communist Hypothesis* (New York: Verso, 2009), is to engage in pyrotechnics. No argument that seeks to substitute the name "communism" for the name "democracy" is convincing—it's a name game. Let's mine the most radical autonomous elements of communist history (for example, workers' councils) for what they are, radical democratic elements, and submit both names to the deconstruction they demand. A notable exception in this playfield is the equation of communism with democracy in the way that Jean-Luc Nancy argued in *The Truth of Democracy* (New York: Fordham University Press, 2010), but in his case the underlying proposition, made explicitly only once but underwriting the text throughout, is that democracy is anarchy, which is precisely my argument here.

2. Quoted in Rüdiger Safranski's *Martin Heidegger: Between Good and Evil* (Cambridge, MA: Harvard University Press, 1998), 229. The exemplary account of this period, from which I have quoted liberally in the text, is to be found at 224-47.

3. I have argued this in relation to the collaborative aesthetics of Brecht and Benjamin in *Does Literature Think?* (Stanford, CA: Stanford University Press, 2003), 186-97.

4. Jacques Rancière, *Hatred of Democracy* (New York: Verso, 2006), 4, 7 (translation modified).

5. "*Archesthai* [being ruled] is not simple passive voice. Animals cannot be *archomena* [ruled], objects of an *archein* [rule]. *Archesthai* means to participate in a political community where one is, by necessity, also 'under authority'—as a subject of power in the double sense." Cornelius Castoriadis, *La cité et les lois—Ce qui fait la Grèce 2* (Paris: Seuil, 2008), 201n.

6. See Elizabeth Baughman, "The Scythian Archers: Policing Athens," *The Stoa* (n.d.), https://stoa.isaw-stoa.hosting.nyu.edu/demos/scythian_archers.pdf.

7. Two points are worth noting even when Aristotle considers the notion of *archē* in a purely philosophical sense, as in the *Metaphysics* when he discusses the matter of first principles and causes: (1) he always speaks in the plural (*archai kai aitiai*), since there can never be *one* first principle or cause in isolation and above all others; (2) nowhere does he place the philosopher—for philosophy is the mode in which first principles and causes are to be contemplated and understood—in the position of *archon* as such (see *Metaphysics*, Book I, 980-85). But insofar as the signifying range of *archē*—or rather, in the plural, *archai*—is limited to the temporal ("beginnings") and not to the political, Aristotle's thinking in *Metaphysics* departs from the differential framework we see in *Politics* and attributes to this term a causal determination as the essence of nature. However, even if naturalized, this determination retains a connection to the inaugural pre-Socratic signification of the inherent finitude (*telos*) made imperative by the *archē* of time.

8. See my essay "On Self-Alteration," in *The Perils of the One* (New York: Columbia University Press, 2019), 59-81. Crucial to the argument in that essay is the epistemology of sexual difference. Even though I am not returning to this here, nonetheless it casts its shadow over the entire argument.

9. See Cornelius Castoriadis, *Thucydide, la force et le droit* (Paris: Seuil, 2011), 291-317.

10. For the most concise exposition of the many modern glosses of the Anaximander fragment, as well as their different registers and translations (from Nietzsche, Heidegger, and Jaeger to Vlastos, Vernant, and Castoriadis), see Vassilis Lambropoulos, "Stumbling Over the 'Boundary Stone of Greek Philosophy,'" in *Justice in Particular: Festschrift in Honour of Professor P. J. Kozyris* (Athens: Sakkoulas, 2007), 193-210.
11. Barry Sandywell, *Pre-Socratic Reflexivity: The Construction of Philosophical Discourse c. 600–450 B.C.* (London: Routledge, 1996), 141. Henceforth cited in the text.
12. See Cornelius Castoriadis, *Philosophia kai Epistēmē* (Athens: Eurasia, 2003), 112.
13. See Cornelius Castoriadis, *Ce qui fait la Grèce* (Paris: Seuil, 2004), 175. Hereafter cited in the text.
14. I am borrowing this notion from Barry Sandywell. Following Aeschylus's cosmological language, Sandywell prefers to see *archē* as a matrix, as a primordial generative force—the mother of all—in full cognizance of how, in this respect, a strictly patriarchal symbology of generation is disrupted (145-46).
15. In his extensive reading of the Anaximander fragment, Castoriadis points out the peculiarity of this creation of the notion of the infinite precisely as an entirely noninstrumental and nondeterminant conceptualization, as thought itself—for him the *archē* (beginning) of philosophy. He would not disagree, I would argue, that this philosophical *archē* is indeed, contra Plato, *poietic* in essence. See *Ce qui fait la Grèce*, 210-14.
16. Jean-Pierre Vernant, *Myth and Thought Among the Greeks* (London: Routledge, 1983), 205. Henceforth cited in the text.
17. See Gregory Vlastos, "Equality and Justice in Early Greek Cosmologies," in *Studies in Greek Philosophy*, Vol. 1, *The Presocratics* (Princeton, NJ: Princeton University Press, 1995), 57-88. Next to Vernant, foremost in placing his commentary on Anaximander at the core of the social-imaginary institution of the polis itself is Castoriadis in *Ce qui fait la Grèce*, 185-224.
18. Pierre Lévêque and Pierre Vidal-Naquet, *Cleisthenes, the Athenian: An Essay on the Representation of Space and Time in Greek Political Thought from the End of the Sixth Century to the Death of Plato* (Amherst, NY: Prometheus Books, 1997), 53. Henceforth cited in the text.
19. Jean-Pierre Vernant, *The Origins of Greek Thought* (Ithaca, NY: Cornell University Press, 1984), 101.
20. See also Martin Ostwald's discussion of this significance of *metechein* in "Shares and Rights: 'Citizenship' Greek Style and American Style," in *Dēmokratia: A Conversation on Democracies, Ancient and Modern*, ed. Josiah Ober and Charles Hedrick (Princeton, NJ: Princeton University Press, 1996), 49-61. Notably, Ostwald reads Aristotle's phrase *exousian einai metechein* not in the sense that *exousia* means sovereignty or even power achieved by right, but rather, "something 'permissible,' 'allowable,' that is open to a person, not something to which a person is 'entitled'" (56).
21. Note also the following: "The nondetermination of what is is not mere 'indetermination' in the privative and ultimately trivial sense. It is creation, namely, emergence of *other* determinations, new laws, new domains of lawfulness.... No state of being is such that it renders impossible the emergence of *other* determinations than those already existing." Castoriadis, "The Logic of Magmas and the Question of Autonomy," in *The Castoriadis Reader*, ed. David Ames Curtis (Oxford: Blackwell, 1997), 308.

22. Much remains to be learned, in this regard, from studying the late work of Friedrich Kittler, who sees in pre-Socratic Greece a revolution in notational systems (alphabet, music, mathematics) that signifies an unprecedented social imaginary (both as ontological and epistemological field), which has otherwise been eclipsed by the advent of Christianity and repercussions of globalatinization. I discuss the significance of writing relative to the tragic world of democracy later on in this essay.
23. The essential meditation on the history and permutations of isonomy remains Gregory Vlastos's essay "*Isonomia*," in *Studies in Greek Philosophy*, 1:89–111.
24. In his exemplary reading of this passage in Herodotus, Castoriadis argues that the essential articulation in Herodotus is the antithesis between freedom and despotism—which, incidentally, can never be reduced to the antithesis between Greeks and barbarians. In this respect, Otanis's phrase makes sense as the ultimate refusal of despotic logic. But, by the same token, it thus remains locked in this specific *existential* antithesis and can never become a springboard for the *political* freedom of autonomy. See *La cité et les lois*, 264–69.
25. I discuss these issues at length in "Political Theology as Monarchical Thought," *Constellations* 23, no. 2 (June 2016): 145–59.
26. Thomas Paine, *Rights of Man* (London: Penguin Books, 1985), 70. Henceforth cited in the text.
27. While not invoking Marx, Hannah Arendt makes the same argument about the Rights of Man in *The Origins of Totalitarianism*, but her attachment to the national-liberal civil apparatus and her (perfectly understandable and historically created) fear of statelessness drives her to the conclusion that this groundlessness—this abstractness, she says—always leads to bare life, a sort of unqualified *human-being*. Hence her disregard of Paine, who is never mentioned, and her defense of Burke's counterrevolutionary position. It is this same fear of groundlessness and attachment to liberal guarantees that also mars her later argument on violence, as we shall see in the next section.
28. See Thomas Jefferson, *Political Writings*, ed. Joyce Appleby and Terence Ball (Cambridge: Cambridge University Press, 1999), 593–98.
29. Jacques Rancière, "Does Democracy Mean Something?" in *Dissensus: On Politics and Aesthetics* (London: Continuum, 2010), 56–57. Henceforth cited in the text.
30. This is the profound significance of one of Edward Said's most incisive quotations: "All criticism is postulated and performed on the assumption that it is to have a future." See "The Future of Criticism," in *Reflections on Exile and Other Essays* (Cambridge, MA: Harvard University, 2000), 171.
31. See Michel Foucault, *On the Government of the Living: Lectures at the Collège de France 1979–1980* (New York: Palgrave MacMillan, 2014).
32. Jeremy Bentham, "Anarchical Fallacies," in *The Works of Jeremy Bentham*, ed. John Bowring (Edinburgh: William Tate, 1843), 2:496–97.
33. Carl Schmitt, *Constitutional Theory*, trans. Jeffrey Seitzer (Durham, NC: Duke University Press, 2008), 272. For an insightful and provocative reading of this text, see Andreas Kalyvas, *Democracy and the Politics of the Extraordinary* (New York: Cambridge University Press, 2008).

34. Hannah Arendt, *On Violence* (New York: Harcourt Brace, 1970), 16. Henceforth cited in the text.
35. See Moten's third volume of the series "consent not to be a single being," *The Universal Machine* (Durham, NC: Duke University Press, 2018). Indeed, the study of Arendt can no longer take place without taking this critique as point of departure.
36. *The Rachel Maddow Show*, MSNBC (January 13, 2011). It's hardly surprising that ten years after this sardonic remark, the same position was echoed—this time in total seriousness—by a person who ran for (and won) a seat in the House of Representatives: "Candidate Running to Primary Elise Stefanik Says People 'Should Be Able to Own a Nuke,'" *Newsweek* (June 31, 2021), https://www.newsweek.com/candidate-running-primary-elise-stefanik-says-people-should-able-own-nuke-1606617.
37. I am referring to an astonishing lecture with the title "Settler Liberalism" that Donald Pease presented at the fiftieth anniversary event of the journal *boundary 2* at Dartmouth College (April 4, 2022), https://www.youtube.com/watch?v=AQl4piQXgYo.
38. John Keane, *Violence and Democracy* (New York: Cambridge University Press, 2004).
39. Robert Paul Wolff, "On Violence," *Journal of Philosophy* 66, no. 19 (October 2, 1969): 609.
40. As I have argued extensively, the transcendental signification of law in liberal-democratic societies, leaning on its silenced lawless underside, is not in fact a "secularized theological concept" (Schmitt) *precisely because it is mythical*. See "Enlightenment and *Paranomia*," in *Does Literature Think?* (Stanford, CA: Stanford University Press, 2003), 49–89, and "Every Religion Is Idolatry," in *The Perils of the One* (New York: Columbia University Press, 2019), 136–98.
41. Robert Paul Wolff, "In Defense of Anarchism," https://theanarchistlibrary.org/library/robert-paul-wolff-in-defense-of-anarchism. Henceforth cited in the text.
42. See *The Perils of the One*, 59–81.
43. *The Force of Nonviolence: An Ethico-Political Bind* (London: Verso, 2020). Henceforth cited in the text.
44. See "Border-Concept (of the Political)," in *Thinking with Balibar: A Lexicon of Conceptual Practice*, ed. Ann Stoler, Stathis Gourgouris, and Jacques Lezra (New York: Fordham University Press, 2020), 28–44.
45. Etienne Balibar, *Violence and Civility: On the Limits of Political Philosophy* (New York: Columbia University Press, 2015), 149. Henceforth cited in the text.
46. Cornelius Castoriadis, "The Greek and the Modern Political Imaginary" (1991), in *World in Fragments* (Stanford, CA: Stanford University Press, 1997), 93.
47. Cornelius Castoriadis, "The Greek Polis and the Creation of Democracy" (1982), in *Philosophy, Politics, Autonomy* (New York: Oxford University Press, 1991), 115.
48. Cornelius Castoriadis, "Democracy as Procedure, Democracy as Regime," *Constellations* 4, no. 1 (1997): 1–18.
49. See M. I. Finley, *Politics in the Ancient World* (New York: Cambridge University Press, 1984).
50. An insightful discussion of this quandary, centering on the problem of audience in Athenian theater, is the collection *Why Athens? A Reappraisal of Tragic Politics*, ed. D. M. Carter (New York: Oxford University Press, 2011).

320 2. Democracy's Anarchy

51. Christian Meier, *Athens: A Portrait of the City in Its Golden Age* (London: John Murray, 1999), 579.
52. Ariane Mnouchkine, whose Théâtre du Soleil demonstrates a profound and unconventional understanding of the tragic element of the theater, celebrates precisely the palindromic contradiction between inevitability and choice in tragedy (which is haunted by the fact that "the wrong choice is fatal" and there is no second chance), as a palpitating rhythm of self-interrogation that makes thought corporeal—"The greatest theatrical invention of the Greeks: giving flesh to questioning." See "The Space of Tragedy: From an Interview with Alfred Simon," in *Collaborative Theater: The Théâtre du Soleil Sourcebook*, ed. David Williams (London: Routledge, 1999), 186–87.
53. This vulnerability to excessive and hubristic behavior is endemic to any radical democratic action we pursue in the present. The project of autonomy itself is a hubristic project. The situation of autonomy is on the cutting edge of what can become *hubris* at any moment—this "what" being as such unknown and unpredictable. This too is another way to conceptualize a tragic way of life where necessary decisions are made in the absence of a priori necessity.
54. Pierre Vidal-Naquet, "Democracy: A Greek Invention," appendix in *Cleisthenes, the Athenian*, 102–18.
55. Vernant, *The Origins of Greek Thought*, 37, 54.
56. Cornelius Castoriadis, "The Logic of Magmas and the Question of Autonomy," in Curtis, *The Castoriadis Reader*, 316.
57. Much can be said of frameworks of the tragic in imaginaries and histories other than Greek, whose language is here the specific object of inquiry, namely the *co-incidence* of Athenian tragedy with Athenian democracy. One such evocation of tragic life (even if it does not bear that name) might be how the biophysicist and philosopher Henri Atlan, proceeding out of a Kabbalistic and Spinozist framework, describes a terrain of human freedom within undeconstructible necessity—so long that we question, however, his antivitalist tendency toward a mechanistic view of the universe. See indicatively Atlan's essay "Is Science Inhuman? An Essay on Free Necessity," in *Selected Writings*, ed. Stefanos Geroulanos and Todd Meyers (New York: Fordham University Press, 2011), 32–64.
58. Jacques Derrida, *Rogues* (Stanford, CA: Stanford University Press, 2005). I discuss this notion extensively in the next section. Henceforth cited in the text.
59. In his *Thucydide, la force et le droit*, Castoriadis makes an adroit argument for Thucydides's *History* being a tragic form, where the public orations documented in the text serve as the tragedy's choral instances and, concerning Athens specifically, the *dēmos* is the tragic hero while Pericles performs what is tantamount to a choral ode. See also Meier, *Athens*, 462.
60. This has been by now extensively addressed. A fine text encountering this problem is Andrew Ford's "*Katharsis*: The Ancient Problem," in *Performativity and Performance*, ed. Andrew Parker and Eve Kosofsky Sedgwick (New York: Routledge, 1995), 109–32. See also the discussions in Carter, *Why Athens?* and Meier, *Athens*, 468.
61. In this regard, Nicole Loraux's argument in her late work that perceived in women's tragic lament what she called tragedy's "anti-political" element is puzzling to me. The argument can only be made on a strict, almost literal, notion of the political where the

polis is equated with the affairs of free male citizens. But in that case, theater itself is not a political space at all. See Nicole Loraux, *La voix endeuillé* (Paris: Gallimard, 1999), and in contrast Helene Foley, "The Politics of Tragic Lamentation," in *Female Acts in Greek Tragedy* (Princeton, NJ: Princeton University Press, 2001), 19-56.

62. For all the years passed since it was written, George Thomson's *Aeschylus and Athens* (London: Lawrence & Wishart, 1941) remains an incomparable source on these issues. I say this despite the limits of its Marxist anthropology as evidenced here: "The use of lot served the same purpose in the new democratic constitution as it had originally served in the democracy of the primitive tribe; it was the safeguard of equality. Ancient democracy was a reversion to tribal democracy on a higher evolutionary plane" (196).

63. Nadia Urbinati and Arturo Zampaglione, *The Antiegalitarian Mutation: The Failure of Institutional Politics in Liberal Democracies* (New York: Columbia University Press, 2013), 105. Henceforth cited in the text.

64. As a result, a great deal has been made of Cleisthenes's possible Pythagorean underpinnings, with the ensuing question as to how to reconcile democratic politics with Pythagorean mystical elitism. In the end, the issue is unresolvable, not least because the numerology can claim varied provenance and the political history of the Pythagoreans themselves in the Italian colonies is quite ambiguous. See extensive discussions in Lévêque's and Vidal-Naquet's *Cleisthenes the Athenian* (52-72); Vernant, *Myth and Thought Among the Greeks* (223-28); Thomson, *Aeschylus and Athens* (197-203). Additionally, Lévêque and Vidal-Naquet underline the persistence of the number 3, whose indisputable cosmological legacy here comes to symbolize the singular significance of *meson*, the democratic mediation of *archē* that undermines its primacy (64-68). Finally, Vernant points out that Plato's own mathematical revision of Cleisthenes's urban geometry returns to the duodecimal system with the sacred space reconstituted at the core (230-33).

65. In his Marxist mindset, Thomson insists that there is indeed a social remainder; the tribal structure is never altogether overcome, if we take seriously the class divisions that remain (*Aeschylus and Athens*, 187-203). In their structuralist sense, Lévêque and Vidal-Naquet do not dispute possible tribal remainders in democracy, but nonetheless they underline the permanent alteration of the very organizational framework of the Athenian polis actualized by an altered social imaginary. In this geometric framework—not strictly geographical and not reducible to pure arithmetic—there is no precise calculus that can account for an indisputably heterogeneous unity. The political cannot be ultimately settled by calculation, even if a recalculation of the social space may alter its terms profoundly; it is a matter of collective and oftentimes violent action. This is encapsulated in Josiah Ober's essential corrective of both Marxist and structuralist analytical tendencies of Greek politics in his *Mass and Elite in Democratic Athens* (Princeton, NJ: Princeton University Press, 1989), *The Athenian Revolution* (Princeton, NJ: Princeton University Press, 1996), and *Political Dissent in Democratic Athens* (Princeton, NJ: Princeton University Press, 1999).

66. Edward Said, "The Future of Criticism," in *Reflections on Exile and Other Essays* (Cambridge, MA: Harvard University Press, 2000), 171.

67. Although the context here is the response to a world post-9/11 and the specific referent is collective trauma, the temporal formulation is perfectly apt. Democracy is not a

trauma—except for the ones who are destroyed by it, the oligarchs—but the conditions of its being are perfectly subversive of all known spatiotemporal parameters in social organization. See *Philosophy in a Time of Terror: Dialogues with Jurgen Habermas and Jacques Derrida*, ed. Giovanna Borradori (Chicago: University of Chicago Press, 2003), 97.

68. No doubt, all invocations of *à-venir* in Derrida's work are implicated in his (I believe unfinished) contemplation of the messianic element. I cannot go into this in any responsible way without writing an entirely different text committed to this inquiry, but I will confess my dissent with this configurative terminology—even with Derrida's caveat of "messianicity without messianism"—which I consider ultimately unnecessary to the notion "democracy-to-come." On another occasion, I would risk opening the perspective of Derrida's *à-venir* to Castoriadis's critique of traditional ontology via his concept of *à-être*, a notion of Being that restores the continuously transitive and dynamic notion of the infinitive form of the verb: *to-be*. Not by any means Heidegger's notion of *Sein-zum-Tod*, which inevitably presupposes Being coming to presence in the clearing (*Lichtung*) of unconcealed existence, but the exact opposite in many ways: an ontological category of continuous *poiēsis* from nonbeing to being, where being is thoroughly both the subject and object of making history, a subject and object whose concealment and unconcealment are both "authentic" gestures—that is, simply, political creations. *L'à-venir* as *l'à-être* enhances the temporal—even if unconditional and unpredictable—necessity of being with an already inherent—even if unconditional and undefinable—necessity of making/altering (*poiein*).

69. Jacques Derrida, *The Politics of Friendship*, trans. George Collins (London: Verso, 1997), 105.

70. Jacques Rancière, "Should Democracy Come? Ethics and Politics in Derrida," in *Derrida and the Time of the Political*, ed. Pheng Cheah and Suzanne Guerlac (Durham, NC: Duke University Press, 2009), 278-80. The exact phrase "democracy without a demos" may have been first invoked by Sheldon Wolin in "Transgression, Equality, and Voice," in Ober and Hedrick, *Dēmokratia*, 63-90.

71. Even Lenin seems to understand this principle when he makes reference to the "*primitive*" democracy (his term, including the italics) that will mark the politics of rule in socialism: "Under socialism all will govern in turn and will soon become accustomed to no one governing." What this famous sentence from *The State and Revolution* (1918) announced, however, proved inadequate in practice, since the first target of Bolshevik autocracy was the anarchic politics of self-government in the soviets themselves.

72. "Democracy entails that there is never merely *one* subject, since political subjects exist in the interval *between* two identities, between *Man and citizen*.... This is what a democratic process entails: creating forms of subjectivation in the interval between two identities; creating cases of universality by playing on the double relation between the universal and the particular" (Rancière, *Dissensus*, 56–57).

73. See Talal Asad, "Free Speech, Blasphemy, and Secular Criticism," in *Is Critique Secular? Blasphemy, Injury, and Free Speech* (Berkeley, CA: Townsend Center for the Humanities, 2009), 24-25. Rancière reminds us that Jean-Claude Milner and Benny Levy take this same position in the name of a Zionism that calls the limitless substitutability of

2. Democracy's Anarchy 323

democracy anti-Semitic, if not outright totalitarian. See "Does Democracy Mean Something?" in *Dissensus*, 48-49.

74. Emily Apter has coined the term "unexceptional politics" to refer to those aspects of politics at the microlevel or outside the "officially" recognized political sphere and therefore often disregarded (although still significantly powerful) or to practices that are considered politically unseemly or uncustomary. She has a different aim specifically but, both in terms of her perspective on the current political moment and from the radical democracy standpoint that I am espousing here, her arguments are quite relevant and insightful in their details. See *Unexceptional Politics: On Obstruction, Impact and the Impolitic* (London: Verso, 2018).

75. Wendy Brown makes the intriguing observation that "sovereignty is never simply held and wielded, but from the beginning *circulates*—it works as currency and through currency, and not only through law or command." See *Walled States, Waning Sovereignty* (New York: Zone Books, 2014), 57. I am not sure this is originary in sovereignty per se—I can certainly see how that point is arguable—but in any case it is surely true and essential to the world of capital.

76. I aim to displace the typical assumptions as to the pathological by invoking here the Greek notion of *pathos*, not simply to denote one's passion—which is hardly aberrant—but to denote the meaning of one who is enacted upon, one being the object of politics, the object of the world, of coming-to-be as one to whom something happens—as the notion of *paskhein* is used in Aristotle's *De Anima*.

77. Considering Solon's famous law against neutrality in the case of *stasis* in ancient Athens, Andreas Kalyvas has spoken precisely of a *nomos* that aims not at conflict resolution but aggravation of conflict as one's resolute political accountability as a citizen. See "Solonian Citizenship: Conflict, Democracy, Participation," in *Athenian Legacies: European Debates on Citizenship*, ed. Paschalis Kitromilidis (Florence: Leo S. Olschki, 2014), 19-36.

78. In one of the instances of discussing governmentality, Foucault includes the negative interrogation that leads to thinking of "how not to be governed," except that he insists this is not some blanket negativity, a general and pointless refusal, but it is always aimed at specific conditions of governmentality: "how not to be governed *like that*"—which is precisely to unconceal the presumption that rule (like legitimacy) is a neutral social domain. Indeed, this is essential democratic thinking. See Michel Foucault, "What Is Critique?" in *The Politics of Truth*, ed. Sylvère Lotringer (New York: Semiotext(e), 1997), 41-81.

79. Jacques Rancière, "Democracy or Consensus" in *Dis-agreement*, trans. Julie Rose (Minneapolis: University of Minnesota Press, 1995), 100.

80. Hannah Arendt, *The Origins of Totalitarianism* (New York: Harcourt, 1994), 200. Henceforth cited in the text.

81. An essential article in this regard is Anna Jurkevics's "Hannah Arendt Reads Carl Schmitt's *The Nomos of the Earth*: A Dialogue on Law and Geopolitics from the Margins," *European Journal of Political Theory* 16, no. 3 (2017): 345-66. Jurkevics bases her argument literally on the marginalia Arendt wrote in her copy of Schmitt's book, noting her evident dissent. What matters for us here is not the differences between the two thinkers,

which are ideologically unbridgeable, but that they are de facto in dialogue in response to their common geohistorical space and time.

82. It is interesting to note that Schmitt, while ignoring More's explicit reference to displaced English farmers from the country to the city where they become thieves and end up gracing the gallows in inordinate numbers, does see in *Utopia* a broader foreshadowing in the terms discussed here: "Behind the image of a new world ordered from the sea, the wider future of the industrial age was dawning." See Carl Schmitt, *The Nomos of the Earth*, trans. Gary Ulmen (New York: Telos Press, 2003), 178.

83. Constantine Tsoukalas, *The Political in the Shadow of the Pandemic* (Athens: Kastaniotis, 2021), 46. My translation.

84. Kalyvas's book-length project on oligarchy is ongoing. As introduction to his position, see his essays "Whose Crisis? Which Democracy? Notes on the Current Political Conjuncture," *Constellations* 26 (2019): 384–90, https://onlinelibrary.wiley.com/doi/10.1111/1467-8675.12438, and "Democracy and the Poor: Prolegomena to a Radical Theory of Democracy," *Constellations* 26 (2019): 538–53, https://onlinelibrary.wiley.com/doi/10.1111/1467-8675.12451.

85. Urbinati and Zampaglione, *The Antiegalitarian Mutation*, 106.

86. Wolfgang Streeck, *Buying Time: The Delayed Crisis of Democratic Capitalism*, trans. Patrick Camillier (London: Verso, 2014). Henceforth cited in the text.

87. See Nadia Urbinati's splendid argument in *Democracy Disfigured: Opinion, Truth, and the People* (Cambridge, MA: Harvard University Press, 2014).

88. Kalyvas, "Democracy and the Poor," 546.

89. One need only recall Fred Jameson's remarkably prescient *Postmodernism, or, the Cultural Logic of Late Capitalism* (Durham, NC: Duke University Press, 1989).

90. I am thinking of Aamir Mufti's insightful point in an interview with me that "one of the most stunning features of the Greek economic crisis was the recurring threat of withdrawal of Europeanness." (See the following note.)

91. This point was developed in the two interviews I conducted with Mufti under the title "Immigration and Neocolonialism in Greece's European Crisis," in *Greek Left Review* (July 14, 2014), https://greekleftreview.wordpress.com/2014/07/14/stathis-gourgouris-interviews-aamir-mufti/, and in *JMGS Occasional Papers* 1 (September 8, 2014), https://www.press.jhu.edu/sites/default/files/2021-12/MGS_OP01.pdf.

92. On the implications of this intrinsic self-contradiction, see Etienne Balibar's "Europe as Borderland," *Environment and Planning D: Society and Space* 27 (2009): 190–215.

93. I draw here extensively from the excellent research of Apostolis Fotiadis in his *Merchants of Borders: The New European Architecture of Surveillance* (Athens: Potamos, 2015). Henceforth cited in the text, my translation.

94. Note the list of names given to the operation of protecting Fortress Europe: Xenios Zeus (this was a Greek operation), Hermes, Triton (previously Frontex Plus), Perseus, Mare Nostrum (Italian), Poseidon Land. The Greco-Roman alphabet of control is to me one of the most cynical expressions of EU bureaucratic elites, and it confirms their appropriation of antiquity as a means of dismissing and discounting the modern realities of southern (or eastern) populations, including of course the civilizational categories of what is presumed to be non-European.

95. Nevertheless, it is interesting to note that on March 23, 2022, the European Parliament voted to rescind the Frontex budget allotted to Greece and Hungary because of "fundamental human rights violations": namely, pushbacks across the border, even if people were stranded at sea, and sometimes even destruction of refugee property and identification papers. Subsequently, on April 28 the executive director of Frontex, Fabrice Leggeri, tendered his resignation after revelations that more than a thousand illegal pushbacks in the Aegean were conducted under his leadership, which his office then proceeded to cover up. On July 28, the European Anti-Fraud Office officially confirmed the cover-up. Meanwhile, the Greek government behaves as if none of this has happened and continues the illegal pushbacks, denying even actual video evidence that journalists have posted in the most mainstream of world media (*The Guardian*, the *New York Times*, etc.). How this EU policy correction will develop and whether it will last is at present unknown.

96. Kostas Zapheiropoulos, Janine Louloudi, and Nikos Morfonios, "Digital Fortress Europe #1: The Ecosystem of European Biometric Monitoring and Surveillance Data," Mediterranean Institute for Investigative Reporting (April 28, 2022), https://miir.gr/the-ecosystem-of-european-biometric-monitoring-and-surveillance-data/.

97. I have not seen a more astute, succinct, and brilliant account of this whole conglomerate of intersections between migration/refugee conditions of sea passage, the politics of rescue, and the necropolitics of sovereignty and capital than in Chloe Howe Haralambous's "The Rescue Plot: Politics, Policing, and Subterfuge in the Mediterranean Migrant Passage" (PhD dissertation, Columbia University, 2024).

98. Jason de Leon, *The Land of Open Graves: Living and Dying on the Migrant Trail* (Berkeley: University of California Press, 2015), 6.

99. Indicatively, see Helaine Olen, "Donald Trump Is the Real Anarchist," *Washington Post*, June 2, 2020, and Melissa Lane, "Why Donald Trump Was the Ultimate Anarchist," *The New Statesman*, February 8, 2021.

100. Fredric Jameson, "Future City," *New Left Review* 21 (May–June 2003): 65–79.

101. Cornelius Castoriadis, "What Democracy?" in *Figures of the Thinkable*, trans. Helen Arnold (New York: Fordham University Press, 2007), 131.

102. "Government and Media Fuel a Vicious Cycle of Distrust" (January 18, 2022), https://www.edelman.com/news-awards/2022-edelman-trust-barometer-reveals-even-greater-expectations-business-lead-government-trust; Dana Millbank, "How Republican Leaders Broke Americans' Confidence," *Washington Post* (July 8, 2022), https://www.washingtonpost.com/opinions/2022/07/08/republicans-broke-americans-confidence-institutions-poll/; Brad Dress, "Nearly One in Three Americans Say It May Soon Be Necessary to Take up Arms Against the Government," *The Hill* (July 24, 2022), https://thehill.com/homenews/3572278-nearly-one-in-three-americans-say-it-may-soon-be-necessary-to-take-up-arms-against-the-government/.

103. While doubts persist about the ideological opacity of the *gilets jaunes* movement, which arguably led to its demise, and while there is no doubt as to its hardcore populist imaginary, which carries a number of antidemocracy traps, as I will discuss at the end, nonetheless it deserves to be included here because of two essential aspects: (1) it is definitely directed against neoliberal economics and its brutal political violence (in the specific Macronist variant), and (2) it belongs to that shift in political movements that,

disgusted with the liberal system, opts for a politics of self-representation. Again, the ideological range in this politics of self-representation is far and wide: from anarchist and fascist *indignados* to the chasm separating BLM and antivaxxers. While the question of where my politics resides in my argument about radical democracy should be clear, nonetheless all aspects of insurgency against neoliberal state violence are in play and need to be examined closely, for their cause and enemy is the same. For a succinct account of the context of *gilets jaunes* see Etienne Balibar, "'Gilets jaunes': The Meaning of the Confrontation," *Open Democracy* (December 20, 2018), https://www.opendemocracy.net/en/can-europe-make-it/gilets-jaunes-meaning-of-confrontation/.

104. See my "Border-Concept (of the Political)," in Stoler, Gourgouris, and Lezra, *Thinking with Balibar*, 28–44.

105. "Crisis governmentality renders crises its own condition of possibility or virtual core that reproduces crisis after crisis to the point of becoming, not a management of the exception, but the crisis-suffused norm." Thanos Zartaloudis, *Giorgio Agamben: Power, Law, and the Uses of Criticism* (London: Routledge, 2011), 52.

106. Kalyvas, "Whose Crisis?" 386.

107. "The Question Is: Society Defended Against Whom? Or What?" *New Philosopher* 1 (May 25, 2013), https://www.newphilosopher.com/articles/the-question-is-society-defended-against-whom-or-what-in-the-name-of-what/.

108. Mehmet Dosemeci brilliantly argues this in "The Kinetics of Our Discontent," *Past and Present* 248, no. 1 (August 2020): 253–89.

109. For the full argument, which proved to be quite controversial at the time and was discussed extensively in Europe, including in its French and Spanish versions, see my essay "The SYRIZA Problem: Radical Democracy and Left Governmentality in Greece," *Open Democracy* (August 6, 2015), http://www.opendemocracy.net/can-europe-make-it/stathis-gourgouris/syriza-problem-radical-democracy-and-left-governmentality-in-g.

110. Michel Foucault, *The Birth of Biopolitics* (New York: Palgrave, 2008), 94.

111. It is useful to consult Chantal Mouffe's succinct interview on left populism today and overall. See Gildas Le Dem, "We Urgently Need to Promote a Left-Populism," interview with Chantal Mouffe (August 4, 2017), https://www.versobooks.com/blogs/3341-chantal-mouffe-we-urgently-need-to-promote-a-left-populism.

112. Urbinati is right to remind us that "a plebiscite expresses a kind of religious consensus." *Democracy Disfigured*, 177.

113. There is much to learn here from how Balibar has asked us to imagine what he has tentatively called "transnational counter-populism," defined precisely as an antidote and an alternative to so-called left populism: a politics that opens up and empowers political subjectivities beyond the institutional parameters of "the people" even in a democracy. See Balibar, "'Populism' and 'Counter-Populism' in the Atlantic Mirror," *Open Democracy* (January 2, 2017), https://www.opendemocracy.net/can-europe-make-it/etienne-balibar/populism-and-counter-populism-in-atlantic-mirror.

CODA

1. Jean-Pierre Dupuy, *The Mark of the Sacred*, trans. M. B. DeBevoise (Stanford, CA: Stanford University Press, 2013), 104. Cited henceforth in the text as MS followed by page number.

2. Gil Anidjar ingeniously shows this to be internal to Agamben's figure by exposing its repressed reversal: *Homo sacer* is he who can be sacrificed but cannot be killed. In this respect, Agamben's *homo sacer* is a quintessentially Christological figure, which its author entirely evades. See "When Killers Become Victims," *Cosmopolis* 3 (2007): 1-24, and "Survival" in *Political Concepts* (2013), https://www.politicalconcepts.org/survival-gil-anidjar/.
3. Thanos Zartaloudis's book *The Birth of Nomos* (Edinburgh: Edinburgh University Press, 2018) remains formidable and inimitable on this subject matter.
4. Carl Schmitt, *The Nomos of the Earth*, trans. G. L. Ulmen (New York: Telos Press, 2006), 71. Henceforth cited in the text.
5. Slavoj Žižek, *The Abyss of Freedom* (Ann Arbor: University of Michigan Press, 1997), 14.
6. Cornelius Castoriadis, *The Imaginary Institution of Society*, trans. Kathleen Blamey (Cambridge, MA: MIT Press, 1989), 372.
7. The work of biologists Humberto Maturana and Francisco Varela, *Autopoiesis and Cognition* (Dordrecht: Springer, 1972), is singularly important in this regard, as is Gary Tomlinson's argument in *A Million Years of Music: The Emergence of Human Modernity* (New York: Zone Books, 2015).
8. Georges Bataille, "The Sacred" (1939), in *Visions of Excess: Selected Writings 1927–1939*, ed. Alan Stoekl (Minneapolis: University of Minnesota Press, 1985), 242.
9. I have discussed this extensively in my essay "Every Religion Is Idolatry," in *The Perils of the One* (New York: Columbia University Press, 2019), 136-98.
10. Interesting in this regard are Walter Benjamin's early thoughts (1916) on the linguistic being of all things, including, of course, *human-being*, but also God, to whose realm he attributes the endpoint of translatability. To proclaim God a linguistic being is a humanist gesture par excellence. See "On Language as Such and on the Language of Man," in *Selected Writings Vol. 1 (1913–1926)*, ed. Marcus Bullock and Michael Jennings (Cambridge, MA: Harvard University Press, 1996), 62-74.

Index

Adorno, Theodor W., 8, 34, 72-73, 182-83, 280, 298n, 307n, 308n
Aeschylus, 160, 162, 204, 209, 311n, 317n, 321n
Agamben, Giorgio, 78, **88-90**, 112, 225, **282-87**, 290-91, 312n, 326-27n
Affirmation, xi-xiii, 12, 36-37, 38, 61, 63, 84, 87, 93, 99-101, 174, 194, 226, 255-56, 264-66, 273, 311n
Africa, 7, 12, 14-15, 19-21, 23, 32-33, 39, 80, 107, 121, 128, 167, 180, 193, 229-31, 234, 245, 246, 298n
Afropessimism, 31, 128
Algorithms, 43-45, 48, 135-36, 139, 305n
Alienation, 22, 32, 36, 38, 56-57, 99, 122, 165
Alt-right, xv, 143, 179, 181, 251, 259-60
Alterity, 50-51, 56, 57, 64, 84-87, 90, 127, 147, 149, 199, 209, 220-23, 261, 267, 271, 310n, 313n
Althusser, Louis, **13-15**, 25, 54, 60, 299n, 302n
Améry, Jean, 26, 302n
Anarchy, x-xii, xvi, 17, 78, 93, 108, 140-41, 145-146, 149-50, 161-63, 169, 172, 187-90, 197-98, 201, 212-13, 221-22, 225, 250-51, 253-54, 262-63, 265, 273, 316n, 319n, 322n, 325n
Anaximander, 64, 86, **150-60**, 195, 214, 307n, 308n, 317n
Anidjar, Gil, 313n, 327n
Animal studies, 1, 5, 35, 79, 89, 309n

Animality, x-xi, xvi, 1-3, 34, 38, 40, 42, 50, 54, 57-58, 67-68, 70-75, 78, **80-91**, 93, 95, 102, 124, 132-33, 139, 310n, 312n
Anthropocene, 29, **120-37**, 314n, 315n
Anthropocentrism, 18-19, 49, 79, 81, 127, 310n; misanthropy, 98-100, 123, 311n
Anthropology, x, xii, 4, 7, 40, 59, 72-75, 78, 89-90, 92-93, 97, 110, 113-14, 116, 123, 130, 135, 137, 155, 164-66, 168, 198, 201, 205, 222-24, 235, 250, 252, 279-84, 288, 290-91, 302n, 306n, 309n, 321n
Anticolonial humanism, xi, **13-33**, 40, 128, 176, 193, 243, 300n
Antihumanism, 5, **7-14**, 20-21, 33, 40, 53, 86, 98, 126, 137, 139, 264, 299n
Apter, Emily, 33, 299n, 312n, 323n
Aquinas, Thomas, 79, 278
Aravamudan, Srinivas, 126-28
Archē, 51, 68, 84, 101, 118, 140-41, 145, **146-63**, 171, 173, 176, 189, 197, 211, 212, 219, 222-25, 289, 308n, 316n, 317n, 321n
Archer, David, 123, 314n
Arendt, Hannah, 24, 39, 93, 148, **175-78**, **182-86**, 187-89, **228-32**, 243, 318n, 319n, 323n
Aristotle, 3, 47, 58, 63, 69, 77-81, **93-95**, 102, **109-17**, 131-32, 138, **145-60**, 195, 198, 207, **209-16**, 222, 224, 267, 287, 310n, 312n, 313n, 316n, 317n, 323n
Artificial intelligence, 6, 35, **43-49**, 135-37, 247, 304n, 305n, 311n, 315n

Asad, Talal, 224, 322n
Assembly, xvi, 21, 145, 169, 170, 173, 176, 204, 249-50, 255-56, 260-61, 267
Assmann, Jan, 286
Atlan, Henri, 297n, 320n
Augustine, 278
Autobiography, 81-85, 105-6, 108
Autodidacticism, 52, **104-9**, 136, 226, 267, 312n
Autoimmunity, 83-84, 209, 214, 218-20
Autonomy, 16-17, 19, 24, 30, 44, 49, 51, 76, 106, 108, 118, 131, 136, 145-49, 154, 160-61, 179, 182, 186, 190-91, 194, 203, 209, 212, 218, 223, 226, 228, 240, 250, 263, 265-68, 274, 278, 289, 291, 293-94, 298n, 316n, 317n, 318n, 319n, 320n
Autopoiesis, xvii, xviii, 3, 23, **28-33**, 55, **106-8**, 134, 136, 138, 288-89, 297n, 298n, 307n, 311n, 312n, 315n, 327n

Badiou, Alain, 316n
Balibar, Etienne, 59, 113, **198-201**, 234, 257, 266, 275, 302n, 306n, 319n, 324n, 326n
Bandung, 12-13, 21, 300n, 302n
Bandung humanism, 12, 18, 21, 24
Barthes, Roland, 259
Bataille, Georges, 280, 290-91
Beaudelaire, Charles, 165
Beaufret, Jean 60-61, 306n, 307n
Beckett, Samuel, 100
Bender, Emily M. 49, 305n
Benjamin, Ruha, 305n
Benjamin, Walter, 51, **60-76**, 197, 261, 308n, 316n, 327n
Bennett, Jane, 297n, 310n
Bentham, Jeremy, 171-72
Benveniste, Emile, 280
Bergson, Henri, 15, 73, 93
Biology, 2-3, 24, 29, 41, 55, 63-64, **67-75**, 84, 96, 107-8, 112, 18, 131-33, 137, 297n, 302n, 307n, 327n
Biopolitics, 69-70, 112, 128, 130, 193, 225-26, 263, 312n
Biotechnology, 6, 50, 72, 246, 325n
Black Panthers, 18, 21, 105-6, 178-79, 267

Black radicalism, 18, 48, 105, 108, 168, 176, 178-79, 232, 255, 271, 301n, 304n, 312n, 315n
Blackness, 15, 20, 22-24, **30-40**, 48, 79-80, 82, 105-6, 108, **128-33**, 168, 179, 185, 193, 228, 231-32, 298n, 302n, 303n, 304n, 315n
Blumenberg, Hans, 309n
Boltanski, Luc, 250, 315n
Bone, Eugenia, 134
Border, xiii-xiv, xvi, 27, 75-76, 184, 200, 232, **242-48**, 257, 274-75, 277, 324n, 325n
Border-concept, 198, 257-58, 265, 274
Bové, Paul, 104, 311n
Braidotti, Rosi, 297n, 311n
Brecht, Bertolt, 293, 316n
Brennan, Peter, 314n
Brennan, Timothy, 300n
Brown, Wendy, 247, 285, 323n
Burke, Edmund, 164-65, 171, 183, 318n
Butler, Judith, **194-99**, 297n

Caillois, Roger, 280
Capitalism, v, xi, xv, 27-28, 35, 40, 44, 46, 56, 70, 72, 100, 112, **124-30**, 134, 137, 164, 173, 180, 224-25, **227-58**, 260, 264, 266, 272-73, 304n, 306n, 314n, 315-16n, 324n
Cassirer, Ernst, 73
Castoriadis, Cornelius, 17, 44, 102-3, 130, 132, 152, 159-60, 201-2, 208, 217, 233, 249, 289, 297n, 302n, 307-8n, 309n, 310n, 311n, 315n, 316n, 317n, 318n, 319n, 320n, 322n, 325n, 327n
Catastrophe, xv, 7, 43, 54, 60, 66, 72, 75, 77-78, 86, 100, **121-26**, 137, 141, 143-44, 166, 176-77, 182, 203, 235, 275, 277, 287, 304n
Césaire, Aimé, 14-15, **19-20**, 28, 30, 301n, 302n
Chakrabarty, Dipesh, 125-28
Chalmers, David, 49, 131-32, 138-39, 315n
Chiapello, Eve, 250, 315n
Chomsky, Noam, 46-47, 305n
Christianity, 6, 7, 61-63, 93, 99-100, 104, 115, 119, 152, 164, 225, 279, 281-83, 293-94, 310n, 311n, 318n

Class, xv, 11, 19, 59, 166, 169, 176, 178, 187, 189, 207, 215-17, 227, 230, 251, 254, 262, 264-66, 276, 321n
Class struggle, 227, 254, 265-66, 271, 275
Clastres, Pierre, 90, 268
Cleisthenes, 113, 117, 155-57, 163, 206, 215-17, 235, 321n
Coetzee, J. M., 309n
Co-incidence, 7, 11, 34, 52-53, 55-56, 66, 71, 76, 89, 92, 104, 129-30, 148-50, 160-61, 166, 173, 180, 209, 211, 221, 267, 305n, 320n
Colonialism, 7, 10, **14-33**, 34, 39-40, 80, 88, 103, 124, 127-29, 167, 180-82, 192-93, **228-33**, 235-36, 239, 243-46, 253, 297n, 300n, 301n, 304n, 324n
Communism, 14, 16-17, 19-20, 61, 125, 222, 254, 265, 300n, 301n, 302n, 316n
Condillac, Etienne Bonnot, 70
Conrad, Joseph, 230
Cooper, John M., 312n
Crary, Alice, 309n, 310n
Crutzen, Paul J., 122, 314n
Cutler, Chris v
Cyberhumanity, 49, 70-72, 77, 83, 136-38, 240, 250, 307n, 311n

Da Vinci, Leonardo, 47
Darwin, Charles, 136
Daskalakis, Constantinos, 304-5n
De Fontenay, Elisabeth, 309n
De Gouges, Olympe, 169
De Leon, Jason, 247-48
De Vries, Hent, 307n
De Waal, Frans, 95
Dean, Jodi, 315-16n
Death-drive, 83-84, 97-99, 101
Decoloniality, 14, 24-30, 33, 192-93
Decolonization, 14, 20, 22-26, 130, 192-93, 244, 301n
Deconstruction, xi, 1, 3, 4, 6, 7, 22, 23, 30, 63, 79, 81, 84, 85, 89, 101, 106, 168, 172, 177, 191, 198, 218, 220, 273, 276, 279, 293, 308n, 316n, 320n

Dehumanization, 2, 11-12, 14, 30, 34-35, 38-39, 56, 82, 97-100, 128-29, 132-33, 257, 299n, 306n
Deleuze, Gilles, 97, 263, 297n
Depersonalization, 22, 25-27, 32, 193, 224
Derrida, Jacques, 78, **80-93**, 98, 106, 110, **115-17**, 129, 214, **217-23**, 283, 297n, 307n, 308n, 309n, 310n, 322n
Descartes, René, 79, 81-82, 138, 223, 310n
Deutscher, Isaac, 10
Diagne, Souleymane Bachir, 14-15, 300n
Dialectics, ix, xi-xiii, 7-9, 14-15, 20, 28, 32, 34, 36, 51, 54, 56, 60, 72-73, 104, 112, 127, 161, 170, 182, 184, 192-93, 287
Diamond, Cora, 309n
Diderot, Denis, 70-72
Dissent, 84, 146, 169, 196, 213, 215, 221, 226-28, 262, 265-66, 269, 273, 322n, 323n
Dosemeci, Mehmet, 326n
Douglass, Frederick, 105, 109
Du Bois, W. E. B., 14, 18-19, 30, 228
Dubreuil, Laurent, 312n
Dupuy, Jean-Pierre, 281, **287-90**, 297n, 326n
Durkheim, Emile, 280

Ecology, 31-32, 84, 123, 137, 177, 251, 259, 276, 314n
Elsayed, Hanan, 302n
Empedocles, 118
Enlightenment, ix, 7-10, 19, 34, 70, 72-73, 98, 103, 109, 126-27, 139, 160, 164, 166, 180, 182, 237, 308n, 309n, 312n, 319n
Epigenetics, 133
Epistemology, x-xii, 4, 6, 10, 15, 18-20, 24-25, 29-30, 40-42, 52, 70-71, 75, 79, 104, 107, 122, 125-26, 128, 130, 155, 164, 177, 182, 189, 195-97, 265-66, 268, 271, 287-88, 302n, 305n, 309n, 316n, 318n
Erikson, Erik, 301n
Eros/eroticism, 43, 99, 114, 115-16, 284
Esposito, Roberto, 112, 312n
Ethics, 14, 43, 44, 46, 48, 77, 82, 114-15, 119, 145-46, 155-56, 161, 176, 185, 193-96, 199-201, 309n, 310n, 311n, 313n, 322n; ethical AI, 48-49, 305n

Euripides, 207-9
Evolution, 3, 29, 66, 127-28, 132, 136-37, 276, 321n
Exception, 69, 85, 117, 162, **224-28**, 248, 259, 264, 268, 275-76, 282, 287, 291, 305n, 323n, 326n

Fanon, Frantz, 3, 14-15, 17, 19, **20-33**, 35, 37, 38, 40, 55, 76, 82, 105, 108, 130-33, **192-94**, 200, 299n, 301n, 302n, 303n, 304n
Fantasy, 36, 45, 91, 94-96, 249, 252, 260, 295
Fascism, xv, 72, 184, 241, 244, 251, 254, 262, 264, 325n
Fassin, Didier, 28
Feuerbach, Ludwig, 59, 70, 306n
Feyerabend, Paul, 189
Ficino, Marcilio, 6
Finitude, 83, 110, 139, 143, **150-60**, 166-67, 169-72, 218, 316n
Flaubert, Gustave, 109
Foley, Helene, 321n
Ford, Andrew, 320n
Fotiadis, Apostolis, 245-46, 324n
Foucault, Michel, xvi, 8, 10, **69-70**, 72, 95, 112, 171, 259, 263, 276, 298-99n, 308n, 318n, 323n, 326n
Fraisse, Jean-Claude, 312n
Frazier, J. G., 280
Freire, Paulo, 103
Freud, Sigmund, 30, 45, 83, 91-92, 94-95, 97, 103, 147, 191, 272, 278, 280, 292, 310n
Friedman, David D., 251-52
Friedman, Milton, 252
Friendship, 92, 109, **113-20**, 218, 312n, 313n
Fugitivity, 35-37

Gandhi, Mahatma, 16, 185
Gawdat, Mo, 135
Gehlen, Arnold 73, 78
Gender, xv, 22, 35, 37, 41, 56, 59, 77, 117, 119, 166, 168, 182, 210, 271, 283, 308n, 317n
Genetics, 6, 30, 97-98, 131, 133, 136, 138
Genre, 3, 29-30, 55-56, 69, 105, 132, 164, 309n
Geology, 121-28, 136-37, 314n
Gilroy, Paul, 26, 33, 299n, 302n

Girard, René, 280
Gleick, James, 68-69
Glissant, Édouard, 35
Globality, 16, 176, 228, 232, 277
Globalization, xiv-xvi, 84, 176, 235, 239, 243-244, 254, 255, 258, 275, 315n
Governance, 147, 161, 202, 236, 256-57, 262-68, 270, 274, 276-77, 300n
Governmentality, xi, 8, 28, 69, 164, 196, 241-42, 255-57, 259, 262-66, 268, 274, 323n, 326n; left governmentality, xi, **255-77**
Gramsci, Antonio, 9
Gray, John, 98, 123, 287
Groundlessness, xii, 4, 43, 55, 58, 87, 104, 144-45, 154, 157, 166, 188, 200-1, 215, 220-22, 226, 248-50, 253, 267, 318n
Guattari, Félix, 297n

Haffner, Sebastian, 143
Haneke, Michael, 100
Haraway, Donna, 78, **84-86**, 297n
Harbisson, Neil 71-72
Hartman, Saidiya, 128, 312n
Hayles, Katherine, 297n
Hegel, G. W. F., 15, 36, 54, 56, 100, 191, 192, 243, 306n, 311n
Heidegger, Martin, 5, 8, 51, 54, **60-67**, 73, 82-83, 90-91, 104, 142-43, 150, 155, 306-7n, 316n, 317n, 322n
Herder, Johann Gottfried, 75
Herodotus, **162-63**, 195, 206, 211, 318n
Hesiod, 86, 160
Heteronomy, 26, 49-51, 54, 108-9, 119, 159-60, 170, 209, 223, 288
Hinton, Geoffrey, 47, 305n
Hippocrates, 195
Hippodamus, 155
Hobbes, Thomas, 78
Hölderlin, Friedrich xi, 5
Holmes, Brooke, 112, 312n
Homer, 111, 117, 150, 157, 160, 208, 212
Hong Qin, 45, 49, 305n
Horkheimer, Max, 8, 34, 72-73, 308n
Houellebecq, Michel, 97-100

Howe Haralambous, Chloe, 325n
Hubris, 77, 118, 153, 163, 201-6, 209-10, 213, 214, 313n, 320n
Humanitarianism, 11, 28, 39, 48, 245, 302n
Human rights, 11, 12, 28, 85, 164, 200, 239, 325n
Humboldt, Wilhelm von, 150
Husserl, Edmund, 73

Identicide, 51, 78, 83-84
Identity, xiv, xv, 10-11, 20, 23, 31, 35-37, 41, 43-44, 50-51, 78, 86, 173, 190, 214, 223, 243, 248, 261, 303n, 313n, 322n
Imagination, 7, 12, 24, 49, 50, 71, 83, 92, 94, 96-101, 109, 111, 124, 127, 153, 160, 177, 216, 231, 238-39, 252, 281-87, 293, 301n, 307n, 309n, 311n
Indigeneity, 7, 31-33, 107-8, 128, 192-94, 217, 230-31, 245, 294
Infinity, 3, 38, 64, 139, **150-60**, 193, 199, 232, 255, 285, 308n, 317n
Internationalism, 12, 16-18, 24, 178, 244, 266, 272-73, 275, 300n, 304n
Irigaray, Luce, 38
Islam, xiv-xv, 6-7, 106, 152, 300n, 310n
Isonomia, 117, 154-58, 161-63, 195, 207, 212, 215-17, 222-23, 236, 273, 287-88, 318n

Jackson, George, 105
Jackson, Zakiyyah Iman, **38-41, 79-82**, 133, 299n, 304n
Jaeger, Werner, 155, 317n
James, C. L. R., 17, 129, 302n
Jameson, Fredric, 252, 324n, 325n
Jefferson, Thomas, 165, 167
Jewishness, 10, 22, 143, 152, 313n, 320n
Judy, R. A., 128, 298n, 303n, 312n
Jurkevics, Anna, 323n
Justinian, 278

Kafka, Franz, 103
Kalyvas, Andreas, 234, 240, 259-60, 318n, 323n, 324n
Kane, Sarah, 100
Kant, Immanuel, 42, 67, 73, 79, 82, 106, 161, 190-91, 197, 223, 250, 310n, 312n

Keane, John, 184-85
Kelley, Robin D. G., 301n
Kind, Carly, 305n
King, Martin Luther, 185
Kittler, Friedrich, 318n
Klein, Naomi, 46, 125, 235, 305n
Klimis, Sophie, 313n
Kristeva, Julia, 301n

La Boétie, Etienne de, 118-19, 148, 190-91, 226, 313n
Lacan, Jacques, 82, 301n
Laclau, Ernesto, 269, 271
Lambropoulos, Vassilis, 317n
La Mettrie, Julien Offray de, 70-72, 308n
Las Casas, Bartolomé de, 108, 129
Latour, Bruno, 297n
Learning, ix, xii, 31, 45-46, 49, 71, 89, 96-97, **101-9**, 141, 145-47, 183, 191, 207, 227, 238, 250, 287, 290, 297n, 305n, 311n, 313n, 315n, 318n, 326n; self-learning, 45-46, 105, 136, 267
Legitimacy, xiv-xv, 119, 141, 174-75, **180-97**, 222, 227, 241-42, 254, 258-59, 289, 323n
Lemoine, Blake, 47-48, 305n
Lenin, V. I., 16, 187, 262, 300n, 322n
Lévêque, Pierre, 155, 157, 163, 321n
Levinas, Emmanuel, 82
Lewis, John, 201
Liberalism, xi-xv, 2, 7, 11, 17, 19, 28, 48, 100, 115, 130, 133, 137, 144-46, 155, 160-61, 167, 169, 173-75, 178, **180-91**, 193-94, 197, 199, 203, 208, 214, 222-25, 233-34, 237-42, 248-56, **259-64**, 273-74, 316n, 318n, 319n, 325n; liberal humanism, **37-41**, 79
Locke, John, 103
Loraux, Nicole, 320-21n
Lovelock, James, 49, 123, **136-38**, 287, 315n
Lubin, Alex, 301n
Luhmann, Niklas, 297n
Lukács, Georg, 9, 279
Luxemburg, Rosa, 200

Macherey, Pierre, 302n
Machiavelli, Niccolo, 6
Maddow, Rachel, 178

Madison, James, 167
Makdisi, George, 6-7
Malabou, Catherine, 38, 310n
Malcolm X, 19, 21, 105-6, 109, 179
Marable, Manning, 105
Marcuse, Herbert, 97
Marx, Karl, 8, 13-15, 22, **51-60**, 65, 67-68, 70, 76, 94-95, 127, 166, 169, 183, 191, 218, 234, 253, 305-6n, 308n, 311n, 318n
Marxism, 13-17, 56, 59, 73, 93-94, 183, 187-89, 227, 234, 253-54, 262-65, 275-76, 299n, 300n, 301n, 305n, 306n, 321n
Mao Zedong, 17, 18, 306n
Margulis, Lynn, 287
Maturana, Humberto, 55, **106-8**, 134, 297n, 307n, 327n
Mauss, Marcel, 280
Mayfield, Curtis, v
Mbembe, Achille, 128, 302n
McGuire, John, 124, 314n
Meier, Christian, 204, 207, 320n
Mezzadra, Sandro, 302n
Migration, xv, 27-28, 39, 246-48, 257, 266, 302n, 324n, 325n
Mnouchkine, Ariane, 310n
Modernity, ix, 37, 67-69, 72, 112, 137, 148, 164-65, 170, 225, 234, 238, 258, 281-92, 298n, 308n, 327n
Monohumanism, 7-8, 29-30, 137, 298n
Monotheism, 86, 89, 240, 252, 294, 298n, 310n
Montaigne, Michel de, 313n
Moore, Jason W., 314n
More, Thomas, 229, 324n
Morin, Edgar, 297n
Moten, Fred, v, **35-40**, 128, 178, 304n, 319n
Mouffe, Chantal, 269, 271, 273, 326n
Mufti, Aamir, 12-13, 244, 299n, 324n
Müller, Heiner, 100
Myth, 5, 13, 19, 29, 188, 193, 217, 234, 237, 252, 292-93, 317n, 319n, 321n

Nancy, Jean-Luc, 316n
Nation (-state; national culture; national sovereignty), xv, 12, 16-17, 23-24, 33-34, 36-37, 130, 167, 180-81, 184, 225, 228-30, 239, **241-47**, 253, 255, 258, 267, 272-75, 278, 290, 300n, 304n, 318n
Nationalism, xv, 10, 17-18, 21, 23-24, 27-28, 36, 96, 168, 179, 181, 228, 232, 235, **241-47**, 254-55, 257, 272, 274, 300n
Native/nativism, 23, 32, 33, 39, 111, 121, 131, 179, 180, 192-93, 231, 245, 303n
Nazism, 73, 143, 228, 244
Negation, ix, xi-xii, 9, 22, 35-39, 53, 100, 108, 127, 130, 174, 190-91, 194, 199, 226, 246, 265-66, 277, 287, 323n
Negativity, 42, 99-100, 146, 215, 226, 323n
Négritude, 14, 19-23, 299n, 300n, 301n, 306n
Neoliberalism, xiv-xvi, 98, 99, **232-42**, 254, 255, 257-60, 274, 315n, 325-26n
Newton, Huey, 18, 105, 301n
Nietzsche, Friedrich, 8, 118, 155, 210, 317n
Nonviolence, 177, 178, 185, 189, **194-99**

Ober, Josiah, 321n
Oligarchy, xvi, 118-19, 144, 161-63, 216, 225, 233-35, 248, 254, **273-77**, 322n, 324n
Ontology, xi, 2-5, 10, 15, 22, 24-27, 29, 31, **35-43**, 50-51, 56, **62-69**, 75, 77-78, 82, **84-91**, 104-5, 108, 115, **124-37**, 159, 161, 184, 258, 279, 284, 286-89, 295, 302n, 303n, 305n, 307n, 308n, 310n, 318n, 322n
Orientalism, 7, 10-11, 234, 299n
Ostwald, Martin, 317n
Otherness, xvii, 26-28, 41, 50, 56-57, 62, 75, 81, 95, 99, 154, 191, 195, 199-200, 220-24, 273, 277, 282, 289, 310n

Paideia, 61-62, 91-92, 103-4, 109
Paine, Thomas, **164-74**, 183, 200, 318n
Palestine, 21, 185
Panourgiá, Neni, 312n
Particularism/particularity, xii-xiv, 1, 11, 20, 29, 31, 37, 44, 53, 55-56, 110-11, 114, 169, 171, 221, 222, 286, 290, 322n
Pasolini, Pier Paolo v
Pease, Donald, 179-80, 319n
Pedagogy, xii, 16-17, 122, 34, 91-92, 103-4, 106, 142, 180, 226, 267, 275, 311n

Performance, 12, 64, 79, 92, 93, 149, 162, 188, 198, 204-7, 209, 218-19, 221, 237, 289, 292, 318n, 320n
Performativity, 21-22, 84, 177, 204, 207-8, 213, 249, 266, 268, 274, 281, 291-92
Peterson, Jordan, 47, 305n
Phantasm, 6, 45, 79, 94-96, 102, 111, 131, 138-39, 155, 191, 193, 284, 292
Physis, 83-87, 92, 96, 101, 103, 110-12, 117-18, 120, 159-61, 284-85, 288
Pico della Mirandola, 6-7
Planetarity, xi, 16, 27, 30, 33, 37, 66, 70, 72, 86, 91, 101, **121-28**, 130, 134, 137, 176-78, 182, 228, 230, 235, 238, 249, 254-55, 259, 273, 276-77, 287, 314n
Plato, 55, 63-64, 79, 81-82, 90, 103, 109-10, 113, 150, 157, 202, **210-13**, 216, 249, 284, 317n, 321n
Plessner, Helmuth, **73-78**, 308-9n
Plutarch, 162
Poetics, 3, 6, 19-21, 25, 29, 31, 36, 43, 66, 81, 113, 151, 155-56, 210, 212-13, 216, 251, 302n, 309n, 314n
Poetry, v, 14, 19, 25, 28, 35, 46, 76, 81, 104, 106, 152-53, 155-56, 207, 210, 212-13, 216, 301n, 309n, 311n
Poiēsis, xvii, 3-4, 6, 19, **23-28**, 31-32, 35, 45, 50, 55, 58, 64, 75, 77, 79, 91, 100-1, 104-6, 111, 153, 156, 165, 173-74, 216, 235-36, 263, 288, 306n, 309n, 310n, 311n, 317n, 322n
Political theology, x, 285-86, 313n, 318n
Populism, xv, 23, 174, 241-44, 251, 259-61, **269-76**, 325n, 326n
Postcoloniality, 9, 17, 23-24, 244, 246
Posthumanism, xi, 1, 5-6, 28, 35, 43, 70, 75, 77, 79, 86, 93, 129, 304n, 311n, 312n
Presocratic, 18, 63-64, 99, 112, 153, 155-57, 284, 316n, 317n, 318n
Protagoras, 19, 207
Psyche, x, xvi, 31-34, 38, 40, 42-44, 49-51, 54, 61-62, 71, 74-76, **91-104**, 120, 124, 126, 131, 133, 138-39, 176, 182, 191, 193, 195-96, 207, 241, 251-52, 254, 266, 270, 272, 280-82, 291-92, 294, 305n, 307n

Psychoanalysis, 20-22, 30, 45, 91-92, 97, 99, 223, 250, 280, 301n, 310n
Pythagoras, 321n

Race, xv, 16, 17, 22, 30, 35, 37, 39, 59, 69, 81, 129, 166, 203, 267, 272, 279, 302n, 305n
Racism, xi, xv, 2, 14, **19-31**, 36, 39-40, 46, 55, 69, 79-82, 105, 115, **128-33**, 168, 176, **178-82**, 193, **228-32**, 241-45, 257, 264, 271, 302n, 305n
Radhakrishnan, R. 299n
Rancière, Jacques, **143-44**, 169, **220-23**, 227, 249, 322n, 323n
Refugees, xv, xvi, 27-28, 36, 245-46, 248, 257, 302n, 325n
Religion, x, 10, 16, 17, 52, 53, 96, 138, 259, 267, 278, 280-81, 290, 307n, 327n
Revolution, 5, 6-7, 16-18, 20-23, 69, 98, 105, 113, 115-17, 122, 15, 129, 142, 164, 166-68, 170-72, 174-84, 189, 191, 193, 198, 210, 211, 216, 227, 233-34, 238-39, 250, 261-62, 265, 274, 282, 291n, 301n, 306n, 312n, 318n, 322n
Rimbaud, Arthur, 223
Robcis, Camille, 301n
Robespierre, Maximilien, 169
Romilly, Jacqueline de, 207
Roose, Kevin, 48, 305n
Rousseau, Jean-Jacques, 103, 173
Roy, M. N., 14, **16-19**, 20, 300n, 301n

Sacred, x-xii, xiv, 26, 82, 157, 160, 168-70, 225, 232-33, 263, 267, 274, **278-95**, **326-27**; sacralization, ix-x, 168, 292; desacralization, ix, 294
Safranski, Rüdiger, 142-43
Said, Edward W., xii, xiii, 5, **8-13**, 21, 30, 104, 127, 218-19, 261, 297n, 298n, 299n, 300n, 305n, 312n, 318n, 321n
Sandywell, Barry, 151, 160, 317n
Sappho, 117
Sartre, Jean-Paul, 14, 22, 61, 109, 301n, 306-7n
Scheler, Max, 73

Schelling, Friedrich Wilhelm Joseph, 286
Schmitt, Carl, 78, 92, 114-15, 118, 120, 144, **172-74**, 225, 228, 243, 247, 282, 285-86, 318n, 319n, 323n, 324n
Scott, David, 29-30, 303n
Secular criticism, ix-x, 11, 298n, 311n, 322n
Self-alteration, 53, 56, 58, 65, 91, 101, 108, 149-50, 170, 191, 223, 250, 273, 289-90, 306n, 307n, 316n
Self-limitation, 76, 148, 154, 201-2, 208-9, 214, 218, 249-50
Senghor, Léopold, 14-15, 19, 30, 299n, 300n, 306n
Sepúlveda, Luis, 108
Sexism, 2, 46, 305n
Sexual difference, 38, 41, 97, 222, 316n
Sexuality, xv, 25, 41-42, 59, 69, 94-99, 131, 222, 248, 271
Shakespeare, William, 47
Simmel, Georg, 73
Simplicius, 150, 154
Slavery, 12, 19, 22-23, 28, 31-33, 38, 40, 80, 105-108, 122, 128, 130, 148, 160, 167, 180, 204, 212, 215-16, 231-33, 245, 253, 294, 312n
Sloterdijk, Peter, 34, 89, 297n, 303n
Smith, Adam, 137, 231, 237
Smith, William Robertson, 280
Social imaginary, xvi, 26, 54, 62, 81, 90, 92, 96, 107, 111, 114, 116, 133, 139, 146, 150, 154-55, 159-160, 164, 182, 188, 193, 195, 199, 205-6, 211, 214, 217, 222, 238, 298n, 303n, 307n, 311n, 317n, 318n, 321n; social imagination, 124, 281, 293
Socialism, 15, 16, 182, 263, 300n, 322n
Sociogenic, 3, 5, 30-31, 130-35, 303n
Socrates, 103, 203, 213
Solon, 215, 235, 323n
Sophocles, 103, 208-10, 267
Sovereignty, x, xiii-xiv, 9, 17, 27, 32, 75-78, 93, 104, 118, 137, 158, 164, 173-74, 182, 184, 188, 192, 199, 225, 228, 229, 239, **241-47**, 251, **253-55**, 257-58, 267, 269, 270, 273-75, 282-87, 291, 317n, 323n; popular sovereignty, 239, 273-74

Species, 24-30, 33, 39-40, 45, 55, 57, **66-69**, 70, 72, 76-78, 80, 83, 85-86, 96-97, 108, 110, 121, 123, 127, 130-33, 138, 143, 192-93, 311n; species-being, **55-59**
Spillers, Hortense, 128
Spivak, Gayatri Chakravorty, 42-43, 127, 135
Stalin, Josef, 16, 300n
Statelessness, 27, 36, 212, 318n
Steiner, Deborah, 207
Stenghers, Isabelle, 297n
Streeck, Wolfgang, **236-39**, 324n
Subjectivity, xiii, 4, 21, 22, 25-26, 28, 31, 33, 36-38, 43, 52-53, 55-58, 61, 63, 65, 62, 75, 103-4, 113, 127, 141, 142, 144, 145, 148-49, 166, 191, 193, 197, 200, 232, 236, 240, 251, 259, 266, 275-76, 313n, 322n, 326n; citizen-subject, **197-200**, 257; desubjectification, 11; intersubjectivity, 26
Sublimation, 97, 101, 132, 28, 287, 311n
Sultan-Galiev, Mirsaid, 300n

Theater, xvi, 22, 139, 162, **203-6**, 210, 213, 286, 319n, 320n, 321n
Theatricality, 22, 204, 206, 223, 293
Theophrastus, 150
Thompson, E. P., 300n
Thomson, George, 321n
Thucydides, 111, 205-6, 208, 210, 320n
Tomlinson, Gary, 327n
Tragedy, 23, 64, 76-77, 103, 113-14, 119, 142, **203-14**, 275, 313n, 319n, 320-21n
Tragic life, 99, 100, 114, 141, 144, 146, 152-53, 160, 189, 200-1, 204, **208-14**, 218, 262, 267, 274-75, 313n, 318n, 320n
Transformation, x, 26, 32-33, 35, 45, 49-50, 56, 58, 91, 94-95, 97, 104, 106, 108, 131, 133, 153, 156, 167, 177, 188, 192-93, 198-99, 207, 214, 216-18, 223, 256, 262, 264, 279, 288, 310n, 311n, 314n
Translation, xv, 14, 25, 26, 29, 32, 55-56, 59, 61, 62-65, 72, 75, 77, 87, 93, 104, 107, 109, 117, 132, 154, 155, 190, 202, 206, 219, 232, 268, 293-94, 299n, 303n, 306n, 308n, 312n, 313n, 317n, 327n

Trier, Lars von, 99–100
Trumpism, 143, 179–80, 241–42, 244, 251, 325n
Tsoukalas, Constantine, 233

Uexküll, Jakob von, 73–75
Universalism, 11, 15–16, 18–20, 56
Universality, 15, 26, 37, 56, 193, 198, 220, 257, 266, 322n
Universalization, 59, 120, 220
Urbinati, Nadia, 236, 270–71, 321n, 324n, 326n

Vardoulakis, Dimitris, 313n
Varela, Francisco, 55, **106–8**, 134, 297n, 302n, 307–8n, 327n
Vergès, Françoise, 314n
Vernant, Jean-Pierre, 153–58, 207, 317n, 321n
Vico, Giambattista, 6, 104, 312n
Vidal-Naquet, Pierre 155, 157, 163, 206, 317n, 321n
Violence, xi–xvi, 21–22, 25–28, 31, 33, 36, 39, 42, 72, 82, 96, 100, 107, 130, 133, 141, **174–201**, 210–11, 226, 230, 233, 243, 245, 247, 256–57, 260, 262, 264, 267, 275, 281–82, 287, 294, 302n, 318n, 319n, 321n, 325–26n
Vitruvius, 155

Vlastos, Gregory, 155, 317n, 318n
Voltaire, 278

Wang, Jackie, 304n
Weber, Max, 73
Weheliye, Alexander, 304n
West, Cornel, 106, 128
Wilder, Gary, 300n
Wittgenstein, Ludwig, 79, 309n
Wolfe, Cary, 41, 78, 297n
Wolff, Robert Paul, **186–91**, 197, 319n
Wolin, Sheldon, 113, 322n
Woodfox, Alfred, 105–6
Wright, Richard, 21
Wynter, Sylvia, 3, 5, **28–33**, 35, 40, 43, 55, 80, 106–8, **128–33**, 230, 298n, 302n, 303n, 304n

Xenophon, 118

Yusoff, Kathryn, 128–29, 315n

Zartaloudis, Thanos, 326n, 327n
Ziarek, Ewa, 301n
Žižek, Slavoj, 286–87
Zoology, 3, 29, 31, 41, 70, 78, 88, 95–96, 103, 112, 122, 132, 310n
Zōon politikon, x, 3–4, 69, 77–78, 81–82, 87, **109–20**, 131–32, 147, 198, 312n